BASIC AND THE
PERSONAL COMPUTER

This book is in the
ADDISON-WESLEY MICROCOMPUTER BOOKS
POPULAR SERIES

BASIC AND THE PERSONAL COMPUTER

Thomas Dwyer

Margot Critchfield

University of Pittsburgh

Illustrations by

Margot Critchfield

ADDISON-WESLEY PUBLISHING COMPANY
Reading, Massachusetts • Menlo Park, California
London • Amsterdam • Don Mills, Ontario • Sydney

The language BASIC was developed at Dartmouth College by John G. Kemeny and Thomas E. Kurtz.

This book was reproduced by Addison-Wesley from camera-ready proof supplied by the authors. The book was designed by Nancy Ross McJennett, set in Palatino, and composed using programs developed by Stephen V. F. Waite at Dartmouth College. The text was prepared on the Dartmouth Time-Sharing System and supplied to a typesetting machine at Imperial Company, Hartford, Vermont.

Eleventh Printing, October 1983

Copyright (c) 1978 by Addison-Wesley Publishing Company, Inc. Philippines copyright 1978 by Addison-Wesley Publishing Company, Inc.

ISBN 0-201-01589-7
    KLMNOPQ-MU-89876543

Contents

PREFACE

Personal computing is an idea that sounds more like science fiction than fact. But it's here, it's real, and it's growing at a rate that has surprised even the experts.

Exactly what is a personal computer? Physically, personal computers are mysterious boxes that house a number of circuit boards (called modules), each containing a large array of solid-state electronics. At a deeper level, they can be described as complex switching networks that orchestrate millions of pulses per second with precise logic.

But it's the human "connection" that explains what all the excitement is about. It's the power of personal computers to act as extensions of the human mind, inviting journeys to worlds few individuals have experienced before.

The technical characteristics of today's personal computers are actually superior to those of the large laboratory computers of the 1960's. Personal microcomputers operate with internal speeds measured in billionths of seconds, they have sophisticated interface capabilities, they can be programmed in high-level computer languages, and best of all they are affordable by individuals. As a result, there is a growing personal computing movement, involving people from all walks of life who find computer pioneering both exciting and rewarding.

This book is meant to be a contribution to this personal movement, especially in the area of applications. It's a collection of ideas that show how to exploit the power of computer "hardware" by an imaginative use of "software".

The word "software" is used to describe the sets of instructions (called programs) that control the flow of information in a computer. Software is important because most modern computers are general purpose. They aren't *a* machine, but *any* machine that can be described to them. This means that in the morning a personal computer can be an accountant for a diet management program, at noon it can speed through the analysis of scouting reports from a football game, and at night become an intriguing space-flight fantasy machine. This chameleon-like behavior is made possible by the programs that describe how the machine is to function.

The programs in this book are based on ideas from several different fields, but no previous experience with computing is required. While many of the applications go beyond those usually found in introductory books, they can be mastered by anyone with the enthusiasm (and perseverance) of the amateur. Also, working with an idea on a computer is very different from just reading about it. In fact, anyone who explores the concepts in this book using a computer can expect to experience a new kind of human learning. Computer explorations combine the insights of do-it-yourself learning with the discipline of logical thinking.

In addition to supporting personal computing, this book will find use in introductory computing courses for both colleges and secondary schools. For this reason, a selection of project ideas has been given at the end of each chapter. Student projects make a good alternative to traditional testing as a way of determining grades in such a course. There are also a number of self-test sections in the book to help clarify new concepts as they arise.

The authors' experience with student programming projects— either in beginning courses or informal study programs—suggests that the best approach is to start with modest ideas that can later be used as parts of larger programs. This takes more planning of course, and it often requires revision of early ideas, but the extra effort soon pays real dividends. Personal computing is one of the few fields where students can contribute new ideas in a relatively short time.

The authors have had the good fortune to see this phenomenon at work over the past few years, and wish to thank the many students and friends whose inventiveness contributed so much to our education. Our special thanks go to Jim Berman, Mary Burleigh, Yale Cohen, Bob Hoffman, Jeff Lederer, Ruth Sabean, Howard Seltman, Cathy McIntire, Mike Shore, Don Simon, and Leon Sweer. We also wish to thank Gordon French, Bill Linder, George Miller and Jack Nevison for their careful reading of the manuscript and their most helpful suggestions, and Bill Gruener for his valued contributions as editor.

BASIC AND THE PERSONAL COMPUTER

1

THE WORLD OF PERSONAL COMPUTING

1.0 INTRODUCTION

The world of personal computing is basically a friendly one, and no special
credentials are needed to become part of it. While it's true that modern
computer systems involve complex technologies and theories, their use is
becoming easier all the time. This means that the mastery of personal
computing can be based on the strategy of doing interesting things first, and
then using the experience gained as the basis for more detailed study.

A key part of this strategy is to use a liberal dose of imagination right
from the start. Computer amateurs aren't afraid to fantasize a bit, knowing
that's where half the fun lies. Surprisingly, most early ideas of this sort have
become reality: color graphics, computer music, computer robots, and even
computers that "speak" (and in a crude way "recognize") English.

Does this mean that computers can eventually be used to do just about
anything—including the making of human judgments? No. The diversity in
personal computing, and the way so many different points of view have
contributed to its growth, makes it clear how impossible (and undesirable)
that would be.

Part of the reason for this diversity is that personal computing spans all
ages. Grade school kids are contributing entries to "computer fair" contests
that have the judges scratching their heads. Popular magazines on the subject
are found nestled between the textbooks of college students. And more than a

few over-forty types report that they are caught up in an involvement that's like nothing they can remember.

While the exact future of personal computing is still an unknown, it's clear that variety will always be a key ingredient. For many, personal computing will be mostly a spectator sport. For others, it will become a powerful tool for exploring all kinds of new ideas. In either case, an excursion behind the scenes to see what's possible—which is where we're now headed—is worth everyone's while.

1.1   ABOUT THE WORD "COMPUTER"

It used to be that computers were easy to spot. They filled large rooms with tons of electronics, crammed behind complex panels dotted with blinking lights. They were understood by only a handful of people, they cost a small fortune, and they were used for the most mysterious of purposes.

But a lot has changed in recent years. Advertisements now proclaim the virtues of everything from "computer-controlled fuel-injection" car engines, to "digital computer displays" for clocks and ovens. And the number of "computer-controlled" game attachments for home TV is growing rapidly. It's reasonable to ask whether all these uses of the word computer mean the same thing.

While there's an element of truth in such popular usage, in many cases the word computer really refers to a special-purpose piece of hardware built for one task. In such instances, it would be more accurate to use the words "microprocessor", "logical circuit", or "digital control circuit". As a rule, consumer products don't qualify as full-fledged computers.

But there's an important exception to this rule: it's the device called the personal, general-purpose, programmable digital computer. As the words say, this is not a machine built for any special purpose at all. In fact it comes out of the factory just waiting to be told what to do—to be *programmed*. It's the closest thing to an "imagination extender" that's ever been invented.

Of course there are some additional questions that need to be asked. Do personal computers really work? Who can afford them? And if my resistance breaks down and I get one, what will it do?

Those are good questions, and the answers to the first two are easy: (1) yes, those made by reputable manufacturers work, and (2) you can buy a modest one for about the price of a component hi-fi system, or a complex one for the price of an automobile.

The third question takes a bit longer to answer. A few hundred pages to be exact, and that's what this book is all about.

We'll begin in Chapter 2 by showing how to program a personal computer, using the high-level programming languages BASIC and EXTENDED BASIC. New ways of using this language to make a general-purpose personal computer do all kinds of special-purpose things will then be introduced in each successive chapter. The topics covered range over most of the areas that both professional and amateur computer users have found useful (and fun).

Before getting started on the business of programming, however, we'd better back off a bit and take a look at a typical personal computing system, and the jargon that's been developed to describe the various components that go into it.

1.2   SOME EXAMPLES OF PERSONAL COMPUTING SYSTEMS; A BRIEF GUIDE TO COMPUTER JARGON

If you read the ads for personal computers or visit a computer store, you very soon run into a new vocabulary: RAM, ROM, BYTE, I/O, SERIAL, PARALLEL, CPU, VDM, ASCII, PROM, EPROM, CRT, — it's all very mysterious at first. Let's try to clear the air by looking at an example of a rather complete personal computing system to see what each of these terms means.

You'll notice that there are several components in our system which interconnect (that's why it's called a computer *system*). There are also alternatives for some of the components, which is why the phrase AND/OR appears on our diagram. (Of course if money is no problem, you can drop the OR).

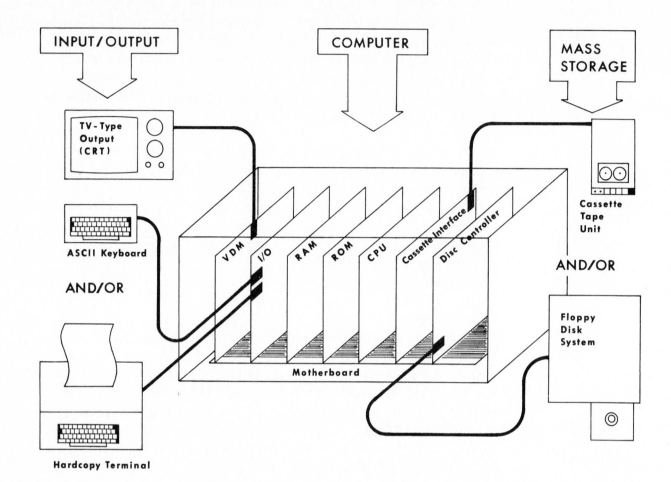

The three headings at the top of the diagram show that a full-fledged computer system consists of three major groups of components. We've labeled these as the INPUT/OUTPUT group, the COMPUTER group, and the MASS STORAGE group. Let's examine the components found in each of these groups in greater detail.

Input/Output Components

The INPUT/OUTPUT components are often called "I/O devices". An *input* device is used to transmit both programs and the data which are to be manipulated by programs *into* the computer. In other words, we want to take information in a form understood by humans, and feed it to the computer in a form that can be handled by machines. The most common input device is what's called an ASCII keyboard. This looks a great deal like a typewriter keyboard. It has all the letters, numbers, and special symbols needed to type programs, math formulas, and even English text. When a key is pressed on this keyboard, a unique "7-bit" code is generated. The word "bit" means a simple 2-valued piece of information (something like the "thumbs-up-thumbs-down" code of the Romans). In computer work the two values of a bit are written as 0 and 1.

For example when you press the key for the letter A, the 7-bit code 1000001 is sent to the computer. The process looks something like this:

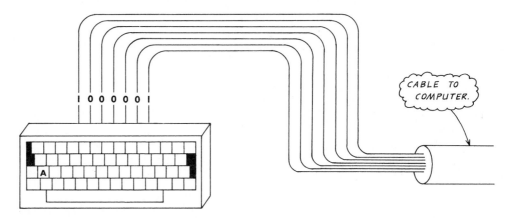

When each of the bits is sent on a separate wire as shown, we speak of a *parallel* connection. When the bits are sent one after the other on a single wire, the connection is called *serial*.

In the computer, bits are represented by two different voltages, usually called "high" (the 1) and "low" (the 0). The 1 and 0 can also be read as "bit on" and "bit off". The important point is that one bit gives only two different codes. We can come up with a lot more codes by using seven bits. With one bit there are $2^1=2$ codes. With seven bits we'll have $2^7=128$ codes, so we can take care of all the alphabet, numbers, and special symbols needed, plus a few extra codes for control functions.

OPTIONAL SELF-TEST:

For most programming, you don't have to know anything about the actual codes. This is all taken care of in the circuits inside the devices. Also, most manufacturers use the same code, so I/O devices can usually be interchanged between systems. The code used is called the *American Standard Code for Information Interchange*, or ASCII for short. The complete ASCII code is shown in Appendix B, and some uses of binary codes are discussed in Chapter 10. Chapter 10 also discusses binary arithmetic—which you don't have to know anything about now. Here are two questions about binary codes to try in case you can't wait until Chapter 10.

1. Use Appendix B to translate the following imaginary conversation.

2. Radio amateurs often use a 5-bit code for transmitting messages. This means there should be $2^5=32$ different patterns of 0's and 1's possible. Make a chart showing all these patterns. If you need help, look at the hot dog problem in Section 2.4, where a 5-bit code is used (in disguise) for another purpose.

Output devices work in a reverse manner. Now the problem is to get the computer to display information in some kind of "human readable" form. For example, many personal computing systems use a TV monitor as an output device. This is either a slightly modified home TV set, or a closed-circuit TV monitor of the kind used in security systems. These are often called CRT displays (because they use *Cathode Ray Tubes*).

For TV output, a special piece of hardware is needed to convert the ASCII codes *inside* the computer back into symbols of the kind we use in ordinary printing (A,B,C,D,...,0,1,2,3,...,#,+,-,etc.). If you look inside the computer shown in our diagram, you'll see a "board" labeled VDM. This means *Video Display Module*. It's a circuit board that takes the ASCII codes from the computer, and converts them into dot patterns which show up on the TV monitor. (The term VDM-1 was coined by Processor Technology Company which makes both boards and computers.) The patterns are chosen as shown in the accompanying photo to look like standard printing.

Another kind of I/O device is the "hard-copy" terminal. This includes both an ASCII keyboard for input, and a mechanism similar to that on an

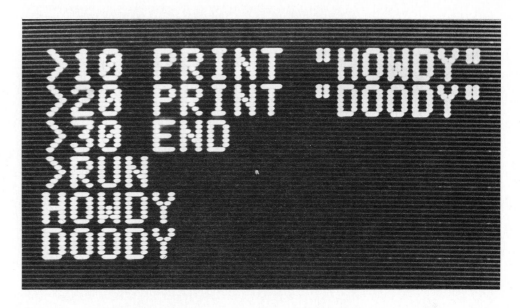

Dot patterns on a CRT screen produced by a video display module.

electric typewriter for output. So "hard-copy" means output printed on paper. This is important for applications where you want to save the output, or reproduce it (as done in this book). Hard-copy terminals do *not* need a VDM board. They contain their own code-conversion circuits. They are connected instead to what's called one "port" on an "I/O board". There are different kinds of ports for different kinds of terminals, but most modern I/O boards can be made to work with any kind of terminal. It's usually just a matter of changing a few wires on the board, following the instructions supplied by the manufacturer.

The Computer Components

The central part of our diagram is labeled "computer". This is shown as a collection of several circuit boards called *modules*. These plug into a common "motherboard". The motherboard has a bunch of printed wires (usually 100) soldered to connectors (called "slots") that accept the modules. This way a computer can grow. As you buy new boards, you simply plug them into an empty motherboard slot. So if you think you'll be expanding some day, it will be worth buying a computer that has a lot of slots available (up to 22 are available on some machines). You'll also want to make sure that the power supply (*not* shown in our diagram) which comes with your computer can handle that many boards. There is usually only one power supply, and it must have the capacity for handling all the boards plugged into the motherboard.

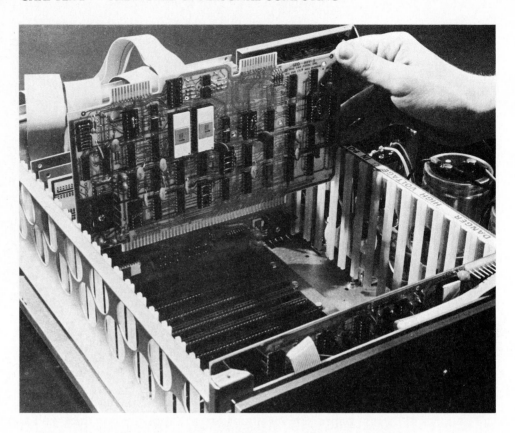

Microcomputer module board being plugged into a slot on the
motherboard of an IMSAI computer.

One of the boards shown inside our computer is labeled RAM. This
means it's a *Random Access Memory* board. It's where the programs and
data we feed our computer are stored. This information is stored in binary
form (all 0's and 1's). As a programmer in BASIC you won't have to worry
about this since BASIC uses normal decimal notation.

In advanced programming (Chapter 10), we'll show how the binary bits
of information are sometimes organized in groups of eight, called *bytes* of
memory. A small RAM board holds 4K bytes. Normally K means 1,000. But
in computer work, 1K means 1024, so a 4K board has 4096 bytes. There are
also boards with 8K, 16K, etc. bytes . Memory can be increased in computers
by plugging in extra boards. The upper limit on many machines is 64K bytes
which is 65,536x8=524,288 bits.

The reason these memories are called random (or direct) access is that
the computer can go directly to any byte, either "reading" its contents, or
"writing" (storing) new information there. The computer can rapidly access
bytes of information at random—there's no need to sequentially search all
through memory looking for something.

A ROM board contains *Read Only Memory*. Individual bytes of this
memory can also be accessed directly (so you could also call it random

access), but now no writing is permitted—only reading. ROM is used for permanent storage of programs or data that will never be changed . Except—well there is a trick for erasing *some* ROM's with a special ultraviolet light. Then you can program new "permanent" data into them. Boards of this type are called EPROM boards, which means *Erasable Programmable Read Only Memory.*

The board labeled CPU (*Central Processing Unit*) is where all the action takes place. The circuits on this board access data from memory, work on it, and ship it back out again. They also make sure the I/O devices get a chance to do their thing.

The heart of the CPU board is a microprocessor "chip", sometimes called a microprocessor unit (MPU). Some of the well-known microprocessor chips are the 8080 (Intel Co.) , the Z-80 (Zilog Co.), the 6800 (Motorola), and the 6502 (MOS Technology). The CPU board also contains "clock" circuitry to keep all this busy activity synchronized. The clock produces several million pulses per second, acting like a *very* fast orchestra leader working to keep everything in step.

The computer box (or "mainframe") also contains the I/O boards we've previously discussed, and the boards that may be needed to connect with mass storage devices. Let's see what these are all about.

Mass Storage Components

Imagine that you've had a busy session with your computer, and you now have a program for a brilliant new game up and running. But it's time to leave for a more gainful occupation, so you turn the computer off. Unfortunately, that act will wipe out all the information stored in RAM memory, so the next time you wish to use the computer you'll have to start all over. A similar problem occurs when you switch to a new program. The old one will have to be "scratched" (erased) before the new one can be typed in.

The solution to this dilemma is mass storage (also called off-line storage). The idea is to save copies of your programs and data in a form that can be re-loaded very rapidly—*without* re-typing at the keyboard.

The two most popular forms of mass storage are tape cassettes, and magnetic disks (sometimes spelled "discs"). The cassettes are the same kind as used in home recording. A special board inside the computer called the "cassette interface" is used to convert the bits in memory into a signal that can be fed into the recording jack of the tape recorder. This allows the *saving* of programs on tape. Conversely, the same board takes the output signal from your recorder (usually from the "monitor" jack), and converts it back into memory bits. This is how you *load* old programs back into memory.

An even better type of mass storage is the "floppy disk". This is about the size of a 45 rpm record, but the information is recorded magnetically.

The transfer speeds for disk are much higher than for tape. Further, disk playback machines can retrieve programs randomly. This is analogous to the way a person can pick up the arm on a record player and select one particular band of music (on tape you'd have to do a fast wind through everything). We'll have more to say about floppy disks and cassettes in Section 3.8, and in most of Chapter 8. We'll also mention a third type of storage, punched paper tape, in Section 3.8.

1.3   PACKAGED COMPUTER SYSTEMS

The previous section showed how a number of components are put together to make a full-fledged computer system. It's a bit like assembling a customized hi-fi system—confusing at first, but the most flexible route for those who want to experiment with all the possibilities of personal computing.

There are also computer amateurs who would rather concentrate more on applying their computer, and not have to worry about much more than plugging the system in and turning it on. There are "packaged" systems that allow one to do just that. At the high end of the price range, these take the form of desk-top computers made for commercial and educational uses. These systems are relatively expensive, and are sold mostly to institutions.

But there are also lower-priced packaged systems made for the consumer market, and the number is growing. Some are neatly enclosed in handsome cabinets with the keyboard built in. Others are a bit less pretentious, and assume you'll make your own enclosure. But most of them are both reliable and sophisticated.

An early example of a low-cost "almost" packaged system that illustrates this last category was the Apple I computer. It had all the circuitry on one board. This board included RAM and ROM memory, the CPU, I/O, a VDM, power supply, and even a tape cassette interface. The only external parts needed were an ASCII keyboard, a TV monitor, and an ordinary cassette tape machine. Although more recent packaged computers simplify things by putting all these parts in one case, it will be informative to show what they'd look like if spread out a bit.

The photo of the Apple I computer on the next page shows what the components look like. The computer to its right has a similar set of components, but they're all in one case.

Despite their apparent simplicity, packaged computers allow the full range of programming. A typical session goes something like this:

1. Plug the system in and turn the power switch to ON.
2. Following a few simple directions, load the BASIC interpreter program from your cassette tape machine. (On some machines you don't even have to do this. BASIC is permanently stored in "read-only" memory.)

The Apple I computer.

The PET computer.

3. Now type in the new BASIC program you've decided to try today. If you make a mistake, just re-type the incorrect lines.
4. Run your program. If you don't like what it's doing, change it or add to it.
5. If you like what you see, save the program on a tape cassette to show your next visitor. Turn the power switch off.

The only things you may not have understood in the above were the references to "loading the BASIC interpreter", "typing in a BASIC program", or "running a BASIC program". So let's turn our attention now to the business of programming, and show some simple examples of what's involved.

1.4   A SIMPLE EXAMPLE OF PROGRAMMING IN BASIC

Once all the hardware is connected and working, it's time to say to our computer system "don't just stand there—do something." However we'll have to be a bit more explicit, and spell out that "do something" in greater detail. This means we're now ready to get into the business of programming, which isn't difficult if you use a high-level language. Actually, it's as simple as

ABC, where A means "get the machine ready", B is "write and load your program", and C is "run it".

Writing a program amounts to making a list of very exact instructions in a language "understood" by your computer. The fundamental language understood by any computer is called "machine language". This is not a good language for people however, so higher level languages like BASIC have been invented. Now the problem is that we'll need an interpreter—a special program that translates BASIC into machine language. BASIC interpreters are supplied by most companies that make personal computers. However these interpreters vary in sophistication, ranging from TINY BASIC to BASIC-PLUS. Some idea of how fancy your interpreter is can be gotten from how much memory it requires. You'll hear references to 4K BASIC, 8K BASIC, 12K BASIC, disk-extended BASIC, and others. In general, the larger versions are more powerful.

The Altair computer with disk mass storage and a hardcopy
terminal for I/O. Its disk-extended BASIC uses 20K of RAM.

Now that we understand the need for an interpreter, we can get back to our ABC's of making a computer do something.

A. Get the machine ready. This means turning everything on, and then following the procedure needed to get your BASIC interpreter in memory. Each machine is different, so you'll have to read your instruction manual at this point. Also, some machines store BASIC permanently in ROM.

B. Write and load your program. How to write programs is the subject of most of this book. Once it's written (on paper), you load it by typing it in at the keyboard (if it's an old program, you load it from tape or disk).

C. Run (or execute) your program. This is easy. All you do is type RUN. If it works as expected, you jump with joy. If not (which is more likely), it's back to the drawing board in order to find your "bugs" (yes, it's probably your error). Actually, finding and fixing bugs is one of the more rewarding parts of beginning programming.

Incidentally, the total amount of memory you'll need will be that required by your BASIC interpreter *plus* that needed by your program. So if your computer has a total of 16K bytes of memory, and if you have an 8K BASIC, then your program will be limited to 8K bytes maximum. Most of the programs in this book will work within that limitation. To handle the larger programs, or to expand on them, a total of 32K bytes will be about right.

Here's what the ABC process looks like to the users of two typical machines. On the left you'll see a simple system with a TV monitor for output, and cassette tape for mass storage. On the right a more complicated system is shown with a hardcopy output terminal, and a floppy disk for mass storage.

A. The BASIC interpreter is loaded from mass storage

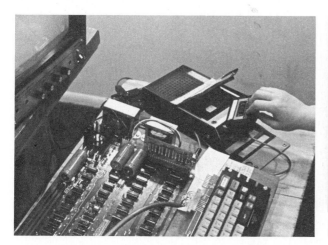

Loading BASIC on the Apple I.   Loading BASIC on the Altair.

B. A program is typed in which looks like this:

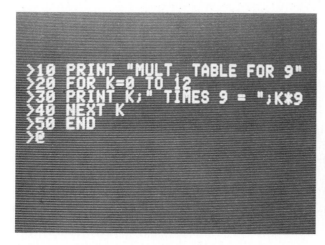

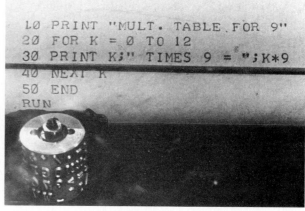

Program typed on the Apple I.   Program typed on the Altair.

C. And now it's run

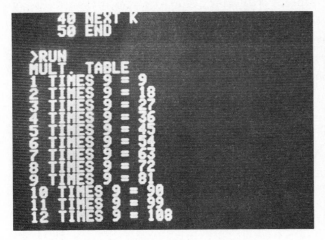

Run of the program on the Apple I.   Run of the program on the Altair.

1.5 A CLOSER LOOK AT A PROGRAMMING SESSION

Now that we've got the big picture, let's zoom in on some of the details that steps B and C involve. Suppose you want to write a program to generate some multiplication tables (just in case your calculator breaks down some day).

If you only want to use the computer to calculate a few values, here's what you type (from now on, we'll only show hardcopy output, but of course the same ideas hold for TV monitor output).

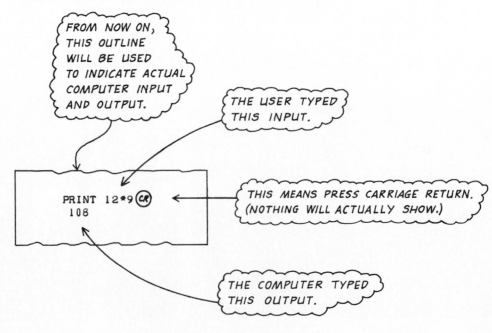

This example uses what's called *direct mode* (also called *immediate* mode) in BASIC. That's because you get an answer directly after you press "carriage return". (The carriage *return* key is always pressed at the end of lines.)

But this only gives us one multiplication. We could get two answers by typing the following direct mode statement:

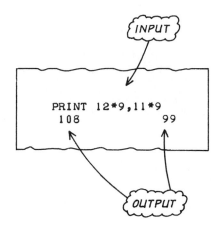

That's still not much of a multiplication table. It's time for a full-fledged *indirect mode* program. Here's what this might look like:

MULT TABLE

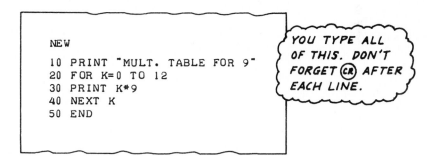

For reference purposes, we've called our program MULT TABLE. All the indirect mode programs in this book will be given a reference name which will be printed in the margin as shown.

Notice that an indirect mode program is made up of several "statements", each of which begins with a line *number*. (Don't worry too much about the details now—this will be explained again in Chapter 2).

So now we have a program, but no answers. That's because an indirect mode program doesn't run (or "execute") until we tell it to by typing the *command* RUN. Watch what happens:

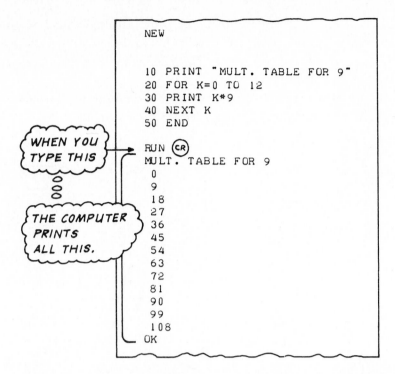

As you can see, our program now produces 12 different products. To label them more neatly, all we have to do is change line 30 a bit. If we type in a new line 30 as follows, it will take the place of the old one. Then running the program will produce the improved output. (The improved output helps someone who doesn't know what our program is all about understand the results).

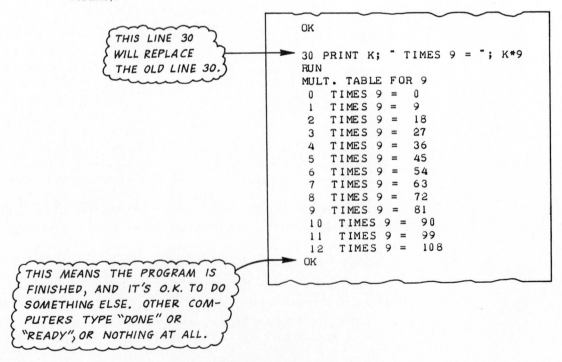

To see what the modified program looks like at any time, simply type the command LIST. This will give you a listing of all the latest statements in your program.

IMPROVED MULT TABLE

```
LIST

10  PRINT "MULT. TABLE FOR 9"
20  FOR K=0 TO 12
30  PRINT K; " TIMES 9 = "; K*9
40  NEXT K
50  END
OK
```

If you want to see the output again, just type RUN. You can do this as often as you wish. To see the program, type LIST; to see it execute and produce output again, type RUN.

Incidentally, if you make typing mistakes, you'll usually get what's called an error message. This may not mean much to you at first, but the cure is simple: retype the offending line. Here's an example where the word RUN was typed incorrectly as RUNG. The computer called it a SYNTAX ERROR. Retyping the word correctly cured the problem.

Correcting an error by retyping a misspelled word.

You may now ask if we can extend this program to print several different multiplication tables. The answer is yes, and it only takes a few more lines. Project #2 at the end of this chapter shows how to do this.

1.6   ANOTHER EXAMPLE OF PROGRAMMING

Suppose that you've just finished the multiplication table program of the previous section, and want to try something else. You decide not to save your program because it's short and can be typed in again any time. For this reason, the first thing to do is to erase the old program from memory. In many versions of BASIC you do this by typing the command SCR (for scratch). Another form of this command is NEW, which means clear out memory because here comes a *new* program. (On a number of computers, you *must* type NEW at the beginning of any session. If you're not sure, try it. You won't hurt anything, but you *will* erase memory.)

Now let's enter a new program which is to calculate how much money will accumulate in a piggy bank. This time, we'll deliberately make some typing mistakes so you can see how this is handled.

PIGGY BANK

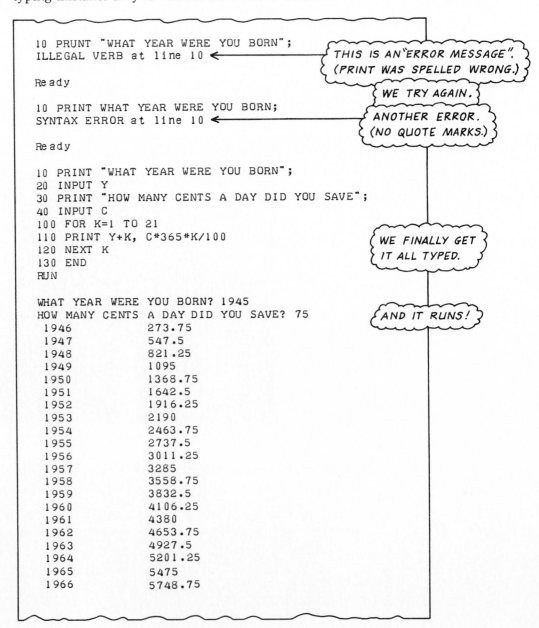

```
10 PRUNT "WHAT YEAR WERE YOU BORN";
ILLEGAL VERB at line 10

Ready

10 PRINT WHAT YEAR WERE YOU BORN;
SYNTAX ERROR at line 10

Ready

10 PRINT "WHAT YEAR WERE YOU BORN";
20 INPUT Y
30 PRINT "HOW MANY CENTS A DAY DID YOU SAVE";
40 INPUT C
100 FOR K=1 TO 21
110 PRINT Y+K, C*365*K/100
120 NEXT K
130 END
RUN

WHAT YEAR WERE YOU BORN? 1945
HOW MANY CENTS A DAY DID YOU SAVE? 75
   1946            273.75
   1947            547.5
   1948            821.25
   1949            1095
   1950            1368.75
   1951            1642.5
   1952            1916.25
   1953            2190
   1954            2463.75
   1955            2737.5
   1956            3011.25
   1957            3285
   1958            3558.75
   1959            3832.5
   1960            4106.25
   1961            4380
   1962            4653.75
   1963            4927.5
   1964            5201.25
   1965            5475
   1966            5748.75
```

THIS IS AN "ERROR MESSAGE". (PRINT WAS SPELLED WRONG.)

WE TRY AGAIN.

ANOTHER ERROR. (NO QUOTE MARKS.)

WE FINALLY GET IT ALL TYPED.

AND IT RUNS!

NOTE 1: When you type in two lines with the same line number, the old line is replaced. If you first type

    10 PRINT "HI"

and then type

    10 PRINT "HOWDY"

only the line 10 PRINT "HOWDY" is in the computer.

NOTE 2: To get rid of a line, just type its line number followed by a carriage return. Typing

    10 (carriage return)

will erase line 10 from the program.

NOTE 3: To get rid of an entire program type SCR or NEW. To double check on what's actually in the computer at any time, simply type LIST.

Suppose we now want to add a few additional lines to the output. Since the old program is still in memory, all we have to do is type in the desired new statements as follows:

IMPROVED PIGGY BANK

```
50  PRINT "MONEY IN PIGGY BANK ON EACH BIRTHDAY --UNTIL 21"
60  PRINT "FROM"; C; "CENTS PER DAY, NO INTEREST"
70  PRINT "-YEAR-------TOTAL DOLLARS"

RUN

WHAT YEAR WERE YOU BORN? 1945
HOW MANY CENTS A DAY DID YOU SAVE? 87
MONEY IN PIGGY BANK ON EACH BIRTHDAY --UNTIL 21
FROM 87 CENTS PER DAY, NO INTEREST
-YEAR-------TOTAL DOLLARS
   1946           317.55
   1947           635.1
   1948           952.65
   1949           1270.2
   1950           1587.75
   1951           1905.3
   1952           2222.85
   1953           2540.4
   1954           2857.95
   1955           3175.5
   1956           3493.05
   1957           3810.6
   1958           4128.15
   1959           4445.7
   1960           4763.25
   1961           5080.8
   1962           5398.35
   1963           5715.9
   1964           6033.45
   1965           6351
   1966           6668.55
```

NOTICE THE ADDITIONAL OUTPUT.

Remember, the carriage *return* key must be pressed after every line *you* type, including the 1945 (year born), and the 87 (cents saved per day). Also remember that you are not supposed to understand how this program works — that's coming in Chapter 2. For now, the idea is just to get the big picture of how a programming session goes together.

Commands in BASIC

Words like RUN and LIST are called *commands*. Notice that they don't have line numbers. Also notice that commands cause something to happen right after you press the return key (CR).

There are several other commands in common use. For example, to store programs on tape or disk, there is usually a SAVE command. To retrieve a program, there is a LOAD command (on some systems, this is called the OLD command, since you're going to retrieve an old program). The SAVE and LOAD commands are not found in all versions of BASIC, so you'll want to check your system manual to see what commands are available.

All versions of BASIC have a command that "erases" the entire program currently in memory. On some systems the command is SCR (short for scratch). On others it is NEW (which means erase the old program, because I want to create a new one).

Some fancier versions of BASIC have a command called DELete for erasing groups of lines. For example,

DEL 50-70

would delete *all* the lines with numbers from 50 up to (and including) 70.

1.7   HOW TO COPE WITH YOUR COMPUTER

By now it should be clear that no two computer systems will be exactly alike. The variety possible in components, together with the fact that the interconnections often have to be customized, means that many individual owners of computers will have unique systems.

Getting your own particular collection of hardware up and running can be both rewarding and frustrating. But help is available in the form of books, magazines, computer clubs, and computer stores. The better stores function something like a good high-fi shop, and offer both advice and service on the components they sell. They can also refer you to others who have put together similar systems, or to personal computing clubs where computer amateurs meet and share ideas.

The closest thing to a common link between the great variety of computer systems is the programming language BASIC. That's why most of the remainder of this book will explain applications in terms of BASIC programs. But even here you must expect some variation. Not all versions of BASIC have the same features. Also, the same features may produce slightly different results in output.

Don't let this discourage you. There's a very simple solution to the problem of adapting to such variations. It's to experiment. You'll be surprised at how good you can get at this (which really amounts to becoming your own teacher) once you see that experimentation won't hurt anything.

We'll try to help by pointing out some of the variations in BASIC as we go along. We'll also demonstrate some techniques for "simulating" fancy features you may not have in your version of BASIC. The best way to evaluate *any* BASIC is to try writing and running some of your favorite programs in it—to set up what are called "benchmarks".

One last suggestion—if you have a choice, get a BASIC that has (among other things) floating point arithmetic, arrays, and strings. Floating point arithmetic assures that you get full decimal values in your answers. For example, in some TINY BASIC interpreters, if you say PRINT 10/3 you'll get 3 for the output. A BASIC with floating point arithmetic will give an answer of 3.333333 which is of course much better (if not downright essential) for many applications.

As to what arrays and strings can do for you, Chapters 4 and 5 give lots of examples. Most versions of BASIC that take 8K bytes or more will have all these features. There's also little doubt that new and better versions will continue to appear. So it's a good idea to set one's sights high right from the beginning.

Timesharing

Using a language like BASIC means that the programs developed can be run on just about any microcomputer. But larger computers can also be used, since most of these can be programmed in BASIC. These machines are too expensive for individuals of course, so they are usually found at institutions where they are "shared" by many users. The technique that makes this possible is called *timesharing*. It works something like a very fast version of a telephone answering service where there is only one operator but lots of phones. Each client gets a fraction of the operator's time. In a similar manner, timesharing users only get a fraction of the computer's time, but the sequence repeats so rapidly there is usually no noticeable waiting for service.

To use timesharing you need a terminal with a keyboard for input, and either a typewriter-like printer or a TV-like screen for output. The terminal must be connected to the large computer either directly with wires, or indirectly with a gadget (called an acoustic coupler) that uses a regular telephone set to communicate with the computer.

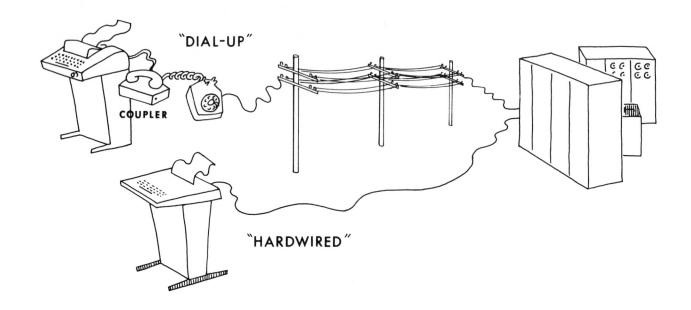

Once connected to the computer, people working at timesharing terminals can try most of the ideas about personal computing discussed in this book. When using BASIC, a timesharing terminal acts pretty much "as if" it were a personal computer.

There *is* one minor difference. Users of timesharing start their session by typing a line or two that gives their *user number* and their *password* (this is to control unauthorized use of the machine). This process is called "logging in". When finished, a timesharing user must also "log out". On many systems this is done by simply typing BYE (which means "goodbye"). An example of how this works for the timesharing system used on a PDP-10 computer is given in Appendix A. (Other systems will differ slightly, and local documentation should be consulted.)

1.8 PROJECTS

The last section in each chapter suggests some project ideas. These will usually be of enough substance to take a few days of on-and-off activity. By exception, we'll only suggest two short projects for Chapter 1. However they're well worth doing, since this will make the reading ahead much easier going.

1. Beg, borrow, or cajole use of a microcomputer that speaks BASIC, and actually type in and run the programs in Sections 1.5 and 1.6. Don't

worry about the fact that the way these programs work hasn't been explained yet. The main point is to get some hands-on experience with the whole process. The project will also get you familiar with the startup procedures needed for future programming.

2. After you have the multiplication table program of Section 1.5 running, try this more advanced version just to see what happens.

```
NEW
5 FOR D=1 TO 9
10 PRINT "MULT. TABLE FOR";D
20 FOR K=0 TO 12
30 PRINT D;" TIMES ";K;" = ";D*K
40 NEXT K
50 PRINT
60 NEXT D
70 END
RUN
```

3. If you have a TRS-80 computer (shown below) with Level II BASIC try the program shown on page 434. Get someone to look over your shoulder and double check your typing. It's a long (but fascinating) program, so you'll probably want to save it on tape.

The TRS-80 personal computer distributed through Radio Shack stores. With this machine use the ENTER key instead of CARRIAGE RETURN.

2

THE 8-HOUR WONDER
All About BASIC Programming
in One Long Day
(or Eight Short Nights)

2.0 INTRODUCTION

Developing an artistic command of BASIC and extended BASIC — which is where we're headed next — will take a while. But getting the fundamentals under control takes very little time—even less than eight hours for most people. This is because the language has a small vocabulary, and the words used pretty well mean what you'd expect.

In this chapter we'll look at about twenty *key words* from this vocabulary. Another dozen or so key words will be explained in Chapters 3 and 4. These, together with a number of programming techniques, will enable you to express ideas with a growing fluency. Add the sage old advice of "practice, practice, practice", and you'll be a virtuoso of the ASCII keyboard in no time at all.

The key words of BASIC are used to make up what are called *statements* (which are something like "sentences" in the language). Statements are then put together to form *programs* . Here's a simple illustration of how this works for the example shown earlier in Chapter 1.

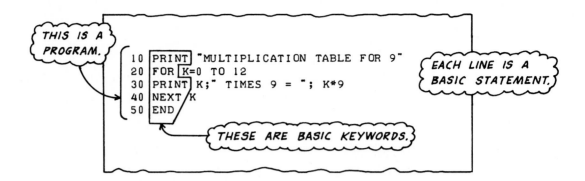

Each statement is an instruction to the computer. You'll notice that statements begin with what is called a *line number* (ln for short). This can be any integer from 1 to 65000 that *you* choose. The computer then uses the order of these numbers to determine the order in which to execute (carry out) the instructions in your statements.

Most programmers use line numbers 10, 20, 30, etc. to leave room for instructions they may have forgotten. For example, if you add a statement 35 at the bottom of a program like this:

```
    .
    .
30 PRINT K
40 NEXT K
50 END
35 PRINT "*************************************"
```

the computer will know you want to print a line of asterisks after line 30. When you LIST this program, you'll find that statement 35 has been inserted between statements 30 and 40 (a very nice feature!).

HOUR 0: TEN WARM-UP EXERCISES

Before attacking the eight sections of this chapter and studying the details of how to write programs, it will be helpful to first try a few things informally. Readers who have had some experience with programming can skip this section. But if you're new at computing, spend as much time with these "warm-up" exercises as you wish.

The approach here will be to present the solutions to some simple problems of the kind that can be studied by imitation. It will soon become clear that most of these problems are not good examples of what computers can do. However the basic ideas shown in the solutions will be useful as later

building blocks. There won't be any detailed explanation of the key words used in this section. The idea is to invent your own explanations based on what happens. The formal explanations will be given shortly, at which time you can see how well your ideas hold up. Here's a brief guide to what the key words used in Chapter 2 are, and where the explanations will be given:

Key Words	Informally Used in Warm-Up Exercise	Explanation Given in Section
INPUT	5	2.1
PRINT	All Exercises	2.1
IF . . . THEN	10	2.1
STOP	10	2.1
GOTO	4	2.1
END	All Exercises	2.1
LET	1, 8	2.2
FOR . . . NEXT	6	2.3
TAB	——	2.4
READ	——	2.5
DATA	——	2.5
RESTORE	——	2.5
RND and RANDOMIZE	——	2.6
ON . . . GOTO	——	2.6
REM	——	2.7
GOSUB and RETURN	——	2.8
DEF FNK	——	2.8
ON . . . GOSUB	——	2.8

As the chart shows, we'll use about ten of the key words informally in the warm-up exercises. It is strongly suggested that you run each of the programs given in these exercises. This will be a good chance to become familiar with the keyboard and output screen (or paper) on your computer.

Also feel free to try variations on the solutions given. NOTE: Before typing in any of these programs, first make sure that the BASIC interpreter is loaded in your computer.

Exercise 1: Use your computer as a calculator.

Solution: There are two approaches you can try. The first uses *direct mode* (also called *immediate* mode). Try typing the following: (Some versions of BASIC do not permit direct mode. If this doesn't work go on to the indirect approach.)

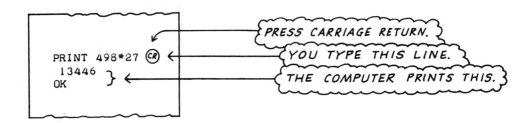

Direct mode statements do *not* have line numbers. Our example calculates the product of 498 and 27. To do this problem as an *indirect mode* program type the following:

PRODUCT

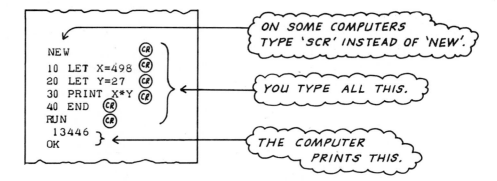

Notice that * means multiply. Similarly + means add, - means subtract, and / means divide.

For this example, using indirect mode (with all those line numbers) is pretty silly. But as you'll soon find, it's the most powerful mode for more important problems.

Exercise 2: The restaurant bill for three people is $18.45, and they want to leave a 15% tip. Calculate how much each person should pay.

Solution: Using direct mode type this:

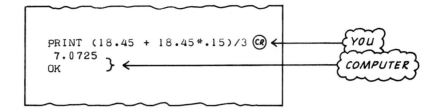

```
PRINT (18.45 + 18.45*.15)/3 (CR)
 7.0725
OK        }
```
YOU
COMPUTER

This tells us that each person owes about $7.07. Notice how parentheses are used to group the bill and tip together so that both are divided by 3. Using indirect mode, the program could be written as follows:

TIP

```
NEW (CR)
10 PRINT (18.45 + 18.45*.15)/3 (CR)
20 END (CR)

RUN (CR)
 7.0725
OK
```

NOTE: Users with a BASIC that doesn't have "floating point" (decimal) arithmetic will have to do everything with whole numbers as follows:

```
PRINT (1845 +1845*15/100)/3 (CR)
 707
OK
```

The answer is 707 cents (which is $7.07).

Exercise 3: Make the computer print some words—say, your name.

Solution: If your name is Bob, you could do this:

BOB

```
NEW

10 PRINT "BOB"
20 END

RUN
BOB
OK
```

FROM NOW ON WE WON'T SHOW THE (CR) WHICH IS TYPED AT END OF EACH LINE.

Exercise 4: That's not very impressive. Make the computer print your name lots of times.

Solution: That's easy. Watch closely.

BOB FOREVER

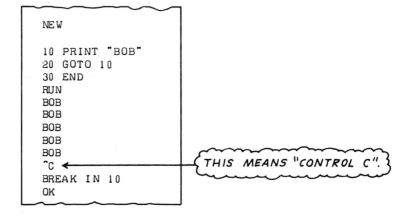

```
NEW

10 PRINT "BOB"
20 GOTO 10
30 END
RUN
BOB
BOB
BOB
BOB
BOB
^C
BREAK IN 10
OK
```

THIS MEANS "CONTROL C".

This program will go on 'forever' unless *you* stop it by pressing "control C". That means holding down the key marked control, while you simultaneously press the key for the letter C. The 'break' message tells you at what line the program was interrupted. Your computer may not print this message. Also some systems use something different from control C for interrupting programs. Check your manual.

Exercise 5: Change the preceding program so it prints any name you wish.

Solution: You can do this by using the key word INPUT as follows:

HI NAME

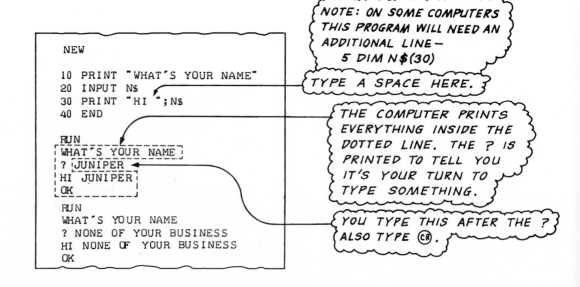

```
NEW

10  PRINT "WHAT'S YOUR NAME"
20  INPUT N$
30  PRINT "HI ";N$
40  END

RUN
WHAT'S YOUR NAME
? JUNIPER
HI JUNIPER
OK
RUN
WHAT'S YOUR NAME
? NONE OF YOUR BUSINESS
HI NONE OF YOUR BUSINESS
OK
```

NOTE: ON SOME COMPUTERS THIS PROGRAM WILL NEED AN ADDITIONAL LINE — 5 DIM N$(30)

TYPE A SPACE HERE.

THE COMPUTER PRINTS EVERYTHING INSIDE THE DOTTED LINE. THE ? IS PRINTED TO TELL YOU IT'S YOUR TURN TO TYPE SOMETHING.

YOU TYPE THIS AFTER THE ? ALSO TYPE (CR).

Notice that you can RUN a program as often as you wish.

Exercise 6: Can you make the computer print lots of numbers— say, the squares and cubes of the first 50 integers?

Solution: The easiest way is to use the key words FOR and NEXT as follows:

SQUARES & CUBES

```
NEW

10  FOR N=1 TO 50
20  PRINT N,  N*N,  N*N*N
30  NEXT N
40  END
OK
RUN
 1              1              1
 2              4              8
 3              9             27
 4             16             64
 5             25            125
 6             36            216
 7             49            343
 8             64            512
 9             81            729
10            100           1000
11            121           1331
12            144           1728
13            169           2197
14            196           2744
15            225           3375
16            256           4096
17            289           4913
18            324           5832
19            361           6859
20            400           8000
21            441           9261
22            484          10648
23            529          12167
24            576          13824
25            625          15625
26            676          17576
```

:
:

ETC. UP TO N = 50

Exercise 7: You're a student, and your teacher wants you to calculate the number of square inches in pizzas of different diameters from 6 to 16 inches. But you only have 10 minutes before class.

Solution: Help is on the way. Try this:

PIZZA

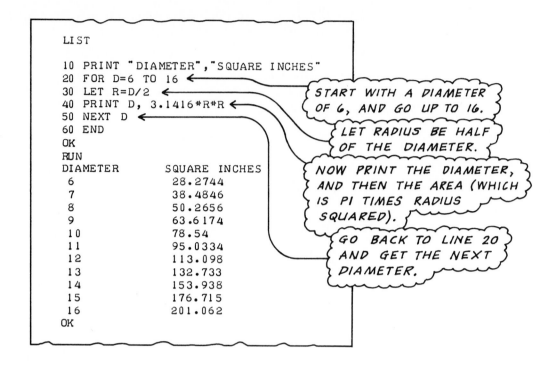

```
LIST

10  PRINT "DIAMETER","SQUARE INCHES"
20  FOR D=6 TO 16          ←
30  LET R=D/2              ←
40  PRINT D, 3.1416*R*R    ←
50  NEXT D                 ←
60  END
OK
RUN
DIAMETER          SQUARE INCHES
6                 28.2744
7                 38.4846
8                 50.2656
9                 63.6174
10                78.54
11                95.0334
12                113.098
13                132.733
14                153.938
15                176.715
16                201.062
OK
```

START WITH A DIAMETER OF 6, AND GO UP TO 16.

LET RADIUS BE HALF OF THE DIAMETER.

NOW PRINT THE DIAMETER, AND THEN THE AREA (WHICH IS PI TIMES RADIUS SQUARED).

GO BACK TO LINE 20 AND GET THE NEXT DIAMETER.

Exercise 8: You're doing a survey of voter preferences on a referendum and need to calculate percentages. How can this be done?

Solution: Here's one way. Let F mean 'number of votes *for* the referendum,' let A mean 'number of votes against,' and T mean '*total* number of votes.' Suppose there are 8,198 *for* , and 7,463 *against*. Here's a program to summarize the results and give percentages:

VOTE PERCENT

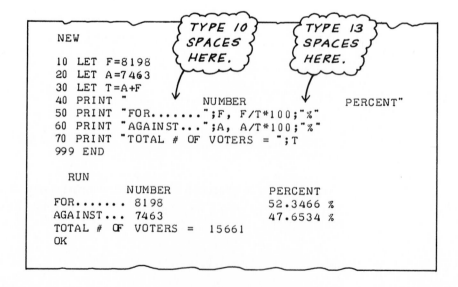

```
NEW

10  LET F=8198
20  LET A=7463
30  LET T=A+F
40  PRINT "            NUMBER        PERCENT"
50  PRINT "FOR......";F, F/T*100;"%"
60  PRINT "AGAINST...";A, A/T*100;"%"
70  PRINT "TOTAL # OF VOTERS = ";T
999 END

RUN
            NUMBER              PERCENT
FOR...... 8198                52.3466 %
AGAINST... 7463               47.6534 %
TOTAL # OF VOTERS =   15661
OK
```

TYPE 10 SPACES HERE.

TYPE 13 SPACES HERE.

Exercise 9: Suppose the votes had to be recounted. Can you run the same program again with new numbers?

Solution: Yes. You only need to change two statements. *Don't* type NEW (or SCR).

```
10 LET F=9483
20 LET A=6213
RUN
              NUMBER            PERCENT
FOR....... 9483                60.4167 %
AGAINST... 6213                39.5833 %
TOTAL # OF VOTERS =   15696
OK
```

Exercise 10: Can you add additional statements to make this program even fancier?

Solution: As long as you don't turn the computer off, or type NEW (or SCR), your program is still in memory. You can add new statements to the old program simply by typing them in. We'll illustrate this by adding an IF...THEN statement, a STOP statement, and two more PRINT statements as follows:

```
80 IF A>F THEN 110
90 PRINT "THE WINNER IS 'FOR' BY";F-A;"VOTES"
100 STOP
110 PRINT "THE WINNER IS 'AGAINST' BY";A-F;"VOTES"

RUN
              NUMBER            PERCENT
FOR....... 9483                60.4167 %
AGAINST... 6213                39.5833 %
TOTAL # OF VOTERS =   15696
THE WINNER IS 'FOR' BY 3270 VOTES
BREAK IN 100   ◄
OK
```

THE PROGRAM WAS INTERRUPTED BY THE 'STOP' AT LINE 100.

Want to see what your improved program looks like? Just type LIST.

VOTE WINNER

```
LIST
10 LET F=9483
20 LET A=6213
30 LET T=A+F
40 PRINT "            NUMBER              PERCENT"
50 PRINT "FOR.......";F, F/T*100;"%"
60 PRINT "AGAINST...";A, A/T*100;"%"
70 PRINT "TOTAL # OF VOTERS = ";T
80 IF A>F THEN 110
90 PRINT "THE WINNER IS 'FOR' BY";F-A;"VOTES"
100 STOP
110 PRINT "THE WINNER IS 'AGAINST' BY";A-F;"VOTES"
999 END
OK
```

That's a pretty fancy program, and it's time to start explaining how it (and the others in this section) work. So let's now look at the business of writing programs in more detail.

2.1 HOUR 1*: A PROGRAM TO HELP JUNIOR PASS ARITHMETIC 101

We'll start out by showing how to write a useful program with only six key words (in the case of IF ... THEN we should strictly talk about a key word "pair"). Our application will be an automated addition practice program that can be both a fun game to play and a painless way to get proficient at arithmetic.

To understand this program, we suggest you first look at what it does when it is executed (RUN). This is a good approach to most programming. It's better to first think about what you want to happen, and then write the program (set of instructions) to do it.

By looking at the RUN, you can see that the first thing this program does is to ask the person running it to type in two numbers. Then the program asks for the sum of these numbers. If the answer given is correct, the program prints TERRIFIC! Otherwise it prints NO, NO, NO followed by the right answer. The program also asks if another problem is wanted. Typing 1 means yes. Typing any other number (like zero) means no.

---

*Hour 1 is the longest since it has a lot of detail. It's probably best to go through it lightly the first time, and re-read it more carefully later.

HERE'S WHAT WE WANT FOR A RUN.

ADDITION PRACTICE

```
LIST
10 PRINT "ADDITION PRACTICE PROGRAM"
20 PRINT "TYPE IN 2 NUMBERS SEPARATED BY A COMMA"
30 INPUT A,B
40 PRINT "WHAT IS ";A;" + ";B;
50 INPUT X
60 IF X = A + B THEN 90
70 PRINT "NO, NO, NO ------ ANSWER IS ";A + B
80 GO TO 100
90 PRINT "TERRIFIC!"
100 PRINT "WANT ANOTHER (YES = 1)";
110 INPUT Y
120 IF Y = 1 THEN 20
130 PRINT "O.K. --- SO LONG."
140 END
```

AND HERE'S THE BASIC PROGRAM THAT MAKES IT HAPPEN.

```
RUN

ADDITION PRACTICE PROGRAM
TYPE IN 2 NUMBERS SEPARATED BY A COMMA
? 24,38
WHAT IS   24   +   38 ? 62
TERRIFIC!
WANT ANOTHER (YES = 1)? 1
TYPE IN 2 NUMBERS SEPARATED BY A COMMA
? 57,64
WHAT IS   57   +   64 ? 111
NO, NO, NO ------ ANSWER IS    121
WANT ANOTHER (YES = 1)? 0
O.K. --- SO LONG.
```

To explain how all this works we'll first explain each of the key words used. This will take a few pages, and will best be done with some simpler examples. Then we'll get back to the addition practice program and see how all the pieces fit together.

First the key words. We'll explain PRINT in a moment, but this will be easier if we first look at INPUT.

INPUT

In lines 30, 50, and 110 the key word used is INPUT. The idea of the INPUT statement is to make a program stop when it reaches that line, print a ? , and wait for the person running the program to type in (input) some "data". Data can be either numbers, or (as we'll explain later in Chapter 4), characters, or even "words". But for now they must be numbers, either integers (like 5, 89, -13) or decimal numbers (like 3.1416 or -.00328). *Fractions may not be used.* To input a number like 1/3, type .333333 instead.

INPUT is always followed by one or more *variable names* (separated by commas if there are two or more variable names). In our example, the variable names we have chosen in line 30 are A and B. To see what INPUT does let's look at a simpler program first:

INPUT

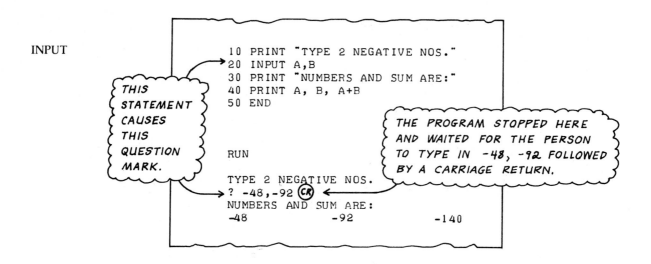

This INPUT statement causes the computer to print ? and then *wait* until the person running the program types two numbers and a carriage return. What happens inside the computer after the carriage return is pushed is that the two memory locations called A and B are set up, and the numbers -48 and -92 are stored in these locations. The situation looks something like the following:

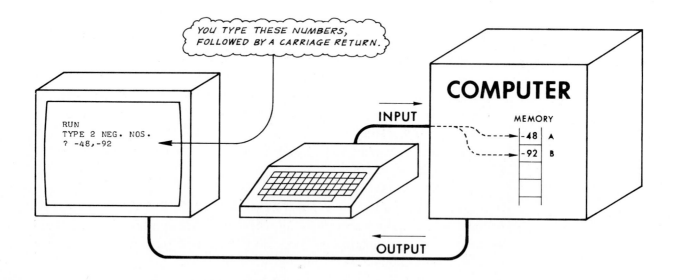

When you type -48, -92, after ? mark, these two numbers are *input* to the computer's memory. (The computer also "echoes" them on the screen so you can see what you've typed.)

> NOTE: In our example two numbers had to be typed because the INPUT statement contained two variables. If it had only one variable (like INPUT A) then you would only type one number. If it had three variables (like INPUT A,B,C) then you would type three numbers, and so on.

Notice that the *name* of a memory location is different from the *contents* of that location. The name is often called a *variable name* (or simply a *variable*) because the contents can be changed (varied) by a program. Thus for each memory location, we can envision a picture like this:

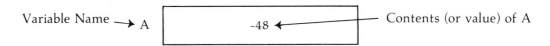

Variable Name → A [-48] ── Contents (or value) of A

PRINT

If a program statement says: 5 PRINT "A" it means print (or display on a screen) the letter A. If a program statement says: 25 PRINT A it *doesn't* mean print the letter A, but rather to print the *contents* of memory location A (which is -48 in our simple example).

If a program says:

40 PRINT A,B,A+B

it means PRINT the *contents* of location A, the *contents* of location B, and the *sum* of the contents in location A and B. The *commas* in the PRINT statement mean that the contents (numbers, in our example) should be printed with enough space between them to make the numbers fall into *fields* that are 14 spaces wide. A space is allowed for the sign in front of the number, but + prints as a blank space. We used negative numbers so you could see the sign.

```
TYPE 2 NUMBERS
? -48, -92
NUMBERS AND SUM ARE:
- 4 8              - 9 2              - 1 4 0
```

0 1 2 3 4 5 6 7 8 9 10 11 12 13 14 15 16 17 18 19 20 21 22 23 24 25 26 27 28 29 30 31 32 33 34 35 36 37 38 39 40 41 42 43 44 45 46 47 48 49 50 51 52 53 54 55

Column Numbers

FIELD 1   FIELD 2   FIELD 3   FIELD 4

To make the numbers in a line of output print closer together, you can use a semicolon instead of a comma. Here's a simple test program that shows what happens:

OUTPUT
SPACING

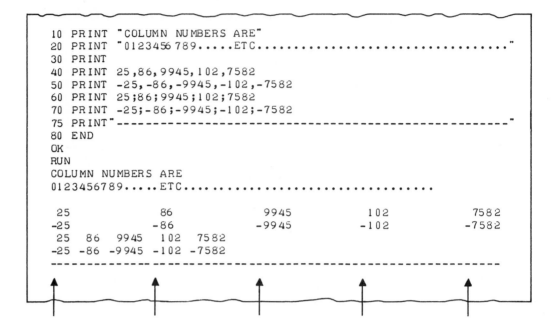

```
10  PRINT "COLUMN NUMBERS ARE"
20  PRINT "0123456789.....ETC........................................"
30  PRINT
40  PRINT 25,86,9945,102,7582
50  PRINT -25,-86,-9945,-102,-7582
60  PRINT 25;86;9945;102;7582
70  PRINT -25;-86;-9945;-102;-7582
75  PRINT"-----------------------------------------------------------"
80  END
OK
RUN
COLUMN NUMBERS ARE
0123456789.....ETC........................................

 25             86              9945            102             7582
-25            -86             -9945           -102            -7582
 25   86  9945  102  7582
-25  -86 -9945 -102 -7582
-----------------------------------------------------------------------
```

The arrows show where the fields caused by a comma begin. On a 70-column terminal, there are five such fields.

> NOTE: The spacing produced by the comma and semicolon in your BASIC may be different. To find out what they are, run the above test program and count what you get.

Notice that the "column" numbers used to describe positions across the output screen (or across the paper in an output printer) are numbered left to right starting with 0 (zero). Large printers can have 132 columns. Most printing terminals have 80 or 72 columns, while TV monitors may be limited to less (e.g. 40 columns). Also, some systems number the first column as 1.

TIME OUT FOR A SELF-TEST

The Self-Test sections in this book are meant to help you check your understanding of the more important ideas. The questions will be mostly in the form of "What does this program do?", or "Write a short program to do the following." These are meant to be pencil and paper exercises. But there will also be test items that say "Write and actually run a program to ... etc." This will usually mean several tries, since unforeseen errors (called "bugs") may creep in.

1. Pretend you're a "computer", and write down the output you would produce when commanded to RUN the following program. This is called "simulating" a computer RUN. It's a good way to check programs. An even better idea is for two people to swap programs they have written and simulate RUNS.

```
10 PRINT "TYPE TWO NUMBERS"
20 INPUT A,B
30 PRINT "SUM =";A+B,"PRODUCT =";A*B
40 PRINT "TYPE ANOTHER NUMBER";
50 INPUT C
60 PRINT "BET YOU CAN'T FIGURE WHERE"
70 PRINT "THESE NUMBERS CAME FROM"
80 PRINT (A+B)*C, A+B*C, A/B+C, A/(B+C)
90 END

RUN
TYPE TWO NUMBERS
?4,2
```

_____ ⎫ Finish the

_____ ⎬ output.

_____ ⎭

2. Write a short program that asks for the dimensions (in feet) of a bedroom, living room, and den, and then prints the total number of square feet of carpeting needed.

3. Write and actually run a program that does the same as Problem 2, and also prints the number of square yards of carpet needed, as well as the total cost. (Note: you'll have to add an INPUT statement that requests cost per square yard.)

Let's now go back to our ADDITION PRACTICE program, and examine the output PRINT statements to see what else is possible. There are really five rules to remember about PRINT.

PRINT Rule 1   Anything in quotes is printed exactly as given when the program is RUN. Example:

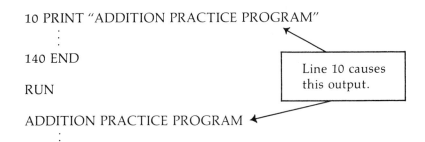

```
10 PRINT "ADDITION PRACTICE PROGRAM"
   ⋮
140 END

RUN

ADDITION PRACTICE PROGRAM
   ⋮
```

Line 10 causes
this output.

PRINT Rule 2

When variable names appear in a PRINT statement (*not* in quotes), the contents of these locations are printed. For example, if A contains 47, the statement

    10 PRINT A

will cause the number 47 to appear on the output device (not the letter A).

PRINT Rule 3

You can mix these two kinds of output (called "items") in one PRINT statement. For example, if A = 24 and B = 38,

    10 PRINT "WHAT IS ";A;" + ";B

causes the output

    WHAT IS 24 + 38

A comma is used between items to place output in separate fields, usually 14 columns wide. A semicolon is used to cause items to print as close together as possible, but leaving a space in front for the sign of a number, and leaving one "trailing" blank after the number. If you want a spacing different from either of these, there is a special item called TAB that can be used in a PRINT statement. It will be explained in Section 2.4.

PRINT Rule 4

A semicolon at the end of a PRINT statement suppresses the normal carriage return (and line feed) that usually takes place automatically when the program is RUN. Look at lines 40 and 50 of the ADDITION program to see how this works:

    40 PRINT "WHAT IS";A;" + ";B;
    50 INPUT X

If the memory locations A and B contain 42 and 17 respectively, here's what we get when these two statements are executed.

    WHAT IS 42 + 17 ?

The question mark came from the INPUT X statement, but it did not appear on the next line because the normal carriage return was suppressed by the semicolon at the end of line 40.

PRINT Rule 5

Arithmetic combinations of variables and numbers (what are called "arithmetic expressions") can be used in PRINT statements. For example you can say:

    200 PRINT "ANS IS";3+(B*B-4*A*C)/4

The combination 3+(B*B-4*A*C)/4 is called an arithmetic expression. If A=5, B=10, and C=2, this statement will produce the output:

ANS IS 18

This is because
3 + (10 * 10 - 4 * 5 * 2)/4 =
3 + (100 - 40)/4 = 3 + 60/4 = 3 + 15 = 18

A Word About Extended BASIC

The explanations so far conform to the minimal standard BASIC defined by a committee of ANSI (American National Standards Institutes). However there are several implementations of BASIC that allow extra features. Two of the most powerful of these are BASIC-PLUS (Digital Equipment Corporation) and Microsoft Extended BASIC (Microsoft Company). The latter is now used by microcomputer manufacturers such as Radio Shack, Pet, Ohio Scientific, Exidy, Apple, SOL, Synertek, Rockwell, Atari, and several others. Microsoft BASIC is summarized on pages 432 and 433. However there *are* a few differences in the way individual companies implement Microsoft BASIC, so you'll always want to check the reference manual for your computer. Project 4 on page 96 shows some of the differences between ANSI BASIC and extended BASIC. Radio Shack TRS-80 owners should also read page 434 for additional information.

More About Expressions; Operations in BASIC

(a) In BASIC, you can form arithmetic expressions using five operators:

   + is used for addition
   - is used for subtraction
   * is used for multiplication
   / is used for division
   ↑ is used for exponentiation (some systems use **)

Exponentiation means "raise to a power". For example, 3↑4 means "3 to the fourth power" which is the same as 3*3*3*3.

(b) Expressions can contain both variables and numbers (called constants). Examples:

(1+2+3+4)/N
(A+4)/16-3.213*B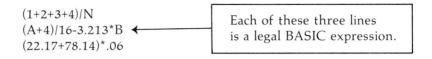
(22.17+78.14)*.06

Each of these three lines
is a legal BASIC expression.

(c) Parentheses are used in expressions to group things together and show in
what order the operations should be done. For example

$$(6+15)/3 \text{ means } 21/3 = 7,$$
but 6+15/3 means 6+5 = 11.

When there are no parentheses, here are the rules the computer follows:

FIRST PRECEDENCE Exponentiations (if any) are done first.
SECOND PRECEDENCE Multiplications and divisions are done next.
THIRD PRECEDENCE Additions and subtractions are done last.
    All operations are done from left to right.
WHEN IN DOUBT, USE PARENTHESES TO CLARIFY YOUR
MEANING.

TIME OUT FOR A SELF-TEST

1. Simulate running this program by completing the output.

```
10 INPUT A,B,C
20 PRINT A,B,C
30 PRINT A;B;C
40 PRINT "(A+B)*C = ";(A+B)*C
50 PRINT "THE";C;"TH POWER OF A+B IS";
60 PRINT (A+B)↑C
70 END
RUN
?20,-18,8
```

2. Write and run a program to convert a person's height into centimeters
using the fact that 2.54 cm = 1 in. Here's what a run should look like:

```
RUN
TYPE IN YOUR HEIGHT (FEET, INCHES)?5,10
THANK YOU.
YOU ARE 177.8 CENTIMETERS TALL
```

Let's now explain the remaining key words used in our program.

END

The END statement is simple to use. It is *always* the last statement of any program, and it has no other parts except a line number. Many programmers use 9999 as the line number for END.

NOTE: Strictly speaking, you don't even need the END statement in many versions of BASIC. But we recommend using it just in case you try running your programs on a computer system that requires it.

GO TO

This is also easy to use. It means that the "execution" of your program should depart from the usual rule of executing in the order given by the line numbers, and instead jump (GO TO) a specified line number. Compare these two examples:

```
10 PRINT 1              10 PRINT 1
20 PRINT 2              20 PRINT 2
30 PRINT 3              30 GO TO 10
40 END                  40 END

RUN                     RUN

1                       1
2                       2
3                       1
                        2
                        1
                        2
                        .
                        .
                        . etc. (forever!)
```

The GO TO in the second example makes it go on "forever" (of course you can always pull the plug). This is called an "infinite loop". On many systems you can stop such loops by typing "control C" (which means hold down the key marked CTRL, and then also press the C key). A better way out is to use an IF...THEN statement, which we'll explain next.

One last comment. You can type either GO TO or GOTO. This is because BASIC ignores most spaces. However it's good to use spaces whenever they make programs more readable (to people, not computers). We'll have more to say about this at the end of Section 2.4.

IF...THEN is a set of key words used in what are called "conditional branching" statements. Such statements are what make programs really interesting. To explain how this statement works, let's look at a simple example:

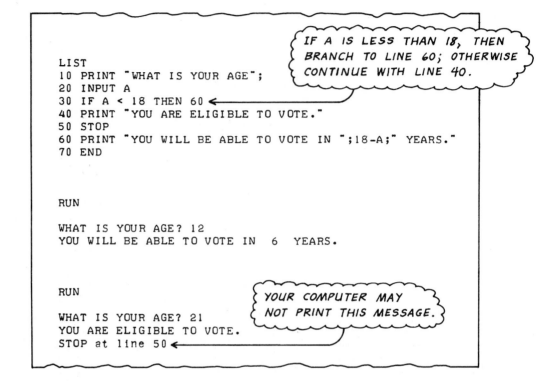

```
LIST
10 PRINT "WHAT IS YOUR AGE";
20 INPUT A
30 IF A < 18 THEN 60
40 PRINT "YOU ARE ELIGIBLE TO VOTE."
50 STOP
60 PRINT "YOU WILL BE ABLE TO VOTE IN ";18-A;" YEARS."
70 END


RUN

WHAT IS YOUR AGE? 12
YOU WILL BE ABLE TO VOTE IN   6   YEARS.


RUN

WHAT IS YOUR AGE? 21
YOU ARE ELIGIBLE TO VOTE.
STOP at line 50
```

IF A IS LESS THAN 18, THEN BRANCH TO LINE 60; OTHERWISE CONTINUE WITH LINE 40.

YOUR COMPUTER MAY NOT PRINT THIS MESSAGE.

Statement 30 is the IF...THEN statement. Here's what it means:

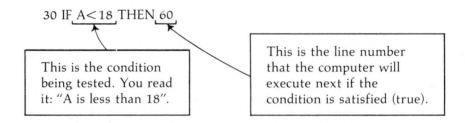

30 IF A<18 THEN 60

This is the condition being tested. You read it: "A is less than 18".

This is the line number that the computer will execute next if the condition is satisfied (true).

"Satisfied" just means that it's *true*—A *is* less than 18. If the condition is *false* (not satisfied) that is, A is either equal to or greater than 18, then the computer will simply go on to the next statement. In our example it would go on to 40. The statement

50 STOP

means that the computer is to stop executing the program at line 50—it should not go on to the END, but stop right where it is. You can have several

STOP statements in a program, but only one END, which *must* be the last statement.

We can illustrate the logical flow of this program with a diagram called a flow chart.

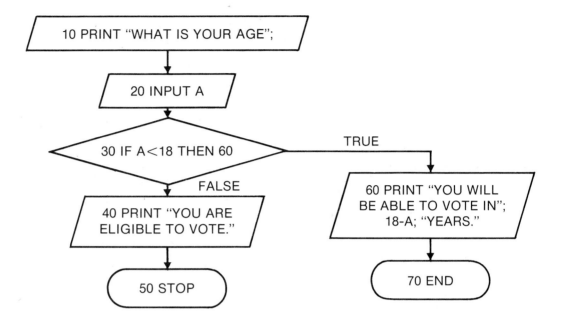

The most important box in our diagram is the diamond-shaped "decision" box, which shows the two possible branches or paths the computer can take. It represents the IF...THEN statement.

Here is how the various conditions are written in BASIC, using the relations <, >, and =.

A<B means "A is less than B".
A>B means "A is greater than B".
A=B means "A is equal to B".

You're also allowed to use the following combinations:

A <= B means "A is less than B *or* A is equal to B".
A >= B means "A is greater than B *or* A is equal to B".
A <> B means "A is not equal to B".

One last (but very important) thing: the parts of a condition can also be expressions. All of the following are correct IF...THEN statements:

```
100 IF A+4 >A-B THEN 120
100 IF X<=B*B-4*A*C THEN 500
100 IF 3*X↑4<.0001 THEN 400
```

Relations have the lowest precedence. They are tested only after all expressions in the condition have been evaluated.

Meanwhile, Back at Our Main Example...

Let's now return to our ADDITION PRACTICE program, and show it in flow chart form. It has two conditional "decision" boxes, one to decide if the answer given to the problem is correct, and the other to decide whether the user wants to do another problem. You'll notice that the GOTO statement doesn't get a box. It's simply written next to the line that shows where the program "goes to" at that point.

Notice that line 120 branches back to line 20 for another problem only if Y=1. Any other number input for Y makes the program go to line 130. Some programmers write line 100 as:

100 PRINT "WANT ANOTHER (YES=1, NO=0)";

Of course, any number except 1 means "No".

The best way to follow this flow chart is to start at the top and trace the arrows. Choose specific numbers for A and B. Trace through the flow chart for two different answers for X, a correct one where X=A+B is *true*, and an incorrect one where X=A+B is *false*.

FINAL SELF-TEST FOR SECTION 2.1

1. Enter and actually RUN the ADDITION PRACTICE program. See if your favorite grade school student can use it, or even suggest some improvements.
2. Modify the program so it gives practice in multiplication.
3. Modify the program so it gives practice in adding three numbers at a time.

NOTE: In addition to the diamond-shaped "decision" box, flow charts use three other standard shapes. Trapezoidal-shaped boxes (slanted sides) are used to show both input and output. Sausage-shaped boxes are used to show the start and end of a flow chart. Rectangular-shaped boxes are used for most other things (LET statements, mostly).

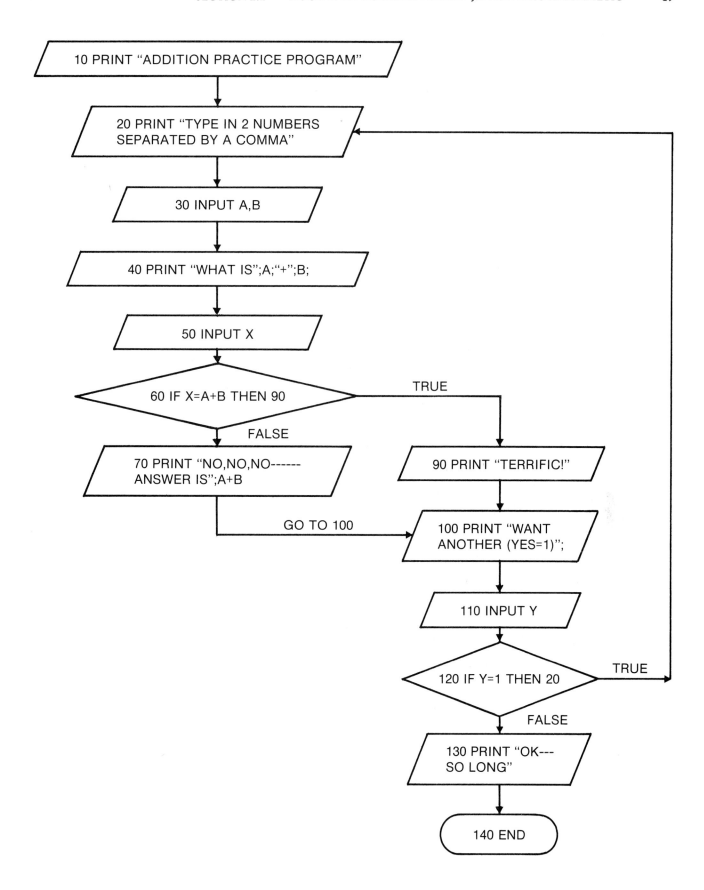

2.2   HOUR 2: ADDING A "COUNTER" TO YOUR
PROGRAM; PRINTING SCORES

The previous program required the "user" (the person running the program) to repeatedly answer the question WANT ANOTHER? This could get pretty tiring for someone who was training for an arithmetic quiz and wanted to do lots of practice problems. Here's a multiplication practice program that allows you to say how many problems you want right at the start. It also prints the percent of correct answers at the end.

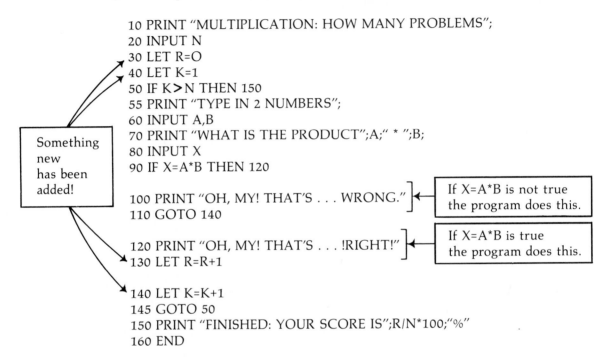

```
10 PRINT "MULTIPLICATION: HOW MANY PROBLEMS";
20 INPUT N
30 LET R=O
40 LET K=1
50 IF K>N THEN 150
55 PRINT "TYPE IN 2 NUMBERS";
60 INPUT A,B
70 PRINT "WHAT IS THE PRODUCT";A;" * ";B;
80 INPUT X
90 IF X=A*B THEN 120

100 PRINT "OH, MY! THAT'S . . . WRONG."
110 GOTO 140

120 PRINT "OH, MY! THAT'S . . . !RIGHT!"
130 LET R=R+1

140 LET K=K+1
145 GOTO 50
150 PRINT "FINISHED: YOUR SCORE IS";R/N*100;"%"
160 END
```

Something new has been added!

If X=A*B is not true the program does this.

If X=A*B is true the program does this.

This program uses a new key word, LET.

LET

As you've probably guessed by now, a computer program can't do very much until data has been stored in the proper memory locations. There are three ways to do this in BASIC. The first is an INPUT statement that let's the person running the program supply this data. The second is the LET statement which allows the program itself to load data in a memory location (the third method uses the READ and DATA statements explained in Section 2.5). LET statements are called *assignment* statements. The statement

```
10 LET  A=54
```

sets up a memory location called A and then "assigns" the number 54 as its contents:

An important feature of the LET statement is that the right side can be any arithmetic expression. For example here's a program that calculates the areas of circles with radii R supplied by the user:

CIRCLE AREA

```
LIST
10  INPUT  R
20  LET  A = 3.1416 * R * R
30  PRINT  R, A
40  GO TO  10
50  END


RUN

?  1
   1                3.1416
?  10
   10               314.16
?  ^C
```

> THE USER PRESSED "CONTROL-C" HERE TO INTERRUPT THE PROGRAM.

Now here's the most interesting feature of LET. You can have the variable on the *left* side of a LET statement become an updated version of its previous value given on the *right* side. Watch this:

COUNT

```
LIST
10  LET  K = 1
20  PRINT  K;
30  LET  K = K + 1
40  IF  K <= 10  THEN 20
50  END


RUN

   1  2  3  4  5  6  7  8  9  10
```

See what happened? K started out as 1. Then it was printed in line 20. Then, in line 30, K was changed to a 2 (a value equal to its previous value + 1). The IF...THEN in line 40 makes the whole process repeat until K is greater than 10.

Suggestion: you should always think of the LET statement as doing what's to the *right* of the = sign first, and *then* storing this value in the variable on the left side. Think of LET K=K+1 as meaning:

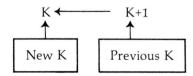

$$K \longleftarrow K+1$$

| New K | Previous K |

The above process is called *incrementing* K. In our case we increment by 1, but of course any increment could be used.

Now Back to the MULTIPLICATION PRACTICE Program

From the discussion of LET, you can now see how our MULTIPLICATION PRACTICE program works. K is a counter that keeps track of how many problems are done. When it finally becomes greater than (>) N, the number of problems which the user wanted to do, the program branches to line 150 and finishes up. Our other counter is R which keeps track of how many problems the user gets right. R only gets incremented (in line 130) if the answer X is correct (that is, when the condition in line 90 is true). This makes the program branch to line 120, followed by line 130 where the incrementing of R takes place.

The percent of correct answers is printed with the expression R/N*100 in line 150. For example, if you do 20 problems (N=20), and get 14 right (R=14), then R/N*100 = 14/20*100 = .7*100 = 70%. Here's a sample RUN of the MULTIPLICATION PRACTICE program:

MULTIPLICATION
PRACTICE

```
LIST
10 PRINT "MULTIPLICATION:  HOW MANY PROBLEMS";
20 INPUT N
30 LET C=0
40 LET K=1
50 IF K > N THEN 150
55 PRINT "TYPE IN 2 NUMBERS";
60 INPUT A,B
70 PRINT "WHAT IS THE PRODUCT ";A;" * ";B;
80 INPUT X
90 IF X = A * B THEN 120
100 PRINT "OH, MY! THAT'S .......WRONG."
105 PRINT "ANSWER IS ";A*B
110 GO TO 140
120 PRINT "OH, MY! THAT'S .......!RIGHT!"
130 LET R=R+1
135 GOTO 50
140 LET K=K+1
145 GO TO 50
150 PRINT "FINISHED:  YOUR SCORE IS ";R/N*100;"%"
160 END

RUN

MULTIPLICATION:  HOW MANY PROBLEMS? 3
TYPE IN 2 NUMBERS? 23,4
WHAT IS THE PRODUCT  23   *   4 ? 92
OH, MY! THAT'S .......!RIGHT!
TYPE IN 2 NUMBERS? 27,8
WHAT IS THE PRODUCT  27   *  8 ? 216
OH, MY! THAT'S .......!RIGHT!
TYPE IN 2 NUMBERS? 2,3
WHAT IS THE PRODUCT   2   *  3 ? 5
OH, MY! THAT'S .......WRONG.
ANSWER IS   6
FINISHED:  YOUR SCORE IS  66.6667 %
```

More About BASIC Variables

This is a good time to answer a question you may have had about what "names" can be used for BASIC variables. The answer is that in minimal BASIC a variable can be

(1) Any single letter, e.g., A, B, C, D, ..., Z.
(2) Any single letter followed by a single decimal digit, e.g., A1, A2, A9, B4, B7, Q7, Q8, Z0, Z3, Z4, Z5.

This means that there are 26 + 10*26 = 286 possible "legal" variable names (additional names for "string" variables will be introduced in Chapter 4.)

SELF-TEST

1. Which are legal variable names? X3, Z, 5K, AB, Q8, W-2, IOU

2. Simulate running this program and write down the output:

```
10 LET A=10
20 LET B=10
30 LET K=1
40 IF K > 5 THEN 100
50 PRINT K,A,B
60 LET A=A+2
70 LET B=A+B
80 LET K=K+1
90 GOTO 40
100 END
```

3. Write a program that acts like (simulates) an adding machine. A run should look like this:

```
RUN
ADDING MACHINE SIMULATOR
ENTER NUMBERS TO BE ADDED AFTER EACH?
ENTER 0 (ZERO) WHEN FINISHED
?142.83
?96.21
?895.04
?7.22
?0
THE NET SUM= 1141.30
```

Hint: Set up an "accumulator" variable for the sum with an initial value 0 (40 LET S=0). Then after you input each number(50 INPUT X), add it to the latest value in the accumulator (60 LET S=S+X).

4. Write and RUN a program to verify your checkbook balance. Hint: There's nothing to do! Simply use the above program, and enter deposits as positive numbers (?605.42), and check or bank charges as negative numbers (?-49.52).

2.3   HOUR 3: GETTING THE COMPUTER TO DO ITS OWN COUNTING; LOOPS

In the last section we showed the technique of using a counter together with an IF...THEN statement to control how many times a program executes a group of statements. This is called "looping" or "iteration", and it's an important type of control in programs. There is another way to control looping that is even simpler. It uses a pair of statements: a FOR statement together with a matching NEXT statement.

FOR...NEXT

Here are two programs that compare the two techniques for controlling loops:

Using a Counter	Using FOR and NEXT Statements
10 LET K = 1	10 FOR K = 1 TO 5
20 IF K > 5 THEN 60	20 PRINT K; K*K; K*K*K
30 PRINT K; K*K; K*K*K	30 NEXT K
40 LET K = K + 1	40 END
50 GO TO 20	
60 END	

Both programs produce the same output:

```
RUN
1 1 1
2 4 8
3 9 27
4 16 64
5 25 125
```

As you can see, the second program is simpler. Here's another example showing how several statements (called the *body* of the loop) can be controlled by FOR...NEXT statements:

SINGLE LOOP

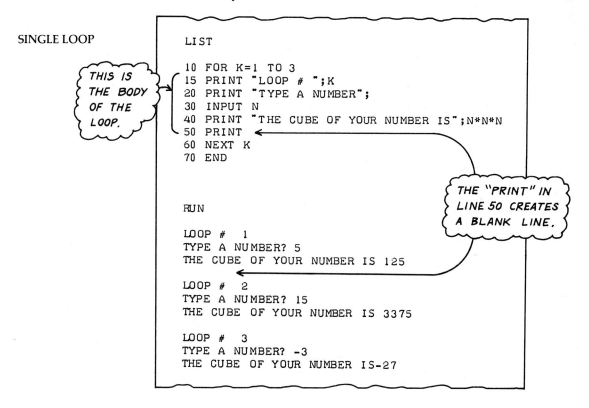

```
LIST

10 FOR K=1 TO 3
15 PRINT "LOOP # ";K
20 PRINT "TYPE A NUMBER";
30 INPUT N
40 PRINT "THE CUBE OF YOUR NUMBER IS";N*N*N
50 PRINT
60 NEXT K
70 END


RUN

LOOP #   1
TYPE A NUMBER? 5
THE CUBE OF YOUR NUMBER IS 125

LOOP #   2
TYPE A NUMBER? 15
THE CUBE OF YOUR NUMBER IS 3375

LOOP #   3
TYPE A NUMBER? -3
THE CUBE OF YOUR NUMBER IS-27
```

THIS IS THE BODY OF THE LOOP.

THE "PRINT" IN LINE 50 CREATES A BLANK LINE.

The full form of the FOR statement is

```
100 FOR K = 1 TO 25 STEP 5
——-(body of the loop)——-
200 NEXT K
```

The FOR statement really has three key words, FOR, TO, and STEP. The word STEP is used to say how much K should be incremented each time around the loop. If STEP is omitted, the STEP size (or increment) is taken to be 1.

Here's an example to show a negative STEP:

NEGATIVE STEP

```
LIST

10  PRINT "STAND BY FOR AIR TIME"
20  FOR K=5 TO 1 STEP -1
30  PRINT K;"SECONDS"
40  NEXT K
50  PRINT "YOU'RE ON!!"
60  END




RUN

STAND BY FOR AIR TIME
 5 SECONDS
 4 SECONDS
 3 SECONDS
 2 SECONDS
 1 SECONDS
YOU'RE ON!!
```

An important feature of the FOR statement is that variables or arithmetic expressions can be used after the = sign, and also after TO and STEP. Here's a simple example showing this feature:

STARS

```
LIST

10  PRINT "HOW MANY STARS DO YOU WANT TO BE PRINTED";
20  INPUT N
30  FOR K=1 TO 2*N
40  PRINT "*";
50  NEXT K
60  PRINT
70  PRINT "HA HA--THAT'S TWICE AS MANY AS YOU WANTED."
80  END




RUN

HOW MANY STARS DO YOU WANT TO BE PRINTED? 5
**********
HA HA--THAT'S TWICE AS MANY AS YOU WANTED.
```

SELF-TEST

1. Simulate running this program and write down the output you get.

   ```
   10 PRINT "IF JAN 1 IS A MONDAY THEN"
   70 FOR K = 1 TO 31 STEP 7
   30 PRINT "JAN";K;"IS A MONDAY"
   40 NEXT K
   50 END
   ```

2. Simulate running this program and write down the output.

   ```
   10 LET N = 10
   20 FOR K = 1 TO N STEP N/5
   30 PRINT K
   40 NEXT K
   50 END
   ```

3. Modify the MULTIPLICATION PROGRAM of Section 2.2 so that the number of problems done is controlled by a FOR...NEXT loop instead of the K counter.

2.4   HOUR 4: PRINTING PATTERNS; THE HOT DOG PROBLEM

Let's start by reminding ourselves of how to use a semicolon to keep printing on the same line, and how to use a PRINT to "undo" the effect of this semicolon. Look at the difference between these two programs:

```
10 FOR K = 1 TO 5          10 FOR K = 1 TO 5
20 PRINT "*";              20 PRINT "*";
30 NEXT K                  30 NEXT K
40 PRINT "FINISHED"        40 PRINT
50 END                     50 PRINT "FINISHED"
                           60 END
RUN
                           RUN
*****FINISHED
                           *****

                           FINISHED
```

In the second program, the PRINT in line 40 was needed to get a line feed and carriage return so that FINISHED appeared on a new line.

Now let's get fancy, and use two FOR loops, one inside the other. The second loop acts like the *body* of the first, and we say we have *nested* FOR loops.

DOUBLE LOOP

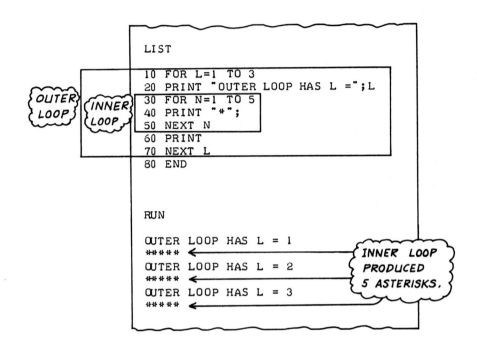

If you think through this program, you'll see that the body of the inner loop (which is simply line 40) gets executed 15 times. Looking at the asterisks printed should make this clear. The variable L controls how many lines get printed (3), while N controls how many asterisks per line (5), so 15 are printed altogether.

Programs with FOR loops can be made easier to read by using indentations that show the bodies of the loops. This will be illustrated at the end of this section. Another technique is to sketch in brackets or boxes that show the bodies of loops. RULE: Bracket or box lines showing the bodies of nested loops should *never* cross.

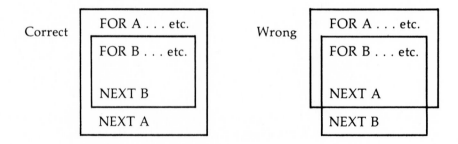

Could we have nested, nested FOR loops? You bet. Here's an example where N controls the number of asterisks per line, L controls how many lines, and B controls how many blocks of lines.

TRIPLE LOOP

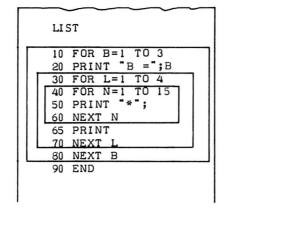

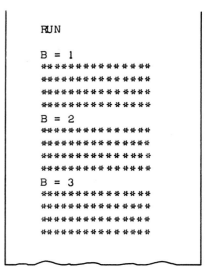

Here's a trickier version of the above which you should study carefully to make sure you understand what's going on.

VARIABLE LOOPS

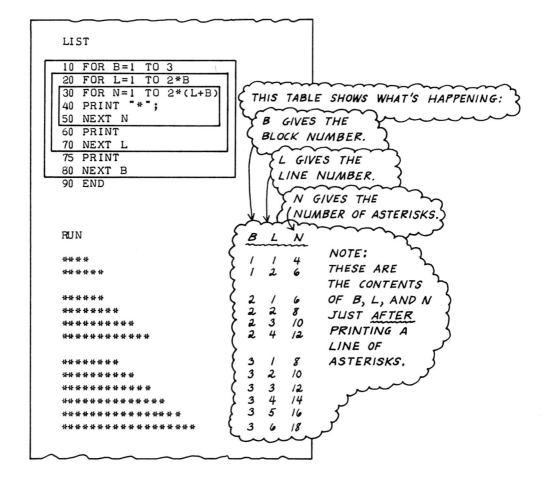

We'll return to the subject of printing patterns later, and show how to make them more interesting by using random numbers and other tricks.

Let's switch to another use of nested loops by showing an application to a fun problem which is also related to the important idea of *tree structures*.

THE HOT DOG PROBLEM

Suppose your're running the hot dog stand at your next club picnic, and you decide to post a computer printout showing how to order all the possible combinations by number. Let's assume that there are only YES/NO decisions allowed for hot dog, bun, mustard, mayonnaise, and catsup. To discourage overindulgence, we'll also print a calorie count for each combination.

The way to think about this problem is to picture what's called a *decision tree*.

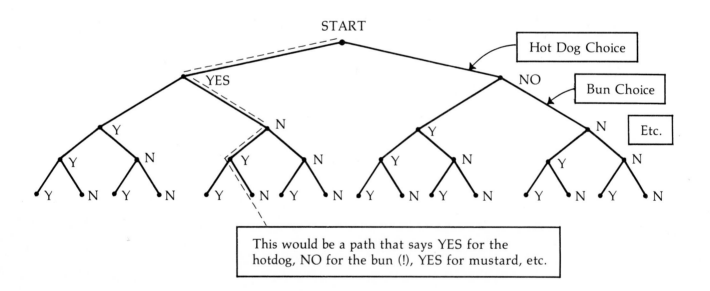

One way to generate a tree structure in BASIC is to use nested FOR loops, one for each level. Our tree will have five levels (one for each ingredient) so there will be five FOR loops. Here's how all the paths through our five-level tree can be tabulated with a BASIC program.

HOT DOG

```
LIST

10 PRINT "        DOG    BUN    MUST.    MAYO.   CATSUP"
15 LET K=1
20 FOR H = 0 TO 1
30 FOR B = 0 TO 1
40 FOR M = 0 TO 1
50 FOR Y = 0 TO 1
60 FOR C = 0 TO 1
70 PRINT "#";K;": ";
80 PRINT H;"      ";B;"      ";M;"      ";Y;"      ";C;
90 PRINT "    CALORIES=";H*140+B*120+M*20+Y*100+C*30
95 LET K=K+1
100 NEXT C
110 NEXT Y
120 NEXT M
130 NEXT B
140 NEXT H
150 END

RUN
```

WEIGHT WATCHER'S SPECIAL

	DOG	BUN	MUST.	MAYO.	CATSUP	
# 1 :	0	0	0	0	0	CALORIES= 0
# 2 :	0	0	0	0	1	CALORIES= 30
# 3 :	0	0	0	1	0	CALORIES= 100
# 4 :	0	0	0	1	1	CALORIES= 130
# 5 :	0	0	1	0	0	CALORIES= 20
# 6 :	0	0	1	0	1	CALORIES= 50
# 7 :	0	0	1	1	0	CALORIES= 120
# 8 :	0	0	1	1	1	CALORIES= 150
# 9 :	0	1	0	0	0	CALORIES= 120
# 10 :	0	1	0	0	1	CALORIES= 150
# 11 :	0	1	0	1	0	CALORIES= 220
# 12 :	0	1	0	1	1	CALORIES= 250
# 13 :	0	1	1	0	0	CALORIES= 140
# 14 :	0	1	1	0	1	CALORIES= 170
# 15 :	0	1	1	1	0	CALORIES= 240
# 16 :	0	1	1	1	1	CALORIES= 270
# 17 :	1	0	0	0	0	CALORIES= 140
# 18 :	1	0	0	0	1	CALORIES= 170
# 19 :	1	0	0	1	0	CALORIES= 240
# 20 :	1	0	0	1	1	CALORIES= 270
# 21 :	1	0	1	0	0	CALORIES= 160
# 22 :	1	0	1	0	1	CALORIES= 190
# 23 :	1	0	1	1	0	CALORIES= 260
# 24 :	1	0	1	1	1	CALORIES= 290
# 25 :	1	1	0	0	0	CALORIES= 260
# 26 :	1	1	0	0	1	CALORIES= 290
# 27 :	1	1	0	1	0	CALORIES= 360
# 28 :	1	1	0	1	1	CALORIES= 390
# 29 :	1	1	1	0	0	CALORIES= 280
# 30 :	1	1	1	0	1	CALORIES= 310
# 31 :	1	1	1	1	0	CALORIES= 380
# 32 :	1	1	1	1	1	CALORIES= 410

The output from this program would be a lot nicer if all the 0's and 1's (NO and YES decisions) lined up. We can make this happen by using the new key word TAB.

The statement 10 PRINT TAB (12) ;"*" will cause the "*" to print in column 12 (don't forget that columns are numbered from left to right starting with *zero*). We'll say more about TAB in Chapter 3, and show how using the form TAB(X) (where X is a variable in your program) can be used to produce graphical output.

To fix up our hot-dog problem all we have to do is change one line.

```
70 PRINT "#";K;TAB(5)":     ";


RUN
           DOG    BUN    MUST.   MAYO.   CATSUP
  # 1  :     0      0      0       0       0      CALORIES=  0
  # 2  :     0      0      0       0       1      CALORIES=  30
  # 3  :     0      0      0       1       0      CALORIES=  100
  # 4  :     0      0      0       1       1      CALORIES=  130
  # 5  :     0      0      1       0       0      CALORIES=  20
  # 6  :     0      0      1       0       1      CALORIES=  50
  # 7  :     0      0      1       1       0      CALORIES=  120
  # 8  :     0      0      1       1       1      CALORIES=  150
  # 9  :     0      1      0       0       0      CALORIES=  120
  # 10 :     0      1      0       0       1      CALORIES=  150
  # 11 :     0      1      0       1       0      CALORIES=  220
  # 12 :     0      1      0       1       1      CALORIES=  250
  # 13 :     0      1      1       0       0      CALORIES=  140
  # 14 :     0      1      1       0       1      CALORIES=  170
  # 15 :     0      1      1       1       0      CALORIES=  240
  # 16 :     0      1      1       1       1      CALORIES=  270
  # 17 :     1      0      0       0       0      CALORIES=  140
  # 18 :     1      0      0       0       1      CALORIES=  170
  # 19 :     1      0      0       1       0      CALORIES=  240
  # 20 :     1      0      0       1       1      CALORIES=  270
  # 21 :     1      0      1       0       0      CALORIES=  160
  # 22 :     1      0      1       0       1      CALORIES=  190
  # 23 :     1      0      1       1       0      CALORIES=  260
  # 24 :     1      0      1       1       1      CALORIES=  290
  # 25 :     1      1      0       0       0      CALORIES=  260
  # 26 :     1      1      0       0       1      CALORIES=  290
  # 27 :     1      1      0       1       0      CALORIES=  360
  # 28 :     1      1      0       1       1      CALORIES=  390
  # 29 :     1      1      1       0       0      CALORIES=  280
  # 30 :     1      1      1       0       1      CALORIES=  310
  # 31 :     1      1      1       1       0      CALORIES=  380
  # 32 :     1      1      1       1       1      CALORIES=  410
```

A Word About Programming Style

Programs should be easy to read. If would also be nice if they were interesting to read—if they had "style". Because of the limited vocabulary in programming languages, it's not too likely that many people will ever curl up in bed to read programs. But making them more readable is nevertheless an important goal. The "Little Book of BASIC Style" by Nevison is recommended as an excellent source of ideas on how to do this.

One technique is to use REMark statements that explain what's going on. Another is to use spaces and indentation. For example, it is helpful to indent the body of the FOR loop. When there are nested FOR loops, several levels of indentation are needed. For the hot dog problem, an indented version would look like this:

HOT DOG
WITH TAB

```
LIST

110 PRINT "------DOG----BUN---MUST.---MAYO.--CATSUP"
115 LET K=1
120   FOR H=0 TO 1
130     FOR B=0 TO 1
140       FOR M=0 TO 1
150         FOR Y=0 TO 1
160           FOR C=0 TO 1
170             PRINT "#";K;TAB(5);":   ";
180             PRINT H;"    B;"    ";M;"    ";Y;"    ";C;
190             PRINT "    CALORIES=";H*140+B*120+M*20+Y*100+C*30
195             LET K=K+1
200           NEXT C
210         NEXT Y
220       NEXT M
230     NEXT B
240   NEXT H
250 END
```

Since it's difficult to type an indented version of a program, special "formatting" programs are sometimes used to do the indenting automatically. However you'll also find that some computer manuals advise *not* using indentation. The reason is that the extra spaces needed increase the size of programs, and also slow down their execution. So you'll see some microcomputer programmers going in the opposite direction, and writing things like this:

10FORX=1TON:PRINTX:NEXTX

This is efficient for the machine, but atrocious for human readers.

The programs in this book were run on microcomputers with limited memory, so fancy indentation wasn't possible. To improve readability, we've used balloons, brackets, and other extra notations instead. More complicated programs have been broken into segments which are distinguished by REMark statements with easily spotted dashed lines. For an example of the dashed line REMark technique, see the horse race program in Section 6.5.

An example of using external brackets to distinguish the nested FOR loops in the hot dog problem is as follows:

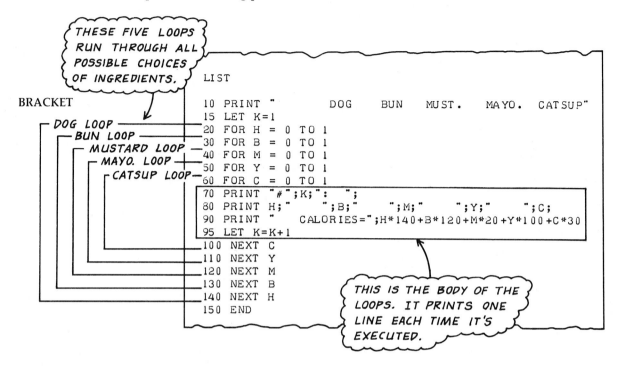

The Style Corner

As computer memories get cheaper and software gets better, versions of BASIC that do automatic formatting are likely to appear. To illustrate the improvement this can make in readability, several examples of programs with careful indentation and spacing are given later in the book. They can be spotted by a scrolled border of the kind used around this note.

SELF-TEST

1. Simulate a run of this program:

```
10 FOR B = 1 TO 2
20 FOR L = 3 TO 1 STEP -1
30 FOR N = 1 TO B*L
40 PRINT "*";
50 NEXT N
60 PRINT
70 NEXT L
80 PRINT
90 NEXT B
100 END
```

2. Write and run a "hot dog" program that allows a triple meat choice of no-dog, beef frank, or kolbassi.

3. Write a program that uses nested FOR loops to print the multiplication tables for 7, 8, and 9. Here's a start:

```
10 FOR T = 7 to 9
20 FOR K = 0 TO 12
30 PRINT K; "TIMES";T;"=";K*T
40 ... etc. ...
```

4. (Optional) Read ahead to the chapter on strings, and see if you can make the hot dog program print words instead of numbers so the lines of output look like this:

28 : DOG   BUN   MAYO.   CATSUP   CALORIES = 390

2.5 HOUR 5: SHELF LABELS AND BATTING AVERAGES

The word is out. You're the first one on your block with a computer and the calls are starting to roll in. First the butcher, then the baker, and now—the local sports writer. Seems he needs to crank out a list of batting averages fast, his calculator is broken, and he never did understand long division. Meanwhile, the corner grocer wonders if you could maybe print him unit-price tags of the kind used in supermarkets. Is there a simple way to handle both requests?

READ...DATA

One way to kill several birds with one stone in the world of computing is to realize that different programs may have similar structures, differing mainly in the data they use. For this reason, it would be nice if the data could be kept more or less separate from the program itself. This also makes it easier to expand or revise data later on. Here's how this idea works in BASIC for the batting average problem:

BATTING AVERAGES

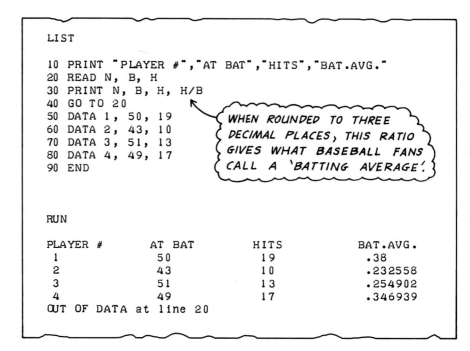

```
LIST

10  PRINT "PLAYER #","AT BAT","HITS","BAT.AVG."
20  READ N, B, H
30  PRINT N, B, H, H/B
40  GO TO 20
50  DATA 1, 50, 19
60  DATA 2, 43, 10
70  DATA 3, 51, 13
80  DATA 4, 49, 17
90  END
```

WHEN ROUNDED TO THREE DECIMAL PLACES, THIS RATIO GIVES WHAT BASEBALL FANS CALL A 'BATTING AVERAGE'.

```
RUN

PLAYER #        AT BAT        HITS        BAT.AVG.
 1                50           19           .38
 2                43           10           .232558
 3                51           13           .254902
 4                49           17           .346939
OUT OF DATA at line 20
```

When this program reaches line 20, it is told to READ enough data to load the variables N, B, and H. So it looks for a DATA statement (which it finds at line 50), and "uses up" the first three pieces of data it finds. You can think of what happens as follows:

20 READ N, B, H

50 DATA 1, 50, 19

You should also picture this data as having been "used up":

50 DATA 1, 50, 19

The program next prints a line of output (line 30), and then does a "GO TO 20". This means it *again* reads data, but starting with the first "fresh" (unused) piece of data it can find. In our example, this is found at line 60, so the second time around our loop we have:

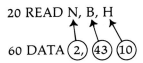

20 READ N, B, H

60 DATA (2,) (43) (10)

This process continues until no more "fresh" data can be found, at which time an "out of data" message is printed. IMPORTANT: The data can be distributed over DATA statements any way you wish, provided it is in the *order* expected by the READ statement. For example, lines 50, 60, 70, and 80 could also be written as two statements:

```
50 DATA 1, 50, 19, 2, 43, 10
60 DATA 3, 51, 13, 4, 49, 17
```

or even as one statement:

```
50 DATA 1,50,19,2,43,10,3,51,13,4,49,17
```

Actually, a program always treats all data as one big list. The READ statement simply goes down the list, "eating up" the data in "gulps". In our example, each "gulp" consists of three numbers, and it's *up to you* to make sure the groups of 3 correspond to N, B, and H.

Here's a similar program for our grocer friend. All we have to do is change our interpretation of what the variables mean, and use data appropriate to grocery prices. We'll also print things a little differently so the grocer can actually cut up the output to make shelf labels.

SHELF LABELS

```
LIST

5 PRINT "----------------------------------------------------------------"
10 READ N, Q, P
20 PRINT "PRODUCT #","QTY.IN OZ.","PRICE","UNIT PRICE"
30 PRINT N, Q, P, 100*P/Q; "CENTS PER OZ."
40 GO TO 5
50 DATA 1, 15, 1.29, 2, 4, .69, 3, 32, 2.49
60 END


RUN

----------------------------------------------------------------
PRODUCT #       QTY.IN OZ.    PRICE       UNIT PRICE
1               15            1.29        8.6 CENTS PER OZ.
----------------------------------------------------------------
PRODUCT #       QTY.IN OZ.    PRICE       UNIT PRICE
2               4             .69         17.25 CENTS PER OZ.
----------------------------------------------------------------
PRODUCT #       QTY.IN OZ.    PRICE       UNIT PRICE
3               32            2.49        7.78125 CENTS PER OZ.
----------------------------------------------------------------
OUT OF DATA at line 10
```

Improving These Programs

One of the nice things about writing programs is that once the basic idea is up and running, it's easy to add improvements. For example, both of the above programs suggest several kinds of additions. We'll describe five of these, and illustrate the last three.

(a) Limit the number of decimals to what people expect: .367 instead of .366666 for a batting average, 13.5 cents instead of 13.49999 for a unit price. There are two ways to do this. One uses the INT function which will be explained in Section 2.7. The other uses PRINT USING, explained in Chapter 3.

(b) It would be nice to have words or names printed instead of product or player numbers. The best way to do this is to use string variables, explained in Chapter 4

(c) It would be convenient to allow grocery data to be given in both pounds and ounces. This is easy to do. Here's one way:

20 READ N, L, Z, P

25 LET Q = 16*L + Z
    •
    • | This means 15 oz. |
    •

50 DATA 1, 2, 7, 1.31, 2, 0, 15, .89

> We agree that this means product #1 contains 2 lbs. 7 oz. and costs $1.31. Statement 25 then converts Q to 39 oz.

(d) The "out of data" message terminates the program. But suppose we want the program to continue and do other things? How do we handle this? (read on!)

(e) We may also want a program to re-use data that's been "scratched out". How do we "restore" such used-up data?

Here's a revision of the batting average program that answers both of these questions:

BATTING GRAPH

```
LIST

10 PRINT "PLAYER #  CLASS  AT BAT   HITS   BAT.AVG."
20 READ N, C, B, H
30 IF N = 0 THEN 110
40 PRINT N; TAB(10);
50 IF C = 0 THEN 90
60 PRINT  "VETERAN";
70 PRINT TAB(18);B;TAB(27);H;TAB(34);H/B
80 GO TO 20
90 PRINT "ROOKIE";
100 GO TO 70
110 RESTORE
115 PRINT
120 PRINT "BAR GRAPH OF PLAYER BATTING AVERAGES"
130 READ N, C, B, H
140 IF N = 0 THEN 220
150 PRINT "PLAYER #";N;
160 FOR K = 1 TO 100*(H/B+.005)
170 PRINT "*";
180 NEXT K
190 PRINT
200 GO TO 130
210 DATA 1,0,50,12,2,1,49,18,3,1,51,17,4,0,43,15,0,0,0,0
220 END
```

> HERE'S WHERE THE DATA POINTER GETS SET BACK TO THE FIRST ITEM.

> THIS EXPRESSION CONVERTS AN AVERAGE OF .24 TO 24 ASTERISKS, .367347 TO 37 ASTERISKS, ETC.

```
RUN

PLAYER #   CLASS  AT BAT   HITS   BAT.AVG.
 1         ROOKIE    50      12      .24
 2         VETERAN   49      18      .367347
 3         VETERAN   51      17      .333333
 4         ROOKIE    43      15      .348837

BAR GRAPH OF PLAYER BATTING AVERAGES
PLAYER # 1 ************************
PLAYER # 2 *************************************
PLAYER # 3 *********************************
PLAYER # 4 **********************************
```

In this program the data is read in groups of four. The second data item in each group of four is a code, with 0 meaning "rookie" and 1 meaning "veteran". For example, the statement

DATA 1, 0, 50, 12

means that player #1 is a rookie (0) who was at bat 50 times and got 12 hits. Line 50 tests C to see what the code is, and then branches to the appropriate PRINT statement.

RESTORE

The revised batting average program uses the DATA in line 210 twice. The first time it's used to produce a table of batting averages. This is done in lines 10 to 100. This part of the program keeps looping back to line 20 to get new data. But the fifth time this happens, it finds the "phoney" data 0,0,0,0. We agree that storing a zero in N signals the end of data. The signal is picked up in line 30 which then causes a branch to the second part of our program (the bar graph routine from lines 120 to 200).

> IMPORTANT: Even though we only need one zero in N to signal end of data, it is essential that four zeros be put at the end of the data statement. This is because the READ statement has four variables to fill, and will squawk with an error message if it doesn't find four data items.

Now you can see what the special statement 110 RESTORE does. The first part of the problem "uses up" all the data. (What happens is that a "pointer" moves along the data to keep track, and when the pointer gets to the end of the list, the program knows it's "out of data".) The RESTORE statement resets this pointer back to the first data item. Now all the data can be used again. (Of course, re-running a program also resets the pointer, but that doesn't help in our example because we would never reach the bar graph part.)

SELF-TEST

1. Simulate running this program:

```
10 LET T1 = 0
20 LET T2 = 0
30 READ A, B
40 IF A = 0 THEN 90
50 PRINT A, B, A/B
60 LET T1 = T2 + A
70 LET T2 = T2 + B
80 GO TO 30
90 PRINT "TOTALS AND OVERALL RATIO"
100 PRINT T1, T2, T1/T2
120 DATA 6, 4, 10, 5, 4, 1
130 DATA 0,0
140 END
```

2. Write and run a program to help balance your checkbook. It should be like Problem 3 at the end of Section 2.2, but use READ and DATA instead of INPUT.

3. Write and run a student record program that has a DATA statement for each student in a class as follows:

100 DATA 101, 16, 75, 80, 65, 90

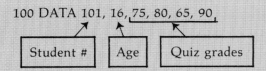

| Student # | Age | Quiz grades |

The program should print out a class roster with the grade average of each student. Finally it should print the average age in the class, the average grade for each quiz, and the overall class average.

2.6   HOUR 6: COMPUTER GAMES OF CHANCE

"What a pity this isn't a sin!" Those are supposed to be the words of the novelist Stendahl upon tasting ice cream for the first time. They sound more like the utterance of a computer center director trying to find a rationale for evicting the game-playing devotees who clutter up his system.

But personal computers are a different story, and the wages of gaming on your own system are an intellectual refreshment that comes in more flavors than found in all the ice cream stands ever franchised.

This section explains the features of BASIC that help make this endless variety possible. We'll start by first answering one of the questions we raised in the last section: How do you make a number like

.343687 print as .344 ?
or .264689 print as 26.46 ?
or .891246 print as 89 ?

INT

One way to control the number of decimal places in a number is to use the INT function of BASIC. If a statement says

10 LET Y = INT(X)

the INT(X) part means that X is to be first "processed" by something called the INT (integer) function. What comes out of the processing is the integer just to the *left* of X on the number scale. Here are some examples:

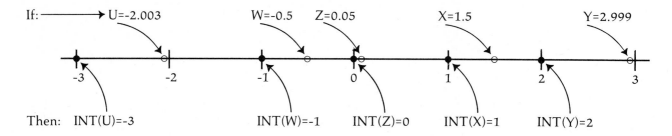

The following program shows some more examples of the differences between X and INT(X)

INT DEMO

```
LIST

5 PRINT "X", "INT(X)", "X/3", "INT(100*X/3)"
10 FOR X = -2 TO 2 STEP .5
20 PRINT X, INT(X), X/3, INT(100*X/3)
30 NEXT X
40 END



RUN

X                 INT(X)            X/3               INT(100*X/3)
-2                -2                -.666667          -67
-1.5              -2                -.5               -50
-1                -1                -.333333          -34
-.5               -1                -.166667          -17
 0                 0                 0                 0
 .5                0                 .166667           16
 1                 1                 .333333           33
 1.5               1                 .5                50
 2                 2                 .666667           66
```

To use INT for getting an answer in dollars and cents with only 2 decimal places (remember the UNIT PRICE program?) we can use the expression INT(100*X)/100. That's because

if	X =	1.36782
then	100*X =	136.782
and	INT(100*X) =	136
so	INT(100*X)/100 =	1.36

To change a batting average to three decimal places we can use a similar trick:

if	A =	.367891
then	1000*A =	367.891
and	INT(1000*A) =	367
so	INT(1000*A)/1000 =	.367

One more thing. To round this answer "up" in the third decimal place, use
INT (1000*A + .5) / 1000 = .368

SELF-TEST

1. Modify and test run the BATTING AVERAGE and UNIT PRICE programs using the above techniques to appropriately change the number of decimal places in the output.

Meanwhile, back at the Casino

RND

One feature no computer language should be without is a random number generator. This is a built-in routine that produces a "surprise" number each time it's used. When a statement like

   10 LET X = RND(0)

is executed, a number between 0 and 1 is produced "randomly", and stored in X. Here's a simple test program you can use to see what these numbers look like in your BASIC.

RND DEMO

```
LIST

10 PRINT "RANDOM NOS. WITH VARIOUS MULTIPLIERS"
20 FOR K = 1 TO 10
30 LET X = RND(0)
40 PRINT X, 10*X, 100*X, INT(100*X)
50 NEXT K
60 END


RUN

RANDOM NOS. WITH VARIOUS MULTIPLIERS
 .771027        7.71027         77.1027         77
 .78183         7.8183          78.183          78
 .75174         7.5174          75.174          75
 .473969        4.73969         47.3969         47
 .781555E-1     .781555         7.81555         7
 .203217        2.03217         20.3217         20
 .5159          5.159           51.59           51
 .266449        2.66449         26.6449         26
 .955597        9.55597         95.5597         95
 .335541        3.35541         33.5541         33
```

THIS STRANGE NUMBER IS .0781555 IN DISGUISE

NOTE: Your version of BASIC will probably produce a different sequence of random numbers, but the general idea is the same. Also, RND(0) may have to be changed to RND(1) in some BASIC's. (In standard BASIC the argument— the number in parenthesis—is ignored, but in other versions it's got to be as specified in the user manual.)

Each time RND is used in line 30, it's as though a new number X from a secret list is revealed. The word "random" means that no one number will appear more frequently than any other. To say it another way, if you generate a lot of random numbers, they should be distributed equally over the interval used. A program that can be used to check out the distribution of numbers produced by the random number generator in your BASIC is suggested in the first SELF-TEST question at the end of this section.

Constants in BASIC

The numbers used in BASIC programs are called constants. So far we have used,

(1) *Integer* constants like -3, 4, 27893, and
(2) *Floating point* (or real) constants like .0831, 3.1416, and -896.28.

Another way to write a floating point constant is shown in the first column of the preceding test program where the number .781555E-1 appears.

This is called the "exponential" or "scientific" notation for writing constants. What .781555E-1 really means is

$$.781555 * 10^{-1}$$

But 10^{-1} means $1/10^1$ (remember, $10^1 = 10$), so this number is really

(.781555) * (1/10) = .0781555. Similarly,

$.781555E-2 = .781555 * 10^{-2} = .00781555$, and
$.781555E-3 = .781555 * 10^{-3} = .000781555$, and so on.

SIMPLE RULE #1   E-3 means "move the decimal point 3 places to the *left*."

.781555E-3 = .000781555

Scientific notation is used to save space when representing very small and very large numbers. (You can see that .781555E-10 takes less room to print than .0000000000781555.)

A similar notation is used to represent large numbers. For example,

$.8965E+1$ means $.8965 * 10^1 = .8965 * 10 = 8.965$
$.8965E+2$ means $.8965 * 10^2 = .8965 * 100 = 89.65$,
$.8965E+3$ means $.8965 * 10^3 = .8965 * 1000 = 896.5$,

and so on. Here, the space saving shows up for very large numbers. For example,

   .8965E+18 = 896500000000000000.

E+18 means "move the decimal point 18 places to the *right*".

Simulated Craps

Now let's get back to the use of RND by writing a program to play craps. The usual rules for this dice game can be summarized in flowchart form as follows:

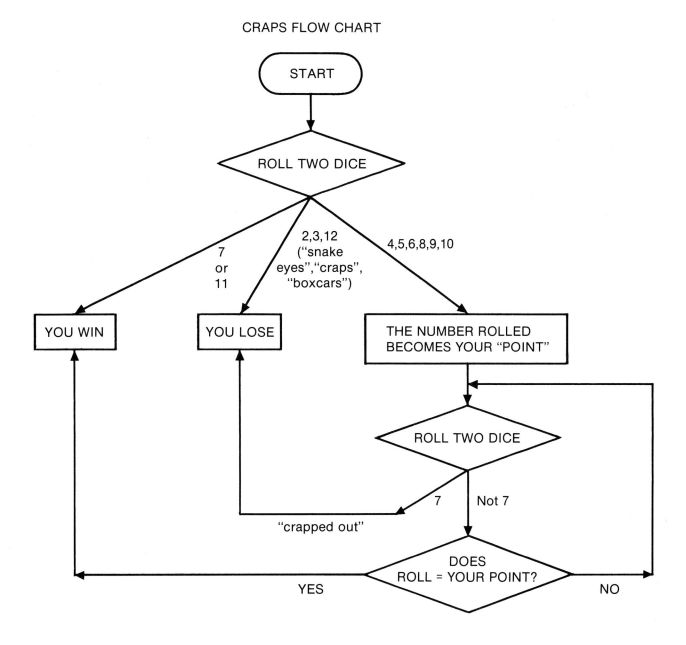

CRAPS FLOW CHART

To write a program that simulates playing this game, we'll need two statements that simulate the roll of two dice by producing random integers from 1 to 6. The statements

```
30 LET D1 = INT(6*RND(0) + 1)
40 LET D2 = INT(6*RND(0) + 1)
```

do this because RND(0) produces numbers from 0 (zero) up to (but not including) 1. So for six decimal places we'd have:

		Lower Value		Upper Value
RND(0)	produces	.0000000	to	.999999
6*RND(0)	produces	.000000	to	5.999994
6*RND(0)+1	produces	1.000000	to	6.999994
INT(6*RND(0)+1)	produces	1	to	6

Thus both D1 and D2 produce integers from 1 to 6. Mathematicians say this by writing that $1 <= D1 <= 6$ and $1 <= D2 <= 6$.

Note for Statistics Buffs: Tossing 2 dice with six sides gives numbers with a total value from 2 to 12. But you will *not* get the same effect by using a "super die" with 11 sides as follows:

```
10 LET D = INT(11*RND(0) +2)
```

It's true that this statement will produce random integers from 2 to 12, but they will not show up with the same distribution you get from adding the results of tossing two 6-sided dice. For example, with one "super die", the number 7 will show up 1/11 of the time. But with two regular dice, the number 7 can be formed in six different ways, each of which shows up 1/36 of the time. So on the average, a 7 will show up $6*(1/36) = 1/6$ of the time, not 1/11.

General Formula for Transforming RND

As just shown, the formula INT(6*RND(0) + 1) transforms the random numbers so that they fall in the interval $1 <= X <= 6$. To generate random numbers in the range $A <= X <= B$ use the formula

```
INT((B-A+1) * RND(0) +A)
```

Examples: To generate integers from 50 to 85 use:

```
20 LET X = INT(36*RND(0) + 50)
```

To generate two-place decimals from .50 to .85 use:

20 LET X = INT(36*RND(0) + 50)/100

To generate integers from -90 to +80 use:

20 LET X = INT(171*RND(0) - 90)

Returning to the CRAPS program, here's a listing followed by a sample run:

CRAPS SIMULATION

```
LIST

5 RANDOMIZE
10 PRINT "SIMULATED CRAPS GAME--YOU START WITH $10"
20 LET D = 10 ←                              D WILL KEEP TRACK
30 PRINT "HOW MUCH DO YOU WANT TO BET";      OF DOLLARS YOU HAVE.
40 INPUT B
50 LET D1 = INT(6*RND(0) + 1)                FIRST ROLL OF DICE.
60 LET D2 = INT(6*RND(0) + 1)
70 LET R1 = D1 + D2 ←
75 PRINT "ROLL IS";R1
80 IF R1=7 THEN 200
90 IF R1 = 11 THEN 200
100 IF R1 = 2 THEN 170
110 IF R1 = 3 THEN 170                        NEXT ROLL OF DICE.
120 IF R1 = 12 THEN 170
130 PRINT "YOUR POINT IS";R1
140 LET R2 = INT(6*RND(0) + 1) + INT(6*RND(0) + 1)←
145 PRINT "NEXT ROLL IS";R2
147 IF R2=7 THEN 170                          YOU LOST, SO YOUR
150 IF R2 = R1 THEN 200                       BET IS SUBTRACTED
160 GOTO 140                                  FROM D.
170 LET D = D - B ←
180 PRINT "TOUGH--YOU LOSE.  YOU NOW HAVE $";D
190 GOTO 220
200 LET D = D + B ←                           YOU WON, SO YOUR
210 PRINT "YOU WIN!  YOU NOW HAVE $";D        BET IS ADDED TO D.
220 PRINT "WANT TO PLAY AGAIN (1=YES)";
230 INPUT A
240 IF A = 1 THEN 30
250 PRINT "YOU ENDED WITH $";D;
260 IF D>10 THEN 290
270 PRINT "WON'T YOU EVER LEARN?"
280 STOP
290 PRINT "TALK ABOUT LUCK!"
300 END
```

This version of the program has been written to make each statement as simple as possible. Questions 5 and 6 of the Self-Test section coming up make some suggestions for shortening the program. Here's a run of the craps program. Your program may give different dice rolls because it has a different random number generator.

```
RUN

SIMULATED CRAPS GAME--YOU START WITH $10
HOW MUCH DO YOU WANT TO BET? 2
ROLL IS 10
YOUR POINT IS 10
NEXT ROLL IS 8
NEXT ROLL IS 3
NEXT ROLL IS 6
NEXT ROLL IS 9
NEXT ROLL IS 6
NEXT ROLL IS 2
NEXT ROLL IS 7
TOUGH--YOU LOSE.   YOU NOW HAVE $ 8
WANT TO PLAY AGAIN (1=YES)? 1
HOW MUCH DO YOU WANT TO BET? 4
ROLL IS 8
YOUR POINT IS 8
NEXT ROLL IS 5
NEXT ROLL IS 7
TOUGH--YOU LOSE.   YOU NOW HAVE $ 4
WANT TO PLAY AGAIN (1=YES)? 1
HOW MUCH DO YOU WANT TO BET? 8
ROLL IS 3
TOUGH--YOU LOSE.   YOU NOW HAVE $-4
WANT TO PLAY AGAIN (1=YES)? 0
YOU ENDED WITH $-4 WON'T YOU EVER LEARN?
STOP at line 280
```

RANDOMIZE

If you run the craps simulation program several times, you'll find that the rolls of the dice are the same for each run.* This is because RND(0) always starts with the same "seed" value, and produces each new number with the same algorithm. This repeatability is very helpful for debugging programs.

To make the numbers really surprise you, there is a feature in most versions of BASIC that creates a new seed number for each run. All you have to do to get this feature is to start your program with the statement

5 RANDOMIZE

To see what happens, run the craps program twice with RANDOMIZE, and twice without.

> *NOTE*: Some versions of BASIC don't have a RANDOMIZE. Their normal way of operating is to give you a different sequence of random numbers on each run. For these systems, if you want the same sequence of random numbers on each run, you must put a statement like 5 Z=RND(-1) at the beginning of the program. (Confusing? Agreed!)

ON...GOTO...

This is sometimes called the "computed GOTO" statement. It branches to different line numbers, depending on the value of a variable placed right after the word ON. Here's a program that demonstrates how it works:

QUIZ

```
LIST

10  PRINT "QUIZ:   WHO WAS THE 4TH MARX BROTHER?"
20  PRINT "1 = ZIPPO, 2 = HARRY, 3 = ZEPPO"
30  INPUT A
40  ON A GO TO 50, 70, 90
50  PRINT "NO, YOU'RE THINKING OF A CIGAR LIGHTER--TRY AGAIN."
60  GOTO 30
70  PRINT "YOU MAY BE WILD ABOUT HARRY, BUT THAT'S NOT RIGHT."
71  PRINT "TRY AGAIN."
80  GOTO 30
90  PRINT "BY GEORGE YOU'VE GOT IT!!"
100 END

Ready

RUN

QUIZ:   WHO WAS THE 4TH MARX BROTHER?
1 = ZIPPO, 2 = HARRY, 3 = ZEPPO
? 2
YOU MAY BE WILD ABOUT HARRY, BUT THAT'S NOT RIGHT.
TRY AGAIN.
? 1
NO, YOU'RE THINKING OF A CIGAR LIGHTER--TRY AGAIN.
? 3
BY GEORGE YOU'VE GOT IT!!
```

IF A=1, GO TO 50
IF A=2, GO TO 70
IF A=3, GO TO 90

Here's a program that uses RND with ON...GOTO... to generate random messages. If you analyze the output, you can see that RND must have produced the integers 4, 4, 4, 2, 1, 1, 3, 2, 4, 2 which caused branches to lines 100, 100, 100, 60, 40, 40, 80, 60, 100, 60.

HICCUP

```
LIST

5   RANDOMIZE
10  FOR N=1 TO 10
20  LET K=INT (4*RND(0)+1)
30  ON K GO TO 40, 60, 80, 100
40  PRINT "HEE-";
50  GO TO 110
60  PRINT "HA-";
70  GO TO 110
80  PRINT "HIC-";
90  GO TO 110
100 PRINT "HO-";
110 NEXT N
120 END



RUN

HO-HO-HO-HA-HEE-HEE-HIC-HA-HO-HA-
```

SELF-TEST

1. Simulate running the following program, using a die to produce the random numbers in line 80. What application do you see for this program?

```
10 LET K1 = 0
20 LET K2 = 0
30 LET K3 = 0
40 LET K4 = 0
50 LET K5 = 0
60 LET K6 = 0
70 FOR N = 1 TO 600
80 LET R = INT(6*RND(0) + 1)
90 ON R GO TO 140, 150, 160, 170, 180, 190
140 LET K1 = K1 + 1
145 GO TO 210
150 LET K2 = K2 + 1
155 GO TO 210
160 LET K3 = K3 + 1
165 GO TO 210
170 LET K4 = K4 + 1
175 GO TO 210
180 LET K5 = K5 + 1
185 GO TO 210
190 LET K6 = K6 + 1
210 NEXT N
230 PRINT K1; K2; K3; K4; K5; K6
240 END
```

2. You didn't really do #1 completely did you? Six hundred die tosses is a bit much. To get some real insight about RND from this program, you should run it on your computer.

3. Play the CRAPS program using the strategy of doubling your bet each time. Will this always guarantee that you eventually come out ahead? What feature can be added to the program to make this strategy less threatening to the "house"?

4. Modify the CRAPS program so a FOR...NEXT loop controls how often it plays. Then run it for a large number of plays (say 100, 200, 300, etc.) printing only the final value of D. The program itself should make the bets, using various strategies (e.g., always bet $1, for example). See what you can discover about the odds of winning this game for various strategies.

5. Can you find five statements in the CRAPS program that can be replaced with a single statement? Hint, try:

   80 ON R1 GOTO 130, 170, 170, 130, 130, 130, 200, 130, 130, 130, 200, 170

6. Can you replace statements 50, 60, 70, and 75 in the CRAPS program with a single statement?

2.7   HOUR 7: PROGRAMS TO HELP MOM AND DAD PASS ARITHMETIC 102

Very few people who have "taken" a foreign language in school are fluent in its use. Little children from countries where that language is spoken do a lot better, and with far less fuss. The same is true of the "languages" of mathematics and science. Achieving fluency in their use is much easier in settings where they are spoken regularly.

Personal computers make it possible to create such settings in some very interesting ways. One of the best involves computer game programs, and there's an entire chapter on games coming up. In this section we'll help prepare the way by explaining some of the techniques used in writing number-oriented games.

ABS   ABS(X) is a function which "processes" X in a very simple manner. It merely changes the sign of X to +. This is useful when we want to check how close some INPUT data supplied by the user comes to another value (say, the one the program expects). The ABS (absolute value) function helps by giving the "distance" between the two numbers . For example,

    ABS(8 - 5) = 3
    ABS(5 - 8) = 3
    ABS(5 - 2) = 3
    ABS(2 - 5) = 3

As you can see, ABS tells us that in all of these cases, the distance between the numbers is 3. Here's an example using this feature:

NUMBER GUESS

```
LIST

3 RANDOMIZE
5 FOR K=1 TO 3
10 LET R = INT(10 * RND(0) + 1)
20 PRINT "PICK A NUMBER FROM 1 TO 10";
30 INPUT N
40 IF R = N THEN 110
50 PRINT "NO, YOU MISSED BY";ABS(N - R)
60 PRINT "TRY ONE MORE TIME.  NUMBER IS";
70 INPUT N
80 IF R = N THEN 110    .
90 PRINT "YOU BLEW IT.  THE NUMBER WAS";R
100 GOTO 120
110 PRINT "RIGHT!!!"
120 NEXT K
130 END


RUN

PICK A NUMBER FROM 1 TO 10? 5
NO, YOU MISSED BY 3
TRY ONE MORE TIME.  NUMBER IS? 8
RIGHT!!!
PICK A NUMBER FROM 1 TO 10? 1
NO, YOU MISSED BY 7
TRY ONE MORE TIME.  NUMBER IS? 8
RIGHT!!!
PICK A NUMBER FROM 1 TO 10? 10
NO, YOU MISSED BY 2
TRY ONE MORE TIME.  NUMBER IS? 8
RIGHT!!!
```

THIS IS THE COMPUTER'S NUMBER

THIS IS YOUR NUMBER.

THIS GIVES THE AMOUNT BY WHICH N MISSED, BUT NOT THE SIGN.

WITH THESE CHOICES YOU CAN ALWAYS GET IT ON THE 2ND CHANCE.

Another use of ABS is for accepting input that is "close enough" even though not exactly the number expected. The art of getting such "ball park" estimates is seldom taught in school, yet it's a valuable one. Here's an example of a program for practicing this:

APPROXIMATE
ARITHMETIC

```
LIST

3 RANDOMIZE
5 FOR K = 1 TO 10
10 LET H = INT(4000 * RND(0) + 1200)/100
20 LET M = INT(1000 * RND(0) + 500)/100
30 LET I = INT(300 * RND(0) + 300)/100
40 LET D = INT(9 * RND(0) + 1)
50 PRINT "APPROXIMATELY HOW MUCH SHOULD YOU BUDGET"
55 PRINT "FOR A TRIP OF";D;"DAYS IF--"
60 PRINT "   HOTEL COST PER DAY   = $";H
70 PRINT "   MEAL COST PER DAY    = $";M
80 PRINT "   INCIDENTALS PER DAY = $";I
90 INPUT A
100 LET C = D * (H + M + I)
110 LET E = ABS(A - C)
120 IF E/C < .10 THEN 160
130 PRINT "YOU MISSED BY $";E
140 PRINT "YOU WERE OFF BY";(E/C)*100;"%"
150 GOTO 180
160 PRINT "VERY GOOD.  YOU WERE OFF BY $";E
170 PRINT "THAT WAS AN ERROR OF ONLY";(E/C)*100;"%"
180 NEXT K
190 END
```

```
RUN

APPROXIMATELY HOW MUCH SHOULD YOU BUDGET
FOR A TRIP OF 5 DAYS IF--
   HOTEL COST PER DAY   = $ 42.84
   MEAL COST PER DAY    = $ 12.81
   INCIDENTALS PER DAY = $ 5.25
? 60
YOU MISSED BY $ 244.5
YOU WERE OFF BY 80.2956 %
APPROXIMATELY HOW MUCH SHOULD YOU BUDGET
FOR A TRIP OF 3 DAYS IF--
   HOTEL COST PER DAY   = $ 15.12
   MEAL COST PER DAY    = $ 7.03
   INCIDENTALS PER DAY = $ 4.54
? 76
VERY GOOD.  YOU WERE OFF BY $ 4.07
THAT WAS AN ERROR OF ONLY 5.08305 %
APPROXIMATELY HOW MUCH SHOULD YOU BUDGET
FOR A TRIP OF 5 DAYS IF--
   HOTEL COST PER DAY   = $ 50.22
   MEAL COST PER DAY    = $ 8.35
   INCIDENTALS PER DAY = $ 4.23
? 320
VERY GOOD.  YOU WERE OFF BY $ 6
THAT WAS AN ERROR OF ONLY 1.91083 %
APPROXIMATELY HOW MUCH SHOULD YOU BUDGET
FOR A TR^C
```

THIS SHOULD HAVE BEEN DONE MENTALLY USING 43 + 13 + 5 = 61 × 5 = 305.

Notice that we used two kinds of "error" formulas in this program. The absolute error E = ABS(A - C) gives the absolute value of the *difference* between the correct answer and the approximate answer, while the relative error E/C shows the *ratio* between this difference and the correct answer.

Why make this distinction? Well suppose you were a contractor who made a bid that missed the true cost by $1000. How serious is this? It all depends. If you take two extreme cases, you'll see why.

Case 1:
$$\begin{aligned}
\text{True cost} &= \$50,000 \\
\text{Your bid} &= \$49,000 \\
\text{Absolute error} &= \$1,000 \\
\text{Relative error} &= 1000/50000 = .02 \\
\text{percent error} &= 2\%
\end{aligned}$$

Case 2:
$$\begin{aligned}
\text{True cost} &= \$2,500 \\
\text{Your bid} &= \$1,500 \\
\text{Absolute error} &= \$1,000 \\
\text{Relative error} &= 1000/2500 = .4 \\
\text{Percent error} &= 40\%
\end{aligned}$$

The absolute error was the same in both cases. It's the relative error that shows which one is a disaster. (Percent error also shows this since it is merely relative error multiplied by 100.)

ABS is also handy in making sure that an input response is as requested. Here's one way this can be done:

INPUT CHECK

```
LIST

10 PRINT "TYPE A POSITIVE INTEGER BETWEEN 50 AND 100."
20 INPUT A
30 IF INT(A) <> A THEN 120
40 IF ABS(75-A) > 25 THEN 140
50 PRINT "YOU HAVE OBEYED A COMPUTER."
60 PRINT "THERE IS NO HOPE."
70 STOP
120 PRINT "THAT'S NOT AN INTEGER."
130 GO TO 10
140 PRINT "OUT OF REQUESTED RANGE."
145 PRINT "READ THE INSTRUCTIONS CAREFULLY."
150 GO TO 10
160 END



RUN

TYPE A POSITIVE INTEGER BETWEEN 50 AND 100.
? 25
OUT OF REQUESTED RANGE.
READ THE INSTRUCTIONS CAREFULLY.
TYPE A POSITIVE INTEGER BETWEEN 50 AND 100.
? 7.5
THAT'S NOT AN INTEGER.
TYPE A POSITIVE INTEGER BETWEEN 50 AND 100.
? 75
YOU HAVE OBEYED A COMPUTER.
THERE IS NO HOPE.
STOP at line 70
```

If you want to be more explicit in your error messages, statement 40 can be replaced by two tests:

```
40 IF A < 50 THEN 140
45 IF A > 100 THEN 142
   .
   .
   .
140 PRINT "TOO SMALL!"
141 GO TO 145
142 PRINT "TOO LARGE!"
   .
   .
   .
```

SQR

We'll finish this section with a math game program that uses the square root function of BASIC . SQR(X) processes the number X by finding its square root and "returning" this value in the place where SQR is used. (The square root of X is a number which when multiplied by itself gives X. This means you must use positive numbers for X. Otherwise you'll get an error message.)

Example:

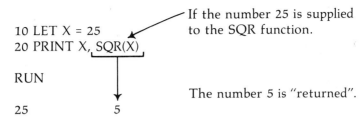

10 LET X = 25
20 PRINT X, SQR(X)

If the number 25 is supplied
to the SQR function.

RUN

The number 5 is "returned".

25   5

Here's a game program to practice estimating square roots:

**SQUARE ROOT
QUIZ**

```
LIST

5 RANDOMIZE
10 LET K = 0
20 PRINT "TO WIN THE GOLD STAR YOU NEED 3 ANSWERS IN A ROW"
25 PRINT "THAT HAVE LESS THAN 5% ERROR."
30 PRINT "------------------------------------------------"
50 LET R = INT(100*RND(0) + 1)
60 PRINT "WHAT IS THE SQUARE ROOT OF";R
70 INPUT A
80 LET C = SQR(R)
90 IF ABS(A - C)/C < .05 THEN 130
100 PRINT "NOT TOO CLOSE.  SQUARE ROOT OF ";R;"IS";C
105 PRINT "YOU MISSED BY";100*ABS(A/C-1);"%"
106 PRINT
110 LET K = 0
120 GO TO 50
130 PRINT "NOT BAD--YOU ONLY MISSED BY";100*ABS(A/C-1);"%"
135 PRINT "SQUARE ROOT OF ";R;"IS";C
136 PRINT
140 LET K = K + 1
150 IF K < 3 THEN 50
160 PRINT "THAT'S 3 IN A ROW!      *****"
170 PRINT "   PASTE STAR HERE--     *   *"
175 PRINT "                         *****"
180 END
```

```
RUN

TO WIN THE GOLD STAR YOU NEED 3 ANSWERS IN A ROW
THAT HAVE LESS THAN 5% ERROR.
------------------------------------------------
WHAT IS THE SQUARE ROOT OF 78
? 8.11
NOT TOO CLOSE.  SQUARE ROOT OF  78 IS 8.83176
YOU MISSED BY 8.17233 %

WHAT IS THE SQUARE ROOT OF 79
? 8.8
NOT BAD--YOU ONLY MISSED BY .992265 %
SQUARE ROOT OF  79 IS 8.88819
```

```
WHAT IS THE SQUARE ROOT OF 76
? 8.5
NOT BAD--YOU ONLY MISSED BY 2.49831 %
SQUARE ROOT OF  76 IS 8.7178

WHAT IS THE SQUARE ROOT OF 48
? 6.10
NOT TOO CLOSE.  SQUARE ROOT OF  48 IS 6.9282
YOU MISSED BY 11.9541 %

WHAT IS THE SQUARE ROOT OF 8
? 6.4
NOT TOO CLOSE.  SQUARE ROOT OF  8 IS 2.82843
YOU MISSED BY 126.274 %

WHAT IS THE SQUARE ROOT OF 21
? 4.68
NOT BAD--YOU ONLY MISSED BY 2.12597 %
SQUARE ROOT OF  21 IS 4.58258

WHAT IS THE SQUARE ROOT OF 52
? 7.57
NOT BAD--YOU ONLY MISSED BY 4.97701 %
SQUARE ROOT OF  52 IS 7.2111

WHAT IS THE SQUARE ROOT OF 27
? 5.15
NOT BAD--YOU ONLY MISSED BY .888204 %
SQUARE ROOT OF  27 IS 5.19615

THAT'S 3 IN A ROW!      *****
   PASTE STAR HERE--     *   *
                        *****
```

Notice that the user had to supply an answer within 5% three times in a row before getting the "gold star".

For a really fiendish game, make the 5% a variable that gets smaller each time. Start with V=.05, and then make V=.7*V each time around.

REM

We have been explaining programs by drawing "balloons" on the side which contain explanatory remarks. Remarks can also be placed within a program by use of the REM statement which looks like this:

10 REM ANYTHING YOU WANT TO SAY

Remark statements only show up when you list a program, *not* during a run. Here's an example of how one of our previous programs might look with REM statements. It also illustrates a feature in *some* BASIC's which allows remarks after the ! or ' symbol.

REMARK
DEMO

```
LIST

10  REM---PROGRAM FOR CHECKING INPUT---------------
15  PRINT "TYPE A POSITIVE INTEGER BETWEEN 50 AND 100"
20  INPUT A
25  REM---FIRST SEE IF MAYBE IT'S NOT AN INTEGER---
30  IF INT(A) <> A THEN 120
35  REM---NOW SEE IF IT'S OUTSIDE RANGE 50 TO 100---
40  IF ABS(75-A) > 25 THEN 140
50  PRINT "YOU HAVE OBEYED A COMPUTER."
60  PRINT "THERE IS NO HOPE."
70  STOP
115 REM---MESSAGE FOR LINE 30 BRANCH---          !
120 PRINT "THAT'S NOT AN INTEGER"                ! THIS IS THE
130 GOTO 10                                      ! SECTION OF
135 REM---MESSAGE FOR LINE 35 BRANCH---          ! THE PROGRAM
140 PRINT "OUT OF REQUESTED RANGE"               ! THAT PRINTS
145 PRINT "READ THE INSTRUCTIONS CAREFULLY"      ! MESSAGES
150 GOTO 10                                      !
160 END
```

SELF-TEST

1. Simulate a RUN of this program:

```
10 FOR K = 1 TO 10
20 LET X = K * K
30 PRINT K, SQR(X)
40 NEXT K
50 END
```

2. Simulate a RUN of this "pattern" program:

```
10 FOR K = 10 TO -10 STEP -1
20 FOR J = 1 TO ABS(K)
30 PRINT "*";
40 NEXT J
50 PRINT
60 NEXT K
70 END
```

3. Write, debug, and run a program that asks for an estimate of the total cost of 5 items on a supermarket receipt. First have the computer print out the simulated receipt. Generate the dollar cost of each item with INT(900*RND(0) + 20) / 100). Then ask for an estimated total, and compare it with the exact sum. Give different kinds of congratulatory (or other) messages that depend on the relative error in each answer.

2.8   HOUR 8: KEEPING CHECK ON A BANK BALANCE

In this section we'll explain two new features of BASIC (subroutines and user-defined functions) by showing how to apply them to the problem of calculating compound interest. Before discussing these features, let's first review what's involved in finding interest that's "compounded" at various intervals.

The idea of compounding shows up in several kinds of problems. For example, in calculating the population growth of some species (say rabbits), you have to allow for the fact that if new rabbits come from the original population, then new, new rabbits come from both the new rabbits and the original population, while new, new, new rabbits come from the new, new rabbits, new rabbits, and original rabbits (assuming no deaths), etc., etc.

The same idea holds for compound interest: it's calculated on the original amount (called the principal), and on the interest on the principal, and on the interest on the interest on the principal, etc., etc. How often this re-calculation gets done is up to the bank. For example, they may do it four times a year (which is called quarterly compounding), or even 365 times a year (called daily compounding). There are two methods for calculating compound interest: (1) use a loop, and (2) use an exponential formula. Let's look at the loop method first.

Here's a loop for finding 5% interest compounded quarterly on a principal of $1000, with a total time in the bank of 1 year.

```
5 LET N = 1000
10 FOR K = 1 TO 4
20 LET N = N + (.05/4) * N
30 NEXT K
40 PRINT "INTEREST IS"; N - 1000
```

The new balance at the end of each quarter (3 months) is calculated in line 20 as follows.

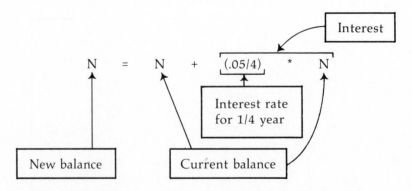

Each time around the FOR...NEXT loop is like another 3 months. At the end of 4 loops, N contains the year-end balance, so N - 1000 gives the compound interest that accumulated in a year.

To do this same calculation for daily compounding, the loop would have to go FOR K = 1 TO 365, while the interest added each day would be at the rate of (.05/365).

GOSUB

The small program we just explained can be used as part of a larger (or "main") program. The small program can be called a "subprogram", or a "subroutine".

The advantage to building a main program partially from subroutines is that it helps organize your thinking. The approach to take is to think of yourself as the VIP (very important programmer). You start by pretending that you don't have to worry about details because you can call on assistants for help. To make the idea even more dramatic, you can picture your executive office on the top floor, while the assistants work at lower levels called subroutines. When you need help from an assistant (say at level 1000) you shout "GOSUB 1000". When the assistant at this location is finished, he yells "RETURN". This image isn't as silly as it may seem. To see why, let's first look at a "program" written by a VIP which only outlines the work to be done.

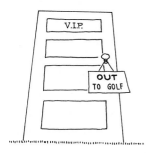

10 Get data on husband's bank account.

　　⋮

50 Get my assistant down on level 1000 to figure out and
　　print husband's interest and balance.

　　⋮

65 Get data on wife's bank account.

　　⋮

90 Ask the same assistant to figure out wife's interest and
　　balance, and print it.
100 Lock up office and go play golf.

If written in BASIC, such a program would partially look like the following:

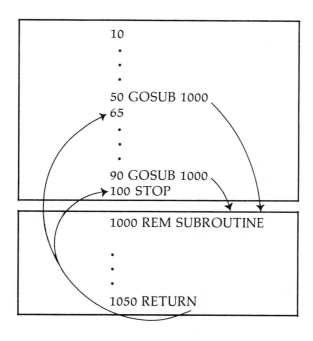

What the statement GOSUB 1000 really means is "go and do the subroutine that starts at line 1000 and then return to the line right after the GOSUB statement that was just executed". To see how this all goes together, look at the following complete program:

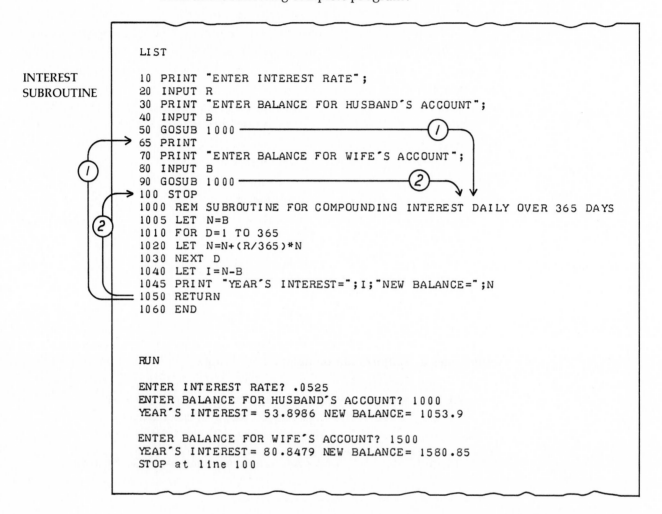

INTEREST
SUBROUTINE

```
LIST

10  PRINT "ENTER INTEREST RATE";
20  INPUT R
30  PRINT "ENTER BALANCE FOR HUSBAND'S ACCOUNT";
40  INPUT B
50  GOSUB 1000
65  PRINT
70  PRINT "ENTER BALANCE FOR WIFE'S ACCOUNT";
80  INPUT B
90  GOSUB 1000
100 STOP
1000 REM SUBROUTINE FOR COMPOUNDING INTEREST DAILY OVER 365 DAYS
1005 LET N=B
1010 FOR D=1 TO 365
1020 LET N=N+(R/365)*N
1030 NEXT D
1040 LET I=N-B
1045 PRINT "YEAR'S INTEREST=";I;"NEW BALANCE=";N
1050 RETURN
1060 END



RUN

ENTER INTEREST RATE? .0525
ENTER BALANCE FOR HUSBAND'S ACCOUNT? 1000
YEAR'S INTEREST= 53.8986 NEW BALANCE= 1053.9

ENTER BALANCE FOR WIFE'S ACCOUNT? 1500
YEAR'S INTEREST= 80.8479 NEW BALANCE= 1580.85
STOP at line 100
```

All the hard work is done in the subroutine from lines 1000 to 1050. When the main program reaches line 50, it "goes to" line 1000, where it continues execution. In our example, it does line 1005, followed by 365 times around the FOR...NEXT loop in 1010 to 1030, followed by 1040, followed by 1045 and 1050. Line 1050 then says RETURN. (Subroutines must always end with a RETURN statement.) Return means go back to the line *right after* the GOSUB. In our example, that's line 65. So 65 is executed right after 1050. The second time the subroutine is called is at line 90. Again all the hard work is done in the subroutine (at no extra cost in programming!), but this time the RETURN is to line 100.

Details, Details

Now that we see the big picture, we can concentrate on explaining how this particular subroutine works. What it does is to start the new balance out as

N = B, calculate the interest for one day as (.0525/365)*N, and then get the revised new balance as N = N + (.0525/365)*N. This process is repeated 365 times in a loop. When the loop is finished, the interest earned for a year will be the final new balance minus the starting balance, that is, I = N - B. Now that we have N and I, we can return to line 65, where the program continues. When the program gets to line 90, this whole process is repeated, but this time B contains the wife's balance, so a completely different calculation is done. In other words, *subroutines in BASIC use the current value that variables have in the main program* .

Question: Could this program have been written as easily using GOTO instead of GOSUB? No, because there would be no way to return to different line numbers the way RETURN does.

Question: Can subroutines sometimes be inefficient? The answer is yes, but after everything is working, you can swap your VIP hat for your STP hat (super terrific programmer), and clean things up a bit. For example, the subroutine we have shown does the division (R/365) seven hundred and thirty times! This inefficiency can be removed by adding the statement

    25 LET F = R/365

and using F instead of R/365 inside the subroutine.

DEF FNX

As just seen, subroutines are small programs, usually involving several lines. Sometimes a "subjob" can be handled by a single LET statement, and using a subroutine is hardly worth the effort. In this case, there's another feature called DEFining a function that can be used instead of GOSUB. We'll illustrate its use with the second method for calculating compound interest.

If you dig through some math books, you'll find the following formula for getting the new balance on an account with compound interest:

$$N = P \ * \ (1 + R/M) \uparrow (M \ * \ T)$$

In this formula,

  P is the starting principal in dollars,
  R is the annual interest rate,
  M is the number of times interest is compounded each year, and
  T is the number of years left in the bank.

For example, for $3000 left for three years in a bank with 5% interest compounded monthly,

    P = 3000
    R = .05
    M = 12
    T = 3

So the new amount at the end of three years is

$$N = 3000 \ * \ (1 + .05/12) \uparrow (12 \ * \ 3).$$

The 'up arrow' means raise to that power (exponentiate), so this is a difficult calculation. It's time for a computer!

Our programming approach will be to place this formula in a special statement that allows the formula to be called upon as often as we wish. The way to "store" a formula like this in a BASIC program is to use the define function statement as follows:

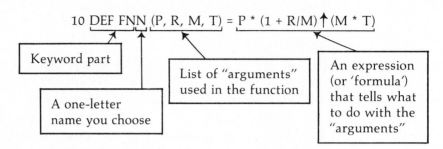

$$10 \ \underline{DEF \ FNN} \ \underline{(P, R, M, T)} = \underline{P * (1 + R/M) \uparrow (M * T)}$$

Keyword part

A one-letter name you choose

List of "arguments" used in the function

An expression (or 'formula') that tells what to do with the "arguments"

The DEF FNN statement can be placed anywhere in a program, and FNN can be used anywhere that an expression can be used. Here's a program that uses our function twice, once in a LET statement, once in a PRINT statement. We called our function FNN. We could just as well have used names like FNA, FNB, FNC, ..., FNZ.

INTEREST
FUNCTION

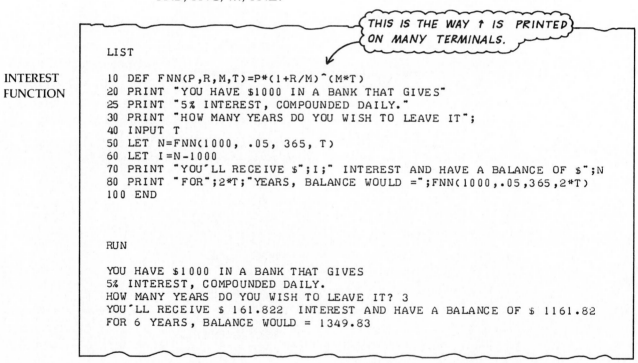

THIS IS THE WAY ↑ IS PRINTED ON MANY TERMINALS.

```
LIST

10 DEF FNN(P,R,M,T)=P*(1+R/M)^(M*T)
20 PRINT "YOU HAVE $1000 IN A BANK THAT GIVES"
25 PRINT "5% INTEREST, COMPOUNDED DAILY."
30 PRINT "HOW MANY YEARS DO YOU WISH TO LEAVE IT";
40 INPUT T
50 LET N=FNN(1000, .05, 365, T)
60 LET I=N-1000
70 PRINT "YOU'LL RECEIVE $";I;" INTEREST AND HAVE A BALANCE OF $";N
80 PRINT "FOR";2*T;"YEARS, BALANCE WOULD =";FNN(1000,.05,365,2*T)
100 END



RUN

YOU HAVE $1000 IN A BANK THAT GIVES
5% INTEREST, COMPOUNDED DAILY.
HOW MANY YEARS DO YOU WISH TO LEAVE IT? 3
YOU'LL RECEIVE $ 161.822  INTEREST AND HAVE A BALANCE OF $ 1161.82
FOR 6 YEARS, BALANCE WOULD = 1349.83
```

As shown in lines 50 and 80, when FNN is used (or "called") it must be given arguments. Notice that these arguments can be replaced with constants, variables, or even expressions.

ON...GOSUB

This statement is similar to the ON...GOTO statement. It directs the program to go to different subroutines, depending on the value of the variable (or expression) right after the keyword ON

```
        .
        .
        .
10 ON K GOSUB 1000, 1500, 2000
20 PRINT
        .
        .
        .
```

means "if K = 1, go to subroutine 1000, return to line 20",
      "if K = 2, go to subroutine 1500, return to line 20",
      "if K = 3, go to subroutine 2000, return to line 20".

It's up to the programmer to make sure that K only takes on values that match the number of subroutines. If, for example, K became 4 in our example, standard BASIC would treat this as an error (some earlier versions treated this as a "default" and continued execution at the next line—line 20 in our example). For an example of ON...GOSUB, see SELF-TEST Question 3.

SELF-TEST

1. Simulate running this program:

```
10 PRINT "TYPE AN INTEGER FROM 1 TO 5"
20 INPUT I
30 IF INT(I)<>I THEN 10
40 IF ABS(I-3)>2 THEN 10
50 PRINT "HOW DO ";
55 LET N = I
60 GOSUB 500
100 PRINT
110 PRINT "OR IS IT ALREADY POSSIBLE ";
120 LET N=2 * I
130 GOSUB 500
140 STOP
500 FOR K = 1 TO N
510 PRINT "YOU KNOW ";
520 NEXT K
530 RETURN
540 END
```

2. Simulate running this program:

```
10 DEF FNA(R) = 3.1416 * R * R
20 FOR K = 1 TO 5
30 PRINT "FOR A RADIUS OF";20+K
40 PRINT "THE AREA OF A CIRCLE IS";FNA(20+K)
50 NEXT K
60 END
```

3. Write and run this program:

```
10 FOR K = 1 TO 10
20 PRINT "MAY ";
30 LET X = INT(4 * RND(0) + 1)
40 ON X GOSUB 100, 200, 300, 400
50 PRINT "SING TO ";
60 LET Y = INT (4 * RND(0) + 1)
70 ON Y GOSUB 100, 200, 300, 400
75 PRINT
80 NEXT K
90 STOP
100 PRINT "AN IMPORTED SALAMI ";
110 RETURN
200 PRINT "YOUR FAITHFUL DOG ";
210 RETURN
300 PRINT "AN ENRAGED CAMEL ";
310 RETURN
400 PRINT "THE EASTER BUNNY ";
410 RETURN
500 END
```

4. Write a program that compares the "loop" method with the "formula" method for getting compound interest. Show the results at the end of each year. A RUN should look like this:

```
PRINCIPAL? 1000
INTEREST RATE? .05
# OF TIMES COMPOUNDED PER YEAR? 365
# OF YEARS? 25
STARTING YEAR? 1976
THANK YOU
```

	LOOP METHOD		FORMULA METHOD	
YEAR	BALANCE	INTEREST	BALANCE	INTEREST
1976	1000	0	1000	0
1977	1051.27	51.2745	1051.27	51.2663
1978	1105.16	53.9032	1105.16	53.8945
1979	1161.82	56.6667	1161.82	56.6574
.	.	.	.	.
.	.	.	.	.
2001	3490.05	170.223	3489.94	170.191

Our program ignored leap years. If you're really ambitious, see if you can take leap years into account. The output of this program will vary slightly on different computers due to what are called "rounding" errors. The only way around this problem is to use a BASIC with double-precision arithmetic.

2.9   PROJECT IDEAS

1. Write a program that allows the user to enter the date of deposit, the amount deposited, the annual interest rate, the number of times compounded per year, and the date of withdrawal. The program should then print the new balance and the interest accumulated. A date like November 18, 1976 can be entered as:

   DATE DEP? 11, 18, 76

   You can ignore leap years if you wish. Another simplification is to treat all months as having 30 days, which means assuming 360 days for one year (some banking systems do this). Sub-project: How can a bank advertise that 5% interest compounded daily amounts to an annual interest rate of 5.47%?

2. Write an arithmetic practice program that uses four subroutines: one for addition problems, one for subtraction, one for multiplication, one for division. The RND function and ON...GOSUB should then be used to select the kind of problem (addition, subtraction, multiplication, or division) to be presented. Also try to use the method of SELF-TEST Question 3 to produce different kinds of messages for wrong answers, and other kinds of messages for correct answers. Here's what a RUN might look like:

   ADDITION QUESTION; 5 + 6 = ? 11
   RIGHT! YOUR REWARD WILL BE RICHES AND RIPE BANANAS.
   SUBTRACTION QUESTION; 33 - 23 = ? 16
   WRONG—ANSWER IS 10
   KEEP THIS UP AND YOU'LL FIND CHICKEN LIVERS IN YOUR SOCKS
   DIVISION QUESTION: ...etc. ...

3. It's legal to have one subroutine call another subroutine in BASIC. The program below illustrates this feature. Study and run the program, and then write it *without* using GOSUB at all. Your program should produce the same output as shown in our example.

SUBMARINE

```
LIST

5 RANDOMIZE
10 PRINT "PLAYER #1 TYPE RANGE (0 TO 50)";
20 INPUT P
30 LET R = 50 * RND(0)
40 LET D1 = ABS(P - R)
50 GOSUB 1000
60 PRINT "PLAYER #2 TYPE RANGE (0 TO 50)";
70 INPUT P
80 LET R = 50 * RND(0)
90 LET D2 = ABS(P-R)
100 GOSUB 1000
110 IF D1 = D2 THEN 170
120 IF D1 < D2 THEN 150
130 PRINT "PLAYER #2 WINS"
140 GOTO 180
150 PRINT "PLAYER #1 WINS"
160 GOTO 180
170 PRINT " TIE SCORE"
180 GOTO 9999
```

```
1000 REM--------TARGET DISPLAY ROUTINE-----
1010 GOSUB 2000
1020 LET X = P
1025 PRINT "SHELL";
1030 GOSUB 3000
1040 GOSUB 2000
1050 LET X = R
1055 PRINT "U-BOAT";
1060 GOSUB 3000
1070 GOSUB 2000
1080 PRINT
1090 RETURN
2000 REM--------LINE ROUTINE-----
2010 FOR K=1 TO 60
2020 PRINT "-";
2030 NEXT K
2040 PRINT
2050 RETURN
3000 REM--------SHELL ROUTINE-----
3010 PRINT TAB(X+8);"<*>"
3020 RETURN
9999 END
```

```
RUN

PLAYER #1 TYPE RANGE (0 TO 50)? 35
------------------------------------------------------------
SHELL                                             <*>
------------------------------------------------------------
U-BOAT                                               <*>
------------------------------------------------------------

PLAYER #2 TYPE RANGE (0 TO 50)? 10
------------------------------------------------------------
SHELL               <*>
------------------------------------------------------------
U-BOAT                                               <*>
------------------------------------------------------------

PLAYER #1 WINS
```

4. Find a program written in an extended version of BASIC, and translate it into a version that runs on your system. The idea is to become familiar with the possibilities of extended BASIC so you can get a feel for those features you want to insist on in buying your next software package. It would also be a good idea to keep a notebook on the special features of your BASIC.

SOLUTION

We'll show a sample solution to this project as a guide to what's involved. Our solution will also help you to read programs written in BASIC-PLUS or EXTENDED BASIC. You'll see that most of the extensions can easily be translated into minimal standard BASIC, but at the cost of extra statements.

Our example will first show a Russian Roulette Game program written in extended BASIC. Then we'll illustrate how each of the extended statements can be replaced by several simpler statements.

**BASIC-PLUS
ROULETTE**

```
LIST

10  RANDOMIZE
20  PRINT "RUSSIAN ROULETTE": PRINT "------------"
30  PRINT "TYPE 1 TO SPIN CHAMBER, 0 TO QUIT"
35  N=0
40  INPUT "YOUR CHOICE IS"; C
60  IF C=1 THEN PRINT "LOTSALUCK" ELSE PRINT "CHICKEN": GOTO 140
70  IF RND(1)>.85 THEN 100 ELSE N=N+1
80  IF N>=10 THEN 120 ELSE PRINT "--CLICK--"
90  PRINT: GOTO 40
100 PRINT "  BANG!!!  YOU'RE DEAD":  PRINT "SORRY ABOUT THAT"
110 PRINT: PRINT "NEXT VICTIM PLEASE":PRINT:GOTO 30
120 PRINT "YOU DID IT!!   10 MISSES! -- YOU WIN"
125 FOR K=1 TO 10: PRINT "YEA! ";: NEXT K: PRINT
130 STOP
140 PRINT "GET SOMEONE ELSE WHO ISN'T SO SMART": PRINT: GOTO 30
150 END
```

STD. BASIC ROULETTE

```
     LIST

     10  RANDOMIZE
①    20  PRINT "RUSSIAN ROULETTE"
     21  PRINT "-----------"
     30  PRINT "TYPE 1 TO SPIN CHAMBER, 0 TO QUIT"
②    35  LET N=0
③    40  PRINT "YOUR CHOICE IS";
     41  INPUT C
     60  IF C=1 THEN 63
④    61  PRINT "CHICKEN"
     62  GOTO 140
     63  PRINT "LOTSALUCK"
⑤    70  IF RND(1)> .85 THEN 100
     71  LET N=N+1
⑤    80  IF N>=10 THEN 120
     81  PRINT "--CLICK--"
①    90  PRINT
     91  GOTO 40
①    100 PRINT "BANG!! YOU'RE DEAD"
     101 PRINT "SORRY ABOUT THAT"
     110 PRINT
①    111 PRINT "NEXT VICTIM PLEASE"
     112 PRINT
     113 GOTO 30
     120 PRINT "YOU DID IT!!   10 MISSES! -- YOU WIN"
     125 FOR K=1 TO 10
①    126 PRINT "YEA! ";
     127 NEXT K
     128 PRINT
     130 STOP
     140 PRINT "GET SOMEONE ELSE WHO ISN'T SO SMART"
①    142 PRINT
     143 GOTO 30
     150 END
```

The numbers in circles on our diagram refer to the following five explanatory notes.

**Notes on the Translation from Extended BASIC
to Minimal BASIC**

1. Many extended BASIC's allow several statements on the same line provided they are separated by colons. To translate, you merely write a separate line for each part. This is what we did with line 20. Other examples are shown in lines 90, 100, 110, 125, and 140.
2. Line 35 shows that many extended BASIC's allow you to omit the word LET.
3. Line 40 shows how a message can be placed within an extended INPUT statement. This translates into a PRINT followed by an INPUT, with the PRINT terminated by a semi-colon.
4. Line 60 shows how the THEN in an IF...THEN statement can be followed by another statement rather than a line number. The translation can be a bit tricky as shown, since ELSE is also used.
5. IF...THEN...ELSE means if true, go to the statement after THEN, if false, go to the statement after ELSE.

Other features of extended BASIC will be introduced as they become useful. Techniques for translating them into minimal BASIC will also be shown.

WARNING: When you're finished with a translation make sure that all your "GOTO" and "IF...THEN" statements branch to the correct line numbers. You may have to make some changes.

Here's a sample RUN of the ROULETTE program to show how it should work if you've done the translation properly. Of course runs will differ with different RND generators (and RANDOMIZE routines).

```
    LIST

    RUSSIAN ROULETTE
    --------------------
    TYPE 1 TO SPIN CHAMBER, 0 TO QUIT
    YOUR CHOICE IS? 1
    LOTSALUCK
      BANG!!!   YOU'RE DEAD
    SORRY ABOUT THAT

    NEXT VICTIM PLEASE

    TYPE 1 TO SPIN CHAMBER, 0 TO QUIT
    YOUR CHOICE IS? 1
    LOTSALUCK
    --CLICK--

    YOUR CHOICE IS? 1
    LOTSALUCK
    --CLICK--

    YOUR CHOICE IS? 1
    LOTSALUCK
    --CLICK--

    YOUR CHOICE IS? 1
    LOTSALUCK
    --CLICK--

    YOUR CHOICE IS? 1
    LOTSALUCK
    --CLICK--

    YOUR CHOICE IS? 1
    LOTSALUCK
    --CLICK--

    YOUR CHOICE IS? 1
    LOTSALUCK
    --CLICK--

    YOUR CHOICE IS? 1
    LOTSALUCK
    --CLICK--

    YOUR CHOICE IS? 1
    LOTSALUCK
    --CLICK--

    YOUR CHOICE IS? 1
    LOTSALUCK
    YOU DID IT!!   10 MISSES! -- YOU WIN
    YEA! YEA! YEA! YEA! YEA! YEA! YEA! YEA! YEA! YEA!
    STOP at line 130
```

3
3
3
3
3
3
3
3

3

SIMPLE COMPUTER GRAPHICS; SUBSCRIPTED VARIABLES

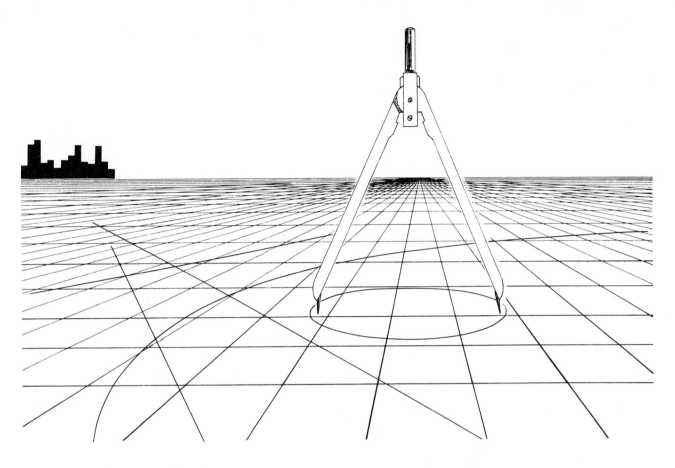

3.0 INTRODUCTION

The ancient wisdom that says "a picture is worth a thousand words" has a special significance for the computer age. With machines that can generate output faster than anyone can read it, there's no doubt that we need new ways to represent this avalanche of data. The best answer (so far) seems to be in computer graphics—sophisticated pictures that show the results of all this computation in a form that is easy to interpret and even easier to remember.

A number of techniques for producing computer graphics will be described in the book. In this chapter, we'll look at simple methods that require only use of a standard "alphanumeric" terminal, either the hard copy or "TV" type. Later chapters will expand on these methods, both in terms of the programs needed to produce graphical displays, and in terms of the hardware required for getting pictures with greater detail.

3.1 Different Kinds of Computer Graphics; Some Terminology

One way to classify computer graphics systems is in terms of the hardware used. A basic distinction that can be made is between "hard copy" (pictures on paper that can be saved for later reference), and "soft copy" (electronic "light" pictures that go away when the machine is shut down). Of course photographs can be taken of soft-copy graphics, but this is not always convenient or easy.

Within each category other distinctions can be made as shown in the chart below. The word "alphanumeric" in the chart means that the terminal can print only standard alphabetic symbols, numbers, and punctuation marks. Some terminals are limited to 64 alphanumeric characters, which means they don't have lower case letters. Other alphanumeric terminals can handle up to 128 characters. However, in both cases, some of these are "control" characters which perform some action (e.g. ring a bell) rather than print anything. By allowing the user to define special characters (e.g. musical notation), an even larger repertoire of symbols can be made available on some alphanumeric terminals.

HARD COPY	H1.	*Standard Alphanumeric Printing Terminals* Usually 10 characters per inch, 6 lines per inch.
	H2.	*Plot-Mode Alphanumeric Printing Terminals* Same as above, plus finer steps for making special shapes out of dots.
	H3.	*X-Y Plotters* Use a pen to make dots, or draw lines connecting any two points.
	H4.	*Other (e.g. Electrostatic, Electrolytic)*
SOFT COPY	S1.	*Cathode-Ray-Tube (CRT) Alphanumeric Displays* Put standard characters on CRT screen.
	S2.	*Raster Scan Color Graphics Displays* Use format similar to home TV (horizontal lines) for both characters and pictures. The entire screen is continuously updated (refreshed).
	S3.	*Cathode-Ray Vector Graphics (also called "stroke writing")* Put characters and/or points and/or continuous lines on CRT screen. Only update (refresh) the parts of the picture being displayed.
	S4.	*Storage Tube Terminals* Put characters, points, and continuous lines on a CRT that does not have to be refreshed.
	S5.	*Dot Matrix Displays* Use a large dot array to get detailed point plots and/or alphanumeric characters.
	S6.	*Other (e.g. futuristic Holographic displays)*

These categories are not exclusive. For example, alphanumeric capability (S1) is frequently found on the other soft copy systems (S2 to S5). And most X-Y plotters (H3) can draw standard characters, often in several styles.

We played it safe and put the word "other" at the end of each list because new ideas keep appearing in the field of graphics. For example, techniques for making hard copies from soft copy terminals already exist. Further down the road, it seems probable that new kinds of thin picture-on-the-wall type color displays will eventually appear for use as both TV and computer display panels. There are even wilder possibilities being explored in the labs, including 3-D holographic projection systems.

For the amateur on a limited budget, the two best bets are currently (1) low-cost alphanumeric terminals (either soft-copy on a TV monitor or hard-copy using a printing mechanism something like an electric typewriter), and (2) graphic systems that use TV-type cathode ray tube (CRT) displays in "raster scan" mode. Vector graphics and dot-matrix displays will also bear investigation when prices come down.

In this chapter we'll look at a number of ways to produce graphics on alphanumeric terminals (H1 and S1). As you'll see, most of the techniques we'll introduce (e.g. scaling) are also applicable to the more advanced graphics systems discussed in later chapters.

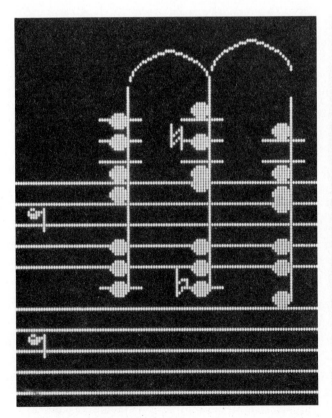

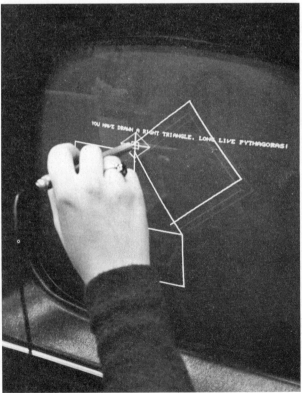

A dot matrix graphics display used with a computer music system (see Section 10.4).

A graphics terminal that accepts input from a light pen (see Section 10.4).

3.2   SIMPLE GRAPHS USING PRINT TAB(X)

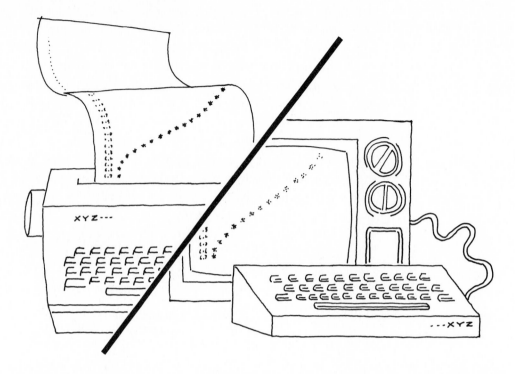

The secret to getting interesting graphical output on an alphanumeric terminal is to find clever ways of controlling the position in which characters print on the paper (or screen) of your terminal. The vertical (up-down) position is usually controlled by the "line-feed" (movement to a new line) that PRINT statements cause. For example, the loop

```
10 FOR X=1 TO 15
20 PRINT "*"
30 NEXT X
```

causes 15 asterisks to print vertically down the left side of the paper. This is because there will be 15 carriage-returns and 15 line-feeds. But if we change line 20 to read

```
20 PRINT TAB(10);"*"
```

something different will happen. The TAB(10) item in the PRINT statement means move *horizontally* ten spaces (0 to 9), and then print the asterisk in the next position (column 10). So now we'll get 15 asterisks printed down the paper, but in column 10.

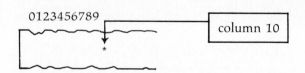

If we change line 20 further to read

20 PRINT TAB(X);"*"

the position from the left will change each time around the loop, and we'll get a slanted line of asterisks like this:

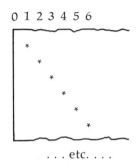

. . . etc. . . .

In other words, TAB(X) means move right to the Xth position before printing the asterisk. (Don't forget—column positions are numbered 0,1,2,3,...).

Now let's get a bit more daring. If we change line 20 to use a more complicated TAB expression like

20 PRINT TAB(X*X/10);"*"

we'll get a "curved" line. This is because increasing X from 1 to 25 will increase X*X/10 from 0.1 to 62.5. Since TAB uses the integer part of its argument, the asterisks will print in positions determined by the numbers in the third column of the following table.

X	X*X/10	TAB(X*X/10)
1	.1	0
2	.4	0
3	.9	0
4	1.6	1
5	2.5	2
6	3.6	3
7	4.9	4
8	6.4	6
9	8.1	8
10	10.0	10
.	.	.
.	.	.
.	.	.

Mathematicians would say we are plotting a "quadratic" curve. Here's what it looks like:

TAB CURVE

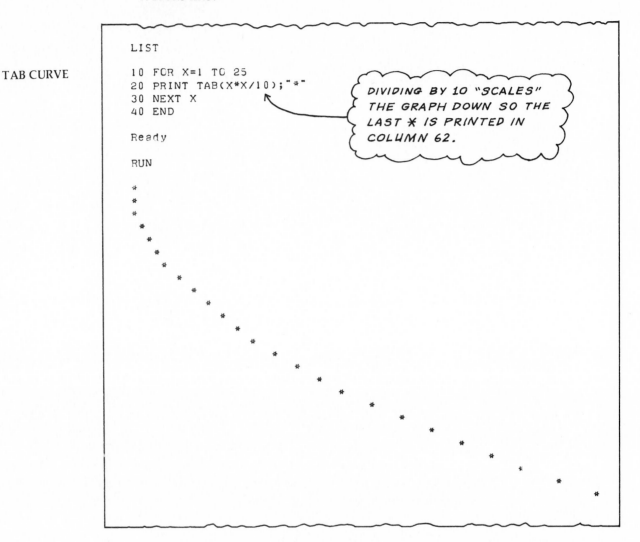

```
LIST

10  FOR X=1 TO 25
20  PRINT TAB(X*X/10);"*"
30  NEXT X
40  END

Ready

RUN
```

> DIVIDING BY 10 "SCALES" THE GRAPH DOWN SO THE LAST * IS PRINTED IN COLUMN 62.

CONFUSION CORNER: The new ANSI standard for BASIC suggests numbering columns 1, 2, 3, . . . etc. However most versions of BASIC follow the 0, 1, 2, 3, . . . scheme we have shown.

TAB can have any legal BASIC expression as its argument, including expressions that use BASIC functions. Here's an example where line 20 prints the symbol "1" in the position determined by TAB(X+3), while line 30 prints the symbol "2" in the position determined by TAB(ABS(3*X-36)+3). The effect is something like graphing the path of two billiard balls. Notice that we are printing the "1" and "2" on alternate lines. (This was done to simplify the program. Section 7.4 explains the techniques needed for printing several symbols on the same line in the proper order.)

TAB LINES

```
LIST

10  FOR X=0 TO 25
20  PRINT "A:";TAB(X+3);"1"
30  PRINT "B:";TAB(ABS(3*X-36)+3);"2"
40  NEXT X
50  END

Ready

RUN

A: 1
B:                                     2
A:  1
B:                                  2
A:   1
B:                               2
A:    1
B:                            2
A:     1
B:                         2
A:      1
B:                      2
A:       1
B:                   2
A:        1
B:                2
A:         1
B:             2
A:          1
B:          2
A:           1
B:       2
A:            1
B:    2
A:             1
B: 2
A:              1
B:    2
A:               1
B:       2
A:                1
B:          2
A:                 1
B:             2
A:                  1
B:                2
A:                   1
B:                   2
A:                    1
B:                      2
A:                     1
B:                         2
A:                      1
B:                            2
A:                       1
B:                               2
A:                        1
B:                                  2
A:                         1
B:                                     2
A:                          1
B:                                        2
```

USING ABS MAKES THE ARGUMENT OF TAB GO FROM +39 TO +3 WHEN X GOES FROM 0 TO +12, AND FROM +6 TO +42 WHEN X GOES FROM +13 TO +25.

Another way to use TAB(X) is to read values of X from data statements. This allows us to print computer graphs that show pictorially what the data "looks" like. For example, we could plot data from the weekly weigh-ins of someone on a reducing diet as follows:

WEIGHT
GRAPH

```
10  PRINT "GRAPH OF WEEKLY WEIGHTS"
20  PRINT "       ";
30  FOR K=100 TO 200 STEP 10:PRINTK;:NEXTK:PRINT
40  PRINT "       ";
50  FOR K= 0 TO 10: PRINT "   +   ";:NEXT K:PRINT
55  LET S = 0
60  FOR X=1 TO 30
70  READ W
80  IF W<0 THEN 150
85  LET S=S+W
90  PRINT X;TAB(4);"I";TAB((W-100)/2+6);"*"
100 NEXT X
110 DATA 155, 149,144, 141, 138, 135, 134.5, 132, 133, 133.7
120 DATA 134, 135, 136, 136, 137, 139, 140.2, 142, 144, 147
130 DATA 150, 143, 135, 130, 126, 123, 121, 120, 119, 119
140 DATA -1
150 PRINT "AVERAGE WEIGHT ="; S/30
160 END

RUN
```

LINES 10-50 PRINT THE 3 "HEADING" LINES.

THIS LINE PRINTS THE GRAPH. THE FORMULAS USED ARE EXPLAINED IN SECTION 3.4.

```
GRAPH OF WEEKLY WEIGHTS
       100   110   120   130   140   150   160   170   180   190   200
        +     +     +     +     +     +     +     +     +     +     +
    1  I                                         *
    2  I                                     *
    3  I                                  *
    4  I                                *
    5  I                               *
    6  I                             *
    7  I                             *
    8  I                            *
    9  I                            *
   10  I                            *
   11  I                            *
   12  I                             *
   13  I                             *
   14  I                             *
   15  I                             *
   16  I                              *
   17  I                               *
   18  I                                *
   19  I                                 *
   20  I                                  *
   21  I                                    *
   22  I                                 *
   23  I                             *
   24  I                          *
   25  I                        *
   26  I                      *
   27  I                     *
   28  I                     *
   29  I                    *
   30  I                    *
AVERAGE WEIGHT = 135.713
```

One difficulty with our program is that it only gives good graphs for someone with weights in the range of 100 to 200 pounds. We'll return to this program in Section 3.4, and show how to make it automatically adapt to a "personalized" scale of weights. The derivation of the formulas used in line 90 will also be explained there.

3.3   MATHEMATICAL FUNCTIONS IN BASIC

SIN, COS, LOG, EXP, TAN, ATN, SGN

The mysterious words SIN, COS, LOG, EXP, TAN, ATN, SGN are abbreviations for what are called *mathematical functions* (their full names are the "sine", "cosine", "logarithmic", "exponential", "tangent", "arctangent", and "sign" functions). Of course you've already seen the ABS, SQR, and INT functions.

A function can be thought of as a "data crunching" machine. You feed it a piece of input data called the *argument* of the function, and get back output data called the *value* of the function. For example, you can think of the SIN function as working something like this:

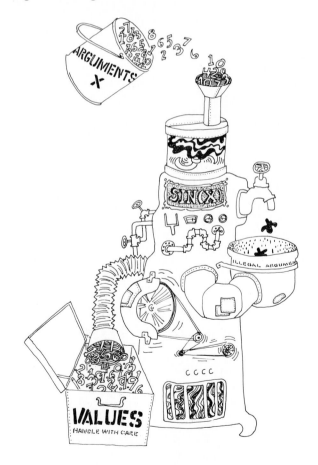

Another way to see what a function does is to make a table. You can do this by writing a program that uses a FOR loop to "plug" different arguments into the function, and then PRINT out the values. Here's such a table for the SIN function:

TABLE

```
LIST

5 PRINT "X", "Y=SIN(X)"
10 FOR X=0 TO 6 STEP 0.5
20 LET Y=SIN(X)
30 PRINT X,Y
40 NEXT X
50 END

Ready

RUN

X                  Y=SIN(X)
 0                  0
 .5                 .479426
 1                  .841471
 1.5                .997495
 2                  .909297
 2.5                .598472
 3                  .14112
 3.5               -.350783
 4                 -.756802
 4.5               -.97753
 5                 -.958924
 5.5               -.70554
 6                 -.279415
```

NOTE: It would be more efficient to replace lines 20 and 30 with one line:

  30 PRINT X, SIN(X)

We used two lines just to clarify what was happening.

We won't go very deeply into the mathematical applications of these functions. However they will be extremely useful to us in writing some of the game programs in Chapter 6, and in producing some of the fancier computer graphics explained in Chapter 10.

As an introduction to these applications, let's see how we can produce some "pictures" that show graphically what some of the mathematical functions look like, and which are also attractive as design elements.

Here's an example showing what the SIN function looks like when graphed.

```
RUN

        -1      -.8     -.6     -.4     -.2      0      .2      .4      .6      .8      1
0                                                       *
.1                                                         *
.2                                                           *
.3                                                             *
.4                                                              *
.5                                                                *
.6                                                                 *
.7                                                                  *
.8                                                                   *
.9                                                                    *
1                                                                     *
1.1                                                                    *
1.2                                                                     *
1.3                                                                      *
1.4                                                                      *
1.5                                                                      *
1.6                                                                      *
1.7                                                                      *
1.8                                                                      *
1.9                                                                     *
2                                                                     *
2.1                                                                   *
2.2                                                                  *
2.3                                                                 *
2.4                                                               *
2.5                                                              *
2.6                                                           *
2.7                                                         *
2.8                                                       *
2.9                                                     *
3                                                     *
3.1                                                 *
3.2                                              *
3.3                                            *
3.4                                          *
3.5                                        *
3.6                                      *
3.7                                    *
3.8                                  *
3.9                                *
4                                 *
4.1                              *
4.2                             *
4.3                            *
4.4                           *
4.5                          *
4.6                          *
4.7                          *
4.8                          *
4.9                          *
5                           *
5.1                          *
5.2                           *
5.3                            *
5.4                             *
5.5                              *
5.6                                *
5.7                                 *
5.8                                   *
5.9                                     *
6                                        *
6.1                                         *
6.2                                           *
6.3                                             *
```

SINE GRAPH

```
LIST

10 FOR F=-1 TO 1.1 STEP .2
20 PRINT TAB(9+30*(F+1));INT(F*100)/100;
30 NEXT F
40 PRINT
50 FOR A = 0 TO 6.3 STEP .1
60 PRINT A;TAB(10+30*(SIN(A)+1));"*"
70 NEXT A
80 END
```

The first loop in lines 10-30 puts numbers across the top of the page to show what values of the SIN function are being graphed. (The numbers were selected as shown because we know from trigonometry* that the SIN function has values that range from -1 to +1).

The second loop in lines 50-70 prints A (the *argument*), and then prints an asterisk in a position determined by the *value* of SIN(A). We used SIN(A)+1 in our TAB so that the values -1 to +1 would be changed to the range 0 to 2 (you can't TAB negative values). We multiplied by 30 to spread the picture out from columns 0 to 60, and then added 10 to shift all values 10 columns to the right (to leave room for printing A). So the final graph goes from 10 to 70. On a terminal with a smaller number of columns the multiplier 30 should be reduced to about 15.

*MATH NOTE: SIN, COS, and TAN are called trigonomeric functions. In many mathematics books, the arguments for these functions are given in degrees. In BASIC, the arguments of these functions must be given in radians. A radian is roughly equivalent to 57 degrees. The exact relation is 2π radians = 360 degrees. Since $2\pi = 6.28$, line 50 of our program makes the argument A go from 0 to about 360 degrees.

Of course we can print other things besides a single asterisk "*". Here's how you can have fun "SIN"ing your name with the same function.

SINE NAME

```
LIST

10 FOR A=0 TO 6.3 STEP .2
20 LET Y= SIN(A)
30 PRINT TAB(20*Y+20);"HARVEY KILOBIT"
40 NEXT A
50 END

Ready

RUN

                        HARVEY KILOBIT
                          HARVEY KILOBIT
                            HARVEY KILOBIT
                             HARVEY KILOBIT
                              HARVEY KILOBIT
                               HARVEY KILOBIT
                                HARVEY KILOBIT
                                 HARVEY KILOBIT
                                 HARVEY KILOBIT
                                 HARVEY KILOBIT
                                HARVEY KILOBIT
                               HARVEY KILOBIT
                              HARVEY KILOBIT
                             HARVEY KILOBIT
                            HARVEY KILOBIT
                          HARVEY KILOBIT
                         HARVEY KILOBIT
                       HARVEY KILOBIT
                     HARVEY KILOBIT
                   HARVEY KILOBIT
                 HARVEY KILOBIT
                HARVEY KILOBIT
                HARVEY KILOBIT
                HARVEY KILOBIT
                HARVEY KILOBIT
                  HARVEY KILOBIT
                    HARVEY KILOBIT
                      HARVEY KILOBIT
                        HARVEY KILOBIT
                          HARVEY KILOBIT
                           HARVEY KILOBIT
```

The COS function can be used to give similar effects. Both SIN and COS "wiggle" between -1 and +1, but with different starting points. Here's what you'll get when you "COS"ign your name:

COSINE NAME

```
LIST

10 FOR A= 0 TO 6.3 STEP .2
20 LET Y=COS(A)
30 PRINT TAB(20*Y+20);"HARVEY KILOBIT"
40 NEXT A
50 END


RUN
                                        HARVEY KILOBIT
                                       HARVEY KILOBIT
                                      HARVEY KILOBIT
                                     HARVEY KILOBIT
                                    HARVEY KILOBIT
                                   HARVEY KILOBIT
                                  HARVEY KILOBIT
                                 HARVEY KILOBIT
                               HARVEY KILOBIT
                             HARVEY KILOBIT
                           HARVEY KILOBIT
                          HARVEY KILOBIT
                        HARVEY KILOBIT
                      HARVEY KILOBIT
                     HARVEY KILOBIT
                    HARVEY KILOBIT
                    HARVEY KILOBIT
                    HARVEY KILOBIT
                     HARVEY KILOBIT
                       HARVEY KILOBIT
                        HARVEY KILOBIT
                          HARVEY KILOBIT
                           HARVEY KILOBIT
                             HARVEY KILOBIT
                              HARVEY KILOBIT
                                HARVEY KILOBIT
                                 HARVEY KILOBIT
                                  HARVEY KILOBIT
                                   HARVEY KILOBIT
                                    HARVEY KILOBIT
                                    HARVEY KILOBIT
```

Combining functions, and putting multipliers in front of the arguments gives tricky "intermodulation" effects. Here's a pleasing pattern that comes from plotting the combined function Y=COS(2*A) + SIN(A). Electronics buffs will see that we are combining two signals that are "90 degrees out of phase", and that the first one has "twice the frequency" of the second.

MODULATED
NAME

```
LIST

10 FOR A=0 TO 9.5 STEP .2
20 LET Y=COS(2*A)+SIN(A)
30 PRINT TAB(15*Y+30);"HARVEY KILOBIT"
40 NEXT A
50 END

RUN
```

```
                                                  HARVEY KILOBIT
                                                   HARVEY KILOBIT
                                                   HARVEY KILOBIT
                                                 HARVEY KILOBIT
                                               HARVEY KILOBIT
                                              HARVEY KILOBIT
                                            HARVEY KILOBIT
                                           HARVEY KILOBIT
                                           HARVEY KILOBIT
                                            HARVEY KILOBIT
                                             HARVEY KILOBIT
                                              HARVEY KILOBIT
                                               HARVEY KILOBIT
                                               HARVEY KILOBIT
                                               HARVEY KILOBIT
                                            HARVEY KILOBIT
                                          HARVEY KILOBIT
                                      HARVEY KILOBIT
                                  HARVEY KILOBIT
                              HARVEY KILOBIT
                          HARVEY KILOBIT
                      HARVEY KILOBIT
                    HARVEY KILOBIT
                    HARVEY KILOBIT
                      HARVEY KILOBIT
                         HARVEY KILOBIT
                            HARVEY KILOBIT
                              HARVEY KILOBIT
                                 HARVEY KILOBIT
                                   HARVEY KILOBIT
                                     HARVEY KILOBIT
                                      HARVEY KILOBIT
                                      HARVEY KILOBIT
                                      HARVEY KILOBIT
                                     HARVEY KILOBIT
                                    HARVEY KILOBIT
                                  HARVEY KILOBIT
                                 HARVEY KILOBIT
                                HARVEY KILOBIT
                                HARVEY KILOBIT
                                 HARVEY KILOBIT
                                  HARVEY KILOBIT
                                    HARVEY KILOBIT
                                     HARVEY KILOBIT
                                     HARVEY KILOBIT
                                     HARVEY KILOBIT
```

There will be other uses of the SIN and COS functions shown in Section 7.3 (for making Lissajous figure art), and in Sections 7.4 and 7.5 (for making polar coordinate graphs).

We won't explain the other mathematical functions here. However applications of the LOG function and EXP function are illustrated in Section 7.5, and the SGN function is used in Section 10.3. (For your information, SGN(X) has the value -1 for all X<0, and +1 for all X>0. For X=0, SGN(X)=0.) If you'd like to experiment with graphs of the other functions, the programs in Sections 7.4 and 7.5 will help. However you will find that for some arguments, you may get error messages. For example, SQR and LOG cannot have negative arguments. Another trouble-maker is TAN. For example, TAN (3.14159265/2) has the value "infinity", so computers can't handle it, and will produce either nonsense or some kind of error message. The best way to identify such cases is to read about these functions in a mathematics book, and then experiment with printing tables of the type shown at the beginning of Section 3.3.

3.4   WHAT TO DO IF YOUR BASIC DOESN'T HAVE TAB; THE SCALING OF GRAPHS

Some of the simpler versions of BASIC may not allow TAB, or they may only allow TAB with a constant (like TAB(5)). You can simulate a statement like

```
30 PRINT TAB(Y);"*"
```

by replacing it with a loop that prints Y blanks, and then follows this with a statement that prints an asterisk on the same line. Here's the code for simulating 30 PRINT TAB(Y);"*"

```
30 FOR T=0 TO Y-1
40 PRINT " ";
50 NEXT T
60 PRINT "*"
```

We let the variable T go from zero to Y-1 because columns on a printer are numbered with zero as the starting position. A program to print a graph of the SIN function using this trick would look like the following:

SIMULATED TAB

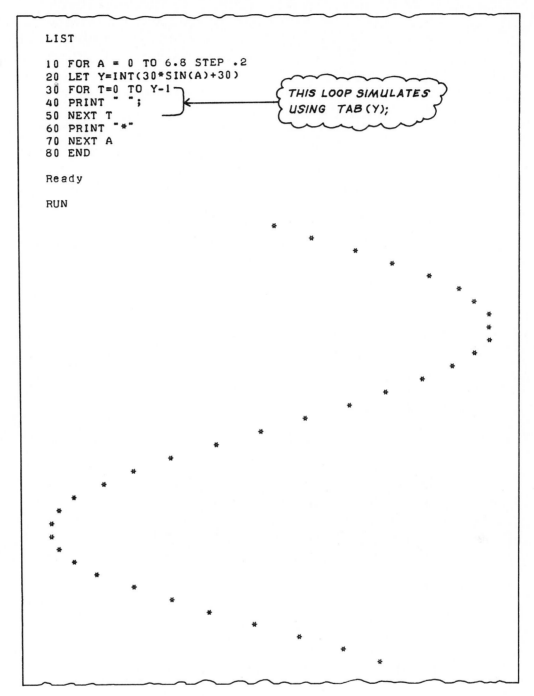

```
LIST

10  FOR A = 0 TO 6.8 STEP .2
20  LET Y=INT(30*SIN(A)+30)
30  FOR T=0 TO Y-1
40  PRINT " ";
50  NEXT T
60  PRINT "*"
70  NEXT A
80  END

Ready

RUN
```

THIS LOOP SIMULATES USING TAB(Y);

Scaling Graphs

You've seen that although the SIN function has values that go from -1 to +1, we were able to spread the graph out over 60 columns. We did this by first adding +1 (which is called *translating* the range of values). This was done to avoid negative numbers, giving a range of values 0 to 2 instead. Then we multiplied by 30 (which is called *scaling* the range of values) so that the range became 0 to 60. In this way we were able to spread 2 units over 60 terminal columns. We can either say that our "scale factor" was 30 terminal spaces per mathematical unit, or conversely, that it was 1/30 of a mathematical unit per terminal space.

Let's now return to the dieter's weight graphing program from Section 3.1 and see how we can add an automatic scaling feature. The diet program was supposed to graph weights from 100 to 200 pounds. To make the left edge of the paper correspond to 100 pounds (instead of zero), the first thing we did was "shift" the whole graph left 100 units. This was done by subtracting 100 from W (a translation).

Our next decision was to scale the weights from 100 to 200 into 50 terminal spaces. To do this we multiplied by a scale factor of

50/(200-100) = 1/2 terminal space per pound

Example: For a weight of 150 pounds, the program should first translate this weight by taking 150-100=50. It should then scale it by taking 50 * (1/2) = 25 terminal spaces. Here's a picture of what happens:

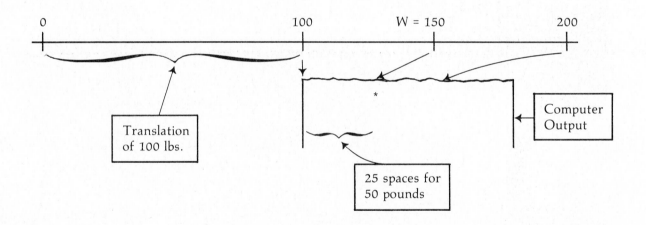

All of this can be done by saying

PRINT TAB ((W-100)*(1/2));"*"

But multiplying by 1/2 is the same as dividing by 2, so this can be written more simply as

PRINT TAB ((W-100)/2);"*"

To improve the readability of the graph, we then allowed six extra spaces for printing X (the week number) followed by the symbol "I" in column 4. Putting all these things together gave line 90 of the original program:

90 PRINT X;TAB(4);"I";TAB((W-100)/2+6);"*"

Thus for X=21 and W=150 we'd have

```
Col.   0123456789...................31 (= 25 + 6)

       20  I
       21  I                    *
            .
            .
            .
```

Automatic Scaling

We can generalize this idea by using a starting weight called A (instead of 100), and a final weight called B (instead of 200). This makes the scale factor 50/(B-A) spaces per pound. The translation is now A pounds (not 100), and the starting weight at the left edge of the graph is W-A (not W-100). This gives us as a generalized print statement:

460 PRINT X;TAB(4);"I";TAB((W-A)*(50/(B-A))+6);"*"

It will also be necessary to generalize the headings at the top of the graph, and this is done in a similar manner. Here's a program that does this "customized" scaling in a subroutine (lines 315 to 480). The first time the subroutine is used, the weights go from 100 to 200 (line 180). But then the user is asked to supply a more personalized set of minimum and maximum weights. These are input as A and B in lines 280 to 301. This program also contains the user's "goal" weight as the first number in DATA statement 900. This way the program can tell the dieter how many "pounds-to-goal" there are. The -1 the the end of the DATA is used to stop the READ loop (see line 80). Here's the improved program and a run.

SCALED
WEIGHT
GRAPH

```
LIST

10 PRINT"WEIGHT WATCHER'S RECORD"
20 PRINT:PRINT"WEEK","WEIGHT","WT. LOSS"
30 S=0: D=0
35 REM-----CALC. & PRINT TABLE----------
40 READ G
45 I=0
50 I=I+1
60 READ W
70 IF I=1 THEN 110
80 IF W<0 THEN 140
90 D=W1-W
100 S=S+D
110 PRINT I,W,D
120 W1=W
130 GOTO 50
140 PRINT:PRINT"AVG. WEEKLY LOSS    ";S/(I-1);"LBS."
150 PRINT"LBS. TO GOAL   ";W1-G
160 PRINT"TOTAL POUNDS LOST SO FAR   ";S
170 PRINT:PRINT"WEIGHT WATCHER'S GRAPH":PRINT
175 REM-----STANDARD SCALE(100-200)-----
180 A=100:B=200
190 GOSUB 315
250 REM-----CUSTOMIZED SCALE----------
260 PRINT:PRINT"WANT A CUSTOMIZED GRAPH";:INPUT A$
270 IF A$="NO" THEN 999
280 PRINT"WHAT IS THE SMALLEST NUMBER YOU WANT(INSTEAD OF 100)";
290 INPUT A
300 PRINT"WHAT IS THE LARGEST NUMBER YOU WANT(INSTEAD OF 200)";
301 INPUT B
303 GOSUB 315
305 PRINT"WANT ANOTHER GRAPH";:INPUT A$
307 IF A$="YES" THEN 280
309 GOTO 999
315 REM-----GRAPH SUBROUTINE-----
316 X=0
317 REM-----HEADING (LINE 1)-----
330 FOR I=A TO B STEP 10
340 PRINT TAB(X*50*(10/(B-A))+5);I;
350 X=X+1
360 NEXT I
370 PRINT
375 REM-----HEADING (LINE 2)-----
380 PRINT"    I";
390 FOR I=0 TO (X-1)
400 PRINT TAB(I*50*(10/(B-A))+7);"+";
410 NEXT I
420 PRINT
425 RESTORE
426 READ G
428 REM-----PRINT GRAPH-----
429 I=0
430 I=I+1
440 READ W
450 IF W<0 THEN 480
460 PRINT I;TAB(4);"I";TAB((W-A)*(50/(B-A))+6);"*"
470 GOTO 430
480 RETURN
900 DATA 122,153,149.5,147.5,147.5,145,144.5,141,141.5,139.25
910 DATA 139.5,137.5,138.5,-1
999 END
```

SUBROUTINE 315-480 IS USED FOR BOTH THE STANDARD AND CUSTOMIZED SCALES. THE VALUES OF A AND B MAKE THE DIFFERENCE.

```
RUN
WEIGHT WATCHER'S RECORD

WEEK          WEIGHT        WT. LOSS
 1             153           0
 2             149.5         3.5
 3             147.5         2
 4             147.5         0
 5             145           2.5
 6             144.5          .5
 7             141           3.5
 8             141.5         -.5
 9             139.25        2.25
10             139.5         -.25
11             137.5         2
12             138.5         -1


AVG. WEEKLY LOSS   1.20833 LBS.
LBS. TO GOAL    16.5
TOTAL POUNDS LOST SO FAR    14.5

WEIGHT WATCHER'S GRAPH

      100   110   120   130   140   150   160   170   180   190   200
   I   +     +     +     +     +     +     +     +     +     +     +
 1 I                                *
 2 I                             *
 3 I                              *
 4 I                              *
 5 I                             *
 6 I                             *
 7 I                          *
 8 I                           *
 9 I                         *
10 I                         *
11 I                        *
12 I                         *


WANT A CUSTOMIZED GRAPH? YES
WHAT IS THE SMALLEST NUMBER YOU WANT(INSTEAD OF 100)? 130
WHAT IS THE LARGEST NUMBER YOU WANT(INSTEAD OF 200)? 150
      130                        140                        150
   I   +                          +                          +
 1 I                                                          *
 2 I                                                     *
 3 I                                               *
 4 I                                               *
 5 I                                         *
 6 I                                      *
 7 I                                *
 8 I                                   *
 9 I                          *
10 I                          *
11 I                   *
12 I                      *
WANT ANOTHER GRAPH? NO
```

THE SECOND GRAPH SHOWS THE SAME DATA AS THE FIRST, BUT IT IS SPREAD OUT OVER A BETTER RANGE.

3.5 SUBSCRIPTED VARIABLES

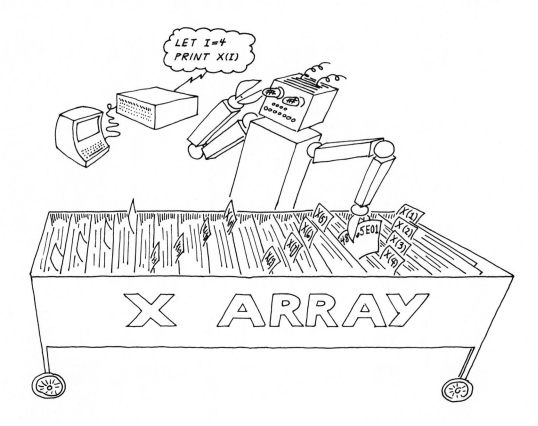

So far we have been limited to variable names made up of a single letter
(A,B,C...,Z), or a single letter followed by a single digit (A1, A2,
A3,...Z8,Z9). One of the problems you eventually run into with such
variables is that you can't always foresee how many are needed, and there's
no way for the computer to add new variable names when this happens. To
see what the problem is, look at the next program which asks a person to
input an unspecified number of weights.

Since we don't know how many weights the person may type in, we ask
the user to type zero to signal when input is finished. Since we want to print
"deviations from the average" of each weight, we'll have to save all the
weights in separate variables until the end (because only then can we
calculate the average). So we "guess" that at most four weights will be input,
and use separate input statements to save these weights in W1, W2, W3, and
W4. As you can see this is a very clumsy and very limited approach. We also

get a ridiculous "deviation from the average" when the user types in the zero. The villain here is line 220 which blindly prints *all* the differences.

HORRIBLE EXAMPLE

```
LIST

10 LET S=0
20 PRINT"TYPE A WEIGHT AFTER EACH ? --TYPE 0 WHEN FINISHED"
30 INPUT W1
40 IF W1=0 THEN 190
50 N=N+1
60 S=S+W1
70 INPUT W2
80 IF W2=0 THEN 190
90 N=N+1
100 S=S+W2
110 INPUT W3
120 IF W3=0 THEN 190
130 N=N+1
140 S=S+W3
150 INPUT W4
160 IF W4=0 THEN 190
170 N=N+1
180 S=S+W4
190 LET A=S/N
200 PRINT "AVERAGE WEIGHT =";A
210 PRINT "DEVIATIONS FROM THE AVERAGE WERE"
220 PRINT W1-A;W2-A;W3-A;W4-A
230 END
OK

RUN
TYPE A WEIGHT AFTER EACH ? --TYPE 0 WHEN FINISHED
? 150
? 175
? 163
? 0
AVERAGE WEIGHT = 162.667
DEVIATIONS FROM THE AVERAGE WERE
-12.6667   12.3333   .333328 -162.667
OK
```

HERE'S JUST ONE OF THE REASONS THIS IS A POOR PROGRAM.

There's got to be a better way! And there is. The new feature that clears up this problem is the ability of BASIC to have what are called "subscripted variables". These look like the following:

$$A(1), A(2), A(3), A(4),...Z(86), Z(87), Z(88),...$$

You use a variable name followed by any positive integer placed in parentheses. $A(3)$ is pronounced "A sub 3", and it really means the third location in an *array* of locations. You can have hundreds (or even thousands) of these locations, depending on how much memory your computer has.

What's an array? It's a concept that allows you to organize your computer's memory in blocks of variables that look something like this:

A(0)	data
A(1)	data
A(2)	data
A(3)	data
A(4)	data
Z(0)	data
Z(1)	data
Z(2)	data
•	•
•	•
•	•
Z(87)	data
Z(88)	data

How many variables are in each block is up to you. You let the program know by using the DIMension statement as follows:

10 DIM A(4), Z(88)

This means reserve a block of five subscripted variables with names from A(0) to A(4), and a block of 89 with names Z(0) to Z(88).

> NOTE: (1) If you don't use DIM, BASIC will assume you meant DIM A(10), Z(10). (2) Some BASIC's don't allow the A(0) or Z(0) names, so they give you one less location in each block than our diagram shows.

And Now for the Really Good News!

The power of arrays (or blocks) of subscripted variables is that the computer can reference them through use of program variables. This is because you can also use *variables* as subscripts. Watch carefully:

ARRAY DEMO

```
LIST

5 DIM W(100)
10 INPUT "HOW MANY WEIGHTS";N
12 PRINT "TYPE A WEIGHT AFTER EACH ?"
15 FOR K = 1 TO N
20 INPUT W(K)
25 NEXT K
30 PRINT "YOUR WEIGHTS IN REVERSE ORDER ARE"
40 FOR K = N TO 1 STEP -1
50 PRINT W(K)
60 NEXT K
70 END

Ready

RUN

HOW MANY WEIGHTS? 4
TYPE A WEIGHT AFTER EACH ?
? 234
? 211
? 213
? 189
YOUR WEIGHTS IN REVERSE ORDER ARE
 189
 213
 211
 234
```

The secret to understanding what happened in this program is to picture memory as follows:

N	4
W(1)	234
W(2)	211
W(3)	213
W(4)	189
W(5)	
•	
•	
•	
W(100)	

In the loop 15 to 25, the user put numbers in the four locations W(1), W(2), W(3), and W(4), so the loop 50 to 70 has no trouble printing them out in reverse (or any other) order. This is because it can reference W(I) for any sequence of I's. The computer can now find variables under *program control*.

WARNING: W(3) is very different from W3. Don't get these confused. Also note that you can use W(K) in a program, but WK is illegal in minimal BASIC.

A program that uses subscripted variables is much more flexible since it can "decide" which variables to manipulate by using a variable for the subscript—like the K and J in W(K) or W(J). Let's see how this idea can make our weight deviation program much more useful.

WEIGHT AVERAGE

```
LIST

10 DIM W(100)
20 LET S=0
30 PRINT "HOW MANY WEIGHTS TO BE AVERAGED";
40 INPUT N
50 PRINT "TYPE A WEIGHT AFTER EACH ?"
60 FOR K=1 TO N
70 INPUT W(K)
80 LET S=S+W(K)
90 NEXT K
95 LET A=S/N
100 PRINT "AVERAGE WEIGHT =";A
110 PRINT "DEVIATIONS FROM THE AVERAGE WERE"
120 FOR K=1 TO N
130 PRINT W(K)-A
140 NEXT K
150 PRINT
160 END

Ready

RUN

HOW MANY WEIGHTS TO BE AVERAGED? 6
TYPE A WEIGHT AFTER EACH ?
? 175
? 163
? 181
? 145
? 162
? 150
AVERAGE WEIGHT = 162.667
DEVIATIONS FROM THE AVERAGE WERE
 12.3333
 .333333
 18.3333
-17.6667
-.666667
-12.6667
```

THIS LOOP PRODUCES THE QUESTION MARKS THAT PROMPT FOR INPUT TO THE W ARRAY.

N	6
W(1)	175
W(2)	163
W(3)	181
W(4)	145
W(5)	162
W(6)	150
•	•
•	•
•	•
W(100)	

K=3 → W(3)

K=6 → W(6)

Notice how easy it is to get the deviations in line 130. This is because the FOR loop of line 120 controls the subscript K. You should think of K as though it were a *pointer*, moving down the list of weights, automatically selecting each in turn until it reaches the Nth one. (N=6 in our example, but it could be as high as 100).

You can have several arrays in a program. (Of course each array uses as many memory locations as you dimension, so you may run out of space unless you have a lot of memory in your machine). Here's an improvement on the previous program that uses two arrays with 100 locations each. This program also contains a useful idea in the subroutine (lines 1000 to 1070). It's an algorithm for finding the largest (max) and smallest (min) item stored in an array. It works by first assuming that W(1) is both the largest (L=W(1)) and smallest (S=W(1)) item. Then it loops down through the array, looking at all the remaining items. If it finds a W(K) that's smaller (line 1020), then *this* W(K) goes into S. Also, we "remember " which subscript corresponded to the latest "smallest" with the variable Y (see line 1050). The same thing is done to find the largest W(K) in lines 1022 and 1030. The subscript of the largest weight is "remembered" with X. Then X and Y can be used to point at the months in which largest and smallest weights occurred (see lines 110 and 120).

MAX-MIN
WEIGHTS

```
LIST

5 DIM W(100),M(100)
10 PRINT "HOW MANY MONTHLY WEIGHTS TO BE AVERAGED";
20 INPUT N
30 PRINT "AFTER EACH ? TYPE MONTH #, WEIGHT"
40 LET S=0
50 FOR I=1 TO N
60 INPUT M(I),W(I)
70 LET S=S+W(I)
80 NEXT I
90 PRINT "AVERAGE WEIGHT WAS";S/N
100 GOSUB 1000
110 PRINT "YOUR LARGEST WEIGHT WAS ";L;"LBS. IN MONTH # ";M(X)
120 PRINT "YOUR SMALLEST WEIGHT WAS ";S;"LBS. IN MONTH # ";M(Y)
130 STOP
999 REM---ROUTINE TO FIND MAX WT., MIN WT., AND CORRESPONDING MONTHS"---
1000 LET L=W(1):LET S=W(1):LET X=1:LET Y=1
1010 FOR K=2 TO N
1020 IF W(K)<S THEN 1050
1022 IF W(K)>L THEN 1030
1024 GOTO 1060
1030 LET L=W(K):LET X=K
1040 GOTO 1060
1050 LET S=W(K):LET Y=K
1060 NEXT K
1070 RETURN
9000 END
```

X AND Y WILL "POINT" AT THE MAXIMUM AND MINIMUM WEIGHTS WHEN THIS LOOP FINISHES.

```
RUN

HOW MANY MONTHLY WEIGHTS TO BE AVERAGED? 5
AFTER EACH ? TYPE MONTH #, WEIGHT
? 4,170
? 5,175
? 6,189
? 7,182
? 8,173
AVERAGE WEIGHT WAS 177.8
YOUR LARGEST WEIGHT WAS   189 LBS. IN MONTH #  6
YOUR SMALLEST WEIGHT WAS  170 LBS. IN MONTH #  4
STOP at line 130
```

The preceding program handles the weights for one person nicely. But suppose you want to keep records for a group of people, and use your program to select and average the data for any one of them. This suggests that it would be nice to have variables with two subscripts, one to "point" out the month, the other to "point" out the person. In other words, we'd like to use a variable like $W(5,4)$ to mean the weight in the 5th month of person #4. This can be done in most versions of BASIC, using two-dimensional arrays. Let's see how they work.

Two-Dimensional Arrays; Double Subscripts

In addition to one-dimensional arrays, it's also possible to set aside two-dimensional or rectangular arrays (blocks) of memory in most versions of BASIC. For example,

10 DIM A(5,4)

means reserve a block of 20 computer memory locations called

$A(1,1)$ $A(1,2),...,$ $A(5,3)$, $A(5,4)$.

You should picture these memory locations as being organized in a block with five rows and four columns as following:

A(1,1) (data)	A(1,2) (data)	A(1,3) (data)	A(1,4) (data)
A(2,1) (data)	A(2,2) (data)	A(2,3) (data)	A(2,4) (data)
A(3,1) (data)	A(3,2) (data)	A(3,3) (data)	A(3,4) (data)
A(4,1) (data)	A(4,2) (data)	A(4,3) (data)	A(4,4) (data)
A(5,1) (data)	A(5,2) (data)	A(5,3) (data)	A(5,4) (data)

I=3 →

J=2

Again the real power of these "doubly-subscripted" variables is that the subscripts themselves can be variables. We can now write $A(I,J)$ to "point" at the data in row I and column J. If $I=3$ and $J=2$, the program will use the data in $A(3,2)$. So this would be a natural way to store the weight of member #2 for month #3 in a diet program. But of course there are many other uses. A more ambitious application will be explained in Chapter 5 where we'll show how a two-dimensional array is a natural way of storing the data for a football scouting report.

For a quick example now, here's a program which prints a table of how many sales of each of three items were made in four months. In other words, our picture of the data structure is the following:

	ITEM 1	ITEM 2	ITEM 3
Month 1	345	687	149
Month 2	344	689	235
Month 3	378	499	245
Month 4	377	568	388

In this example think of ROW as meaning "MONTH", and COLUMN as meaning "ITEM". The main thing to observe is that two nested FOR loops are needed for both INPUT (lines 60 to 110) and OUTPUT (lines 150 to 200). The outer loop on I controls the row subscript, while the inner loop on J controls the column subscript. The comma at the end of line 170 forces all the items controlled by the J loop to print on one line. The PRINT statement in line 190 produces a carriage return and line feed to get ready for the next time the J loop is executed.

ARRAY DEMO 2

```
LIST

10 DIM D(10,4)
20 PRINT "HOW MANY ROWS OF DATA";
30 INPUT M
40 PRINT "HOW MANY COLUMNS PER ROW";
50 INPUT N
60 FOR I=1 TO M
70 PRINT "TYPE";N; "ITEMS FOR ROW";I
80 FOR J=1 TO N
90 INPUT D(I,J)
100 NEXT J
110 NEXT I
120 PRINT "DATA SUMMARY"
130 FOR I=1 TO N:PRINT "ITEM";I,:NEXT I:PRINT
140 PRINT"------------------------------------"
150 FOR I=1 TO M
160 FOR J=1 TO N
170 PRINT D(I,J),
180 NEXT J
190 PRINT
200 NEXT I
210 END
```

ARRAY INPUT

ARRAY OUTPUT

```
RUN

HOW MANY ROWS OF DATA? 4
HOW MANY COLUMNS PER ROW? 3
TYPE 3 ITEMS FOR ROW 1
? 345
? 687
? 149
TYPE 3 ITEMS FOR ROW 2
? 344
? 689
? 235
TYPE 3 ITEMS FOR ROW 3
? 378
? 499
? 245
TYPE 3 ITEMS FOR ROW 4
? 377
? 568
? 388
DATA SUMMARY
ITEM 1          ITEM 2          ITEM 3
------------------------------------------
   345             687             149
   344             689             235
   378             499             245
   377             568             388
```

This program doesn't do very much at present, but we'll return to it in Section 5.1 and make it more useful.

SELF-TEST

1. Simulate running the following program on paper, and then check your results on a computer.

```
10 LET A(1)=1
20 LET A(2)=1
30 PRINT A(1);
40 PRINT A(2);
50 FOR K = 3 TO 10
60 LET A(K) = A(K-1) + A(K-2)
70 PRINT A(K);
80 NEXT K
100 PRINT "END OF FIBONACCI DEMO"
110 END
```

2. Simulate running this program, writing the output you'd expect on paper, along with the proper spacing. Then try it on a computer.

```
10 FOR I = 1 TO 3
20 FOR J = 1 TO 4
30 LET A(I,J) = I * J
40 PRINT A(I,J);
50 NEXT J
60 PRINT
70 NEXT I
80 END
```

3.6   BAR GRAPHS; PINBALL SIMULATION

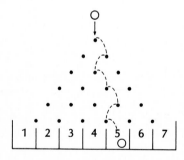

Graphical output is often useful in displaying the results of what are called "computer simulations". These are programs that make the computer imitate some other process. We'll look at the idea of simulation in greater detail in Chapter 9. For the present, let's look at one specific example of a simulation.

Our simulation program will imitate a pinball machine with rigid (non-moving) pins on a slanted table, and pockets at the bottom. The program "drops" balls in the opening indicated by the arrow. As each simulated ball rolls down, it strikes pins and bounces randomly to the left or right, finally landing in one of the pockets.

We would like to know how many balls end up in each pocket after a large number of trials. One way to find out would be to build the pinball machine and spend days rolling balls and counting how many land in each pocket. Instead, let's write a program to simulate such a machine. We'll use seven pockets in our example.

To begin with, let's set up a "pointer" P which describes where the ball is at any given time. Another way to explain P is to say it points at the pcoket position directly under the ball. At the beginning of the simulation, the ball would fall into pocket 4 if no pins were in the way, so we'll start by setting P = 4. Since there are 6 levels of pins, we'll need a loop "FOR L = 1 TO 6" to simulate the entire drop. At each level, the ball will hit a pin and bounce either to the left or to the right.

This is random process, so let's use random numbers to decide the ball's path. If the ball does hit a pin we'll assume it's knocked one-half pocket to either side, that is, we'll assume the pins are always in the middle of the ball's path. We'll set P = P + .5 or P = P - .5, depending on which direction the ball goes. When the ball finally lands in a pocket we'll keep score by adding one to that pocket's contents. Then we'll drop the next ball. After all the balls have been dropped, we'll print a table of pockets and the corresponding number of balls.

PINBALL COUNT

```
100  REM---PUT RANDOMIZE STATEMENT HERE IF NEEDED
110  FOR N=1 TO 7
120      LET C(N)=0
130  NEXT N
140  PRINT "POCKET","COUNT"
160  FOR B=1 TO 100
170      LET P=4
180      FOR L=1 TO 6
190          LETX=RND(1)
200          IF X<.5 THEN 230
210          LET P=P-.5
220          GOTO 240
230          LET P=P+.5
240      NEXT L
250      LET C(P)=C(P)+1
260  NEXT B
270  FOR N=1 TO 7
280      PRINT N, C(N)
290  NEXT N
300  END
```

NOTICE HOW THE POINTER P IS ALSO USED AS A SUBSCRIPT: THIS MAKES THE VARIABLE C(P) COUNT THE NUMBER OF BALLS FALLING INTO THE POCKET TO WHICH P FINALLY POINTS.

```
'IN BASIC-PLUS 3 LINES LIKE THIS CAN BE
'WRITTEN AS 1 BY USING A 'FOR MODIFIER':
'270 PRINT N, C(N)   FOR N=1 TO 7
```

```
RUN
POCKET          COUNT
  1               0
  2               9
  3               19
  4               35
  5               25
  6               8
  7               4
OK
  RUN
POCKET          COUNT
  1               1
  2               7
  3               21
  4               37
  5               24
  6               7
  7               3
OK
RUN
POCKET          COUNT
  1               4
  2               4
  3               23
  4               33
  5               25
  6               8
  7               3
OK
```

You can see that most of the balls land in pockets 3, 4, and 5. If we plot the distribution of balls, we get a graph something like this:

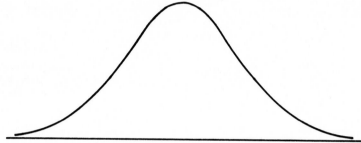

```
        35        x
        30            x   x
# BALLS 25
        20
        15    x           x
        10
         5
              1 2 3 4 5 6 7
                POCKETS
```

This is a rather crude graph. Theoretically, the graph should approximate what is called a "normal" or bell-shaped curve that looks like this:

To get a better approximation to this curve, we'll have to run more trials. Suppose we change our program so there are 31 pockets with pins at 30 levels, and drop 5,000 balls into this pinball machine. Let's also make our program graph the results.

For this problem, a good way to display results is to use a histogram, or bar graph. Here's a short program segment that illustrates the basic technique needed for making a bar-graph on an alphanumeric terminal. Suppose we wanted to graph the contents of 3 pockets that had 50, 110, and 87 balls each. Here's what we could do:

BAR GRAPH

```
LIST

10 LET C(1) = 50
20 LET C(2) = 110
30 LET C(3) = 87
40 FOR I =1 TO 3
45 PRINT I; TAB(5);C(I);TAB(10);"I";
50 FOR K=1 TO C(I)/10
60 PRINT "<*>";
70 NEXT K
80 PRINT
90 NEXT I
100 END

Ready

RUN

   1    50   I<*><*><*><*><*>
   2   110   I<*><*><*><*><*><*><*><*><*><*><*>
   3    87   I<*><*><*><*><*><*><*><*>
```

The loop 50-60-70 prints one "bar" in our bar graph, using the symbol <*> for every 10 balls that reach pocket C(I). The outer loop 40-90 controls the number of bars, one for each pocket.

SELF-TEST

1. Write a program that displays the results of dropping 5,000 balls in a pinball machine with 31 pockets. Print one graphing symbol (say "0") for every 10 balls if you're using a 72 column terminal, or one symbol for every 20 balls on a 40 column terminal. The output should look something like that in the sample run we've shown.

   WARNING: This program will take a long time to run!

```
RUN

PKT COUNT GRAPH

  1    0  :
  2    0  :
  3    0  :
  4    0  :
  5    0  :
  6    0  :
  7    4  :
  8   10  :0
  9   23  :00
 10   61  :000000
 11  148  :0000000000000
 12  248  :000000000000000000000000
 13  407  :0000000000000000000000000000000000000000
 14  604  :000000000000000000000000000000000000000000000000000000000000
 15  644  :0000000000000000000000000000000000000000000000000000000000000000
 16  719  :0000000000000000000000000000000000000000000000000000000000000000000000000
 17  640  :0000000000000000000000000000000000000000000000000000000000000000
 18  578  :00000000000000000000000000000000000000000000000000000000000
 19  418  :000000000000000000000000000000000000000000
 20  240  :000000000000000000000000
 21  151  :000000000000000
 22   62  :000000
 23   28  :00
 24   10  :0
 25    5  :
 26    0  :
 27    0  :
 28    0  :
 29    0  :
 30    0  :
 31    0  :
```

3.7 PRINT USING; FRACTURED FRACTIONS

Some extended versions of BASIC permit what is called "formated" output. This means that you can specify the format (or arrangement) of items in a line of output, and avoid some of the limitations of the "standard" spacing for numbers and characters. In particular, you can specify the number of decimal digits to be printed, the position of the decimal, the size of the field, and the position of the digits within that field. Here's a simple example that shows how it works.

```
10  LET A$= "  ###.####"
20  PRINT USING A$; 355/113
30  END
OK
RUN
      3.1416
```

We left room for 3 digits, a decimal, and 4 more digits
We forced two spaces at the beginning of the "field"

Thus the field we specified is 10 positions wide.

In line 10 we used what's called a string variable, A$. This is a variable in which characters are stored instead of numbers. The characters to be stored are placed between quotation marks. In our example, the string A$ consists of two blanks, three pound signs (#), a decimal, and four more pound signs. The blanks (or spaces) force spaces in the output field, while the pound signs say exactly how many positions are available for digits before and after the decimal.

If you wish, the two parts of PRINT USING can be written as a single statement:

```
10 PRINT USING "   ###.####"; 355/113
```

There are other symbols that can be included in the format string, allowing things like $,*, or spaces to be made part of the output. Since these features are not standardized, you'll have to read your own BASIC reference manual to get further detail.

The PRINT USING and the TAB statements complement each other, allowing you to produce just about any kind of output format. Let's look at an example that illustrates how both features might be used in the same program.

Fractured Fractions

You have probably seen the fraction 22/7 used as an approximation for PI, correct to 3 significant figures. The example just given used 355/113 as a much better approximation. This raises the question of whether we could find a fraction that does even better. A more general question is this: can we find fractions that approximate any decimal number to any required accuracy?

An Algorithm for Finding Approximating Fractions

The answer is that we *can* find fractions which produce decimal numbers to any degree of accuracy. (However, if we use a computer, then there will be a limit on accuracy imposed by the BASIC interpreter, which may not handle more than 6 or 7 significant figures. To go beyond this limit requires software with "multiple precision" arithmetic. Our example will illustrate this by showing what happens on a system that allows 15 significant digits.)

The algorithm we'll use first generates what are called continued fractions, which are like fractions within fractions within fractions, etc.

General Algorithm	*Example*
Y_0 is the decimal we start with	$Y_0 = 2.55$
Let $R_0 = $ the integer part of Y_0	$R_0 = 2$
$Y_1 = \dfrac{1}{Y_0 - R_0}$	$Y_1 = \dfrac{1}{2.55 - 2} = \dfrac{1}{.55} = 1.81818\ldots$
$R_1 = \text{INT}\,(Y_1)$	$R_1 = 1$
$Y_2 = \dfrac{1}{Y_1 - R_1}$	$Y_2 = \dfrac{1}{1.818\ldots - 1} = \dfrac{1}{.81818\ldots} = 1.222\ldots$
$R_2 = \text{INT}\,(Y_2)$	$R_2 = 1$
$Y_3 = \dfrac{1}{Y_2 - R_2}$	$Y_3 = \dfrac{1}{1.222\ldots - 1} = \dfrac{1}{.222\ldots} = 4.5000$
$R_3 = \text{INT}\,(Y_3)$	$R_3 = 4$
In general, $R_i = \text{INT}\,(Y_i)$	$Y_4 = \dfrac{1}{4.5 - 4} = \dfrac{1}{.5} = 2$
$Y_{i+1} = \dfrac{1}{Y_i - R_i}$	$R_4 = 2$

Since $R_4 = Y_4$ we have gone as far as we can.

The continued fraction then looks like this:

$$Y_0 = R_0 + \cfrac{1}{R_1 + \cfrac{1}{R_2 + \cfrac{1}{R_3 + \cdots \cfrac{1}{R_n}}}}$$

$$2.55 = 2 + \cfrac{1}{1 + \cfrac{1}{1 + \cfrac{1}{4 + \cfrac{1}{2}}}}$$

Since a continued fraction is hard to use, we must next convert it to a simple fraction. This is done by starting at the bottom and working up, using a second algorithm as follows:

$$4 + \frac{1}{2} = \frac{9}{2}$$ The fraction is now $$2 + \cfrac{1}{1 + \cfrac{1}{1 + \cfrac{1}{\frac{9}{2}}}}$$

$$\frac{1}{\frac{9}{2}} = \frac{2}{9}$$

$$1 + \frac{2}{9} = \frac{11}{9}$$ Now we have $$2 + \cfrac{1}{1 + \cfrac{1}{\frac{11}{9}}}$$

$$\frac{1}{\frac{11}{9}} = \frac{9}{11}$$

$$1 + \frac{9}{11} = \frac{20}{11}$$ So now we have $$2 + \cfrac{1}{\frac{20}{11}}$$

Finally, we get $$2 + \frac{11}{20} = \frac{51}{20}$$

Here's a listing of a computer program which combines these two algorithms, followed by a run using 2.55 as input.

CONTINUED
FRACTIONS

```
LIST

10 DIM R(20)
20 A$="###.############"
30 B$="   ############"
40 PRINT
50 PRINT "THIS PROGRAM CONVERTS DECIMALS TO FRACTIONS."
60 PRINT
80 INPUT Y
90 PRINT "HOW MANY LEVELS (1 TO 12)?"
100 INPUT T
110 PRINT
120 FOR A=1 TO T
130 R(A)=INT(Y+.00001)
140 IF ABS(R(A)-Y)<.00001 THEN 180
150 Y=1/(Y-R(A))
160 NEXT A
170 GOTO 190
180 T=A
190 PRINT R(1);"  +   1"
```

HERE'S WHERE THE FORMATS USED IN LINES 330, 350, AND 360 ARE DEFINED.

```
200 FOR A=2 TO T-1
210 PRINT TAB(A*6-7);"---------"
220 PRINT TAB(A*6-6);R(A);"  +   1"
230 NEXT A
240 PRINT TAB(T*6-7);"-----"
250 PRINT TAB(T*6-6);R(T)
260 N=R(T)
270 D=1
280 FOR B=T-1 TO 1 STEP -1
290 A=N
300 N=R(B)*N+D
310 D=A
320 NEXT B
330 PRINT USING B$,N
340 PRINT "=  ------------- = ";
350 PRINT USING A$,N/D
360 PRINT USING B$,D
370 END
```

```
RUN


THIS PROGRAM CONVERTS DECIMALS TO FRACTIONS.

? 2.55
HOW MANY LEVELS (1 TO 12)?
? 12

  2   +   1
          ---------
          1   +   1
                  ---------
                  1   +   1
                          ---------
                          4   +   1
                                  -----
                                    2

                   51
=  ------------- =    2.550000000000
                   20
```

Here's a run of this same program on a system with a BASIC that has "multiple-precision floating point arithmetic". Up to 15 decimal digits of accuracy can be handled by this system, which is why we used fifteen # symbols in defining A$:

A$ ="###.############"

Since we allowed for three digits in front of the decimal, this leaves room for twelve digits after the decimal. As you can see, our final fraction was equal to the decimal

3.141592653580

which agrees with the input decimal's 12 significant digits. Since different versions of BASIC have different "precisions" of arithmetic, you may not obtain exactly the same results.

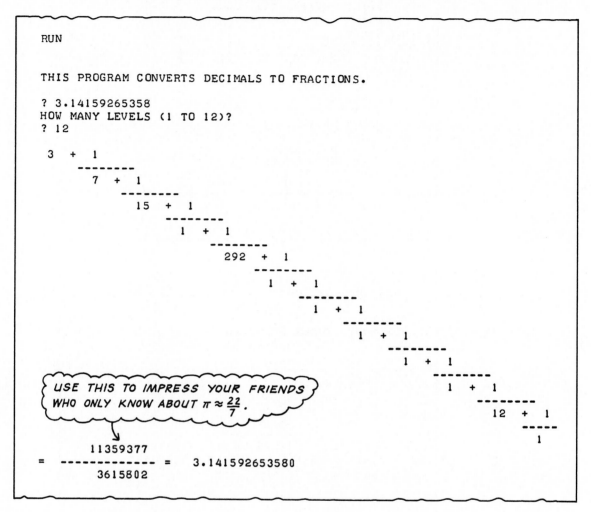

3.8   SAVING YOUR PROGRAMS

Now that your programs are getting a bit lengthy, you will be looking for some method of storing them outside the computer's memory for later use. Three kinds of "external" storage are usually used: punched paper tape, magnetic disk, and magnetic tape (usually in the form of cassettes or cartridges).

Saving Programs on Paper Tape

Until lately a widespread (and cheap) way of storing programs externally was on punched paper tape. The popularity of this method was due to the use of terminals in schools and industry which had a paper tape punch and paper tape reader built in. Here's what the usual 8-channel paper tape looks like:

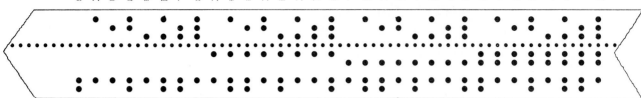

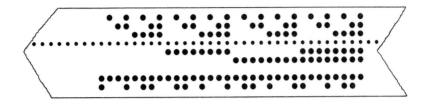

NOTE: The lower tape is spaced normally. The upper tape has "null" (no punch) typed in between each character. The ASCII (American Standard Code for Information Interchange) meaning of the punched codes is shown above it. A chart of all these codes is given in Appendix B.

Paper tape has eight positions for holes but only seven are used for the bits of the ASCII code. For example, for the letter L the ASCII code is

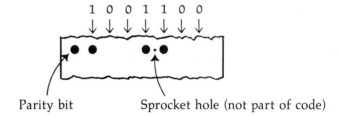

The eighth punched hole (at the left) is called a "parity bit" and it's used to make the total number of bits even for error checking (if the computer doesn't find an *even* number of bits "on", there's an error).

Punching a paper tape copy of a program is only a little more complicated than getting a listing. The main thing to keep in mind is that when you later read the tape back in, the computer will react just as if someone were typing the program into the terminal. So you should be careful when you turn on the paper tape punch that whatever gets punched will be acceptable when it is later read back in. That's the reasoning behind the following steps:

1. Make sure the program you want to save is in memory. If your BASIC has a NULL command, type NULL 3 (CR) (This puts 3 extra blank codes at the ends of lines which makes the tapes easier to read later on.)
2. Switch the terminal to "local".
3. Turn on the paper tape punch.
4. Hold down the "null" key to get a blank length of paper tape for a leader. (On some terminals, a different key may have to be used, e.g., "here is").
5. Turn *off* the paper tape punch.
6. Switch the terminal back to "line".
7. Type the command LIST—*do not type carriage return.*
8. Turn *on* the paper punch; *now type carriage return*

The computer will print out a listing, and it will be recorded on the paper tape. When the listing and punching is finished,

9. Switch the terminal to "local".
10. Hold down the "null" key to get a blank length of tape for a tail.
11. Turn *off* the paper tape punch.
12. Detach the paper tape, roll it up before it gets stepped on, label the leader with the program name and date (it helps to know when to throw it out). Rubberband it. (Adhesive type tape will get gummy on oiled paper tape in time.)

What you have actually recorded on punched tape is:

carriage return,
line feed,
your program,
carriage return,
line feed,
'OK' (or whatever your computer says when it completes a LIST).

Loading Programs from Paper Tape

Reading in the paper tape should be thought of like typing in a program. Start by doing whatever your computer requires before typing in a NEW program, then:

1. Insert your paper tape in the reader.
2. Turn on the reader, and sit back and watch.
3. Remove tape when finished, roll it up again before it gets stepped on. Turn off reader.

Ignore the error message that may be triggered by the 'OK' (or whatever) that was recorded on the tape.

4. To see what got read in, type LIST.
5. Examine the listing for obvious mistakes—paper tape readers have been known to lose a bit here and there.
6. Make corrections in exactly the same manner as you would for a program that had just been typed in.

In spite of the problems noted above, paper tape does provide a reasonably reliable method of storing programs. Even if you have magnetic storage, paper tape provides a good backup.

Saving Program Output on Punched Paper Tape

For those who have the paper tape reader-punch on their terminal, the following trick is possible. When you need several copies of the same output (to give to friends or decorate your wall, etc.) copy it onto punched tape. Then, instead of recomputing this output, just read the tape with the terminal on "local".

Saving and Loading Programs on Disk

If paper tape is the least sophisticated way of getting data in and out of a computer, magnetic disk is the most sophisticated. There are a number of systems on the market which use a disk to save both programs and data. The procedure described here is for an Altair with one floppy disk drive.

In addition to physically inserting and removing the disk, you must "logically" connect and disconnect it using the commands MOUNT and UNLOAD (not DISMOUNT as you might expect). This lets your computer system know that the disk is there and allows it to do all the preliminary operations that make data transfer so simple. After inserting the disk, you type:

MOUNT 0

(Zero is the number of the first disk drive. If you only have one, it's zero.)
Before removing the disk at the end of a session, you type:

UNLOAD 0

After a disk has been mounted, you can save a program you have written by simply typing

SAVE "DIET4"

where DIET4 is the name under which you "file" the program. The computer then takes care of finding a free space on the disk and storing your program in it. Rules for naming files on this system are: (1) it must be one to eight characters long, and (2) there can be no numbers or special characters as the first character.

To see what programs (or data files) you have saved, type:

FILES

The computer will print out all the names of files on the disk currently in the disk drive. A program already saved on disk is loaded into memory by typing:

LOAD "DIET4"   or   RUN "DIET4"

In both cases the disk is searched for the file you name, memory is erased and the file DIET4 is loaded into memory. In the second case, it is also immediately run.

If you decide to change the name of a stored file, type:

NAME "DIET4" AS "DIET2"

You can get rid of a stored file by simply typing:

KILL "DIET2"

Some of the above commands (not MOUNT or UNLOAD) can be used within a program. Other commands for working with files will be introduced in Chapter 8.

Saving and Loading Programs on Cassette Tape

Cassette storage systems are at a level of sophistication in between punched paper tape and disk. They are faster than most paper tape systems but slower and less flexible than disk. Here is a procedure on an Altair cassette system for saving a file you name "HAROLD":

1. Turn on the tape recorder and position the tape cassette to a free space.
2. Type CSAVE "HAROLD", *do not type carriage return.*
3. Start the tape recorder recording. *Type carriage return.*
   Only the first character of HAROLD is used as the label of the saved file.
4. When the computer prints OK, turn off the tape recorder.
5. Write the file name and date on the cassette label.

To load files from cassette:

1. Turn on the recorder, insert the cassette and rewind it.
2. Type CLOAD "HAROLD", *do not type carriage return.*
3. Press "play". *Type carriage return.*
4. When the computer prints OK, turn off the recorder.

The computer will clear memory, search the cassette tape until it finds the file name HAROLD (just the first character) and load it into memory. If this doesn't work don't be surprised—cassette storage is sometimes erratic. Try again.

3.9   PROJECT IDEAS

1. Write a program to print Pascal's triangle. This is a triangular pattern of numbers which has 1's along the edges. All the other numbers have the property that they equal the sum of the two numbers just above them in the pattern. It also turns out that the numbers across row K give the combinations of K things taken 0 at a time, 1 at a time, etc. For example, row 5 has the numbers 1,5,10,10,5,1. If you think of these as giving how many "combination sandwiches" are possible, first from 5 ingredients taken 0 at a time (the null sandwich), then 1 at a time, 2 at a time, etc., you see that the total number of combinations is 1+5+10+10+1=32. Now go back and look at the hot dog problem in Section 2.4 and you'll see that we have discovered a new way of solving the same problem. It's a small world.

   Here's what a run of your program should look like:

```
RUN

HOW MANY LEVELS (MAX.= 12)? 12
                                          1
                                       1     1
                                    1     2     1
                                 1     3     3     1
                              1     4     6     4     1
                           1     5    10    10     5     1
                        1     6    15    20    15     6     1
                     1     7    21    35    35    21     7     1
                  1     8    28    56    70    56    28     8     1
               1     9    36    84   126   126    84    36     9     1
            1    10    45   120   210   252   210   120    45    10     1
         1    11    55   165   330   462   462   330   165    55    11     1
      1    12    66   220   495   792   924   792   495   220    66    12     1
```

2. One of the difficulties with making graphs on an alphanumeric terminal is that you can't always put the plotting characters exactly where they belong. Sometimes it's better to leave out characters that would plot in "bad" positions, and let the viewer mentally fill in what's missing. Write a program that does this for a circle, with an output that "suggests" a perfect circle. The equation for a circle of radius R is:

$$Y = SQR(R*R - X*X)$$

Since the SQR function only gives + values, you'll have to take care of also plotting the - values. Here's an example of what the output might look like.

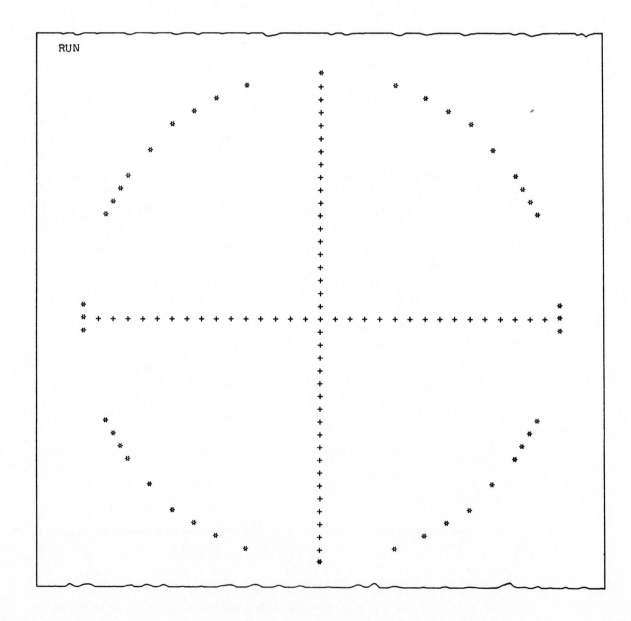

3. Rewrite one of the programs from this chapter in minimal BASIC, using remarks and indentations to clarify the program's structure. An example showing some techniques that can be used is given in the "style corner".

THE STYLE
CORNER

```
100 REM     WATCHER     28 SEPTEMBER 1977     JOHN M. NEVISON
105
110 REM     THIS PROGRAM IS A STYLED VERSION OF AN ORIGINAL
115 REM     PROGRAM BY T. DWYER AND M. CRITCHFIELD.
120
125 REM     REFERENCE:   DWYER, T. AND CRITCHFIELD, M., "BASIC AND
130 REM                  THE PERSONAL COMPUTER," READING, MASS:
135 REM                  ADDISON-WESLEY PUBLISHING COMPANY, 1978.
140
145 REM     PRINT A TABLE AND A GRAPH OF A WEIGHT-WATCHER'S
150 REM     PROGRESS.  PRINT A CUSTOMIZED GRAPH IF ONE
155 REM     IS REQUESTED.
160
165 REM     VARIABLES:
170 REM          A.....LOW END OF THE GRAPH
175 REM          B.....HIGH END OF THE GRAPH
180 REM          A$....ANSWER TO A QUESTION
185 REM          D.....DIFFERENCE BETWEEN TWO WEIGHTS
190 REM          I.....INDEX VARIABLE
195 REM          S.....SUM OF THE WEIGHT LOST
200 REM          W.....PREVIOUS WEEK'S WEIGHT
205 REM          X.....INTERVAL COUNTER
210
215 REM     CONSTANTS:
220     LET G9 = 122                    'THE GOAL WEIGHT
225     LET N9 = 12                     'THE NUMBER OF WEEKS DONE
230     DIM W(12)
235     FOR I = 1 TO N9
240        READ W(I)                    'THE WEEKLY WEIGHTS
245     NEXT I
250     DATA 153, 149.5, 147.5, 147.5, 145, 144.5, 141, 141.5, 139.25
255     DATA 139.5, 137.5, 138.5
260
265
270 REM     MAIN PROGRAM
275
280     GO SUB 390                      'PRINT TABLE
285     LET A = 100
290     LET B = 200
295     GO SUB 520                      'PRINT GRAPH
300
305     PRINT
310     PRINT "WANT A CUSTOMIZED GRAPH";
315     INPUT A$                        '*
320        IF A$ <> "YES" THEN 370
325           PRINT "WHAT IS THE SMALLEST NUMBER THAT ";
330           PRINT "YOU WANT (INSTEAD OF 100)";
335           INPUT A
340           PRINT "WHAT IS THE LARGEST NUMBER THAT ";
345           PRINT "YOU WANT (INSTEAD OF 200)";
350           INPUT B
355           GO SUB 520                 'PRINT GRAPH
360           PRINT "WANT ANOTHER GRAPH";
365     GO TO 315                       '*
370
375     STOP
380
385
```

```
390 REM     SUBROUTINE:  PRINT TABLE
395 REM        IN:  G, W()
400 REM        OUT:
405
410     PRINT "WEIGHT WATCHER'S RECORD"
415     PRINT
420     PRINT "WEEK", "WEIGHT", "DIFFERENCE"
425     LET S = 0
430
435     PRINT 1, W(1), 0
440     LET W = W(1)
445     FOR I = 2 TO N9
450        LET D = W(I) - W
455        LET S = S + D
460        PRINT I, W(I), D
465        LET W = W(I)
470     NEXT I
475
480     PRINT
485     PRINT "AVG. WEEKLY LOSS  "; S/ I   ; "POUNDS"
490     PRINT "POUNDS TO GOAL  "; W-G9
495     PRINT "TOTAL POUNDS LOST SO FAR  "; S
500     PRINT
505
510 RETURN
515
520 REM     SUBROUTINE:  PRINT GRAPH
525 REM        IN:  A, B, W()
530 REM        OUT:
535
540 REM     PRINT THE HEADING LINE 1, THE HEADING LINE 2,
545 REM     AND THE LINES OF THE GRAPH.
550
555     PRINT "WEIGHT WATCHER'S GRAPH"
560     PRINT
565
570     LET X = 0
575
580
585     FOR I = A TO B STEP 10
590        PRINT TAB(X*50* (10/(B-A)) + 5); I;
595        LET X = X + 1
600     NEXT I
605     PRINT
610
615     PRINT "    I"
620     FOR I = 1 TO (X-1)
625        PRINT TAB(I*50* (10/(B-A)) + 7); "*";
630     NEXT I
635     PRINT
640
645     FOR I = 1 TO N9
650        PRINT I; TAB(4); "I"; TAB((W(I)-A) *(50/(B-A)) + 6); "+"
655     NEXT I
660
665 RETURN
670
675     END
```

```
100 REM             CHAPTER 3, PROJECT IDEA #4
105 REM
110 REM             WRITE A PROGRAM THAT CONSISTS ENTIRE-
120 REM             LY OF REMARK STATEMENTS AT FIRST.
125 REM
130 REM             THEN EXPAND THE REMARK IDEAS
140 REM             INTO BLOCKS OF EXECUTABLE STATEMENTS
155 REM
160 REM                       EXAMPLE
170 REM
199 REM-------------------------------------
200 REM    BLOCK 200 STATEMENTS ARE TO READ
201 REM    IN WEEKLY STOCK PRICES OVER YEAR
299 REM-------------------------------------
300 REM    BLOCK 300 STATEMENTS ARE TO PRINT
301 REM    A TABLE OF PRICES FOR EACH WEEK
399 REM-------------------------------------
400 REM    BLOCK 400 WILL FIND MAX AND MIN PRICES
499 REM-------------------------------------
500 REM    BLOCK 500 WILL ASK THE USER HOW MANY
501 REM    COLUMNS ARE AVAILABLE FOR A GRAPH
502 REM    AND THEN CALCULATE SCALE FACTORS
599 REM-------------------------------------
600 REM    BLOCK 600 WILL MAKE A GRAPH OF PRICES
699 REM-------------------------------------
999 END
```

Who What Where Please Hello

paid copy pulp past upon drop plan pl

The   pay ape top pal apt lip put tap pen

Tu seras aimé.   Il sera aimé.   Nous serons aimés. Il

ss less pass class cross issue ass

the its act ten ate but try Ute get

Oratio ad s... vpriũ angelũ ftos omũ

BE

the, we, great, each them sky, like by

For about not

as

qua quo quad quay quey quid quip quit

discovered

4 WORD PROCESSING IN BASIC

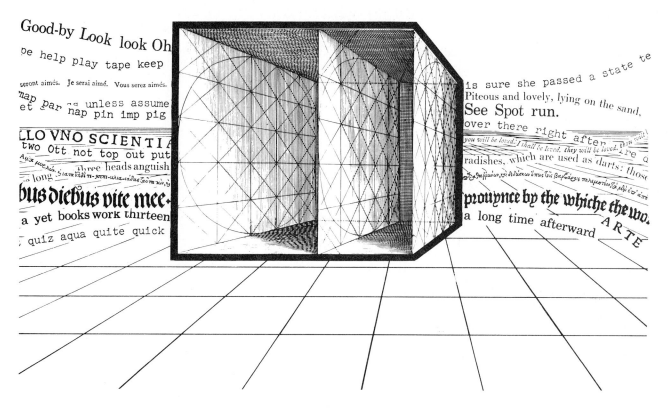

4.0 INTRODUCTION; STRING VARIABLES AND STRING ARRAYS

The word "computer" makes most people think of a machine that can only be used for numerical computation. Fortunately that's not true. We say fortunately, because many of the greatest ideas of civilization are expressed best through non-numerical means: with music, art, crafts,—and of course words. In this chapter we'll look at some of the ways in which personal computers can be used as tools for manipulating "symbols" and "words". Since "words" really don't have meaning to a computer, we prefer calling them *strings*. A string is nothing more than a sequence of symbols like "CAT", "MIKE", "OOMPH", "ARGYLE-88", or even "##!!!*@??$%&+>>?!!!". The length of a string is the number of characters it contains: the length of "CAT" is 3, the length of "X" is 1, and the length of the empty string "" is zero! (Notice that we're using quotation marks to show the start and finish of the string; quotation marks are the one symbol you try not to use in strings*).

---

*If you must, see if the following works in your BASIC:

```
10 PRINT "THIS IS A "; CHR$(34);" MARK"
RUN
THIS IS A " MARK
```

String Variables

In BASIC you can store strings in memory by using *string variables*. These have a $ sign added to a single letter, so there are 26 possible names for simple string variables: A$, B$, C$, ..., Z$. Here's an example using the string variable N$.

```
10 PRINT "WHAT'S YOUR NAME";
20 INPUT N$
30 PRINT "HI ";N$;" YOU OLD SO & SO"
RUN
WHAT'S YOUR NAME? ISABEL
HI ISABEL YOU OLD SO & SO
```

Notice that we had to put a space after HI and before YOU. This is because the PRINT statement packs strings tightly together.

4.1   STRING ARRAYS; THE AUTOMATED WISH GENERATOR

String Arrays

The more sophisticated versions of BASIC also allow string arrays. This means you can have whole blocks of string variables. For example, the names of the months could be stored in an array with locations M$(1), M$(2), and so on.

M$ (1)	JANUARY
M$ (2)	FEBRUARY
M$ (3)	MARCH
•	
•	
•	

> WARNING: Many of the simpler versions of BASIC don't have string arrays. In some versions it may appear that there are string arrays, but the notation M$(3) may have a completely different meaning. See Section 4.3 for further information.

Here's an example using string arrays that improves on the program of Section 3.5 by using month names instead of numbers.

STRING
ARRAY

```
LIST

5 DIM W(100),M$(100)          M$ IS NOW A STRING ARRAY
10 PRINT "HOW MANY MONTHLY WEIGHTS TO BE AVERAGED";   WITH 100 LOCATIONS
20 INPUT N
30 PRINT"AFTER EACH ? TYPE MONTH, WEIGHT"
40 LET S=0
50 FOR I=1 TO N            SO NOW YOU TYPE MARCH, 189 AFTER THE INPUT ?
60 INPUT M$(I),W(I)
70 LET S=S+W(I)                     AND THE COMPUTER
80 NEXT I                           CAN PRINT OUT WORDS
90 PRINT "AVERAGE WEIGHT WAS";S/N   INSTEAD OF NUMBERS.
100 GOSUB 1000
110 PRINT "YOUR LARGEST WEIGHT WAS";L;"LBS. IN THE MONTH OF ";M$(X)
120 PRINT "YOUR SMALLEST WEIGHT WAS";S;"LBS. IN THE MONTH OF ";M$(Y)
130 STOP
999 REM---ROUTINE TO FIND MAX WT., MIN WT., AND CORRESPONDING MONTHS
1000 LET L=W(1):LET S=W(1):LET X=1:LET Y=1
1010 FOR K=2 TO N
1020 IF W(K)<S THEN 1050
1022 IF W(K)>L THEN 1030
1024 GOTO 1060
1030 LET L=W(K):LET X=K
1040 GOTO 1060
1050 LET S=W(K):LET Y=K
1060 NEXT K
1070 RETURN
9000 END

Ready

RUN

HOW MANY MONTHLY WEIGHTS TO BE AVERAGED? 5
AFTER EACH ? TYPE MONTH, WEIGHT
? JAN,176
? FEB,175
? MARCH,189
? APRIL,182
? MAY,180
AVERAGE WEIGHT WAS 180.4
YOUR LARGEST WEIGHT WAS 189 LBS. IN THE MONTH OF MARCH
YOUR SMALLEST WEIGHT WAS 175 LBS. IN THE MONTH OF FEB
STOP at line 130
```

The Automated Wish Generator

The nice thing about string arrays (if your BASIC allows them) is that when you say N$(X), you are using X to point to the Xth string in a whole array of strings. Here's an example that uses the READ statement to put noun phrases in the array locations given by N$(I), verb phrases in V$(I), and "wishee" phrases in S$(I). Then the random number generator is used to create subscripts which "point" to various items in each array. The results are put together in a PRINT statement (line 80) that produces some outrageous results.

WISH GENERATOR

```
LIST

1 RANDOMIZE
5 INPUT"HOW MANY WISHES";X
10 FOR I=1 TO 10
20 READ N$(I),V$(I),S$(I)
30 NEXT I
40 FOR I=1 TO X
50 LET R1 = INT(10*RND(0)+1)
60 LET R2 = INT(10*RND(0)+1)
70 LET R3 = INT(10*RND(0)+1)
80 PRINT"MAY ";N$(R1);" ";V$(R2);" YOUR ";S$(R3)
85 PRINT
90 NEXT I
100 GOTO 999
110 DATA"AN ENRAGED CAMEL","SEND A MASH NOTE TO","MOTHER-IN-LAW"
120 DATA"AN ANCIENT PHILOSOPHER","GET INSPIRATION FROM","PSYCHOANALYST"
130 DATA"A COCKER SPANIEL","REDECORATE","RUMPUS ROOM"
140 DATA"THE EIFEL TOWER","BECOME AN OBSESSION OF","FERN"
150 DATA"A COWARDLY MOOSE","MAKE A SALT LICK OUT OF","GARAGE"
160 DATA"THE SILENT MAJORITY","BUY AN INTEREST IN","LOVE LETTERS"
170 DATA"THE LAST PICTURE SHOW","OVERWHELM","PIGGY BANK"
180 DATA"A FURIOUS TRUMPET PLAYER","POUR YOGURT ON","HAMBURGER"
190 DATA"MISS AMERICA","SING AN OPERATIC SOLO TO","DILL PICKLE"
200 DATA"SEVEN LARGE CHICKENS","LAY AN EGG ON","HONDA"
999 END


RUN

HOW MANY WISHES? 10
MAY AN ANCIENT PHILOSOPHER MAKE A SALT LICK OUT OF YOUR FERN

MAY A COCKER SPANIEL MAKE A SALT LICK OUT OF YOUR MOTHER-IN-LAW

MAY THE LAST PICTURE SHOW POUR YOGURT ON YOUR PIGGY BANK

MAY AN ENRAGED CAMEL REDECORATE YOUR MOTHER-IN-LAW

MAY AN ENRAGED CAMEL OVERWHELM YOUR GARAGE

MAY AN ANCIENT PHILOSOPHER LAY AN EGG ON YOUR DILL PICKLE

MAY THE LAST PICTURE SHOW BECOME AN OBSESSION OF YOUR HAMBURGER

MAY MISS AMERICA REDECORATE YOUR LOVE LETTERS

MAY SEVEN LARGE CHICKENS SING AN OPERATIC SOLO TO YOUR LOVE LETTERS

MAY SEVEN LARGE CHICKENS POUR YOGURT ON YOUR DILL PICKLE
```

THESE ARRAYS ARE LOADED WITH THE PHRASES IN THE DATA STATEMENTS. NOTICE THAT ARRAYS WITH 10 OR LESS LOCATIONS DON'T HAVE TO BE DIMENSIONED.

THIS WISH WAS GENERATED BECAUSE RND MADE R1=2, R2=5, AND R3=4.

If you don't have string arrays, you can use the ON...GOTO statement plus a lot of PRINT statements to write programs like the above. However the program will be longer. This technique is explained in Section 4.3.

4.2 WORDS AND PERMUTATIONS

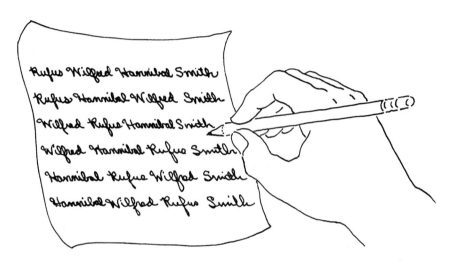

An interesting use of the computer is to generate all possible permutations of several words. For example, you may wish to give a new child several names, but need help in seeing what all the possibilities look like. A re-arrangement of the order in which words (or other objects) appear is called a permutation of those objects.

For two words—say BABY and BUGSY—life is simple. There are only two permutations: BUGSY BABY and BABY BUGSY

For three words there are six (3*2*1) permutations. For example:

SEE	SPOT	RUN
SEE	RUN	SPOT
SPOT	SEE	RUN
SPOT	RUN	SEE
RUN	SEE	SPOT
RUN	SPOT	SEE

For four words there are 4*3*2*1 = 24 permutations, for five there are 120, and—well, you get the picture. It's time for a computer.

One way to create the permutations of N objects is to use N nested FOR loops. For example, if we wanted to show the permutations of the digits 1, 2, and 3 we could write:

PERMUTATION
DEMO

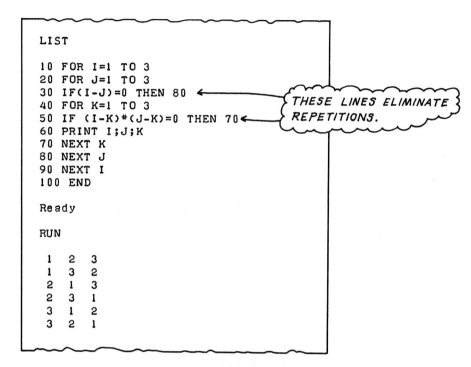

```
LIST

10 FOR I=1 TO 3
20 FOR J=1 TO 3
30 IF(I-J)=0 THEN 80       ←
40 FOR K=1 TO 3
50 IF (I-K)*(J-K)=0 THEN 70←
60 PRINT I;J;K
70 NEXT K
80 NEXT J
90 NEXT I
100 END

Ready

RUN

    1   2   3
    1   3   2
    2   1   3
    2   3   1
    3   1   2
    3   2   1
```

THESE LINES ELIMINATE REPETITIONS.

To see how this works, first take out lines 30 and 40 and try it. You'll find you get all possible ways of printing 1, 2, 3, *including* repetitions. The program will print what are called all possible "samples".

I	J	K
1	1	1
1	1	2
1	1	3
1	2	1
1	2	2
1	2	3
. . . etc . . .		

The sixth line 1, 2, 3 is a true permutation, but the first five are not because they include repetitions. They should be rejected either because I=J, or I=K, or J=K. Statement 30 of our program rejects the cases where I=J (because IF I-J=0 the program branches to line 80, thereby skipping the PRINT). Similarly, line 50 rejects the cases where either I=K or J=K (because then either I-K=0 or J-K=0 so that their product is zero and the program branches to line 70, thereby skipping the PRINT).

To apply this technique to permuting words, all we have to do is use I,J, and K as subscripts that "point" to the proper strings in an array. Let's do this with four strings stored in the array N$ as follows:

N$(1)	BOB
N$(2)	TED
N$(3)	ALICE
N$(4)	CAROL

We'll now need FOR loops on I, J, K, and L to handle the four strings.

Here's a program and run to show all the permutations of these four words (and perhaps help you decide which one you like best).

PERMUTING NAMES

```
LIST

5 REM_____LOAD STRING ARRAY____
10 LET N$(1) = "BOB"
20 LET N$(2) = "TED"
30 LET N$(3) = "ALICE"
40 LET N$(4) = "CAROL"
45 REM-----USE NESTED LOOPS TO FIND ALL PERMUTATIONS-----
50 FOR I=1 TO 4
60 FOR J=1 TO 4
70 IF (I-J)=0 THEN 230
80 FOR K=1 TO 4
90 IF (I-K)*(J-K)=0 THEN 220
100 FOR L=1 TO 4
110 IF (I-L)*(J-L)*(K-L)=0 THEN 210
200 PRINT N$(I);" & ";N$(J);" & ";N$(K);" & ";N$(L)
210 NEXT L
220 NEXT K
230 NEXT J
240 NEXT I
999 END


RUN

BOB & TED & ALICE & CAROL
BOB & TED & CAROL & ALICE
BOB & ALICE & TED & CAROL
BOB & ALICE & CAROL & TED
BOB & CAROL & TED & ALICE
BOB & CAROL & ALICE & TED
TED & BOB & ALICE & CAROL
TED & BOB & CAROL & ALICE
TED & ALICE & BOB & CAROL
TED & ALICE & CAROL & BOB
TED & CAROL & BOB & ALICE
TED & CAROL & ALICE & BOB
ALICE & BOB & TED & CAROL
ALICE & BOB & CAROL & TED
ALICE & TED & BOB & CAROL
ALICE & TED & CAROL & BOB
ALICE & CAROL & BOB & TED
ALICE & CAROL & TED & BOB
CAROL & BOB & TED & ALICE
CAROL & BOB & ALICE & TED
CAROL & TED & BOB & ALICE
CAROL & TED & ALICE & BOB
CAROL & ALICE & BOB & TED
CAROL & ALICE & TED & BOB
```

As you can see, we got the necessary spaces as well as the "&" sign between words simply by including them as string "constants" inserted in the PRINT statement between the string variables.

Another (and very interesting) way to look at our permutation program is to compare it with the hot dog problem back in Section 2.4. There we saw that using nested FOR loops was equivalent to searching down all the branches of a tree structure. In our BOB & TED & ALICE & CAROL program we also have nested FOR loops, so we are also searching through a tree—*but* the tests like IF (I-K)=0 THEN... mean we are eliminating branches in the tree that correspond to repetitions (like BOB & BOB & TED & ALICE). So you could say that the structure we are using is a "pruned tree", with the repetition branches being eliminated before any time is wasted searching them.

4.3   WHAT TO DO IF YOUR BASIC DOESN'T HAVE STRING VARIABLES OR STRING ARRAYS

4.3(a) No String Variables

If you are temporarily limited to a BASIC that doesn't have string variables, but which does have the ON K GOSUB statement, here's how you can write the permutation program:

SIMULATED STRING VARIABLES

```
LIST

1 REM----FOR BASICS WITHOUT STRING VARIABLES
45 REM-----USE NESTED LOOPS TO FIND ALL PERMUTATIONS-----
50 FOR I=1 TO 4
60 FOR J=1 TO 4
70 IF (I-J)=0 THEN 230
80 FOR K=1 TO 4
90 IF (I-K)*(J-K)=0 THEN 220
100 FOR L=1 TO 4
110 IF (I-L)*(J-L)*(K-L)=0 THEN 210
130 ON I GO SUB 300, 310, 320, 330
140 PRINT " & ";
150 ON J GO SUB 300, 310, 320, 330
160 PRINT " & ";
170 ON K GO SUB 300, 310, 320, 330
180 PRINT " & ";
190 ON L GO SUB 300, 310, 320, 330
200 PRINT
210 NEXT L
220 NEXT K
230 NEXT J
240 NEXT I
250 GOTO 999
300 PRINT "BOB";
305 RETURN
310 PRINT "TED";
315 RETURN
320 PRINT "ALICE";
325 RETURN
330 PRINT "CAROL";
335 RETURN
999 END
```

EACH 'ON' STATEMENT BRANCHES DOWN AND PICKS OUT ONE WORD DEPENDING ON WHAT VALUE THE VARIABLE FOLLOWING 'ON' HAS.

```
RUN

BOB   & TED   & ALICE & CAROL
BOB   & TED   & CAROL & ALICE
BOB   & ALICE & TED   & CAROL
BOB   & ALICE & CAROL & TED
BOB   & CAROL & TED   & ALICE
BOB   & CAROL & ALICE & TED
TED   & BOB   & ALICE & CAROL
TED   & BOB   & CAROL & ALICE
TED   & ALICE & BOB   & CAROL
TED   & ALICE & CAROL & BOB
TED   & CAROL & BOB   & ALICE
TED   & CAROL & ALICE & BOB
ALICE & BOB   & TED   & CAROL
ALICE & BOB   & CAROL & TED
ALICE & TED   & BOB   & CAROL
ALICE & TED   & CAROL & BOB
ALICE & CAROL & BOB   & TED
ALICE & CAROL & TED   & BOB
CAROL & BOB   & TED   & ALICE
CAROL & BOB   & ALICE & TED
CAROL & TED   & BOB   & ALICE
CAROL & TED   & ALICE & BOB
CAROL & ALICE & BOB   & TED
CAROL & ALICE & TED   & BOB
```

As you can see, the trick is to piece together a number of PRINT "STRING"; type statements. Since they each end with a semi-colon, they'll all print on the same line. To start a new line, an extra PRINT statement is then needed (see line 200).

4.3(b) Getting Along Without String Arrays

In looking at various BASIC programs you'll find dimension statements for string variables that look like this:

10 DIM A$(20)

> WARNING: This can mean two very different things, depending on which BASIC you're using. Read on, and then check your BASIC manual to see how your version works.

1. In the more advanced versions (like BASIC-PLUS and Altair EXTENDED BASIC)

   10 DIM A$(20)

A$(1)	KLUNK
A$(2)	473-2800
⋮	⋮
A$(20)	ZANZIBAR

means that you have set up a one-dimensional array of strings like that shown. Each string can have many characters (usually up to 255). So if you write a program like this:

```
10 FOR K=1 TO 20
20 PRINT A$(K)
30 NEXT K
```

you'll get a list of 20 strings, each of which may contain up to 255 characters.

2. In some simpler versions of BASIC

```
10 DIM A$(20)
```

means that you have set up room for only *one* string called A$, and that it can have up to 20 characters. In other words you get something like this:

A$="THIS STRING HAS 20 C"

In this case, saying PRINT A$ means print this one string:

```
10 PRINT A$
20 END
RUN
THIS STRING HAS 20 C
```

Now for the confusing part. With this simpler approach to strings, there may still be a need to *simulate* an array of strings. You can do this if you limit the length of strings, and pack them end to end like the following:

N$ = "BOB TED ALICECAROL"

12345123451234512345

Here we have decided to use five positions for each name, so N$(20) is thought of as having four strings of five characters each. To "extract" the strings, these versions of BASIC use the notation N$(I,J) to mean the *sub*-string found in N$ between characters I and J. So N$(1,5) means BOB, while N$(11,15) means ALICE.

> NOTE: When N$(I,J) is used in BASIC-PLUS or Altair EXTENDED BASIC, it means much more: it means the Ith row and Jth column of a whole array of strings. In other words, you are referencing one string in a rectangular array. So all the power of two-dimensional numerical arrays discussed in Sections 3.5, 5.0, and 5.1 is available. In these extended BASICs, DIM B$(10,4) means give me 40 different string locations, each with any length needed up to 255 characters. For a use of such an array, see the LP Record program in Section 5.6.

Exercise For Users Without String Arrays

Try writing the BOB & TED & ALICE & CAROL program in your BASIC. Here are some suggestions:

1. Start with the program in Section 4.2 but delete lines 5, 10, 20, 30, 40, and 200.

2. Add the following statements at the beginning of the program:

```
5 REM—-FOR BASICS WITHOUT STRING ARRAYS
10 DIM A$(20)
20 LET A$="BOB   TED   ALICECAROL"
```

3. Add the following steps to "locate" sub-string positions:

```
120 LET I1 = 5*I-4
130 LET J1 = 5*J-4
140 LET K1 = 5*K-4
150 LET L1 = 5*L-4
160 LET I5 = I1+4
170 LET J5 = J1+4
180 LET K5 = K1+4
190 LET L5 = L1+4
```

4. Change the PRINT statement to the following:

```
200 PRINT N$(I1,I5);"&";N$(J1,J5);"&";N$(K1,K5);"&";N$(L1,L5)
```

As you can see, the lack of standardization on strings can cause lots of problems. This is an area where you'll want to read your BASIC manual carefully, and not be afraid to experiment.

In the remainder of this book we'll use the string *array* approach found in BASIC-PLUS and Altair EXTENDED BASIC since this makes the logic of programs much easier to follow. Because true arrays are powerful "data structures", future higher level languages will undoubtedly include this feature.

One last note: if you are using a BASIC with string arrays, but find you also want to extract sub-strings, or do other fancy things with parts of strings, that's easy to do. Section 4.7 shows how, using the special string functions found in these BASICs.

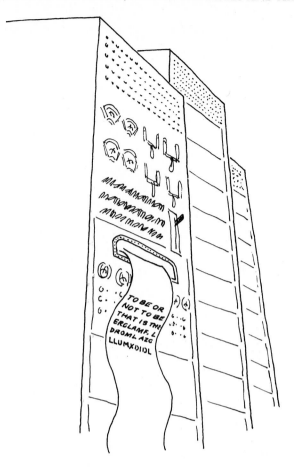

4.4 COMPUTER "POEMS"

A good way to get a pitying look from a good writer is to declare you're going to use your computer to "write poetry". It can't be done! However the computer can be a nice tool for playing with words, allowing a non-poet to experiment, and perhaps eventually become inspired to try the real thing.

Here's a program that might be used to help students think about using words poetically in one particular form. As you'll see, it's pretty simple. For example, the statement INPUT N$ prints a question mark, and saves whatever noun the person types in the memory location N$. Then it later prints this noun in the proper place in the simple poetical form being used.

> NOTE: Remember, for BASICs without string arrays you'll have to add a dimension statement like the following: 5 DIM N$(20), A$(20), B$(20), P$(50), C$(20), D$(20), V$(20)

POEM
FORM

```
LIST

10 PRINT"THIS PROGRAM CAN HELP YOU BECOME A "POET"."
20 PRINT"PLEASE TYPE IN THE FOLLOWING KINDS OF WORDS OR PHRASES"
30 PRINT"AS THE PROGRAM ASKS FOR THEM:"
40 PRINT"NOUN--";:INPUT N$
50 PRINT"ADJECTIVE DESCRIBING THE NOUN--";:INPUT A$
60 PRINT"ANOTHER ADJECTIVE--";:INPUT B$
```

```
70  PRINT"A PREPOSITIONAL PHRASE TELLING"
75  PRINT"WHERE OR WHEN SOMETHING CAN HAPPEN TO YOUR NOUN--";:INPUT P$
80  PRINT"A VERB--";:INPUT V$
90  PRINT"AN ADVERB DESCRIBING HOW YOUR NOUN DOES IT--";:INPUT C$
95  PRINT"ANOTHER ADVERB--";:INPUT D$
100 PRINT:PRINT"HERE IS THE 'POEM':":PRINT
110 PRINT"THE ";N$
120 PRINT"      ";A$;", ";B$
130 PRINT P$
140 PRINT"      ";C$;", ";D$
150 PRINT V$;"."
155 PRINT
160 PRINT"WANT TO MAKE ANOTHER 'POEM'";:INPUT Z$
170 IF Z$="YES" THEN 40
180 END

Ready

RUN

THIS PROGRAM CAN HELP YOU BECOME A 'POET'.
PLEASE TYPE IN THE FOLLOWING KINDS OF WORDS OR PHRASES
AS THE PROGRAM ASKS FOR THEM:
NOUN--? SNOW
ADJECTIVE DESCRIBING THE NOUN--? GRAY
ANOTHER ADJECTIVE--? RAGGED
A PREPOSITIONAL PHRASE TELLING
WHERE OR WHEN SOMETHING CAN HAPPEN TO YOUR NOUN--? BETWEEN THE BUILDINGS
A VERB--? FALLS
AN ADVERB DESCRIBING HOW YOUR NOUN DOES IT--? SLOWLY
ANOTHER ADVERB--? UNCERTAINLY

HERE IS THE 'POEM':

THE SNOW
     GRAY, RAGGED
BETWEEN THE BUILDINGS
     SLOWLY, UNCERTAINLY
FALLS.

WANT TO MAKE ANOTHER 'POEM'? NO
```

Here's another RUN to show how one might use completely different words in writing a poem with the same form.

```
RUN

THIS PROGRAM CAN HELP YOU BECOME A 'POET'.
PLEASE TYPE IN THE FOLLOWING KINDS OF WORDS OR PHRASES
AS THE PROGRAM ASKS FOR THEM:
NOUN--? PROFESSOR
ADJECTIVE DESCRIBING THE NOUN--? TIRED
ANOTHER ADJECTIVE--? HARASSED
A PREPOSITIONAL PHRASE TELLING
WHERE OR WHEN SOMETHING CAN HAPPEN TO YOUR NOUN--? IN THE OFFICE
A VERB--? MUMBLES
AN ADVERB DESCRIBING HOW YOUR NOUN DOES IT--? INCOHERENTLY
ANOTHER ADVERB--? SOFTLY
```

```
HERE IS THE 'POEM':

THE PROFESSOR
      TIRED, HARASSED
IN THE OFFICE
      INCOHERENTLY, SOFTLY
MUMBLES.

WANT TO MAKE ANOTHER 'POEM'? NO
```

4.5 A COMPUTERIZED LETTER WRITER

It's rumored that a magazine once sent a letter to "Mrs. Ecumenical Movement" soliciting a subscription. The letter assured "Mrs. Movement" that not everyone on "Diaconate Studies" street had received a similar once-in-a-lifetime offer. Yes, you guessed it. The evils of computer data processing and purchased-for-a-price mailing lists had finally caught up with one another.

To see how such nonsense works, let's look at a program that writes letters by inserting data about the addressee into a "standard" form letter. We'll also try to generate a little variety by having the program branch to special phrases that depend on the person's age.

As you'll see, the results are a bit silly, and not recommended as a replacement for the real thing. Unfortunately, more and more business correspondence is being generated by similar "word processing" systems. So perhaps one useful application of the program ideas shown here would be to show people how to use their personal computers to start writing back to all those big computers.

The string variables used in BASIC make this an easy program to write. Study it by first looking at the run below. You'll see that three letters are generated (because there are presently only three people on file). The data on these people is stored in DATA statements at lines 600, 700, and 800, and read by statement 70. A more extensive version of the program would probably use BASIC cassette or disk files for storing data (see Chapter 8). Another change you might try is to do a more realistic calculation of the "closest" birthday, rather than always picking the next birthday as we did.

```
RUN

TYPE TODAY'S DATE (E.G. 3,23,78)? 11,8,77
LATEST PURCHASE? RUG
NEEDED ITEM? ROCKING CHAIR


                                      11 / 8 / 77

MR. JOHN SMITH
130 WAYNE AVE.
FERNWOOD, OH  45438

DEAR JOHN:

     WELL HOW HAVE YOU BEEN JOHN?  AND HOW
ARE THINGS IN GOOD OLD FERNWOOD?  ANY
NEW NEIGHBORS ON WAYNE AVE.?  WE'RE ALL
WELL HERE, BUSY FIXING UP THE HOUSE.  WE
JUST BOUGHT A NEW RUG.  NEXT WEEK WE'LL
ADD A ROCKING CHAIR. SOME COMBINATION!!

     BEFORE I FORGET, LET ME WISH YOU A
HAPPY BIRTHDAY.  I KNOW IT'S NOT FOR 11
MONTHS YET, BUT NOTHING LIKE LOOKING
AHEAD!  AND BECOMING 35 YEARS OLD MEANS
THE END OF FOOTLOOSE AND FANCY FREE (SIGH).
PLEASE KEEP IN TOUCH.

                    CHEERS AND KEEP WELL


                    ELWOOD, BRUNHILDA,
                    AND ALL THE KIDS
```

By looking at these runs you can see which parts of the letter are the "boiler plate" standard text, and which parts are inserted from the name and address data. The sentence that talks about M months until a birthday always calculates M for the *next* birthday. (A trickier calculation would be to find the nearest birthday). Our program calculates M in line 80 if the person's birth month (M2) is greater than the current month (M1). Otherwise, line 90 is used because we have to add 12 in order to not get a negative value for M.

```
                                    11 / 8 / 77
MISS LUCY BROWN
8042 APPLE ST.
PIXLEY, NJ   07753

DEAR LUCY:

     WELL HOW HAVE YOU BEEN LUCY?  AND HOW
ARE THINGS IN GOOD OLD PIXLEY?  ANY
NEW NEIGHBORS ON APPLE ST.?  WE'RE ALL
WELL HERE, BUSY FIXING UP THE HOUSE.  WE
JUST BOUGHT A NEW RUG.  NEXT WEEK WE'LL
ADD A ROCKING CHAIR. SOME COMBINATION!!

     BEFORE I FORGET, LET ME WISH YOU A
HAPPY BIRTHDAY.  I KNOW IT'S NOT FOR 4
MONTHS YET, BUT NOTHING LIKE LOOKING
AHEAD!  AND BECOMING 20 YEARS OLD MEANS
YOU'LL BE MAKING YOUR MARK PRETTY SOON.
PLEASE KEEP IN TOUCH.

                         LOADS OF LOVE FROM


                         ELWOOD, BRUNHILDA,
                         AND ALL THE KIDS




                                    11 / 8 / 77

DR. ARNOLD UPDIKE
42 1/2 MAIN STREET
ALABASTER, AL   35708

DEAR ARNOLD:

     WELL HOW HAVE YOU BEEN ARNOLD?  AND HOW
ARE THINGS IN GOOD OLD ALABASTER?  ANY
NEW NEIGHBORS ON MAIN STREET?  WE'RE ALL
WELL HERE, BUSY FIXING UP THE HOUSE.  WE
JUST BOUGHT A NEW RUG.  NEXT WEEK WE'LL
ADD A ROCKING CHAIR. SOME COMBINATION!!

     BEFORE I FORGET, LET ME WISH YOU A
HAPPY BIRTHDAY.  I KNOW IT'S NOT FOR 9
MONTHS YET, BUT NOTHING LIKE LOOKING
AHEAD!  AND BECOMING 55 YEARS OLD MEANS
WE CAN TURN TO YOU FOR SENIOR ADVICE (!).
PLEASE KEEP IN TOUCH.

                         CHEERS AND KEEP WELL


                         ELWOOD, BRUNHILDA,
                         AND ALL THE KIDS


OUT OF DATA at line 70
```

Here's a listing of the program.

LETTER WRITER

```
LIST
10 PRINT "TYPE TODAY'S DATE (E.G. 3,23,78)";
20 INPUT M1,D1,Y1
30 PRINT "LATEST PURCHASE";
40 INPUT P$
50 PRINT "NEEDED ITEM";
60 INPUT I$
70 READ T$, F$, L$, N$, S$, C$, Z$, M2, D2, Y2, C  ⟵
80 IF M2 > M1 THEN LET M = M2 - M1: LET Y= Y1: GOTO 100
90 LET M = M2 - M1 + 12: LET Y = Y1 + 1
100 LET A = Y - Y2
110 PRINT: PRINT: PRINT
120 PRINT TAB(30); M1; "/"; D1; "/"; Y1
130 PRINT T$; " "; F$; " "; L$
140 PRINT N$; " "; S$
150 PRINT C$; ", "; Z$
160 PRINT
170 PRINT "DEAR "; F$; ":"
180 PRINT
190 PRINT "      WELL HOW HAVE YOU BEEN "; F$; "?  AND HOW"
200 PRINT "ARE THINGS IN GOOD OLD "; C$; "?  ANY"
210 PRINT "NEW NEIGHBORS ON "; S$; "?  WE'RE ALL"
220 PRINT "WELL HERE, BUSY FIXING UP THE HOUSE.  WE"
230 PRINT "JUST BOUGHT A NEW "; P$".  NEXT WEEK WE'LL"
240 PRINT "ADD A "; I$; ". SOME COMBINATION!!":PRINT
250 PRINT "      BEFORE I FORGET, LET ME WISH YOU A"
260 PRINT "HAPPY BIRTHDAY.  I KNOW IT'S NOT FOR"; M
270 PRINT "MONTHS YET, BUT NOTHING LIKE LOOKING"
340 PRINT "AHEAD!  AND BECOMING" A; "YEARS OLD MEANS"
350 IF A < 21 THEN 390
360 IF A < 40 THEN 405
370 PRINT "WE CAN TURN TO YOU FOR SENIOR ADVICE (!)."
380 GOTO 410
390 PRINT "YOU'LL BE MAKING YOUR MARK PRETTY SOON."
400 GOTO 410
405 PRINT "THE END OF FOOTLOOSE AND FANCY FREE (SIGH)."
410 PRINT "PLEASE KEEP IN TOUCH.":PRINT
420 IF C > 0 THEN 450
430 PRINT TAB(20); "CHEERS AND KEEP WELL"
440 GOTO 460
450 PRINT TAB(20); "LOADS OF LOVE FROM"
460 PRINT:PRINT
470 PRINT TAB(20) "ELWOOD, BRUNHILDA,"
475 PRINT TAB (20); "AND ALL THE KIDS"
480 PRINT:PRINT:PRINT
490 GOTO 70
600 DATA "MR.", "JOHN", "SMITH", "130", "WAYNE AVE.", "FERNWOOD"
601 DATA "OH  45438", 10, 4, 43, 0
700 DATA "MISS", "LUCY", "BROWN", "8042", "APPLE ST.", "PIXLEY"
701 DATA "NJ  07753", 3,11,58,1
800 DATA "DR.", "ARNOLD", "UPDIKE", "42 1/2", "MAIN STREET", "ALABASTER"
801 DATA "AL  35708", 8, 15, 23, 0
999 END
```

THESE VARIABLES HOLD THE TITLE, FIRST NAME, LAST NAME, NUMBER, STREET, CITY, STATE AND ZIP, MONTH, DAY, AND YEAR OF BIRTH, AND A CODE: C=0 FOR "CHEERS", C=1 FOR "LOVE".

HERE'S WHERE A SPECIAL PHRASE IS SELECTED DEPENDING ON AGE A.

4.6   THE MONSTER WORD GAME

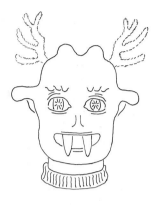

Word games are fun, and also a great way to increase vocabulary and spelling skills. Here's a game that helps do both. The words are stored as DATA statements, and as you can see, we've used some tough ones (taken from an esoteric list recommended for cerebral college students). You can of course change the DATA statements to include other words—perhaps a list from a child's spelling book. You could also put in a foreign language vocabulary, or a list of technical terms being studied.

The idea of the game is for you to guess a letter in a word that has been randomly selected from the DATA list. If you guess correctly the program shows you where the letter fits in the word. Then you get a chance to guess the entire word. If any of your guesses are wrong, a picture of a monster starts to arise. Eight wrong guesses means you lose, and you're eaten by the monster.

Let's first look at a run where the person wins.

```
RUN
WORD GUESSING GAME
IF YOU GET 8 WRONG GUESSES, THE MONSTER WILL EAT YOU!
WANT MONSTER TO BE VISIBLE? YES


-------

GUESS A LETTER? E
SORRY,NOT IN WORD.
   ((        ))
   ( ** ** )
LETTERS YOU USED:
E


-------

GUESS A LETTER? A


-A---A-

GUESS THE WORD?
NO--TRY ANOTHER LETTER
LETTERS YOU USED:
E,A

-A---A-

GUESS A LETTER? I
SORRY,NOT IN WORD.
   ((        ))
    ( ** ** )
    **  *  **
LETTERS YOU USED:
E,A,I
```

```
    -A---A-

GUESS A LETTER? T
SORRY,NOT IN WORD.
  ((        ))
   ( ** ** )
    ** * **
   *        *
LETTERS YOU USED:
E,A,I,T

    -A---A-

GUESS A LETTER? O


    -A--OA-

GUESS THE WORD? PAYLOAD
RIGHT!!! YOU TOOK 5 GUESSES.
WANT ANOTHER WORD
? NO
SO LONG.
```

Now let's look at a run where the monster arises fully and eats its victim. Where you see the lines

GUESS THE WORD?
NO—TRY ANOTHER LETTER

the user typed a carriage return after the ? which didn't print, but which was interpreted as "NO."

```
    RUN
    WORD GUESSING GAME
    IF YOU GET 8 WRONG GUESSES, THE MONSTER WILL EAT YOU!
    WANT MONSTER TO BE VISIBLE? YES


    -----

    GUESS A LETTER? E
    SORRY,NOT IN WORD.
      ((        ))
       ( ** ** )
    LETTERS YOU USED:
    E


    -----

    GUESS A LETTER? A
```

```
SORRY,NOT IN WORD.
   ((      ))
   ( ** ** )
   **  *  **
LETTERS YOU USED:
E,A

-----

GUESS A LETTER? I
SORRY,NOT IN WORD.
   ((      ))
   ( ** ** )
   **  *  **
   *        *
LETTERS YOU USED:
E,A,I

-----

GUESS A LETTER? O


--O--

GUESS THE WORD?
NO--TRY ANOTHER LETTER
LETTERS YOU USED:
E,A,I,O

--O--

GUESS A LETTER? U
SORRY,NOT IN WORD.
   ((      ))
   ( ** ** )
   **  *  **
   *        *
***  W   W  ***
LETTERS YOU USED:
E,A,I,O,U

--O--

GUESS A LETTER? Y
SORRY,NOT IN WORD.
   ((      ))
   ( ** ** )
   **  *  **
   *        *
***  W   W  ***
 ** (0) (0) **
LETTERS YOU USED:
E,A,I,O,U,Y

--O--
```

```
GUESS A LETTER? T
SORRY,NOT IN WORD.
   ((      ))
   ( ** ** )
   **  *  **
   *        *
***  W   W  ***
 ** (0) (0) **
   *    I    *
LETTERS YOU USED:
E,A,I,O,U,Y,T

--O--

GUESS A LETTER? S
SORRY,NOT IN WORD.
   ((      ))
   ( ** ** )
   **  *  **
   *        *
***  W   W  ***
 ** (0) (0) **
   *    I    *
   * ----- *
LETTERS YOU USED:
E,A,I,O,U,Y,T,S

--O--

GUESS A LETTER? Y
YOU GUESSED THAT BEFORE
LETTERS YOU USED:
E,A,I,O,U,Y,T,S

--O--

GUESS A LETTER? B
SORRY,NOT IN WORD.
   ((      ))
   ( ** ** )
   **  *  **
   *        *
***  W   W  ***
 ** (0) (0) **
   *    I    *
   * ----- *
    * -V-V- *
     *     *
     IIIIIII
GULP--YUM,YUM!!
SORRY, YOU LOSE. THE MONSTER HAS EATEN YOU.
THE WORD WAS WHORL
WANT ANOTHER WORD
? NO
SO LONG.
```

Here's a listing of the monster word game. The monster picture is stored in the array P$, with the first line of the picture in P$(1), the second line in P$(2), and so on. The picture is printed with the FOR loop in line 810. Since this loop only prints W1 lines, and since W1 is determined by the number of wrong guesses, the "fraction" of the monster printed depends on how many wrong guesses have been made.

MONSTER WORD GAME

```
LIST

10 RANDOMIZE
20 PRINT"WORD GUESSING GAME"
30 PRINT"IF YOU GET 8 WRONG GUESSES, THE MONSTER WILL EAT YOU!"
40 PRINT"WANT MONSTER TO BE VISIBLE";:INPUT B$
50 IF B$="YES" THEN 70
60 F=1
70 DIM P$(12),L$(20),D$(20),N$(26),U(50)
80 P$(1)="  ((        ))  "
90 P$(2)="  ( ** ** )  "
100 P$(3)="   **  *  **   "
110 P$(4)="   *        *   "
120 P$(5)="***   W   W   ***"
130 P$(6)=" ** (0) (0) ** "
140 P$(7)="  *     I     *  "
150 P$(8)="  *   -----   *  "
160 P$(9)="    *  -V-V-  *    "
170 P$(10)="    *        *    "
180 P$(11)="      IIIIIII      "
190 P$(12)="GULP--YUM,YUM!!"
200 C=0: N=50
210 REM-----INITIALIZE ARRAYS FOR NEW GAME----------
220 C=C+1: IF C<N THEN 240
230 PRINT"YOU USED ALL THE WORDS!!": GOTO 970
240 FOR I=1 TO 20: D$(I)="-": NEXT I
250 FOR I=1 TO 50: U(I)=0: NEXT I
260 FOR I=1 TO 26: N$(I)="": NEXT I
270 REM-----FIND NEW WORD----------
280 Z=INT(N*RND(0)+1)
290 IF U(Z)<>1 THEN 310
300 Z=Z+1: Z=Z-INT(Z/(N+1)*50): GOTO 290
310 U(Z)=1
320 RESTORE
330 FOR I=1 TO Z: READ A$: NEXT I
340 L=LEN(A$)
350 FOR I=1 TO L: L$(I)=MID(A$,I,1): NEXT I
360 T=0: W=0
370 REM-----START TURN----------
380 IF T<1 THEN 460
390 PRINT"LETTERS YOU USED:"
400 FOR I=1 TO 26
410 PRINT N$(I);
420 IF N$(I+1)="" THEN 460
430 PRINT",";
440 NEXT I
```

```
450 REM-----DISPLAY WORD CLUE----------
460 PRINT:PRINT:FOR I=1 TO L:PRINT D$(I);:NEXT I:PRINT:PRINT
470 PRINT"GUESS A LETTER";:INPUT G$: R=0
480 FOR I=1 TO 26
490 IF N$(I)="" THEN 540
500 IF G$<>N$(I) THEN 520
510 PRINT"YOU GUESSED THAT BEFORE": GOTO 390
520 NEXT I
530 STOP
540 N$(I)=G$: T=T+1
550 REM-----IS GUESS IN WORD----------
560 FOR I=1 TO L
570 IF L$(I)<>G$ THEN 590
580 D$(I)=G$: R=1
590 NEXT I
600 IF R<>0 THEN 630
610 PRINT"SORRY,NOT IN WORD.": W=W+1: GOTO 770
620 REM-----IS WORD FILLED IN----------
630 FOR I=1 TO L
640 IF D$(I)="-" THEN 680
650 NEXT I
660 PRINT"YOU FOUND THE WORD!": GOTO 730
670 REM-----GUESS WHOLE WORD----------
680 PRINT:PRINT:FOR I=1 TO L:PRINT D$(I);:NEXT I:PRINT:PRINT
690 PRINT"GUESS THE WORD";: INPUT B$
700 IF B$=A$ THEN 720
710 PRINT"NO--TRY ANOTHER LETTER": GOTO 390
720 PRINT"RIGHT!!! YOU TOOK";T;"GUESSES."
730 PRINT"WANT ANOTHER WORD":INPUT W$
740 IF W$="YES" THEN 220
750 PRINT"SO LONG.": GOTO 970
760 REM-----MONSTER PICTURE----------
770 IF F=1 THEN 820
780 W1=W+1
790 IF W<8 THEN 810
800 W1=12
810 FOR I=1 TO W1: PRINT P$(I): NEXT I
820 IF W=8 THEN 840
830 GOTO 390
840 PRINT"SORRY, YOU LOSE. THE MONSTER HAS EATEN YOU."
850 PRINT"THE WORD WAS ";A$
860 GOTO 730
870 DATA"ABATE","ABHORE","BANAL","CYNIC","DADO"
880 DATA "AVATAR","BUSKIN","CURSIVE","DURESS","FROND"
890 DATA"FUSTIAN","GLOSSARY","HYBRID","INVEIGH","JUNCTURE"
900 DATA"KINETIC","LUDICROUS","MISOGYNIST","NEGOTIABLE","ORTHOGRAPHY"
910 DATA"PACHYDERM","PUSILLANIMOUS","QUINTESSENCE","RETROSPECTIVE"
920 DATA"SUBLIMINAL","SYNTHESIS","SURVEILLANCE","TERMAGANT","RUDIMENTARY"
930 DATA"SALUBRIOUS","TALON","SADISM","ROBOT","NUCLEUS","NASCENT"
940 DATA"TAUTOLOGY","PAYLOAD","ORGY","MULCH","QUORUM"
950 DATA"ZENITH","WHORL","WELTER","VERBOSE","USURY","THWART"
960 DATA"TURGID","URBANE","VINDICTIVE","ZENOPHOBE"
970 END
```

4.7   STRING RELATIONS, OPERATORS, AND FUNCTIONS

Most of our examples so far have used strings "as is". But there are times when you may want to manipulate strings, or "get at" substrings inside of strings. Most BASIC's will allow you to do this and more. Here is a brief summary of the features to look for.

String Relations

<, = ,> can be used to put strings in order. They are based on the ASCII codes for the characters. The codes have been chosen so that $0 < 1 < \ldots < 9 < A < B < \ldots < Z$. Strings are compared, character for character until a difference is found. Then the alphabetical order prevails.

```
10 A$="JONES"
20 B$="JONAS"
30 IF A$>B$ THEN 60
40 PRINT B$;"IS'GREATER'THAN ";A*
50 STOP
60 PRINT A$; "IS'GREATER'THAN ";B$
RUN
JONES IS'GREATER'THAN JONAS
```

These relations are usually used to alphabetize data.

The String Operator +

+ can be used to 'concatenate' strings, string variables, and string functions. For example:

```
10 A$="HIND"
20 B$="SIGHT"
30 PRINT A$+B$
RUN
HINDSIGHT
```


String Functions

ASC(X$) gives the ASCII code (in decimal notation) of the first character of a string:

```
10 PRINT ASC("A-B-C")
RUN
65
    (65 is the ASCII code for A.)
```

CHR$(I) returns a string one character long, which has the ASCII code I. (The ASCII codes are given in Appendix B.)

```
10 PRINT CHR$(65);CHR$(45);CHR$(66);CHR$(45);CHR$(67)
RUN
A-B-C
```

LEFT$(X$,I) gives the leftmost I characters of X$.

```
10 PRINT LEFT$("APPLESAUCE",5)
RUN
APPLE
```

LEN(X$) gives the length (number of characters) of X$.

```
10 PRINT LEN("NUTCRACKERS")
RUN
11
```

MID$(X$,I,J) gives a string J characters long, starting at the Ith character of X$. J is optional. Without it, MID$ gives the rightmost characters of X$ starting at I.

```
10 PRINT MID$("CANDLESTICK", 7,3)
RUN
STI
10 PRINT MID$("CANDLESTICK",7)
RUN
STICK
```

RIGHT$(X$,I) gives the rightmost I characters of X$.

```
10 PRINT RIGHT$("HAPHAZARD", 6)
RUN
HAZARD
```

SPACE $(I) gives a string of spaces I long.

STR$(N) translates a number into a string that looks like it.

```
10 A$=STR$(.1234)
20 PRINT RIGHT$(A$,4)
RUN
1234
```

VAL(X$) converts a string made up of decimal digits into a number. (VAL can be used to ask "Is it a number?" since VAL returns a 0 if the string has anything but a +, -, or a digit as the first character.)

```
10 A$=STR$(.1234)
20 B$=RIGHT$(A$,4)
30 B=VAL(B$)*2
40 PRINT B
RUN
2468
```

INSTR(X$,Y$) tells you at what position the second string is found in the first string.

```
10 PRINT INSTR("BUGGYBUMPER", "BUMP")
RUN
6
```

Since INSTR returns a 0 if the string is not found, it can be used to ask "Is Y$ in X$?".

```
10 PRINT 'WHO LIKES YOU BEST';
20 INPUT M$
30 IF INSTR(M$,"MOTHER")=0 THEN 60
40 PRINT" YOU SEEM TO HAVE A MOTHER FIXATION"
50 GO TO 70
60 PRINT"AHA...YOU DIDN'T MENTION YOUR MOTHER!"
70 PRINT"TELL ME MORE."
RUN
WHO LIKES YOU BEST?MY DEAR MOTHER
YOU SEEM TO HAVE A MOTHER FIXATION
TELL ME MORE.
RUN
WHO LIKES YOU BEST?DADDY
AHA...YOU DIDN'T MENTION YOUR MOTHER!
TELL ME MORE.
```

If you don't have INSTR in your BASIC, here's a trick you can use instead:

```
10 PRINT"WHO LIKES YOU BEST";
20 INPUT M$
30 FOR I=1 TO 20
32 IF MID$(M$,I,I+5)="MOTHER" THEN 40
34 NEXT I
36 PRINT"AHA...YOU DIDN'T MENTION YOUR MOTHER!"
38 GOTO 50
40 PRINT" YOU SEEM TO HAVE A MOTHER FIXATION"
50 PRINT"TELL ME MORE."
RUN
WHO LIKES YOU BEST?MY DEAR MOTHER
YOU SEEM TO HAVE A MOTHER FIXATION
TELL ME MORE.
RUN
WHO LIKES YOU BEST?DADDY
AHA...YOU DIDN'T MENTION YOUR MOTHER!
TELL ME MORE.
```

4.8 PROJECTS

1. Write an improved poem generating program. You can use READ and DATA statements to supply the words instead of (or in addition to) INPUT statements. There are many short poetic forms that are suitable, such as the Japanese haiku. Consult a poetry anthology. It is possible to have the program produce poetry where *all* the words are variables.

2. Write a program that modifies a children's story to include names of friends, relatives, pets, favorite foods and toys of a particular child. Such a program could combine features of the poem generator and letter writing program. The program could first ask the child for the names of friends, pets, toys, etc. and then insert them as variables into a "form story" like a form letter.

3. The word guessing game can be modified very simply by changing the contents of the DATA statements to hold vocabulary words for different age levels or specific areas (all automobile names, state capitals, hero's and heroine's names, aircraft models, ballet steps, etc.) It then becomes a relatively painless way of practicing spelling and general familiarity with the words. A further modification would have the program *ask* the user for his age or the type of vocabulary he wants. The program would then call a subroutine containing a 'dummy' READ loop (one that just reads and does nothing else) in order to push the pointer to the correct DATA.

4. Write a program that produces TV scripts, movie plots, or outlines for popular novels. These often have plots which use the same kinds of characters and situations over and over with variation only in specific detail. For example, in a 'monster-type' horror film the monster can be a giant gorilla, giant ants, mutant turtles, berserk birds, etc. but the general problem situations are the same: (1) hero is not believed at first, (2) he is believed but by now the monster(s) have destroyed half the human race, (3) a new weapon or hidden flaw must be invented/discovered, and (4) the monster(s) are destroyed or just go away. These similarities can become the basis of a script or plot generating program. The level of detail is up to you. The program could produce a brief summary consisting of a few sentences or a detailed narrative of several pages.

5. Write a program that "talks", that is, appears to have a conversation with the user. The most famous program of this kind is ELIZA, a program written by Dr. Joseph Weizenbaum of M.I.T. This program imitates a certain style of psychotherapy in which the "therapist" (computer program) replies briefly, using words picked out of the "patient's" (human user's) inputs. If the program does not "understand" (does not have a way of dealing with) a particular input, it can always print out

VERY INTERESTING, PLEASE GO ON.

This sort of program requires a repertoire of "form replies" like the form letter, plus a way of extracting words from the user's input (string functions), plus a set of *rules* (IF statements) for recognizing certain common words and matching them with the form replies. A good imitation requires a lot of forethought and a large repertoire of replies, but a less-than-perfect imitation is still a lot of fun. A version of ELIZA written in BASIC appeared in *Creative Computing* for July-August, 1977 (Vol. 3, No. 4).

5
5
5
5
5
5
5

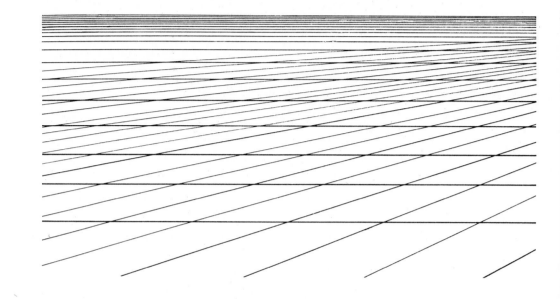

COMPUTERS IN SPORTS AND RECREATION; SORTING ALGORITHMS

5.0 INTRODUCTION; A WORD ABOUT DATA STRUCTURES

If we could see inside a computer's memory, what we'd find would be both amazing and confusing. The representation of data and programs in a 64K machine would be in terms of hundreds of thousands of binary electrical signals. Even if translated into "numbers", all we would see would be incomprehensible patterns of 0 and 1 symbols. There wouldn't be any discernible human-oriented structure to all these "bits" of information.

Fortunately, people don't have to think in terms of binary bits when they use a language like BASIC. As we've seen, programmers can use normal decimal numbers, or even strings of English symbols for data. Further, we can think of this data as being organized, or *structured* within single variables, or interrelated blocks of variables. These blocks can be one-dimensional arrays, or even two-dimensional arrays.

Part of the secret to writing more advanced programs is to choose the right structures. This helps you organize your thinking. It also simplifies the logic of the program, and makes it easy to follow. In this section we're going to look at some moderately advanced programs which will be made easier to understand because we'll use one or two-dimensional arrays for our data. Later in Section 5.8 we'll use another data structure (the *stack*), and in Sections 9.2 and 9.3 we'll use a data structure called a *queue* or FIFO.

177

5.1   MORE ABOUT TWO-DIMENSIONAL ARRAYS; THE MAT STATEMENTS

We briefly introduced the idea of two dimensional arrays at the end of Section 3.5. Let's now take the program we wrote there and make it more useful.

Suppose you want to keep track of how well three items are selling in your new health-food store on a monthly basis. The natural data structure is a two-dimensional (or "rectangular") array. The rows can represent months, and the columns the items. For four months, the data might look like the following:

	ITEM 1	ITEM 2	ITEM 3
MONTH 1	345	687	149
MONTH 2	344	689	235
MONTH 3	378	499	245
MONTH 4	377	568	388

D(3,2)

This rectangular array of numbers can be called a "4 by 3 array", or a "4 x 3 matrix". Each number is called an *element* of the matrix. For example, the number of sales of item 2 in month 3 is the element 499. In BASIC, we can store this element in a data location called D(3,2). That's nice—you can immediately tell from the name of this location that it holds data for the third month and second item. The numbers 3 and 2 are called the *subscripts* of the variable. By agreement, the first subscript points out the row, while the second points out the column. In general

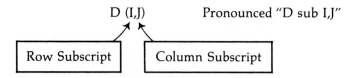

holds data for row I and column J. To print out an MxN matrix (or array) we use nested FOR loops as follows:

```
150 FOR I=1 TO M
160 FOR J=1 TO N
170 PRINT D (I,J),
180 NEXT J
190 PRINT
200 NEXT I
```

Line 150 first sets I=1 (first row). Then the inner loop (160,170,180) makes J=1 (first column), J=2 (second column), and so on to J=N (Nth column). The corresponding data items print on the same line because of the comma at the end of line 170. Now the program goes to line 190 where the PRINT says start a new line by doing a carriage return (back to the left margin) and line feed (down one line). The next I=2, so now we're ready to repeat the whole process for the second row.

NOTE: Using a comma usually puts items in fields 14 columns wide. If you want a different width (say 8 columns) try this trick:

170 PRINT TAB(8*(J-1)); D(I,J);

For numbers, room is left for a sign, so the actual numbers will start in columns 1,9,17,25,etc.

A similar method is used to "load" up the array, either with the INPUT statement (as will be shown in lines 60 to 110 of the next program), or with a READ statement (which we'll illustrate in Section 5.2).

Calculations Within A Matrix

Suppose you'd like a report on the total number of items sold in each month, and also a report on the total number sold of each item for all the months. In other words, you'd like the sums for all the numbers *across* each row, and also sums for all the numbers *down* each column. We can accumulate these sums by sneaking two extra lines inside the PRINT loop:

```
165 LET R(I) = R(I) + D(I,J)
166 LET C(J) = C(J) + D(I,J)
```

R(I) starts out as zero (in BASIC variables are usually initialized to zero). It accumulates the sum for row I by adding D(I,J) to the old R(I) each time around the loop. In our example there will be four such sums (one for each month) accumulated in R(1), R(2), R(3), R(4). The magic of subscripts is that only the items from row 1 will be added to R(1) because when I=1 line 165 reads LET R(1) = R(1) + D(1,J). Similarly when I=2, it reads LET R(2) = R(2) + D(2,J), so now only the items from row 2 are accumulated, etc.

The column sums are accumulated in a similar manner in C(1), C(2), and C(3). To print out the four row sums, a simple loop on I in lines 220 to 240 does the trick. To print out the column sums, a simple loop on J does the job in lines 260 to 280. Here's our final program and a run.

ARRAY SUMS

```
LIST

10 DIM D(10,4)
20 PRINT "HOW MANY ROWS OF DATA";
30 INPUT M
40 PRINT "HOW MANY COLUMNS PER ROW";
50 INPUT N
60 FOR I=1 TO M
70 PRINT "TYPE";N; "ITEMS FOR ROW";I
80 FOR J=1 TO N
90 INPUT D(I,J)
100 NEXT J
110 NEXT I
115 PRINT
120 PRINT "DATA SUMMARY"
130 FOR I=1 TO N:PRINT "ITEM";I,:NEXT I:PRINT
140 PRINT"------------------------------------"
150 FOR I=1 TO M
160 FOR J=1 TO N
165 LET R(I)=R(I)+D(I,J)
166 LET C(J)=C(J)+D(I,J)
170 PRINT D(I,J),
180 NEXT J
190 PRINT
200 NEXT I
205 PRINT
210 PRINT "SUMS BY ROWS"
220 FOR I=1 TO M
230 PRINT "FOR ROW #";I;"SUM =";R(I)
240 NEXT I
245 PRINT
250 PRINT "SUMS BY ITEMS"
260 FOR J=1 TO N
270 PRINT "FOR ITEM #";J;"SUM =";C(J)
280 NEXT J
290 END
```

HERE'S WHERE THE ROW SUMS ARE ACCUMULATED.

AND HERE'S WHERE THE COLUMN SUMS BUILD UP.

```
RUN

HOW MANY ROWS OF DATA? 4
HOW MANY COLUMNS PER ROW? 3
TYPE 3 ITEMS FOR ROW 1
? 345
? 687
? 149
TYPE 3 ITEMS FOR ROW 2
? 344
? 689
? 235
TYPE 3 ITEMS FOR ROW 3
? 378
? 499
? 245
TYPE 3 ITEMS FOR ROW 4
? 377
? 568
? 388
```

```
DATA SUMMARY
ITEM 1              ITEM 2              ITEM 3
------------------------------------------------
   345                687                 149
   344                689                 235
   378                499                 245
   377                568                 388

SUMS BY ROWS
FOR ROW # 1 SUM = 1181
FOR ROW # 2 SUM = 1268
FOR ROW # 3 SUM = 1122
FOR ROW # 4 SUM = 1333

SUMS BY ITEMS
FOR ITEM # 1 SUM = 1444
FOR ITEM # 2 SUM = 2443
FOR ITEM # 3 SUM = 1017
```

The MAT Statements; Initializing Variables in BASIC

As you have seen, manipulating two-dimensional matrices takes two nested FOR loops. That's usually the best way, because then you can make modifications by sneaking in other statements (the way we did in lines 165 and 166). However if you want certain standard operations, some versions of BASIC have statements like MAT PRINT and MAT INPUT which have all the double FOR-looping done automatically. The way these statements work varies slightly between different versions of BASIC. Your manual should be consulted for further detail.

There are also MAT statements for "adding", "multiplying", and "taking the inverse" of matrices. We won't have any use for these operations in this book, and so they won't be discussed. Also remember that the MAT statements are a convenience. You can always do the same things with FOR loops.

Use of some simple MAT statements is illustrated in the Crazy-Eights program given in Section 6.4. For example,

```
120 DIM G(52),D(52)
450 MAT G = ZER
```

means initialize the matrix (or array) G with all zeros.

```
510 MAT D = CON
```

means initialize the matrix D with all 1's (CON means 'constant').

```
511 MAT D = (-1) * D
```

means multiply all the 1's in D by -1. If you don't have MAT statements, you can initialize G and D as follows

```
10 DIM G(52), D(52)
20 FOR K = 1 TO 52
30 LET G(K) = 0
40 LET D(K) = -1
50 NEXT K
```

NOTE: BASIC normally initializes all variables with the value 0 (zero) at the beginning of a RUN. However it is good practice not to depend on this, and do all initializing with assignment statements placed near the beginning of a program. For simple variables, use statements like

```
5 LET S = 0
```

To initialize one-dimensional arrays, use a FOR loop as shown above. To initialize two-dimensional arrays, use two FOR loops

```
10 DIM A(20,5)
20 FOR I = 1 TO 20
30 FOR J = 1 TO 5
40 LET A(I,J) = 0
50 NEXT J
60 NEXT I
```

5.2   A FOOTBALL SCOUTING PROGRAM

A football scout who covers one of the games of a future opponent must gather a lot of "raw" data. A natural way to organize this data is in the form of a two-dimensional array. Each row in the array would correspond to the data for a given play. The columns would show the things about that play of interest to a coach. For example, the columns could be used to record the down number, yards to go for a first down, field position, position of the tight end, type of formation, type of play, runner or passer number, receiver number, and yards gained on the play. Put in this concise form, here's what some typical scouting data would look like:

DOWN	YARDS TO GO	FIELD POSITION	TIGHT END	FORMATION	PLAY	PUNTER PASSER RUNNER	RCVR	YARDS GAINED
1	10	2	1	4	1	31	0	3
2	7	2	2	4	3	33	0	−1
3	8	3	2	3	5	31	22	35

. . . etc. . .

In order to enter everything as a number, some sort of coding scheme is needed for some of the items. For example, we might use 7 codes for plays as follows:

1 = Buck to right
2 = Buck to left
3 = Sweep around right end
4 = Sweep around left end
5 = Completed Pass
6 = Incomplete Pass
7 = Punt

We'll also agree that when a play is not a pass, the RCVR number will be entered as zero.

There could obviously be additional codes, but we'll stick to these in our example. Similar codes would have to be developed for field position, tight-end position, and formation.

In addition to this kind of play-by-play data, we'll also want data on which teams played, which was the home team, who the scouts were, and what the data was. Finally, it would be convenient to have kickoff data recorded separately (although you might "fudge" it as data for a down # zero).

Now for the Problem

The problem is that handing this raw data to a coach on the day after a game isn't much help. It needs to be analyzed. The coach would like to see summary statistics on the whole game, statistics about individual players, and some kind of "trend" analysis that might give away team tendencies.

These statistics and analyses have traditionally been done by hand, taking up a lot of valuable time. Using a computer to extract this information from the raw data makes a lot of sense.

We'll show a program to do this which could eventually become rather large. So we'll organize our work in a way that illustrates the technique of writing a large program in terms of program "modules". A program module is simply a small subprogram that can be tested independently of the rest of the program. This way, the program can grow in stages. By testing the program at each stage, you can be pretty sure that any problems that show up are located in the last module that was added.

To illustrate this growth, a "barebones" program outline will first be shown. Then it will be expanded in three stages as follows:

Stage 0   Bare bones program outline

Stage 1   Raw data will be read into arrays
                 General information will be summarized
                 Overall team data will be summarized

Stage 2   In addition to the above, individual player statistics will be printed.

Stage 3   In addition to the above, an analysis of team tendencies by downs will be made.

Additional stages can be added of course (which is suggested as a project), so the other advantage to structuring a program like this is that it can easily be expanded.

Before starting to write any of the modules for this program, it will be a good idea to decide on the variables and arrays needed—to lay out the "data structures" that will be used.

The data for the plays will be stored by downs in the array D(20,9). This allows for 20 plays, with 9 items of data for each play using the scheme we introduced earlier. If you want to store data for more plays (say 100), then you'll need a bigger array D(100,9), and of course more bytes of memory will be required. For row R, D(R,1) holds the down number for the Rth play, D(R,2) holds the yards to go for this play, and so on, up to D(R,9) which holds the yards gained on the play.

An array Y(42,4) will be used to store yardages gained (or lost) by individual players. We've assumed a poor team with jerseys numbered only 1 to 42, so we'll be able to handle up to 42 players using the rows of Y. The four columns of Y will be used to hold yards gained rushing, punting, passing, and receiving.

Kickoff data will be stored in the array K(6,2) which allows for 6 kickoffs. The first column will be used to store the yardline where the ball was received, and the second will hold the number of yards run back.

The array P(42) is used to "point" to those players who were involved in gaining yardage. If P(I)=0, this means player "I" wasn't involved in any yardage gain. If P(I)=I, this means player I contributed to moving the ball. This way we can handle both passers and receivers. Column 8 of the D array will hold a non-zero player number only for receivers of completed passes. Column 7 of D will hold a non-zero player number for runners, passers, and punters. (Lines 615 and 675 will show how this information is used in stage 3 of our program development.)

Four arrays are used as counters for gathering statistics. First, if we use the variable C as follows:

C =   1 for "short yardage situation"
C =   2 for "medium yardage situation"
C =   3 for "long yardage situation"

then we can keep yardage statistics for each situation by letting

B(C)   count the number of bucks in a C yardage situation
S(C)   count the number of sweeps in a C yardage situation
V(C)   count the number of passes in a C yardage situation
U(C)   count the number of punts in a C yardage situation

The array M(C) will count the total number of plays for a C yardage situation. This way we can get percentages. For example, 100*B(C)/M(C) will give the percent of bucks in a C yardage situation. Individual variables used are as follows:

N =   total number of plays
N1 =   total number of kickoffs
Y1 =   sum of yard-lines reached on kickoffs
Y2 =   sum of yards run back from kickoffs
Y3 =   total number of yards gained rushing
Y5 =   total number of yards gained passing
Y7 =   total number of yards gained punting
N5 =   total number of completed passes
N6 =   total number of incomplete passes
N7 =   total number of punts
E =   down number
S$ =   name of first scout
T$ =   name of second scout
A$ =   name of team scouted
B$ =   Name of their opponent
D$ =   date
H$ =   home team

With these variables and arrays defined, we can now proceed to develop our program.

Stage 0 Outline the Program

Our program will contain 9 modules as follows:

1. A module to print headings (lines 30-90), and a module to print dashed lines (subroutine 800) between sections of output.
2. A module to read and complete kickoff data (subroutine 500)
3. A module to read in and total raw data for plays (subroutine 700)
4. A module to print overall team statistics (lines 110-200)
5. A module to calculate and print individual player statistics (subroutine 600)
6. A module to calculate and print analysis of trends by downs and yardage situation (subroutine 400)
7. Team and kickoff data (lines 900-920)
8. Play-by-play data (lines 1001-1999)
9. A module to print an echo check of data (lines 990-999)

Stage 1 Normally, one might only attempt a few modules for a start—say numbers 1, 2, 3, and 9. These modules would allow our program to read all the data into the proper arrays and variables, and then print it back out in "raw" form. This is called an "echo check", and it's done mainly to make sure all the data is getting into the program correctly.

To save time, we'll show a program that also includes modules 4, 7 and 8. Most of this stage 1 program is pretty easy to follow. However module 3 (subroutine 700) needs some explanation.

Line 710 reads through all the data for the plays. This read is stopped by line 716 which detects a "phoney" down number 5 (which is our signal for end of data). Line 715 reads across each row of data and stores the numbers in the D array. Line 725 counts how many plays there were. Line 730 tests to find out if the type of play stored in $D(I,6)$ was rushing (types 1,2,3 or 4), line 735 finds incomplete passes (type 5), line 740 finds completed passes (type 6), and line 745 finds punts (type 7). Depending on what's found, the appropriate total is incremented in lines 760-775. Here's a listing of our stage 1 program followed by a run. Notice that we have left "blank" sections for the modules to be added in later stages. Our run uses only a small amount of test data for a hypothetical scouting report on the Midwest Occult School of Science and Technology (MOSS Tech).

SCOUT ONE

```
LIST

10  DIM Y(50,4),D(15,9),K(10,2)
20  REM-----WE ASSUME ALL VARIABLES ZEROED----------
30  READ S$,T$,A$,B$,D$,H$,N1
40  GOSUB 500
50  GOSUB 800
60  PRINT"OFFENSIVE SCOUTING REPORT BY ";S$;" AND ";T$
70  GOSUB 800
80  PRINT"TEAM SCOUTED: ";A$;TAB(30);"OPPONENT: ";B$
90  PRINT"DATE: ";D$;TAB(30);"HOME TEAM WAS ";H$
```

```
100 GOSUB 800
110 PRINT"OVERALL DATA ON ";A$;"'S OFFENSIVE GAINS"
120 PRINT
130 GOSUB 700
140 PRINT:PRINT"TOTAL YARDS GAINED BY RUSHING = ";Y3
150 PRINT"TOTAL # OF PASSES ATTEMPTED = ";N5+N6
160 PRINT"TOTAL # OF PASSES COMPLETED = ";N5;",     # INCOMPLETE = ";N6
170 PRINT"TOTAL YDS GAINED BY PASSING = ";Y5;"FOR AVG PER PASS OF";Y5/N5
180 PRINT"TOTAL # OF PUNTS =";N7;"FOR AVG OF";Y7/N7;"YARDS"
190 PRINT"TOTAL # OF KICKOFFS =";N1
195 PRINT"KICKOFFS AVERAGED TO THE";Y1/N1;"YD LINE WITH AVG RETURN =";Y2/N1
200 GOSUB 800
210 PRINT"INDIVIDUAL PLAYER STATISTICS
220 PRINT
230 REM-----FUTURE GOSUB 600 WILL BE USED HERE----------
240 GOSUB 800
250 PRINT"ANALYSIS BY DOWNS"
260 PRINT
270 REM-----FUTURE GOSUB 400 WILL BE USED HERE----------
280 GOSUB 800
290 GOTO 990
500 REM-----SUBR FOR READING & SUMMING KICKOFF DATA-----
510 FOR I=1 TO N1:FOR J=1 TO 2:READ K(I,J):NEXT J:NEXT I
520 FOR I=1 TO N1
530 LET Y1=Y1+K(I,1):LET Y2=Y2+K(I,2)
540 NEXT I
550 RETURN
700 REM-----SUBR TO READ IN D(I,J) AND CALC TOTALS-----
710 FOR I=1 TO 50
715 FOR J=1 TO 9:READ D(I,J):NEXT J
716 IF D(I,1)>4 THEN 785
725 LET N=N+1
730 IF ABS(D(I,6)-2.5)<1.6 THEN 760
735 IF D(I,6)=5 THEN 765
740 IF D(I,6)=6 THEN 770
745 IF D(I,6)=7 THEN 775
750 PRINT "ILLEGAL PLAY CODE #";D(I,6);"IN LINE";1000+I
755 STOP
760 LET Y3=Y3+D(I,9): LET N3=N3+1: GOTO 780
765 LET Y5=Y5+D(I,9): LET N5=N5+1: GOTO 780
770 LET N6=N6+1: GOTO 780
775 LET Y7=Y7+D(I,9): LET N7=N7+1
780 NEXT I
785 RETURN
800 REM-----SUBR FOR DASHED LINE----------
810 FOR K= 1 TO 56:PRINT"-";:NEXT K:PRINT
820 RETURN
900 DATA"J. EAGLEYE","R. SUPERSPOT"
901 DATA"MOSS TECH","SLIPPERY SOCK"
902 DATA"10/14/77","MOSS TECH"
920 DATA 6
921 DATA 4,2
922 DATA 20,-4
923 DATA 15,20
924 DATA 25,10
925 DATA 7,25
926 DATA 10,5
990 PRINT"ECHO CHECK OF SCOUT DATA FORM"
992 FOR I=1 TO N:FOR J=1 TO 9
994 PRINT TAB(4*(J-1));D(I,J);
996 NEXT J:PRINT:NEXT I
999 GOTO 9999
1001 DATA 1,10,2,1,4,1,31,0,3
1002 DATA 2,7,2,2,4,3,33,0,-1
```

```
1003 DATA 3,8,3,2,3,5,31,22,35
1004 DATA 1,10,2,3,2,2,42,0,5
1005 DATA 2,5,1,1,4,4,42,0,6
1006 DATA 1,10,2,3,1,2,41,0,4
1007 DATA 2,6,1,2,1,3,31,0,3
1008 DATA 3,3,1,2,2,6,33,0,0
1009 DATA 4,3,2,1,4,7,42,0,45
1010 DATA 1,10,2,2,3,1,31,0,11
1011 DATA 1,10,3,3,2,2,42,0,5
1012 DATA 2,5,2,2,3,4,41,0,0
1013 DATA 3,5,3,1,4,5,31,23,4
1014 DATA 4,1,1,1,2,7,42,0,55
1999 DATA 5,5,5,5,5,5,5,5,5
9999 END
```

```
RUN


-----------------------------------------------------------
OFFENSIVE SCOUTING REPORT BY J. EAGLEYE AND R. SUPERSPOT
-----------------------------------------------------------
TEAM SCOUTED: MOSS TECH        OPPONENT: SLIPPERY SOCK
DATE: 10/14/77                 HOME TEAM WAS MOSS TECH
-----------------------------------------------------------
OVERALL DATA ON MOSS TECH'S OFFENSIVE GAINS


TOTAL YARDS GAINED BY RUSHING =  36
TOTAL # OF PASSES ATTEMPTED =  3
TOTAL # OF PASSES COMPLETED =  2 ,    # INCOMPLETE =  1
TOTAL YDS GAINED BY PASSING =  39 FOR AVG PER PASS OF 19.5
TOTAL # OF PUNTS = 2 FOR AVG OF 50 YARDS
TOTAL # OF KICKOFFS = 6
KICKOFFS AVERAGED TO THE 13.5 YD LINE WITH AVG RETURN = 9.66667
-----------------------------------------------------------
INDIVIDUAL PLAYER STATISTICS


-----------------------------------------------------------
ANALYSIS BY DOWNS


-----------------------------------------------------------
ECHO CHECK OF SCOUT DATA FORM
  1    10  2   1   4   1    31   0    3
  2    7   2   2   4   3    33   0   -1
  3    8   3   2   3   5    31  22   35
  1    10  2   3   2   2    42   0    5
  2    5   1   1   4   4    42   0    6
  1    10  2   3   1   2    41   0    4
  2    6   1   2   1   3    31   0    3
  3    3   1   2   2   6    33   0    0
  4    3   2   1   4   7    42   0   45
  1    10  2   2   3   1    31   0   11
  1    10  3   3   2   2    42   0    5
  2    5   2   2   3   4    41   0    0
  3    5   3   1   4   5    31  23    4
  4    1   1   1   2   7    42   0   55
```

THERE'S NOTHING HERE SINCE WE HAVEN'T WRITTEN THE NEEDED SUBROUTINES YET.

5.3   A MANAGEMENT INFORMATION SYSTEM

In this section we're really just going to continue the football scouting program. We've given it the fancy name of "management information system" (or MIS for short) to point out that programs similar to this in style can be used to prepare concise reports for managers who need to see trends in data. In our example, the coach is the manager, and our program is meant to help him absorb all the information hidden in the scouting data very quickly.

To give the coach some new management information, let's now go to stage 2 and add module 6 (the individual player statistics). This module will be written as a subroutine (lines 600-699). This subroutine searches through all the data stored in array D. The first thing it does with each row of data is to change the zeros in the player "pointer" array to the actual player numbers recorded in D(I,7) for rushing, punting, or passing, and in D(I,8) for receiving. Then actual yardages gained (or lost) by these players are stored in the corresponding rows of Y. After this is finished, the individual yardages stored in Y are printed out in line 685.

Here's a listing of the stage 2 program followed by a run. To double check on the first program, an extra line of play data has been added in line 1015. Notice that the new totals on passing are changed as a result, which is what should happen.

SCOUT TWO

```
LIST

10 DIM D(16,9),Y(42,4),K(6,2),P(42)
20 REM-----WE ASSUME ALL VARIABLES ZEROED----------
30 READ S$,T$,A$,B$,D$,H$,N1
40 GOSUB 500:GOSUB 800
60 PRINT"OFFENSIVE SCOUTING REPORT BY ";S$;" AND ";T$
70 GOSUB 800
80 PRINT"TEAM SCOUTED: ";A$;TAB(30);"OPPONENT: ";B$
90 PRINT"DATE: ";D$;TAB(30);"HOME TEAM WAS ";H$
100 GOSUB 800
110 PRINT"OVERALL DATA ON ";A$;"'S OFFENSIVE GAINS"
120 PRINT: GOSUB700
140 PRINT:PRINT"TOTAL YARDS GAINED BY RUSHING = ";Y3
150 PRINT"TOTAL # OF PASSES ATTEMPTED = ";N5+N6
160 PRINT"TOTAL # OF PASSES COMPLETED = ";N5;",     # INCOMPLETE = ";N6
170 PRINT"TOTAL YDS GAINED BY PASSING = ";Y5;"FOR AVG PER PASS OF";Y5/N5
180 PRINT"TOTAL # OF PUNTS =";N7;"FOR AVG OF";Y7/N7;"YARDS"
190 PRINT"TOTAL # OF KICKOFFS =";N1
195 PRINT"KICKOFFS AVERAGED TO THE";Y1/N1;"YD LINE WITH AVG RETURN =";Y2/N1
200 GOSUB 800
210 PRINT "INDIVIDUAL PLAYER STATISTICS":PRINT
230 GOSUB 600: GOSUB 800
250 PRINT "ANALYSIS BY DOWNS":PRINT:GOSUB 400: GOSUB 800: GOTO 990
400 REM---SUBRTN FOR ANALYSIS BY DOWNS
499 RETURN
500 REM-----SUBR FOR READING & SUMMING KICKOFF DATA-----
510 FOR I=1 TO N1:FOR J=1 TO 2:READ K(I,J):NEXT J:NEXT I
520 FOR I=1 TO N1
530 LET Y1=Y1+K(I,1):LET Y2=Y2+K(I,2)
540 NEXT I
550 RETURN
```

```
600 REM---SUBRTN FOR INDIVID. PLAYER YDGS
610 FOR I=1 TO N
615 R=D(I,7):P(R)=R:P(D(I,8))=D(I,8)
620 IF ABS(D(I,6)-2.5)<1.6 THEN 650
625 IF D(I,6)=7 THEN 655
630 IF D(I,6)=5 THEN 660
650 Y(R,1)=Y(R,1)+D(I,9):GOTO 670
655 Y(R,2)=Y(R,2)+D(I,9):GOTO 670
660 Y(R,3)=Y(R,3)+D(I,9):Y(D(I,8),4)=Y(D(I,8),4)+D(I,9)
670 NEXT I
672 PRINT"YARDS RUSHING-PUNTING-PASSING-RCVING"
675 FOR I=1 TO 42: IF P(I)=0 THEN 695
685 PRINT"#";I;:FOR J=1 TO 4:PRINT TAB(7+8*(J-1));Y(I,J);:NEXT J
690 PRINT
695 NEXT I
699 RETURN
700 REM-----SUBR TO READ IN D(I,J) AND CALC TOTALS-----
710 FOR I=1 TO 42
715 FOR J=1 TO 9:READ D(I,J):NEXT J
716 IF D(I,1)>4 THEN 785
725 LET N=N+1
730 IF ABS(D(I,6)-2.5)<1.6 THEN 760
735 IF D(I,6)=5 THEN 765
740 IF D(I,6)=6 THEN 770
745 IF D(I,6)=7 THEN 775
750 PRINT "ILLEGAL PLAY CODE #";D(I,6);"IN LINE";1000+I
755 STOP
760 LET Y3=Y3+D(I,9): LET N3=N3+1: GOTO 780
765 LET Y5=Y5+D(I,9): LET N5=N5+1: GOTO 780
770 LET N6=N6+1: GOTO 780
775 LET Y7=Y7+D(I,9): LET N7=N7+1
780 NEXT I
785 RETURN
800 REM-----SUBR FOR DASHED LINE----------
810 FOR K= 1 TO 56:PRINT"-";:NEXT K:PRINT
820 RETURN
900 DATA"J. EAGLEYE","R. SUPERSPOT"
901 DATA"MOSS TECH","SLIPPERY SOCK"
902 DATA"10/14/77","MOSS TECH"
920 DATA 6,4,2,20,-4,15,20,25,10,7,25,10,5
990 PRINT"ECHO CHECK OF SCOUT DATA FORM"
992 FOR I=1 TO N:FOR J=1 TO 9
994 PRINT TAB(4*(J-1));D(I,J);
996 NEXT J:PRINT:NEXT I
999 GOTO 9999
1001 DATA 1,10,2,1,4,1,31,0,3
1002 DATA 2,7,2,2,4,3,33,0,-1
1003 DATA 3,8,3,2,3,5,31,22,35
1004 DATA 1,10,2,3,2,2,42,0,5
1005 DATA 2,5,1,1,4,4,42,0,6
1006 DATA 1,10,2,3,1,2,41,0,4
1007 DATA 2,6,1,2,1,3,31,0,3
1008 DATA 3,3,1,2,2,6,33,0,0
1009 DATA 4,3,2,1,4,7,42,0,45
1010 DATA 1,10,2,2,3,1,31,0,11
1011 DATA 1,25,3,3,2,2,42,0,5
1012 DATA 2,5,2,2,3,4,41,0,0
1013 DATA 3,5,3,1,4,5,31,23,4
1014 DATA 4,1,1,1,2,7,42,0,55
1015 DATA 1,10,2,2,4,5,33,23,15
1'999 DATA 5,5,5,5,5,5,5,5,5
9999 END
```

```
RUN


------------------------------------------------------------
OFFENSIVE SCOUTING REPORT BY J. EAGLEYE AND R. SUPERSPOT
------------------------------------------------------------
TEAM SCOUTED: MOSS TECH         OPPONENT: SLIPPERY SOCK
DATE: 10/14/77                  HOME TEAM WAS MOSS TECH
------------------------------------------------------------
OVERALL DATA ON MOSS TECH'S OFFENSIVE GAINS


TOTAL YARDS GAINED BY RUSHING =  36
TOTAL # OF PASSES ATTEMPTED =  4
TOTAL # OF PASSES COMPLETED =  3 ,    # INCOMPLETE =  1
TOTAL YDS GAINED BY PASSING =  54 FOR AVG PER PASS OF 18
TOTAL # OF PUNTS = 2 FOR AVG OF 50 YARDS
TOTAL # OF KICKOFFS = 6
KICKOFFS AVERAGED TO THE 13.5 YD LINE WITH AVG RETURN = 9.66667
------------------------------------------------------------
INDIVIDUAL PLAYER STATISTICS

YARDS RUSHING-PUNTING-PASSING-RCVING
# 22    0       0       0       35
# 23    0       0       0       19
# 31   17       0      39        0
# 33   -1       0      15        0
# 41    4       0       0        0
# 42   16     100       0        0

------------------------------------------------------------
ANALYSIS BY DOWNS


------------------------------------------------------------
ECHO CHECK OF SCOUT DATA FORM
 1   10   2   1   4   1   31    0    3
 2    7   2   2   4   3   33    0   -1
 3    8   3   2   3   5   31   22   35
 1   10   2   3   2   2   42    0    5
 2    5   1   1   4   4   42    0    6
 1   10   2   3   1   2   41    0    4
 2    6   1   2   1   3   31    0    3
 3    3   1   2   2   6   33    0    0
 4    3   2   1   4   7   42    0   45
 1   10   2   2   3   1   31    0   11
 1   25   3   3   2   2   42    0    5
 2    5   2   2   3   4   41    0    0
 3    5   3   1   4   5   31   23    4
 4    1   1   1   2   7   42    0   55
 1   10   2   2   4   5   33   23   15
```

Team Tendencies

As our final improvement, we'll go to stage 3 and add module #6 which calculates the tendencies the scouted team has shown for calling certain plays on a given down, and for a given "yards to go" situation.

Module 6 is written as subroutine 400. Line 410 sets E to a down number, and then all the data is searched to find plays with that down number (line 414). Lines 420 and 421 determine whether it was a short, medium, or long yards-to-go situation. Lines 430-450 determine what kind of play was called. Lines 455-470 then increment the appropriate counter for this kind of play for this particular yardage situation.

The results of all these calculations are printed out in lines 482-494. By using the string array Y$ as defined in line 405, we can have the words "SHORT", "MEDIUM", or "LONG" printed for when C = 1, 2, or 3.

To make the output a little more realistic, we've added some more play-by-play data (up to line 1019). Of course a real game would have more than 19 plays, so the program would be even longer. This suggests that data might better be kept on "files" rather than in DATA statements. Files are discussed in Chapter 8.

Here's a listing of the stage 3 program, followed by a run.

SCOUT THREE

```
LIST
10 DIM D(20,9),Y(42,4),K(6,2),P(42)
20 REM-----WE ASSUME ALL VARIABLES ZEROED----------
30 READ S$,T$,A$,B$,D$,H$,N1
40 GOSUB 500:GOSUB 800
60 PRINT"OFFENSIVE SCOUTING REPORT BY ";S$;" AND ";T$
70 GOSUB 800
80 PRINT"TEAM SCOUTED: ";A$;TAB(30);"OPPONENT: ";B$
90 PRINT"DATE: ";D$;TAB(30);"HOME TEAM WAS ";H$
100 GOSUB 800
110 PRINT"OVERALL DATA ON ";A$;"'S OFFENSIVE GAINS"
120 PRINT: GOSUB700
140 PRINT:PRINT"TOTAL YARDS GAINED BY RUSHING = ";Y3
150 PRINT"TOTAL # OF PASSES ATTEMPTED = ";N5+N6
160 PRINT"TOTAL # OF PASSES COMPLETED = ";N5;",     # INCOMPLETE = ";N6
170 PRINT"TOTAL YDS GAINED BY PASSING = ";Y5;"FOR AVG PER PASS OF";Y5/N5
180 PRINT"TOTAL # OF PUNTS =";N7;"FOR AVG OF";Y7/N7;"YARDS"
190 PRINT"TOTAL # OF KICKOFFS =";N1
195 PRINT"KICKOFFS AVERAGED TO THE";Y1/N1;"YD LINE WITH AVG RETURN =";Y2/N1
200 GOSUB 800
210 PRINT "INDIVIDUAL PLAYER STATISTICS":PRINT
230 GOSUB 600: GOSUB 800
250 PRINT "ANALYSIS BY DOWNS":PRINT:GOSUB 400: GOSUB 800: GOTO 990
400 REM---SUBRTN FOR ANALYSIS BY DOWNS
405 Y$(1)=" SHORT ":Y$(2)=" MEDIUM ":Y$(3)=" LONG "
410 FOR E=1 TO 4
412 FOR C=1 TO 3:M(C)=0:B(C)=0:S(C)=0:V(C)=0:U(C)=0:NEXT C
414 FOR I=1 TO N: IF D(I,1)<>E THEN 475
420 IF D(I,2)<3 THEN LET C=1:GOTO 425
421 IF D(I,2)<7 THEN LET C=2 ELSE C=3
425 M(C)=M(C)+1
430 IF ABS(D(I,6)-1.5)<.6 THEN 455
435 IF ABS(D(I,6)-3.5)<.6 THEN 460
440 IF ABS(D(I,6)-5.5)<.6 THEN 465
450 IF D(I,6)=7 THEN 470
455 B(C)=B(C)+1:GOTO 475
460 S(C)=S(C)+1:GOTO 475
465 V(C)=V(C)+1:GOTO 475
470 U(C)=U(C)+1
475 NEXT I
```

```
480 PRINT "HERE'S WHAT ";A$;" TENDS TO DO ON DOWN #";E:PRINT
482 FOR C=1 TO 3
483 IF M(C)=0 THEN PRINT "NO DATA FOR A";Y$(C);"YARDAGE SITUATION":GOTO 494
484 PRINT "FOR A";Y$(C);"YARDAGE SITUATION THEY WILL"
486 PRINT TAB(20);"BUCK";100*B(C)/M(C);"% OF TIME"
488 PRINT TAB(20);"SWEEP";100*S(C)/M(C);"% OF TIME"
490 PRINT TAB(20);"PASS";100*V(C)/M(C);"% OF TIME"
492 PRINT TAB(20);"PUNT";100*U(C)/M(C);"% OF TIME"
493 PRINT
494 NEXT C
498 NEXT E
499 RETURN
500 REM-----SUBR FOR READING & SUMMING KICKOFF DATA-----
510 FOR I=1 TO N1:FOR J=1 TO 2:READ K(I,J):NEXT J:NEXT I
520 FOR I=1 TO N1
530 LET Y1=Y1+K(I,1):LET Y2=Y2+K(I,2)
540 NEXT I
550 RETURN
600 REM---SUBRTN FOR INDIVID. PLAYER YDGS
610 FOR I=1 TO N
615 R=D(I,7):P(R)=R:P(D(I,8))=D(I,8)
620 IF ABS(D(I,6)-2.5)<1.6 THEN 650
625 IF D(I,6)=7 THEN 655
630 IF D(I,6)=5 THEN 660
650 Y(R,1)=Y(R,1)+D(I,9):GOTO 670
655 Y(R,2)=Y(R,2)+D(I,9):GOTO 670
660 Y(R,3)=Y(R,3)+D(I,9):Y(D(I,8),4)=Y(D(I,8),4)+D(I,9)
670 NEXT I
672 PRINT"YARDS RUSHING-PUNTING-PASSING-RCVING"
675 FOR I=1 TO 42: IF P(I)=0 THEN 695
685 PRINT"#";I;:FOR J=1 TO 4:PRINT TAB(7+8*(J-1));Y(I,J);:NEXT J
690 PRINT
695 NEXT I
699 RETURN
700 REM-----SUBR TO READ IN D(I,J) AND CALC TOTALS-----
710 FOR I=1 TO 42
715 FOR J=1 TO 9:READ D(I,J):NEXT J
716 IF D(I,1)>4 THEN 785
725 LET N=N+1
730 IF ABS(D(I,6)-2.5)<1.6 THEN 760
735 IF D(I,6)=5 THEN 765
740 IF D(I,6)=6 THEN 770
745 IF D(I,6)=7 THEN 775
750 PRINT "ILLEGAL PLAY CODE #";D(I,6);"IN LINE";1000+I
755 STOP
760 LET Y3=Y3+D(I,9): LET N3=N3+1: GOTO 780
765 LET Y5=Y5+D(I,9): LET N5=N5+1: GOTO 780
770 LET N6=N6+1: GOTO 780
775 LET Y7=Y7+D(I,9): LET N7=N7+1
780 NEXT I
785 RETURN
800 REM-----SUBR FOR DASHED LINE----------
810 FOR K= 1 TO 56:PRINT"-";:NEXT K:PRINT
820 RETURN
900 DATA"J. EAGLEYE","R. SUPERSPOT"
901 DATA"MOSS TECH","SLIPPERY SOCK"
902 DATA"10/14/77","MOSS TECH"
920 DATA 6,4,2,20,-4,15,20,25,10,7,25,10,5
990 PRINT"ECHO CHECK OF SCOUT DATA FORM"
992 FOR I=1 TO N:FOR J=1 TO 9
994 PRINT TAB(4*(J-1));D(I,J);
996 NEXT J:PRINT:NEXT I
999 GOTO 9999
```

```
1001 DATA 1,10,2,1,4,1,31,0,3
1002 DATA 2,7,2,2,4,3,33,0,-1
1003 DATA 3,8,3,2,3,5,31,22,35
1004 DATA 1,10,2,3,2,2,42,0,5
1005 DATA 2,5,1,1,4,4,42,0,6
1006 DATA 1,10,2,3,1,2,41,0,4
1007 DATA 2,6,1,2,1,3,31,0,3
1008 DATA 3,3,1,2,2,6,33,0,0
1009 DATA 4,3,2,1,4,7,42,0,45
1010 DATA 1,10,2,2,3,1,31,0,11
1011 DATA 1,25,3,3,2,2,42,0,5
1012 DATA 2,5,2,2,3,4,41,0,0
1013 DATA 3,5,3,1,4,5,31,23,4
1014 DATA 4,1,1,1,2,7,42,0,55
1015 DATA 1,10,2,2,4,5,33,23,15
1016 DATA 1,10,2,2,2,3,19,0,6
1017 DATA 3,4,2,2,2,2,19,0,2
1018 DATA 4,2,3,4,3,1,41,0,1
1019 DATA 4,12,3,2,2,7,41,0,28
1999 DATA 5,5,5,5,5,5,5,5,5
9999 END
```

```
RUN

--------------------------------------------------------
OFFENSIVE SCOUTING REPORT BY J. EAGLEYE AND R. SUPERSPOT
--------------------------------------------------------
TEAM SCOUTED: MOSS TECH        OPPONENT: SLIPPERY SOCK
DATE: 10/14/77                 HOME TEAM WAS MOSS TECH
--------------------------------------------------------
OVERALL DATA ON MOSS TECH'S OFFENSIVE GAINS


TOTAL YARDS GAINED BY RUSHING =  45
TOTAL # OF PASSES ATTEMPTED =  4
TOTAL # OF PASSES COMPLETED =  3 ,    # INCOMPLETE =  1
TOTAL YDS GAINED BY PASSING =  54 FOR AVG PER PASS OF 18
TOTAL # OF PUNTS = 3 FOR AVG OF 42.6667 YARDS
TOTAL # OF KICKOFFS = 6
KICKOFFS AVERAGED TO THE 13.5 YD LINE WITH AVG RETURN = 9.66667
--------------------------------------------------------
INDIVIDUAL PLAYER STATISTICS

YARDS RUSHING-PUNTING-PASSING-RCVING
# 19      8          0         0         0
# 22      0          0         0         35
# 23      0          0         0         19
# 31     17          0        39         0
# 33     -1          0        15         0
# 41      5         28         0         0
# 42     16        100         0         0
--------------------------------------------------------
ANALYSIS BY DOWNS

HERE'S WHAT MOSS TECH TENDS TO DO ON DOWN # 1

NO DATA FOR A SHORT YARDAGE SITUATION
NO DATA FOR A MEDIUM YARDAGE SITUATION
FOR A LONG YARDAGE SITUATION THEY WILL
                BUCK 71.4286 % OF TIME
                SWEEP 14.2857 % OF TIME
                PASS 14.2857 % OF TIME
                PUNT 0 % OF TIME


HERE'S WHAT MOSS TECH TENDS TO DO ON DOWN # 2
```

```
NO DATA FOR A SHORT YARDAGE SITUATION
FOR A MEDIUM YARDAGE SITUATION THEY WILL
                        BUCK 0 % OF TIME
                        SWEEP 100 % OF TIME
                        PASS 0 % OF TIME
                        PUNT 0 % OF TIME

FOR A LONG YARDAGE SITUATION THEY WILL
                        BUCK 0 % OF TIME
                        SWEEP 100 % OF TIME
                        PASS 0 % OF TIME
                        PUNT 0 % OF TIME
HERE'S WHAT MOSS TECH TENDS TO DO ON DOWN # 3

NO DATA FOR A SHORT YARDAGE SITUATION
FOR A MEDIUM YARDAGE SITUATION THEY WILL
                        BUCK 33.3333 % OF TIME
                        SWEEP 0 % OF TIME
                        PASS 66.6667 % OF TIME
                        PUNT 0 % OF TIME

FOR A LONG YARDAGE SITUATION THEY WILL
                        BUCK 0 % OF TIME
                        SWEEP 0 % OF TIME
                        PASS 100 % OF TIME
                        PUNT 0 % OF TIME

HERE'S WHAT MOSS TECH TENDS TO DO ON DOWN # 4

FOR A SHORT YARDAGE SITUATION THEY WILL
                        BUCK 50 % OF TIME
                        SWEEP 0 % OF TIME
                        PASS 0 % OF TIME
                        PUNT 50 % OF TIME

FOR A MEDIUM YARDAGE SITUATION THEY WILL
                        BUCK 0 % OF TIME
                        SWEEP 0 % OF TIME
                        PASS 0 % OF TIME
                        PUNT 100 % OF TIME

FOR A LONG YARDAGE SITUATION THEY WILL
                        BUCK 0 % OF TIME
                        SWEEP 0 % OF TIME
                        PASS 0 % OF TIME
                        PUNT 100 % OF TIME
-------------------------------------------------------------
ECHO CHECK OF SCOUT DATA FORM
   1    10   2   1   4   1   31   0    3
   2    7    2   2   4   3   33   0   -1
   3    8    3   2   3   5   31  22   35
   1    10   2   3   2   2   42   0    5
   2    5    1   1   4   4   42   0    6
   1    10   2   3   1   2   41   0    4
   2    6    1   2   1   3   31   0    3
   3    3    1   2   2   6   33   0    0
   4    3    2   1   4   7   42   0   45
   1    10   2   2   3   1   31   0   11
   1    25   3   3   2   2   42   0    5
   2    5    2   2   3   4   41   0    0
   3    5    3   1   4   5   31  23    4
   4    1    1   1   2   7   42   0   55
   1    10   2   2   4   5   33  23   15
   1    10   2   2   2   3   19   0    6
   3    4    2   2   2   2   19   0    2
   4    2    3   4   3   1   41   0    1
   4    12   3   2   2   7   41   0   28
```

5.4   SIMPLE SORTING ALGORITHMS

An algorithm is like a recipe. It gives a set of exact instructions on how to take input "ingredients", and transform them into something different (the output).

To be more precise, an algorithm is "a finite set of rules which gives a sequence of operations for solving a problem". Algorithms have five properties:

(1) They must stop after a *finite* number of steps.
(2) Each step must be *unambiguous,* that is, have only one meaning.
(3) Algorithms accept zero or more *inputs.*
(4) Algorithms produce one or more *outputs.*
(5) They are *effective,* that is, each step can be done on a finite machine in a finite time.

To satisfy property (2), algorithms have to be expressed in unambiguous languages like BASIC. Correct BASIC programs are really algorithms expressed in a special form.

An important class of algorithms used in computing has to do with the problem of sorting. *Sorting* is the process of putting a list of things in order. The list may contain numbers, and look like this:

INPUT: 2.34, 7.8, -2, 3.2

Sorted in increasing order, this list becomes:

OUTPUT: -2, 2.34, 3.2, 7.8

We can also sort alphabetic data, like this:

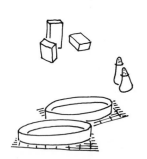

INPUT: Zeke, Abe, Sally, Charlie

Sorted alphabetically, this list becomes:

OUTPUT: Abe, Charlie, Sally, Zeke

There are many algorithms for sorting. Most of them depend on *comparing* items in the list and then *swapping* pairs of items. This process must be repeated many times to sort a large list. This means sorting can take lots of computer time. Let's look at the problem more closely.

Swapping; The Bubble Sort

The typical computer code for swapping pairs of items requires three steps. Here's a program to swap the contents of A with the contents of B:

	PROGRAM		T	A	B ◀VARIABLES
	10 LET A=5:	LET B=3		⑤	③ Start
These are the	20 LET T=A		5	5	3
steps for	30 LET A=B		5	3	3
swapping.	40 LET B=T		5	③	⑤ Swapped

The temporary variable T is needed to save A because line 30 "writes over" A.

Let's now use the swapping idea as part of a sorting program called *Bubble Sort*. In this algorithm, the first two items of an unsorted list are compared and, if out of order, swapped to place them in the correct order. Then the second and third items are compared, and so on. For instance, here's how we would do the swapping for the list of numbers 4, 1, 5, 3, 2:

need swapping? YES
$\begin{bmatrix} 4 \\ 1 \\ 5 \\ 3 \\ 2 \end{bmatrix}$
need swapping? NO
$\begin{bmatrix} 1 \\ 4 \\ 5 \\ 3 \\ 2 \end{bmatrix}$
need swapping? YES
$\begin{bmatrix} 1 \\ 4 \\ 5 \\ 3 \\ 2 \end{bmatrix}$
need swapping? YES
$\begin{bmatrix} 1 \\ 4 \\ 3 \\ 5 \\ 2 \end{bmatrix}$
$\begin{bmatrix} 1 \\ 4 \\ 3 \\ 2 \\ 5 \end{bmatrix}$

As you can see, in this first "pass" through the numbers, the largest number is moved to the bottom of the list. (To see why this method is called bubble sorting, imagine you are standing on your head. Now, what used to be the bottom of the list is the top. You can think of the largest number "bubbling" to the top of the list.)

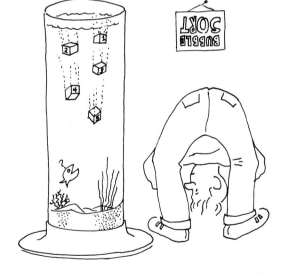

Notice that the numbers 1,4,3,2,5 aren't in order yet. We must therefore repeat the swapping process, but only for the numbers 1, 4, 3, 2. This is called the second "pass". With each pass through the program, the largest unsorted item "bubbles" to the top (remember, you're still standing on your head!). When no more swaps can be made, the list is sorted. You can see that *at most*, N-1 passes will be needed for sorting N items.

Confused? Maybe the computer can help. Here is a demonstration program which shows each pass in the sorting procedure. (An explanation of how the bubble sort part of this program works will be given shortly. For the present, think of this as a "teaching" or "demonstration" program).

BUBBLE
DEMO

```
LIST
5 DIM A(100)
10 READ N
20 READ A(B) FORB = 1 TO N
30 PRINT "UNSORTED LIST:"
40 PRINT A(B); FOR B=1 TO N
50 PRINT:PRINT
60 FOR B=1 TO N-1
70 PRINT "PASS #";B
80 F=0
90 FOR C=1 TO N-B
100 B(C,D)=A(D) FOR D=1 TO N
110 IF A(C+1)>=A(C) THEN 160
120 T=A(C)
130 A(C)=A(C+1)
140 A(C+1)=T
150 F=1
160 NEXT C
170 B(N-B+1,D)=A(D) FOR D=1 TO N
180 FOR D=1 TO N
190 IF D=1 THEN PRINT " [";  :D1=-1: GOTO 270
200 D1=D-2
210 D1=N-B+1 IF D1>=N-B
220 PRINT TAB(E*6-3);B(E,D); FOR E=1 TO D1
230 IF D>N-B+1 GOTO 280
240 PRINT TAB(6*D1+2); "[";  B(D1+1,D);
250 IF D>N-B THEN PRINT TAB(6*D1+9);B(D1+2,D);:GOTO 280
260 PRINT TAB(6*D1+8); "[";
270 PRINT TAB(E*6-3); B(E,D); FOR E=D1+2 TO N-B+1
280 IF D<>N-B+1 THEN 310
290 PRINT
300 PRINT "-"; FOR E=1 TO 6*(N-B+1)
310 PRINT
320 NEXT D
330 IF F=0 THEN PRINT: PRINT "AHA!! NO SWAPS!! WE CAN QUIT" : GOTO 350
340 PRINT : NEXT B
350 PRINT: PRINT "SORTED LIST:"
360 PRINT A(B); FOR B=1 TO N
370 DATA 5
380 DATA 4,1,5,3,2
390 END
```

NOTE: The BUBBLE programs on pp. 198, 202, and 203 use the BASIC-PLUS 'FOR suffix' (explained on page 131). This translates into three statements in standard BASIC. For example, line 20 of BUBBLE DEMO becomes

20 FOR B=1 TO N
21 READ A(B)
22 NEXT B

A similar translation is needed for lines 40, 100, 170, 220, 270, 300 and 360. Line 210 must also be changed, and a new line 215 should be added (see p. 434 for further detail).

Here's what a run looks like. Follow the [symbols down to see the swapping in each pass. The dashed line shows that each pass looks at fewer and fewer items.

```
RUN

UNSORTED LIST:
 4   1   5   3   2

PASS # 1
[ 4       1       1       1       1
  [ 1     [ 4     4       4       4
    5     [ 5     [ 5     3       3
    3       3     [ 3     [ 5     2
    2       2       2     [ 2     5
---------------------------------------

PASS # 2
[ 1       1       1       1
  [ 4     [ 4     3       3
    3     [ 3     [ 4     2
    2       2     [ 2     4
-----------------------------------
    5       5       5       5

PASS # 3
[ 1       1       1
  [ 3     [ 3     2
    2     [ 2     3
-------------------
    4       4       4
    5       5       5

PASS # 4
[ 1       1
  [ 2     2
------------
    3       3
    4       4
    5       5

AHA!! NO SWAPS!! WE CAN QUIT

SORTED LIST:
 1   2   3   4   5
```

Let's look at a more complicated example. This time we'll change the DATA statements to hold 10 numbers. As you can see, the number of comparisons needed (where the square brackets are) is much larger. We'll have more to say about the number of comparisons needed by Bubble Sort in Section 5.7.

```
370 DATA 10
380 DATA 5,23,67,1,26,90,4,62,4,22

RUN
UNSORTED LIST:
 5   23  67  1   26  90   4  62   4  22

PASS # 1
[ 5       5      5      5      5      5      5      5      5      5
  [ 23  [ 23     23     23     23     23     23     23     23     23
    67  [ 67  [ 67     1      1      1      1      1      1      1
    1      1    [ 1    [ 67     26     26     26     26     26     26
    26     26     26   [ 26   [ 67     67     67     67     67     67
    90     90     90     90   [ 90   [ 90     4      4      4      4
    4      4      4      4      4    [ 4    [ 90     62     62     62
    62     62     62     62     62     62   [ 62   [ 90     4      4
    4      4      4      4      4      4      4    [ 4    [ 90     22
    22     22     22     22     22     22     22     22   [ 22     90
----------------------------------------------------------------------

PASS # 2
[ 5       5      5      5      5      5      5      5      5
  [ 23  [ 23     1      1      1      1      1      1      1
    1    [ 1    [ 23     23     23     23     23     23     23
    26     26   [ 26   [ 26     26     26     26     26     26
    67     67     67   [ 67   [ 67     4      4      4      4
    4      4      4      4    [ 4    [ 67     62     62     62
    62     62     62     62     62   [ 62   [ 67     4      4
    4      4      4      4      4      4    [ 4    [ 67     22
    22     22     22     22     22     22     22   [ 22     67
----------------------------------------------------------------
    90     90     90     90     90     90     90     90     90

PASS # 3
[ 5       1      1      1      1      1      1      1
  [ 1    [ 5      5      5      5      5      5      5
    23   [ 23   [ 23     23     23     23     23     23
    26     26   [ 26   [ 26     4      4      4      4
    4      4      4    [ 4    [ 26     26     26     26
    62     62     62     62   [ 62   [ 62     4      4
    4      4      4      4      4    [ 4    [ 62     22
    22     22     22     22     22     22   [ 22     62
--------------------------------------------------------
    67     67     67     67     67     67     67     67
    90     90     90     90     90     90     90     90

PASS # 4
[ 1       1      1      1      1      1      1
  [ 5    [ 5      5      5      5      5      5
    23   [ 23   [ 23     4      4      4      4
    4      4    [ 4    [ 23     23     23     23
    26     26     26   [ 26   [ 26     4      4
    4      4      4      4    [ 4    [ 26     22
    22     22     22     22     22   [ 22     26
--------------------------------------------------------
    62     62     62     62     62     62     62
    67     67     67     67     67     67     67
    90     90     90     90     90     90     90
```

```
PASS # 5
 [  1      1      1      1      1      1
   [ 5    [ 5     4      4      4      4
     4    [ 4    [ 5     5      5      5
     23     23   [ 23   [ 23     4      4
     4      4      4    [ 4    [ 23    22
     22     22     22     22   [ 22    23
--------------------------------------------
     26     26     26     26     26     26
     62     62     62     62     62     62
     67     67     67     67     67     67
     90     90     90     90     90     90

PASS # 6
 [  1      1      1      1      1
   [ 4    [ 4     4      4      4
     5    [ 5    [ 5     4      4
     4      4    [ 4    [ 5     5
     22     22     22   [ 22    22
-------------------------------------
     23     23     23     23     23
     26     26     26     26     26
     62     62     62     62     62
     67     67     67     67     67
     90     90     90     90     90

PASS # 7
 [  1      1      1      1
   [ 4    [ 4     4      4
     4    [ 4    [ 4     4
     5      5    [ 5     5
------------------------------
     22     22     22     22
     23     23     23     23
     26     26     26     26
     62     62     62     62
     67     67     67     67
     90     90     90     90

AHA!! NO SWAPS!! WE CAN QUIT

SORTED LIST:
 1   4   4   5   22   23   26   62   67   90
```

A More Normal Bubble Sort Program

The preceding program was written to help you understand how Bubble Sort works. But, when actually sorting data, you don't need to see each pass. A more normal (and more efficient) Bubble Sort run would only print the final sorted list.

Here's a listing and run of a normal Bubble Sort program written in standard BASIC:

BUBBLE SORT

```
LIST
10 DIM A(100)
20 READ N
25 FOR B=1 TO N
30 READ A(B)
35 NEXT B
40 PRINT "UNSORTED LIST:"
50 PRINT A(B) FOR B=1 TO N
55 FOR B=1 TO N-1         ←    B CONTROLS THE
60 F=0                         NUMBER OF PASSES.
70 FOR C=1 TO N-B         ←
80 IF A(C+1) >=A(C) THEN 130    C MOVES US DOWN
90 T=A(C)                       THE LIST DURING
100 A(C)=A(C+1)                 EACH PASS.
110 A(C+1)=T
120 F=1
130 NEXT C
140 IF F=0 THEN 155
150 NEXT B
155 PRINT
160 PRINT "SORTED LIST:"
165 FOR B=1 TO N
170 PRINT A(B)
175 NEXT B
180 DATA 5
185 DATA 4,1,5,3,2
190 END

Ready

RUN

UNSORTED LIST:
 4
 1
 5
 3
 2

SORTED LIST:
 1
 2
 3
 4
 5
```

If we want to sort alphabetic data, the program must be modified slightly. A string array A$ can be used to hold the data. The comparison and swap statements should then be rewritten to use these string array variables, and the DATA statements modified to hold string data. BASIC interprets a test like IF A$(C+1)>A$(C) to mean "IF A$(C+1) comes after A$(C) in an alphabetic listing". Here's a string version of Bubble Sort:

STRING BUBBLE

```
LIST
10 DIM A$(100)
20 READ N
25 FOR B=1 TO N
30 READ A$(B)
35 NEXT B
40 PRINT "UNSORTED LIST:"
50 PRINT A$(B) FOR B=1 TO N
55 FOR B=1 TO N-1
60 F=0
70 FOR C=1 TO N-B
80 IF A$(C+1)>=A$(C) THEN 130
90 T$ = A$(C)
100 A$(C)=A$(C+1)
110 A$(C+1)=T$
120 F=1
130 NEXT C
140 IF F=0 THEN 155
150 NEXT B
155 PRINT
160 PRINT "SORTED LIST:"
165 FOR B=1 TO N
170 PRINT A$(B)
175 NEXT B
180 DATA 6
190 DATA "CHARLIE", "ABE", "ZEKE", "SALLY", "SUZY", "SUSY"
200 END

Ready

RUN

UNSORTED LIST:
CHARLIE
ABE
ZEKE
SALLY
SUZY
SUSY

SORTED LIST:
ABE
CHARLIE
SALLY
SUSY
SUZY
ZEKE
```

You can also use this "string version" on numbers, providing: (a) all the numbers have the same number of digits, (b) the same sign, and (c) the decimal point is in the same place. Here's an example where the DATA statements are changed to hold decimal numbers as 6 character strings.

STRING NUMBERS

```
LIST
10 DIM A$(100)
20 READ N
25 FOR B=1 TO N
30 READ A$(B)
35 NEXT B
40 PRINT "UNSORTED LIST:"
50 PRINT A$(B) FOR B=1 TO N
55 FOR B=1 TO N-1
60 F=0
70 FOR C=1 TO N-B
80 IF A$(C+1)>=A$(C) THEN 130
90 T$ = A$(C)
100 A$(C)=A$(C+1)
110 A$(C+1)=T$
120 F=1
130 NEXT C
140 IF F=0 THEN 155
150 NEXT B
155 PRINT
160 PRINT "SORTED LIST:"
165 FOR B=1 TO N
170 PRINT A$(B)
175 NEXT B
180 DATA 4
190 DATA "128.45", "053.25", "001.99", "101.11"
200 END

RUN

UNSORTED LIST:
128.45
053.25
001.99
101.11

SORTED LIST:
001.99
053.25
101.11
128.45
```

SELF-TEST

1. The two previous programs used a variable F (see lines 60, 120, 140) which is sometimes called a "flag" variable. What is its purpose? Hint: Try running the program with and without these three lines, using as DATA to be sorted 1,9,2,3,4,5,6,7,8. Put in an extra "trace" statement

145 PRINT "PASS #";B

2. One of the techniques used in "debugging" programs is to use "trace" statements which show the values of variables at important places in the program. Find a program with a "bug" in it (that should be easy!) and use trace statements to find out what's wrong.

Records

No, the word record as used here doesn't mean a hi-fi music disc. It refers to a collection of associated data that needs to be kept together. So a program to sort records may have to do a lot of swapping. To see why, consider three records, where each record contains three items or *fields*: a name, a phone number, and the balance owed to a loan company.

RECORD 1 → (Smith   487-2306   48.47)

RECORD 2 → (Jones   242-9611   162.22)

RECORD 3 → (Baker   487-2606   4.98)

                     Field 1   Field 2   Field 3

There are three ways we might want to sort these records: By name (in which case the first field is called the sorting *key*):

Baker	487-2606	4.98
Jones	242-9611	162.22
Smith	487-2306	48.47

By phone (now the second field is the sorting key):

Jones	242-9611	162.22
Smith	487-2306	48.87
Baker	487-2606	4.98

By balance (the third field is the sorting key):

Baker	487-2606	4.98
Smith	487-2306	48.87
Jones	242-9611	162.22

In each case, *all* the items of a given record need to be swapped, although the comparisons are only done on the key item. Most records contain both numerical and string (alphabetical) data. One way to store the data is in a string array A$(I,J). For example, if each record contained a baseball player's name, team affiliation, and batting average, the storage would be:

RECORD 1	A$ (1,1) = "Ruth, Babe"	A$ (1,2) = "Yankees"	A$ (1,3) = ".375"
RECORD 2	A$ (2,1) = "Clemente, R."	A$ (2,2) = "Pirates"	A$ (2,3) = ".342"
RECORD 3	etc.	etc.	etc.

To "swap" record 1 and record 2 in this example, you can use a loop as follows:

```
200 FOR J=1 TO 3
210 LET T$=A$(1,J)
220 LET A$(1,J)=A$(2,J)
230 LET A$(2,J)=T$
240 NEXT J
```

SELF-TEST

1. Modify the Bubble Sort program to handle records with three fields in each record

We'll return to the problem of sorting records in Sections 5.5 and 5.6. But let's first look at another sorting algorithm called *Selection* Sort.

Straight Selection Sort

Most sorting algorithms depend on comparing items in a list and swapping if necessary. In Bubble Sort we compared pairs of items. Let's look at a different type of comparison.

Straight Selection Sorting is based on a comparison of a given item A(I) with every other item below it in the list. In this way the smallest element is found, then swapped with A(I). The process is repeated with A(I+1) and so on down the list.

Let's look at an example where there are four items to be sorted:

```
A(1) = 8
A(2) = 6
A(3) = 5
A(4) = 3
```

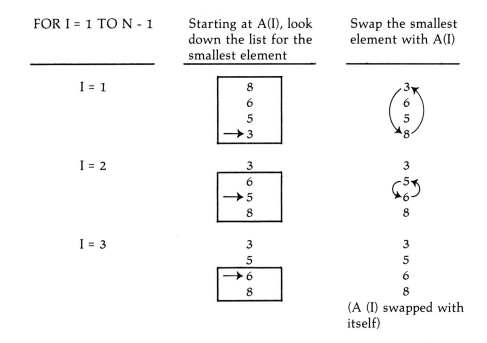

FOR I = 1 TO N - 1	Starting at A(I), look down the list for the smallest element	Swap the smallest element with A(I)
I = 1	8 6 5 → 3	3 6 5 8
I = 2	3 6 → 5 8	3 5 6 8
I = 3	3 5 → 6 8	3 5 6 8 (A (I) swapped with itself)

After N-1 passes the list is sorted (in our example N=4, so three passes were needed). Here's a list and run of a Selection Sort program:

SELECTION SORT

```
LIST

10 REM FIRST WE'LL PUT 10 RANDOM NOS IN A(I)
20 DIM A(10)
30 LET N=10
35 PRINT "NUMBERS TO BE SORTED ARE:"
40 FOR I=1 TO N
50 LET A(I)=INT(100*RND(0))
60 PRINT A(I);
70 NEXT I
80 PRINT
90 REM NOW WE'LL USE THE STRAIGHT SELECTION SORT
95 REM THE OUTER LOOP RUNS THROUGH THE DATA N-1 TIMES
100 FOR I=1 TO N-1
110 REM WE'LL START BY ASSUMING A(I) IS THE MINIMUM
120 LET M=A(I)
130 REM WE'LL REMEMBER WHERE THE MINIMUM IS WITH J
140 LET J=I
150 REM NOW WE'LL FIND THE REAL MINIMUM BY COMPARING
160 REM A(I) WITH ALL THE ELEMENTS BELOW IT
170 FOR K=I+1 TO N
180 IF A(K)>=M THEN 210
190 LET M=A(K)
200 LET J=K
210 NEXT K
220 REM NOW SWAP MINIMUM WITH A(I)
230 T=A(I)
240 A(I)=A(J)
250 A(J)=T
260 REM RECOGNIZE THE SWAPPING ROUTINE JUST USED?
270 NEXT I
```

```
280 REM PRINT OUT SORTED LIST
290 PRINT "SORTED NUMBERS ARE:"
300 FOR I=1 TO N
310 PRINT A(I);
320 NEXT I
330 PRINT
340 PRINT "FINISHED"
350 END

RUN

NUMBERS TO BE SORTED ARE:
 77  78  75  47   7  20  51  26  95  33
SORTED NUMBERS ARE:
  7  20  26  33  47  51  75  77  78  95
FINISHED
```

SELF-TEST

1. Modify the Straight Selection Sort program so that (a) it first asks you how many numbers are to be sorted, (b) it then requests these numbers from your terminal by using an INPUT statement in a loop, (c) finally, it prints the numbers in increasing order
2. Modify the Bubble Sort program so it prints the output list in decreasing order, for example:

INPUT: 17.2, -8.2, 49, 3.14
OUTPUT: 49, 17.2, 3.14, -8.2

5.5 NOT-SO-SIMPLE SORTING ALGORITHMS

Indexed Sorting

Most real-world applications of sorting involve what are called "records", that is, groups of data. Let's look at the example from Section 5.4 again:

	FIELD 1	FIELD 2	FIELD 3
RECORD 1	A$ (1,1) = "Ruth, Babe"	A$ (1,2) = "Yankees"	A$ (1,3) = ".375"
RECORD 2	A$ (2,1) = "Clemente, R."	A$ (2,2) = "Pirates"	A$ (2,3) = ".342"
RECORD 3	etc.	etc.	etc.

Suppose we wanted to sort these records alphabetically by team name (field 2). We would then call field 2 the *sorting key*.

As you can see, the sorting of records by a given key means that the comparisons need only be made for the key item. For example, to compare field 2 we can change one statement inside the C loop of our Bubble Sort program to the following:

80 IF A$(C+1,2)>=A$ (C,2) then 130

FIELD 2

There is, however, a problem with this method. Suppose each record has P fields (in our example, P=3). If the key fields are out of order, we must swap all P of the fields in the corresponding records (to keep the player's name, team, and batting average together). We need to insert a loop like the following into our Bubble Sort program to perform all these swaps:

```
90 FOR L=1 TO P
95 LET T$=A$(C,L)
100 LET A$(C,L)=A$(C+1,L)
105 LET A$(C+1,L)=T$
110 NEXT L
```

Since each swap takes three statements (lines 95-105), 3*P statements must be executed to sort all the records. That's a lot of program execution time if P is large. So let's look at another way to sort records, which eliminates most of the swapping by using subscripted subscripts. (No, that's not a mistake.)

To see how this method works, let's try some experiments. First, imagine that the following data have been stored in your computer, using the two-dimensional array A(I,J) plus an additional one-dimensional array X(I).

A (1,1) = 67	A (1,2) = 2	A (1,3) = 6	X (1) = 1
A (2,1) = 33	A (2,2) = 10	A (2,3) = 8	X (2) = 2
A (3,1) = 47	A (3,2) = 9	A (3,3) = 7	X (3) = 3
A (4,1) = 19	A (4,2) = 14	A (4,3) = 3	X (4) = 4

Now suppose we write a program called INDPRT (for INDexed PRinT), that uses this data as follows:

```
10 FOR I=1 TO 4
20 FOR J=1 TO 3
30 PRINT A(X(I),J),
40 NEXT J
50 PRINT
60 NEXT I
70 END
```

What would we get? If you go through the program carefully, you'll see that we should get the following output:

67	2	6
33	10	8
47	9	7
19	14	3

This is exactly the same as the original A(I,J) array.

Now suppose that somehow or other the X(I) array (called the index array) is re-ordered, so that:

X(1)=4
X(2)=2
X(3)=3
X(4)=1

If you now run INDPRT, you'll get this output:

19	14	3
33	10	8
47	9	7
67	2	6

Notice that (a) the records have stayed together, and (b) they have been sorted with item 1 as the key.

SELF-TEST

The idea of ordering an index array and using it to sort records is a bit tricky, so don't proceed until you at least answer questions 1 and 2.

1. What should the index array X(I) be so that the program sorts the A(I,J) array with item 2 as the sorting key?
2. What should X(I) be so that A is sorted by item 3?
3. (Difficult) Write a program in which you input the item number you want to use as the key. The program then swaps the numbers in the *index array* X(I) so that the INDPRT program will print the records correctly sorted by the key. Here are the major parts of your program:

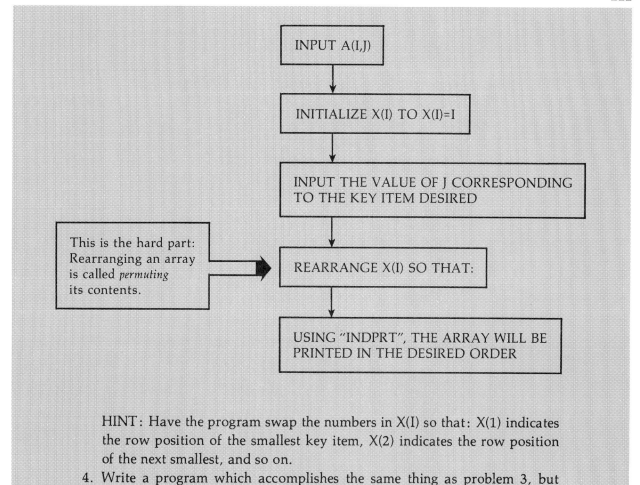

HINT: Have the program swap the numbers in X(I) so that: X(1) indicates the row position of the smallest key item, X(2) indicates the row position of the next smallest, and so on.

4. Write a program which accomplishes the same thing as problem 3, but without using *any* swaps. This is a tough question, so we'll show a solution in the next section. But give it a try first.

Sorting by Counting

In this section we'll show a sorting algorithm that doesn't do any swapping. Let's first look at a listing and run:

INDEXED SORT

```
LIST
10 INPUT "HOW MANY RECORDS";N
20 INPUT "HOW MANY ITEMS PER RECORD";L
50 FOR R=1 TO N
55 PRINT "TYPE";L;"ITEMS FOR RECORD";R
57 FOR I=1 TO L
60 INPUT N$(R,I)
65 NEXT I
70 NEXT R
80 REM
```

```
90 PRINT:INPUT "WHICH ITEM # IS THE SORTING KEY ";J
100 K$(R)=N$(R,J) FOR R=1 TO N
120 GOSUB 900
130 REM
140 PRINT:PRINT "SORTED RECORDS ARE: " : PRINT
150 FOR R=1 TO N
160 PRINT N$(X(R),I); " "; FOR I=1 TO L:PRINT
170 NEXT R
180 REM
190 PRINT:INPUT "CONTINUE" ;Y$
200 IF ASCII(Y$)=89 GOTO 90
210 GOTO 990
900 FOR A=1 TO N
910 P=1
920 FOR B=1 TO N
930 IF K$(A)>K$(B) THEN P=P+1
940 IF K$(A)=K$(B) AND A>B THEN P=P+1
950 NEXT B
960 X(P)=A
970 NEXT A
980 RETURN
990 END
```

THIS MEANS THAT BOTH $K\$(A)=K\$(B)$ _AND_ $A>B$ MUST BE TRUE. IF YOUR BASIC DOESN'T ALLOW "AND", DO THIS:

```
940 IF K$(A)=K$(B) THEN 945
941 GOTO 950
945 IF A>B THEN 948
946 GOTO 950
948 LET P=P+1
```

```
RUN

HOW MANY RECORDS? 4
HOW MANY ITEMS PER RECORD? 3
TYPE 3 ITEMS FOR RECORD 1
? SMITH
? 671-5555
? MCKEES ROCKS
TYPE 3 ITEMS FOR RECORD 2
? LUKASIEWICZ
? 999-8100
? WARSAW
TYPE 3 ITEMS FOR RECORD 3
? BROWN
? 653-7564
? WASHINGTON
TYPE 3 ITEMS FOR RECORD 4
? FEATHERGILL
? 555-2345
? TIMBUKTU

WHICH ITEM # IS THE SORTING KEY ? 1

SORTED RECORDS ARE:

BROWN 653-7564 WASHINGTON
FEATHERGILL 555-2345 TIMBUKTU
LUKASIEWICZ 999-8100 WARSAW
SMITH 671-5555 MCKEES ROCKS

CONTINUE? YES

WHICH ITEM # IS THE SORTING KEY ? 2

SORTED RECORDS ARE:

FEATHERGILL 555-2345 TIMBUKTU
BROWN 653-7564 WASHINGTON
SMITH 671-5555 MCKEES ROCKS
LUKASIEWICZ 999-8100 WARSAW

CONTINUE? YEP
```

```
WHICH ITEM # IS THE SORTING KEY ? 3

SORTED RECORDS ARE:

SMITH 671-5555 MCKEES ROCKS
FEATHERGILL 555-2345 TIMBUKTU
LUKASIEWICZ 999-8100 WARSAW
BROWN 653-7564 WASHINGTON

CONTINUE? NO
```

NOTE: The word "AND" in statement 940 is called a Boolean operator. The explanation in the balloon shows what to do if you don't have "AND" in your BASIC. Another Boolean operator is "OR". If you don't have it in your BASIC, here's what you do

    100 IF A>X OR B>X THEN 150

can be replaced by:

    100 IF A>X THEN 150
    102 IF B>X THEN 150

The secret to this program is, given a key field J, to fill the index array X(R) with exactly the right numbers, so that line 160 will print the records N$(X(R),I) sorted by field J. (Notice that the FOR I=1 to L loop in line 160 keeps the records intact by printing all the items on one line.)

How are "exactly the right numbers" put in X(R)? This is done in subroutine 900, where the list of N key items is worked through N times as follows:

1. Set a counter P=1. Use P to count how many times the first item is >= the other items (including itself). Then set X(P)=1.
2. Reset P=1 and count how many times the *second* item is >= the other items. Then set X(P)=2.
3. Reset P=1, repeat process for third item, setting X(P)=3. Repeat process as many times as you have items, so that for the Nth item X(P)=N.

In our subroutine, the outer A loop controls these N steps, and the inner B loop goes through the list, doing the counting.

Note what happens when we return from subroutine 900 and print N$(X(R),I). When R=1, X(R) will indicate the record in which the key item is the smallest (P is the lowest). Thus this record will be printed first. When R=2, the record with the second smallest key item will be printed, and so on.

Let's look at an example. Suppose we have four records with each containing a name, phone number, and zip code, and suppose we designate the name as the key item.

K$(1)="SMITH"
K$(2)="BAKER"
K$(3)="JONES"
K$(4)="ZILCH"

When we compare each of these items with all the other key items in subroutine 900, we have the following relationships:

	A=1	A=2	A=3	A=4
B=1	=	<	<	>
B=2	>	=	>	>
B=3	>	<	=	>
B=4	<	<	<	=

Using P to count the number of times each item is $>=$ the other items, (including itself) we find:

P=3   P=1   P=2   P=4

Next, we set X(P)=A:

X(3)=1   X(1)=2   X(2)=3   X(4)=4

$$\boxed{P}\ \boxed{ITEM\ \#}$$

This says that the *first* item in the unsorted list (SMITH) is greater than or equal to 3 other items (including itself). Thus it should be printed third in the sorted list. In other words, the record containing SMITH should be printed when R=3. We set the index array X(R)=1, so that, in line 160,

N$(X(R),I)=N$(X(3),I)=N$(1,I)

and the first record (whose key item is SMITH) is printed third.

In sum, you can think of X(R) as a pointer, indicating which record should be printed for each R. In our example, when R=3, X(R) points to record #1 as the one to print. Similarly,

LINE BEING PRINTED	POINTER TO	ITEM
R = 1	X (1) = 2	BAKER
R = 2	X (2) = 3	JONES
R = 3	X (3) = 1	SMITH
R = 4	X (4) = 4	ZILCH

Verify for yourself that this method works by going through the example in detail, doing every step the way a computer would.

SELF-TEST

1. Test the preceding program with "records" taken from your record collection (no, that's not a pun). For example, the "record" for each phonograph record could consist of shelf #, album #, composer, and composition. (Shelf # is an arbitrary number you give each phono record as soon as you buy it. The first record you buy is #1, the next #2, etc.). If necessary, first rewrite the program in standard BASIC.

2. Compare the computer times needed to sort 100 records of five fields each, using (a) the above method, and (b) a method based on Bubble Sort where all the fields of a record are swapped if the key fields are out of order.

5.6   Computerizing Your Record Library (or Recipe File (or Date Book)).

Self-Test question #1 in the previous section asked you to use a sorting program to organize your record collection. In this section we'll expand on that idea, and use READ and DATA statements instead of INPUT statements. Our goal will be to allow a person to add new DATA statements when new records are bought, and then get fresh lists that are sorted by various key items. For example, one list could show the records in alphabetical order by composer, another ordered by type of music, another by performer, and so on. The same idea applies to other lists—say your recipe file. Lists ordered by category (meat, vegetable, etc.), lists ordered by nationality of dish, lists ordered by preparation time; all would be useful. (As to which categories you might want to use in ordering your date book—you probably know best there.)

The approach we'll take is to use one data statement for each record. We'll agree on the following organization of data within each statement.

1001 DATA "101-CLASSIC", "BACH", "PRELUDE IN F", "GOULD,G."

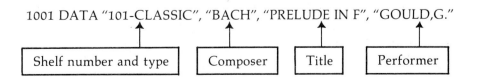

The shelf number is assigned by the buyer in increasing order for each new purchase. If you are up to 177, then your next record becomes 178, and you simply put it on the shelf right after 177. You also decide on categories. We'll use four: CLASSIC, SYNTHetic, SHOW tune, and RAGTIME to illustrate the idea. We'll put the shelf number and type together as one string to show how string functions can be used to extract substrings when needed. The data structure we'll use is a string array with four columns, and as many rows as records. Our example uses only ten rows.

> NOTE: There will be a limit to how big you can make this array, depending on how much memory you have. The only way around this limitation is to combine sorting with tape file storage, and then use "merging" techniques. This is an advanced topic which will not be covered here.

Here's our program with a sample run:

RECORD SORT

```
LIST

1 DIM N$(10,4),K$(10)
5 N=0
10 FOR R=1 TO 100
20 FOR I=1 TO 4
30 READ N$(R,I)
40 IF N$(R,I)="0" THEN 90
50 NEXT I
60 N=N+1
70 NEXT R
90 PRINT "SORT KEYS ARE: 0= TYPE      1=SHELF NUMBER"
91 PRINT "                    2=COMPOSER 3=TITLE 4=ARTIST"
92 PRINT "TYPE SORT KEY";:INPUT J: IF ABS(J-2)>2 THEN 90
95 IF J=0 THEN 300
100 K$(R)=N$(R,J) FOR R=1 TO N
120 GOSUB 900
140 PRINT : PRINT "SORTED RECORDS ARE: " : PRINT
150 FOR R=1 TO N
160 FOR I=1 TO 4: PRINT TAB(15*(I-1));N$(X(R),I);:NEXT I:PRINT
170 NEXT R
190 PRINT : INPUT "CONTINUE ";Y$
200 IF LEFT (Y$,1)="Y" THEN 92
210 GO TO 9999
300 REM-----EXTRACT CLASSIFICATION FROM SHELF #-----
310 J=1
320 FOR R=1 TO N:K$(R)=RIGHT(N$(R,J),5): NEXT R
325 GOTO 120
899 REM-----SORTING SUBR.----------
900 FOR A=1 TO N
910 P=1
920 FOR B=1 TO N
930 IF K$(A)>K$(B) THEN P=P+1
940 IF K$(A)=K$(B) AND A>B THEN P=P+1
950 NEXT B
960 X(P)=A
970 NEXT A
980 RETURN
981 STOP
982 J=1
983 LET K$(R)=RIGHT(N$(R,J),5) FOR R=1 TO N
984 GOTO 120
```

```
1000 REM-----DATA(SHELF#-TYPE,COMPOSER,TITLE,ARTIST)-----
1001 DATA"101-CLASSIC","BACH","GOLD.VAR.","GOULD,G."
1002 DATA"102-SYNTH","EMERSON LAKE","TARKUS","EMERSON LAKE"
1003 DATA"103-SHOW","YOUMANS,V.","NO NO NANETTE","CRAZY HORSE"
1004 DATA"104-RAGTIME","JOPLIN,S.","ENTERTAINER","BLAKE,E."
1005 DATA"105-CLASSIC","BEETHOVEN,L.","SYMPHONY #5","KRIPS,J."
1006 DATA"106-SHOW","BERNSTEIN,L.","WEST SIDE STY.","DRAGON,C."
1007 DATA"107-CLASSIC","BRAHMS,J.","PIANO CONC.#1","ARRAU,C."
1100 DATA"0","0","0","0"
9999 END
```

```
RUN

SORT KEYS ARE:  0= TYPE      1=SHELF NUMBER
                2=COMPOSER 3=TITLE 4=ARTIST
TYPE SORT KEY? 1

SORTED RECORDS ARE:

101-CLASSIC     BACH           GOLD.VAR.       GOULD,G.
102-SYNTH       EMERSON LAKE   TARKUS          EMERSON LAKE
103-SHOW        YOUMANS,V.     NO NO NANETTE   CRAZY HORSE
104-RAGTIME     JOPLIN,S.      ENTERTAINER     BLAKE,E.
105-CLASSIC     BEETHOVEN,L.   SYMPHONY #5     KRIPS,J.
106-SHOW        BERNSTEIN,L.   WEST SIDE STY.  DRAGON,C.
107-CLASSIC     BRAHMS,J.      PIANO CONC.#1   ARRAU,C.

CONTINUE ? YES
TYPE SORT KEY? 0

SORTED RECORDS ARE:

101-CLASSIC     BACH           GOLD.VAR.       GOULD,G.
105-CLASSIC     BEETHOVEN,L.   SYMPHONY #5     KRIPS,J.
107-CLASSIC     BRAHMS,J.      PIANO CONC.#1   ARRAU,C.
104-RAGTIME     JOPLIN,S.      ENTERTAINER     BLAKE,E.
103-SHOW        YOUMANS,V.     NO NO NANETTE   CRAZY HORSE
106-SHOW        BERNSTEIN,L.   WEST SIDE STY.  DRAGON,C.
102-SYNTH       EMERSON LAKE   TARKUS          EMERSON LAKE

CONTINUE ? YEP
TYPE SORT KEY? 2

SORTED RECORDS ARE:

101-CLASSIC     BACH           GOLD.VAR.       GOULD,G.
105-CLASSIC     BEETHOVEN,L.   SYMPHONY #5     KRIPS,J.
106-SHOW        BERNSTEIN,L.   WEST SIDE STY.  DRAGON,C.
107-CLASSIC     BRAHMS,J.      PIANO CONC.#1   ARRAU,C.
102-SYNTH       EMERSON LAKE   TARKUS          EMERSON LAKE
104-RAGTIME     JOPLIN,S.      ENTERTAINER     BLAKE,E.
103-SHOW        YOUMANS,V.     NO NO NANETTE   CRAZY HORSE

CONTINUE ? YOWSAH
TYPE SORT KEY? 3

SORTED RECORDS ARE:

104-RAGTIME     JOPLIN,S.      ENTERTAINER     BLAKE,E.
101-CLASSIC     BACH           GOLD.VAR.       GOULD,G.
103-SHOW        YOUMANS,V.     NO NO NANETTE   CRAZY HORSE
107-CLASSIC     BRAHMS,J.      PIANO CONC.#1   ARRAU,C.
105-CLASSIC     BEETHOVEN,L.   SYMPHONY #5     KRIPS,J.
102-SYNTH       EMERSON LAKE   TARKUS          EMERSON LAKE
106-SHOW        BERNSTEIN,L.   WEST SIDE STY.  DRAGON,C.
```

```
CONTINUE ? YETH
TYPE SORT KEY? 4

SORTED RECORDS ARE:

107-CLASSIC     BRAHMS,J.        PIANO CONC.#1   ARRAU,C.
104-RAGTIME     JOPLIN,S.        ENTERTAINER     BLAKE,E.
103-SHOW        YOUMANS,V.       NO NO NANETTE   CRAZY HORSE
106-SHOW        BERNSTEIN,L.     WEST SIDE STY.  DRAGON,C.
102-SYNTH       EMERSON LAKE     TARKUS          EMERSON LAKE
101-CLASSIC     BACH             GOLD.VAR.       GOULD,G.
105-CLASSIC     BEETHOVEN,L.     SYMPHONY #5     KRIPS,J.

CONTINUE ? NO
```

You'll notice that we read the data into the string array N$(R,I) by using two nested FOR loops (lines 10 to 70). The zeros in the last data statement signal when to stop reading. The number of records read in are counted by N. The rest of the program is similar to that in Section 5.5 except for one extra trick. If the user asks to sort on TYPE of record by using the sorting code J=0, we branch to line 300. There we change J back to 1 (column 1), and use the statement

LET K$(R)=RIGHT(N$(J),5)

to extract the right part of N$(R,1) starting with character number 5.

56789..

101-[CLASSIC] ◄———— This is RIGHT(N$(R,J),5)

So you see we get only the "type" substring for use in the sorting key K$(R).

SELF-TEST

1. What changes would have to be made in this program in order to run it using a BASIC that does not have string arrays?
HINT: Re-read Section 4.3(b).

NOTE: In some versions of BASIC the name of the RIGHT string function is RIGHT$.

5.7 SHELL SORT

The sorting algorithms given so far can take a lot of time when N (the number of items to be sorted) is large. There are more efficient sorting algorithms available, and we'll show two of these in this and the next section. The first is called the Shell Sort (named after its inventor). The second is called Quicksort (not named after its inventor). First, the Shell Sort.

SHELL SORT

```
LIST

5 LET S=0:LET C=0
10 DIM X(100)
15 N=100
20 REM---PUT UNSORTED NUMBERS IN THE X ARRAY----
40 FOR K=1 TO 100
42 LET X(K)=INT(100*RND(0))
48 NEXT K
55 PRINT "THE UNSORTED ARRAY IS"
56 GOSUB 900
59 REM----NOW SORT THEM---
60 GOSUB 1000
70 REM----PRINT THE SORTED ARRAY----
72 PRINT "THE SORTED ARRAY IS"
75 GOSUB 900
85 PRINT C; "COMPARISONS"
86 PRINT S; "SWAPS"
90 GOTO 9000
900 REM----PRINT ROUTINE FOR 10 COLUMNS--
901 FOR K=1 TO N
905 LET Z=K-10*INT((K-1)/10)
910 PRINT TAB(4*(Z-1));X(K);
920 IF Z>=10 THEN PRINT
930 NEXT K
940 RETURN
1000 REM----SHELL SORT-----
1010 G=N
1020 IF G<=1 THEN RETURN
1030 G=INT(G/2)
1040 M=N-G
1050 F=0
1060 FOR I=1 TO M
1070 P=I+G
1075 C=C+1
1080 IF X(I)<=X(P) THEN 1130
1085 S=S+1
1090 T=X(I)
1100 X(I)=X(P)
1110 X(P)=T
1120 F=1
1130 NEXT I
1140 IF F>0 THEN 1050
1150 GOTO 1020
9000 END
```

```
RUN

THE UNSORTED ARRAY IS
 77  78  75  47   7  20  51  26  95  33
 41  45   2   5   6  92  92  23  10  53
 25  74  15  17  66  47  82  70  77  28
 76   1  19   5  58  97  56  66  91  45
 50  98  36  32  64  89  58  48  59  26
 18  78  99  96  79  10  46  87   3  32
 63  87  53  32  12  83  91  96  55  63
 80  13  55  14  82  69  75  23  60  53
 77  78  76  52  23  67  93  53  77  77
 74  44  99  96  80  13  54  11  74  46
THE SORTED ARRAY IS
  1   2   3   5   5   6   7  10  10  11
 12  13  13  14  15  17  18  19  20  23
 23  23  25  26  26  28  32  32  32  33
 36  41  44  45  45  46  46  47  47  48
 50  51  52  53  53  53  53  54  55  55
 56  58  58  59  60  63  63  64  66  66
 67  69  70  74  74  74  75  75  76  76
 77  77  77  77  77  78  78  78  79  80
 80  82  82  83  87  87  89  91  91  92
 92  93  95  96  96  96  97  98  99  99
2616 COMPARISONS
399 SWAPS
```

Two questions we can ask are how good is Shell compared to the Bubble or Straight Selection Sort, and if it's better, why? To answer the first question, we'll present a table of numbers below, which shows that for 500 items of random data, if a Shell Sort would take 10 minutes, a Bubble Sort would take six times as long—about 1 hour. (You'll also see that Quicksort should take about 2 or 3 minutes for this same data. However there are some "catches" to these figures which we'll point out later.)

The reason Shell Sort is usually faster than Bubble or Selection Sort is the following.

As you know, sorting is done by *comparing* items in the list, and then (if they are out of order) *swapping* them. Bubble and Selection Sort always compare pairs of *adjacent* items, so they must go through all N items on the first "pass". If the data is badly out of order, there will have to be up to N-1 passes on the unsorted part of the data. It can be shown that this could take up to $N^2/2$ comparisons. For N=500, this gives 125,000 comparisons. If we assume that swaps are needed half the time (62,000 swaps), we see that Bubble could require roughly 180,000 "operations". Here's a table which verifies these numbers. It was produced by actually running sorts of random data, and putting in counters in front of the comparison and swapping statements (1075 C=C+1 and 1085 S=S+1). The same thing was done for the Quicksort programs shown in Section 5.8. As you can see, Shell Sort doesn't get out of hand as rapidly as Bubble. It can be shown that it grows in proportion to $N^{1.5}$(not to N^2).

| N | BUBBLE SORT | | SHELL SORT | | QUICKSORT | |
	Comparisons	Swaps	Comparisons	Swaps	Comparisons	Swaps
100	4,900	2,100	2,700	400	600	200
200	20,000	9,600	7,200	980	1,500	500
300	45,000	23,000	10,200	1,400	2,600	900
400	80,000	40,000	21,200	2,600	3,600	1,200
500	125,000	63,000	26,000	3,200	5,000	1,600

Remember that these numbers are only valid for data which is randomly generated to begin with. If you are sorting data that is already nearly in order, you may very well find that the Bubble Sort is best. This is because the Bubble Sort uses a "flag" that makes it stop as soon as the data is in order. In general, if you don't know what kind of data you'll have, Shell Sort is a good choice.

So how does Shell work? The idea is to be more "daring", and to start out by comparing items that are far apart. The assumption is that making a swap over a bigger "distance" will be more efficient than methodically making swaps of just one position at a time. The "distance" between items being compared is called the *gap*, and in line 1010 it is initialized to G=N, but changed to G/2 in line 1030. So for N=500 items, the starting gap is INT(500/2)=250. Each time around the main loop for controlling successive "big gap" sorting (lines 1020 to 1150) G is cut in half. So it is eventually reduced to a "little gap" of 1. In other words, the last time around the main loop, the program is just like the Bubble Sort. But by this time the data will be "almost" in order. The variable F is a flag that makes the program stop when no more swaps can be made (F=0). To fully understand the program, you should trace it through with about 16 numbers for data, using a starting comparison gap of 8. You'll see that the first time you'll make M=N-G=8 comparisons per pass (in loop 1060 to 1130). Then when the gap is changed to 4, you'll make M=N-G=12 comparisons, then 14, and finally 15 per pass (there may be several passes for each of these gaps as determined by the flag in line 1140).

SELF-TEST

1. Put a loop for N=100 TO 500 STEP 100 *around* the Shell Sort program to set how closely your numbers match those in the table. (Since you have a different RND function, they won't be exactly the same.) Don't forget to DIM X(500).
2. Do the same thing for the Bubble and Selection Sorts of Section 5.4. Here you'll also have to add statements for generating the random data to be sorted.

5.8 QUICKSORT

The table in Section 5.7 comparing three different sorting algorithms shows that the winner is Quicksort. Whether it will always be the winner depends on how much the data being sorted is out of order. For data that is "almost"in order to begin with, the Bubble Sort might actually be best. But in general, the Quicksort algorithm is rated very highly by professional users. They point out that it is of "order n*log n", rather than "order n²" like Bubble Sort. For n = 1000, this means roughly the difference between 3,000 (n*log n) and 1,000,000 (n²).

Actually, a mathematical analysis is not needed to understand how Quicksort works. In fact it is very similar to the way some people do sorting "naturally".

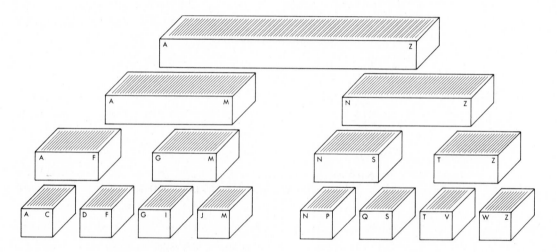

Imagine you have a big stack of unsorted 3 x 5 library cards which you want to put in alphabetical order. What you can do is first toss them into piles labeled A-M, and N-Z. So now you have split the original problem into two smaller problems. This process can be repeated, splitting each of the smaller piles into two, giving a total of four piles. Depending on how large n is, this can be done a few more times. When you get tired of splitting, you can then use something like Bubble Sort to finish off sorting the small piles. At this point, the value of n for each pile is very small, so an n² method isn't too bad.

For example, if n = 1000, and you split the cards into 16 piles of about 62 each, then the "order" of the problem has gone from 1000^2 = 1,000,000 to $16*62^2$ = 62,000 (roughly). That's still pretty large, but you can see we're heading in the right direction.

Let's now look at the actual algorithm we'll use to do Quicksort. To start, we need to decide how to do our first "split". The easiest thing to do is to choose the first card in our stack of library cards as our reference point. We'll call this card a *super-record*. So if the card says "KILROY", what we'll do is split all our cards into two piles, one from A to "KILROY", and one from "KILROY" to Z.

To express these ideas in a computer program, let's assume that the n items to be sorted are stored in an array X which goes from X(1) to X(N). Picture it as going from left to right. To make things easier to show, we'll sort numbers (instead of names like Kilroy). For example, if we have 8 numbers to sort, here's what our array might look like:

X(1)	X(2)	X(3)	X(4)	X(5)	X(6)	X(7)	X(8)
65	28	44	99	75	34	88	44
↑							↑
I							J

Two pointers called I and J will be used to keep track of what's going on. With this notation, here's the basic idea behind the Quicksort algorithm.

1. Initialize pointers I and J to opposite ends of the array; define X(I) as the super-record. (In our example the super-record will be 65).
2. Compare the super-record with the number referenced by the "opposite" pointer. (In our example, we're now comparing 65 with 44.)
3. If these numbers are out of order, swap them (in our example the 65 and 44 are out of order, so we will swap them).
4. Move the pointer "opposite" the super-record one step toward the super-record (in our example I will be moved, since the super-record is now on the right).
5. If I=J, go to step 6; otherwise go back to step 2. Note that when I=J, all possible comparisons have been made. The super-record now splits the list into two sub-lists, *and* it is in its final position.
6. Repeat the whole process in steps 1 to 5 for each of the remaining sub-lists.

Here's part of what will happen to our example list of numbers if we apply this algorithm. The position of the pointers is shown by using parentheses. The super-record is 65.

COMPARE	(65)	28	44	99	75	34	88	(44)	
SWAP	(44)	28	44	99	75	34	88	(65)	MOVE I
COMPARE	44	(28)	44	99	75	34	88	(65)	MOVE I
COMPARE	44	28	(44)	99	75	34	88	(65)	MOVE I
COMPARE	44	28	44	(99)	75	34	88	(65)	MOVE I
SWAP	44	28	44	(65)	75	34	88	(99)	MOVE J
COMPARE	44	28	44	(65)	75	34	(88)	99	MOVE J

. . . etc. . . .

SWAP	44	28	44	34	(65)	(75)	88	99	MOVE J
GO TO 6	44	28	44	34	(65)	75	88	99	

SELF-TEST

Complete this sort by hand using the Quicksort algorithm. Here's what you should have each time you get to step 6, using the rule of choosing the left sub-file where possible.

A. The first time step 6 is reached you should have

LEFT SUB-FILE	RIGHT SUB-FILE
[44 28 44 34] (65)	[75 88 99]

B. Now you apply steps 1-5 to the left sub-file (numbers to left of 65). *When finished* you should have:

[34   28   44]   (44)   65   [75   88   99]

C. Again applying steps 1-5 to the new left sub-file you should get, *when finished*,

28   (34)   44   44   65   [75   88   99]

D. Now applying it to the *right* sub-file which we had back at stage A, you should get:

28   34   44   44   65   [(75)   88   (99)]

which becomes this:

28   34   44   44   65   (75)   [88   99]

E. Finally, applying steps 1-5 to the final right sub-file, you will get:

28   34   44   44   65   75   (88)   99

There are really two parts to the Quicksort algorithm that will have to show up in our program. The first will take care of steps 1-5. These steps compare and swap items with the goal of splitting the list into left and right sub-files. The second part is a bookkeeping system which remembers which sub-file we are working on by keeping track of the "boundaries" of the sub-files. It corresponds to step 6.

Here's a flow chart for steps 1 to 5. The variables L and R give the subscripts of the left and right records of our file or subfile. The variables I and J give the subscripts of the records being compared. The variable S takes on the value 1 if the super-record is at location J, and -1 if it is at location I of our file. The array X contains the n items to be sorted.

FLOW CHART 1

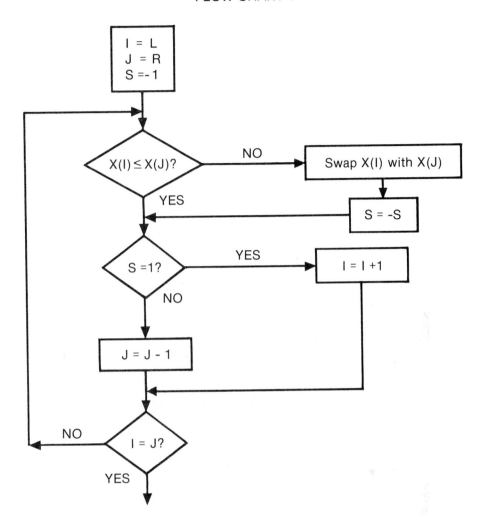

The flow chart for step 6 is more complicated. It has the job of keeping track of the sub-files. When we finish dividing a file, the boundaries of the two sublists are (L,I-1) and (I+1,R). The old super-record will be at location I. Since we can only work on one sublist at a time, we "remember" the boundaries of the other sublists in what's called a stack.

A stack is a last-come-first-served list. We'll set up two stacks with a doubly subscripted array S(P,K). Variable P is the stack pointer. It starts at P = 0 and is increased whenever there is a subfile to "remember". Here is how to save (PUSH) a subfile's boundaries onto the two stacks.

P = P+1: S(P,1) = I+1: S(P,2) = R

Whenever the next subfile to be divided has only one record, we ignore it and dip into our stack and POP out saved subfile boundaries.

L = S(P,1): R=S(P,2): P = P-1

We can only POP a subfile as long as the stack is not empty. Once the stack is empty (P=0), we have no subfiles left to sort.

Here's a flow chart showing how this all works. Notice that it contains the previous flow chart, so it is really a master flow chart for the whole program.

FLOW CHART 2

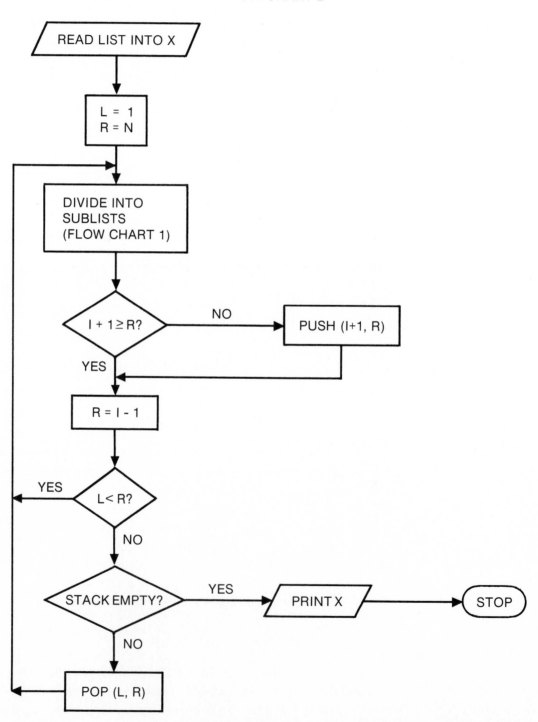

The key to understanding flow chart 2 is to picture the X array and the stack as follows:

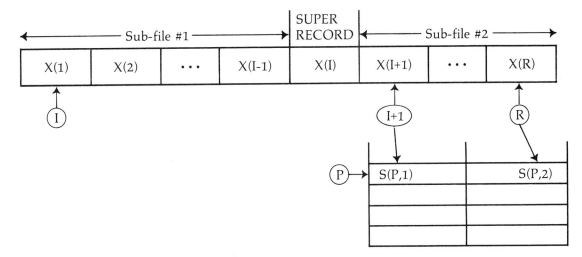

The first stack S(P,1) "remembers" the left boundary of subfile #2, and the second stack "remembers" the right boundary.

Here's a listing of a BASIC Quicksort program based on our flow charts. The SWAP is handled in line 160, PUSH is found in line 270, and the POP is in line 350. Line 180 uses the function SGN(-S) to change S to +1 if S=-1, and to -1 if S was +1. You could just as well make line 180 LET S=-S. To check the program out, 100 random numbers are initially stored in the X array, The array is then sorted, and printed as output. The program also prints the number of comparisons and swaps that were required.

QUICKSORT

```
LIST

5 C1=0:S1=0
10 DIM X(100),S9(20,2)
20 N=100
30 FOR K=1 TO N
40 LET X(K)=INT(N*RND(0))
50 NEXT K
55 PRINT "THE UNSORTED ARRAY IS"
56 GOSUB 900
100 I1=1:J1=N
120 I=I1:J=J1:S=-1
150 C1=C1+1
160 IF X(I)<=X(J) THEN 200
165 S1=S1+1
170 T=X(I) : X(I)=X(J) : X(J)=T
180 S=SGN(-S)
200 IF S=1 THEN I=I+1 ELSE J=J-1
240 IF  I<J THEN 150
260 IF I+1>=J1 THEN 300
270 P=P+1 : S9(P,1)=I+1 : S9(P,2)=J1
300 J1=I-1
330 IF I1<J1 THEN 120
340 IF P=0 THEN 370
350 I1=S9(P,1) : J1=S9(P,2) : P=P-1
360 GOTO 120
```

```
370 PRINT "THE SORTED ARRAY IS"
375 GOSUB 900
390 PRINT N; "RANDOM NUMBERS"
400 PRINT C1; "COMPARISONS"
410 PRINT S1; "SWAPS"
420 GOTO 1000
900 FOR K=1 TO N
905 LET Z=K-10*INT((K-1)/10)
910 PRINT TAB(4*(Z-1));X(K);
920 IF Z>=10 THEN PRINT
930 NEXT K
940 RETURN
1000 END
```

```
RUN

THE UNSORTED ARRAY IS
  77  78  75  47   7   20  51  26  95  33
  41  45   2   5   6   92  92  23  10  53
  25  74  15  17  66   47  82  70  77  28
  76   1  19   5  58   97  56  66  91  45
  50  98  36  32  64   89  58  48  59  26
  18  78  99  96  79   10  46  87   3  32
  63  87  53  32  12   83  91  96  55  63
  80  13  55  14  82   69  75  23  60  53
  77  78  76  52  23   67  93  53  77  77
  74  44  99  96  80   13  54  11  74  46
THE SORTED ARRAY IS
   1   2   3   5   5    6   7  10  10  11
  12  13  13  14  15   17  18  19  20  23
  23  23  25  26  26   28  32  32  32  33
  36  41  44  45  45   46  46  47  47  48
  50  51  52  53  53   53  53  54  55  55
  56  58  58  59  60   63  63  64  66  66
  67  69  70  74  74   74  75  75  76  76
  77  77  77  77  77   78  78  78  79  80
  80  82  82  83  87   87  89  91  91  92
  92  93  95  96  96   96  97  98  99  99
 100  RANDOM NUMBERS
 591  COMPARISONS
 205  SWAPS
```

The WHILE Control Structure

Some programming languages (e.g. PASCAL) use a WHILE statement to control looping. They do this to avoid GOTO statements (and some of the confusion these can cause). For example, to print all the factorials less than 1000, they would do something like the following:

```
10 N=0
20 F=1
30   WHILE F<1000 DO
40   BEGIN
50     PRINT N,F
60     N=N+1
70     F=F*N
80   END
90 REM-----BEGIN NEXT PART OF PROGRAM-----
```

This says "do everything from line 40 to line 80 repeatedly WHILE (as long as) F is less than 1000". Even though standard BASIC doesn't have this construct, you can still think this way, and then translate to standard BASIC as follows:

```
10 LET N=0
20 LET F=1
30 REM-----BEGIN WHILE LOOP-----
40   IF F>=1000 THEN 90
50     PRINT N,F
60     LET N=N+1
70     LET F=F*N
80   GOTO 40
90 REM-----BEGIN NEXT PART OF PROGRAM-----
```

BASIC-PLUS actually allows a form of WHILE which is illustrated in the following Quicksort program. Notice that WHILE's can be nested, and that there are no explicit GOTO statements. This is an example of what is called "structured top-down programming". The details (like SWAP, POP, and PUSH) are "down" at the bottom of the list of things to do. This structure shows up in the program if you change the word "down" to "right". The lines which have no line number are really extensions of the previous line. To obtain such extensions in BASIC-PLUS, you press LINEFEED (instead of CARRIAGE RETURN) at the end of the line which is to be extended.

QUICKSORT 2

```
1     REM   THIS IS A QUICKSORT WRITTEN IN BASIC-PLUS
2     REM   BY JEFF LEDERER. FOR OTHER BASIC'S, TRANSLATE
3     REM   "WHILE A<B" TO "IF B>= A THEN LN" WHERE LN
4     REM   IS THE LINE NUMBER FOLLOWING THE CORRESPONDING
5     REM   "NEXT", AND CHANGE "NEXT" TO A "GOTO" TOP OF LOOP.
6     REM   S% IS A LOGICAL VARIABLE.
7     REM   S%=-1 MEANS TRUE, AND S%=0 MEANS FALSE.
8     REM-------------------------------------------------------
100   DIM X(100),S9(10,2):
      N=100:
      FOR K=1 TO N:
          X(K)=INT(100*RND(0)):
      NEXT K
200   PRINT "THE UNSORTED LIST:":
      MAT PRINT X(N);:
      PRINT:
      P,S9(1,1)=1:
      S9(1,2)=N:
      WHILE P>0:
          I1=S9(P,1):                              '-----
          J1=S9(P,2):                              ' POP
          P=P-1:                                   '-----
          WHILE I1<J1
300           I=I1:
              J=J1:
              S%=-1%:
              WHILE I<J:
                  IF X(I)>X(J) THEN
                      T=X(I):                      '-----
                      X(I)=X(J):                   ' SWAP
                      X(J)=T:                      '-----
                      S%=-(S%+1%)
400               IF NOT S% THEN J=J-1 ELSE I=I+1  'SWITCH
500           NEXT
510           IF I+1<J1 THEN
                  P=P+1:                           '-----
                  S9(P,1)=I+1:                     ' PUSH
                  S9(P,2)=J1                       '-----
600           J1=I-1
610       NEXT
620   NEXT
630   PRINT "THE SORTED LIST:":
      MAT PRINT X(N);:
      PRINT:
      END
```

5.9 PROJECT IDEAS

1. Talk to your local football coach about the information he'd like to see come out of the scouting program in Section 5.3. Try to add program modules to handle these ideas, and/or come up with better ones. In short, look into the possibility of gradually developing (and debugging) a professional scouting program.

2. The program at the beginning of Section 5.4 showed the progress of all the intermediate steps in a Bubble Sort. Write a program that shows the progress of a Quicksort. Show the position of the pointers by printing parentheses around the corresponding numbers, and indicate the sub-files by some other symbol. The idea is to help someone understand Quicksort by seeing all the comparisons, swaps, and file subdivisions.

3. Modify the LP record sorting program so that the item being alphabetized always prints in the first column.

4. Rewrite one of the programs from this chapter in minimal BASIC, using remarks and indentations to clarify the program's structure. Two examples showing some techniques that can be used are given in the "style corner".

THE STYLE
CORNER

```
100 REM    QUICKSORT    28 SEPTEMBER 1977    JOHN M. NEVISON
105
110 REM    THIS PROGRAM IS A STYLED VERSION OF AN ORIGINAL
115 REM    BASIC-PLUS PROGRAM BY J. LEDERER
120
125 REM    REFERENCE:  DWYER, T. AND CRITCHFIELD, M., "BASIC AND
130 REM                THE PERSONAL COMPUTER," READING, MASS:
135 REM                ADDISON-WESLEY PUBLISHING COMPANY, 1978.
140
145 REM    VARIABLES:
150 REM        C1......COUNTER OF COMPARISONS
155 REM        C2......COUNTER OF SWAPS
160 REM        I1......LEFT END OF THE CURRENT LIST
165 REM        I.......INDEX VARIABLE FOR LEFT SIDE OF LIST
170 REM        J1......RIGHT END OF THE CURRENT LIST
175 REM        J.......INDEX VARIABLE FOR RIGHT SIDE OF LIST
180 REM        K.......INDEX VARIABLE
185 REM        P.......POINTER TO THE TOP OF THE STACK OF SUBLISTS
190 REM        S(P,1).THE  LEFT END OF THE NEXT SUBLIST
195 REM        S(P,2).THE RIGHT END OF THE NEXT SUBLIST
200 REM        S.......DIRECTION SWITCH(-1 AT I, +1 AT J)
205 REM        T.......TEMPORARY EXCHANGE VARIABLE
210 REM        X().....LIST OF  NUMBERS TO BE SORTED
215
220 REM    CONSTANTS:
225     LET N9 = 200                          'NUMBER OF  NUMBERS
230
235 REM     DIMENSIONS:
240     DIM X(200), S(10,2)
245
250
255 REM    MAIN PROGRAM
260
265 REM    PERFORM A 'QUICK' SORT ON A BATCH OF NUMBERS, X().
270 REM    SEE REFERENCE FOR DETAILS.
275
280     FOR K = 1 TO N9
285        LET X(K) = INT(N9*RND)
290     NEXT K
295     LET P = 1
300     LET S(P,1) = 1
305     LET S(P,2) = N9
310
315     IF P <= 0 THEN 345              '*
320        LET I1 = S(P,1)
325        LET J1 = S(P,2)
330        LET P = P - 1
335        GO SUB 385                   'SORT OR STACK
340     GO TO 315                       '*
345
350     PRINT N9; "RANDOM NUMBERS"
355     PRINT C1; "COMPARISONS"
360     PRINT C2; "SWAPS"
365
370     STOP
375
380
```

```
385 REM     SUBROUTINE:  SORT OR STACK
390 REM       IN:   I1, J1, P, C1, C2
395 REM       OUT:  P, S(), C1, C2
400
405 REM     STARTING  FROM THE RIGHT-HAND SIDE,
410 REM     BREAK OFF AND STACK POINTERS TO THE UNSORTED
415 REM     SUBLISTS.  SORT THE LEFT-MOST LIST.
420 REM     (SEE REFERENCE FOR A MORE COMPLETE EXPLANATION.)
425
430     LET T = 0
435     IF J1 <= I1 THEN 595              '*
440       LET I = I1
445       LET J = J1
450       LET S = -1
455       IF I >= J THEN  535             '*
460         LET C1 = C1 + 1
465         IF X(I) <= X(J) THEN 495
470           LET C2 = C2 + 1
475           LET T = X(I)
480           LET X(I) = X(J)
485           LET X(J) = T
490           LET S = -S
495
500           IF S < 0 THEN 515
505             LET J = J - 1
510             GO TO 525                 'THEN BOTTOM
515
520             LET I = I + 1
525
530         GO TO 455                     '*
535
540 REM     IF I DID NOT GET ALL THE WAY TO J1, THEN
545 REM     STACK THE UNSORTED RIGHT HAND PART OF
550 REM     THE CURRENT LIST, (I+1--J1).
555
560         IF I+1 >= J1 THEN 580
565           LET P = P + 1
570           LET S(P,1) = I + 1
575           LET S(P,2) = J1
580
585         LET J1 = I-1
590     GO TO 435                         '*
595
600 RETURN
605
610     END



291 MAT PRINT X;
361 MAT PRINT X;
```

THE STYLE CORNER

```
100 REM      SHLSORT: SHELL SORT   17 JULY 77  J.M. NEVISON
110
112 REM    SORTS A MIXED BATCH OF NUMBERS, B(), INTO ASCENDING
114 REM    ORDER.  ESPECIALLY GOOD FOR BATCHES OF MORE THAN 50.
116
120 REM      REFERENCE:  D.L. SHELL, "A HIGH-SPEED SORTING
130 REM                    PROCEDURE," COMMUNICATIONS OF THE ACM,
160 REM                    VOL. 2, (JULY, 1959), PP. 30-32.
170
180 REM    VARIABLES:
190 REM        B()...THE BATCH OF NUMBERS
200 REM        E$....EXCHANGE MARKER
210 REM        G.....THE GAP
220 REM        I.....INDEX VARIABLE
230 REM        S.....THE STEP ACROSS THE GAP
240 REM        T.....THE TOP OF THE PASS THROUGH THE NUMBERS
250 REM        X.....EXCHANGE VARIABLE
260
270 REM    CONSTANT:
280     LET N9 = 55                          'NUMBER OF DATA
290
300 REM    DIMENSIONS:
310     DIM B(55)
320
330 REM    MAIN PROGRAM
340
350 REM    COMPARES ITEMS ACROSS A GAP N9/2 WIDE UNTIL THERE ARE NO
360 REM    MORE EXCHANGES, THEN CUTS THE GAP IN HALF AND REPEATS.
370
380     FOR I = 1 TO N9
390        LET B(I) = INT(RND*25 + 1)
400        PRINT B(I);
410     NEXT I
420     PRINT
430     PRINT
440
450     LET E$ = " "
460     LET S = 0
470     LET T = 0
480     LET X = 0
490     LET G = N9
500
510     IF G <= 1 THEN 680
520        LET G = INT(G/2)
530        LET T = N9 - G
540        LET E$ = "NO EXCHANGE"
550           FOR I = 1 TO T
560              LET S = I + G
570              IF B(I) <= B(S) THEN 620
580                 LET X = B(I)
590                 LET B(I) = B(S)
600                 LET B(S) = X
610                 LET E$ = "EXCHANGE"
620
630           NEXT I
640           IF E$ = "NO EXCHANGE" THEN 660
650        GO TO 540
660
670     GO TO 510
680
690     FOR I = 1 TO N9
700        PRINT B(I);
710     NEXT I
720     PRINT
730
740     END
```

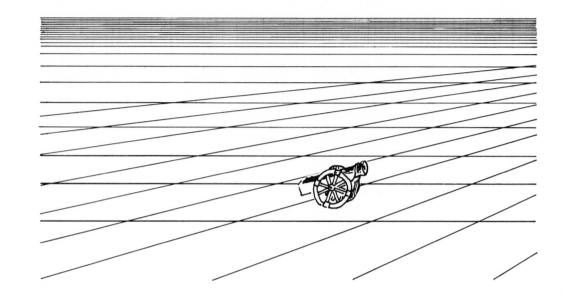

6

COMPUTER GAMES

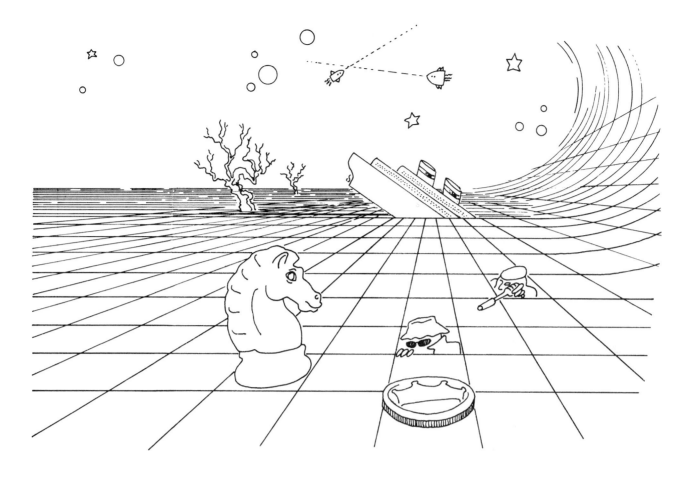

6.0 INTRODUCTION

And now for a subject that needs no introduction — Computer Games.

6.1 DIFFERENT VIEWS OF GAMES

The word "game" has several different meanings, all of which lead to interesting computer programs. Before looking at some of these programs, it will be helpful to distinguish between three uses of the word "game".

1. Mathematical Games—This phrase is usually used in a technical sense to mean systems based on the mathematical theories developed by John von Neumann in the 1940's. We'll look at an example of how this theory works in Section 6.2, and get a feel for the concept of "optimal strategy".

2. Recreational Games—These are as old as mankind itself, and include everything from make-the-rules-up-as-you-go children's games, to sophisticated games like Chess and GO (a Chinese invention). Of course many recreational games can also be analyzed as mathematical games,

and the recreational Morra game we'll show illustrates this possibility. Other recreational games include games of chance, board games of all kinds, and a whole new group of computer sci-fi games.

3. Simulation Games—These are "let's pretend" situations which usually have a "serious" (educational?) purpose. Military people play war games, business students play management games, and engineers play "land the new space-craft" games. We'll see an example of a spacecraft simulation in this section, and present a political simulation game later in Section 9.6.

These three categories often overlap, of course, and we needn't worry about deciding whether something is a fun-game or a simulation. Actually, just about everything done on a computer is a simulation, since the word simulate means "to imitate". So when you think about it, a card game, a business game, a space travel game, a stock market game, or a chess game, when played on a computer, is really a form of simulation. The computer program is "imitating" something else.

However, not all simulations are games. The essence of a game is that there be a "payoff" — there must be the element of winning or losing something (money, points, checker pieces). Usually that's an easy feature to add to a simulation. For example, you could give X points for every successful landing in a lunar-lander simulation (or take away Y points for every crash) and thus also have a game. So don't hesitate to try inventing new games; it's one of the most intriguing learning strategies around. A personal computer used in this way is undoubtedly an excellent educational investment for the whole family.

6.2 MATRIX GAMES; OPTIMAL STRATEGIES

The mathematical theory of games is most easily explained in terms of what is called a two-player zero-sum matrix game. The idea is to describe the game in terms of a square matrix that shows all the possible "payoffs". The "zero-sum" part means that the sum of what one player wins and what the other player loses is always zero. In other words, the total wealth of the two players remains constant. Let's look at an example of a matrix game based on a version of the game called Morra.

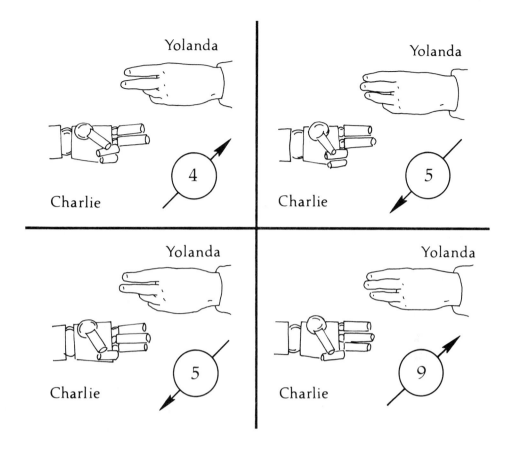

As the sketches show, there are two players who extend either 2 or 3 fingers simultaneously. Let's call the players Yolanda and Charlie (which will later translate into You versus the Computer, using the variables Y and C).

The rules of the game are as follows. If the total number of fingers is even, then Charlie pays Yolanda the product; if odd, then Yolanda pays Charlie the sum. We can exhibit these rules in a 2 x 2 "payoff" matrix as follows:

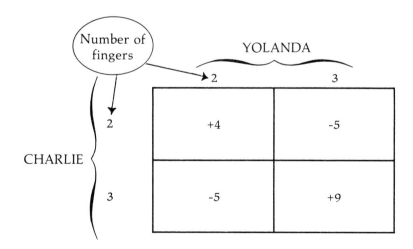

The numbers in the matrix show the payoff *from* Charlie *to* Yolanda. For example, the entry +4 means Charlie pays Yolanda +4 points (or dollars, or chips, or anything else). This also means of course that 4 points are subtracted from Charlie's bankroll. So the total wealth remains constant. The *sum* of the changes has been *zero*. The entry -5 means that 5 points go the other way, from Yolanda to Charlie.

Here's a sample sequence of plays to show how the payoffs work. To make the situation more concrete, we'll suppose that both players start with a bankroll of $100.

CHARLIE'S FINGERS	YOLANDA'S FINGERS	PAYOFF	CHARLIE'S BANKROLL	YOLANDA'S BANKROLL
— START —			$100	$100
2	2	+4	96	104
3	2	−5	101	99
3	3	+9	92	108
2	3	−5	97	103
2	3	−5	102	98
.	.	.	.	.
.	.	.	.	.
.	.	.	.	.

You may very well ask if this is a "fair" game. The answer is no; it's slightly rigged in favor of Yolanda. *If* both players play the "best" they can, it can be shown mathematically that on the average Yolanda will gain $11/23 (about 48 cents) per play. This means that Charlie can expect to lose that much per game. So playing the "best" possible game means that Yolanda tries to maximize gains, while Charlie tries to minimize losses. Of course if either player plays a poor strategy, things could turn out differently.

So what's the best strategy for each player? It can be shown (using von Neumann's Mini-Max theory) that over the *long* haul both Yolanda and Charlie should play two fingers about 14/23 of the time. The reason for Yolanda favoring two is that while playing three fingers has the prospect of gaining a big fat +9 (if Charlie also plays a 3), Charlie knows this too! So a smart Charlie will therefore favor playing two fingers. But Yolanda figures this will happen, and therefore also favors two. Of course both players have to mix up their plays, otherwise they would give away their plans (like a football team that *always* went around right end).

Here are two runs of a program that allows Y (You, not Yolanda) to play C (the Computer, not Charlie). The first run shows what happens when the computer is "not too smart", which means it plays more 3's than 2's. This is because the computer determines its play by first choosing a random number X between 0 and 1 (see line 520). If this random number X falls below a number we called B (X<B), the computer will play two fingers (see

lines 530 and 550). *But,* back up in line 55 we made B=9/23 if the user *didn't* say "YES" to the question about making the computer smart. So we have:

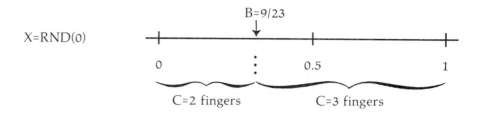

As you can see, our "not too bright" computer will play more 3's than 2's.

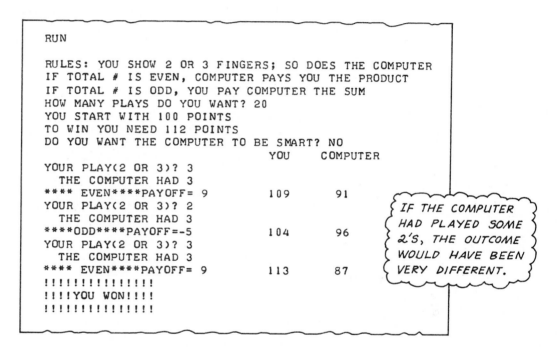

```
RUN

RULES: YOU SHOW 2 OR 3 FINGERS; SO DOES THE COMPUTER
IF TOTAL # IS EVEN, COMPUTER PAYS YOU THE PRODUCT
IF TOTAL # IS ODD, YOU PAY COMPUTER THE SUM
HOW MANY PLAYS DO YOU WANT? 20
YOU START WITH 100 POINTS
TO WIN YOU NEED 112 POINTS
DO YOU WANT THE COMPUTER TO BE SMART? NO
                                  YOU     COMPUTER
YOUR PLAY(2 OR 3)? 3
   THE COMPUTER HAD 3
**** EVEN****PAYOFF= 9            109       91
YOUR PLAY(2 OR 3)? 2
   THE COMPUTER HAD 3
****ODD****PAYOFF=-5             104       96
YOUR PLAY(2 OR 3)? 3
   THE COMPUTER HAD 3
**** EVEN****PAYOFF= 9           113       87
!!!!!!!!!!!!!!!!
!!!!YOU WON!!!!
!!!!!!!!!!!!!!!!
```

IF THE COMPUTER HAD PLAYED SOME 2'S, THE OUTCOME WOULD HAVE BEEN VERY DIFFERENT.

Now let's look at a run where the computer tries to play the optimal strategy of two fingers 14/23 of the time. In this run the human (YOUR PLAY) chose two fingers 9/20 of the time (which is about 10/23). The computer actually chose two fingers 14/20 of the time (which is about 16/23). The reason for this is found in line 55 where we let B=14/23 when the user says "YES" to making the computer smart. So down in lines 530 and 550 we get more C=2 than C=3 choices

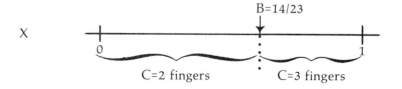

The number of C=2 choices won't be precisely 14/23 because of short-term variations in the behavior of the random generator. But for a

large number of plays, the ratio of C=2 to C=3 choices should approach 14/23.

```
RUN

RULES: YOU SHOW 2 OR 3 FINGERS; SO DOES THE COMPUTER
IF TOTAL # IS EVEN, COMPUTER PAYS YOU THE PRODUCT
IF TOTAL # IS ODD, YOU PAY COMPUTER THE SUM
HOW MANY PLAYS DO YOU WANT? 20
YOU START WITH 100 POINTS
TO WIN YOU NEED 112 POINTS
DO YOU WANT THE COMPUTER TO BE SMART? YES
                                   YOU      COMPUTER
YOUR PLAY(2 OR 3)? 2
   THE COMPUTER HAD 3
****ODD****PAYOFF=-5               95        105
YOUR PLAY(2 OR 3)? 2
   THE COMPUTER HAD 3
****ODD****PAYOFF=-5               90        110
YOUR PLAY(2 OR 3)? 3
   THE COMPUTER HAD 3
**** EVEN****PAYOFF= 9             99        101
YOUR PLAY(2 OR 3)? 3
   THE COMPUTER HAD 2
****ODD****PAYOFF=-5               94        106
YOUR PLAY(2 OR 3)? 2
   THE COMPUTER HAD 2
**** EVEN****PAYOFF= 4             98        102
YOUR PLAY(2 OR 3)? 2
   THE COMPUTER HAD 2
**** EVEN****PAYOFF= 4            102         98
YOUR PLAY(2 OR 3)? 3
   THE COMPUTER HAD 2
****ODD****PAYOFF=-5               97        103
YOUR PLAY(2 OR 3)? 3
   THE COMPUTER HAD 2
****ODD****PAYOFF=-5               92        108
YOUR PLAY(2 OR 3)? 3
   THE COMPUTER HAD 3
**** EVEN****PAYOFF= 9            101         99
YOUR PLAY(2 OR 3)? 3
   THE COMPUTER HAD 2
****ODD****PAYOFF=-5               96        104
YOUR PLAY(2 OR 3)? 2
   THE COMPUTER HAD 2
**** EVEN****PAYOFF= 4            100        100
YOUR PLAY(2 OR 3)? 3
   THE COMPUTER HAD 2
****ODD****PAYOFF=-5               95        105
YOUR PLAY(2 OR 3)? 3
   THE COMPUTER HAD 2
****ODD****PAYOFF=-5               90        110
YOUR PLAY(2 OR 3)? 2
   THE COMPUTER HAD 2
**** EVEN****PAYOFF= 4             94        106
YOUR PLAY(2 OR 3)? 2
   THE COMPUTER HAD 2
**** EVEN****PAYOFF= 4             98        102
YOUR PLAY(2 OR 3)? 2
   THE COMPUTER HAD 3
****ODD****PAYOFF=-5               93        107
YOUR PLAY(2 OR 3)? 2
   THE COMPUTER HAD 3
****ODD****PAYOFF=-5               88        112
YOUR PLAY(2 OR 3)? 3
```

```
     THE COMPUTER HAD 2
****ODD****PAYOFF=-5              83        117
YOUR PLAY(2 OR 3)? 3
     THE COMPUTER HAD 2
****ODD****PAYOFF=-5              78        122
YOUR PLAY(2 OR 3)? 3
     THE COMPUTER HAD 2
****ODD****PAYOFF=-5              73        127
THE COMPUTER WINS+*-/ FIE ON HUMANS
!#$%&()=@+*?,.<>#$%&()=+*
STOP at line 240
```

THIS IS THE SCORE AFTER 20 PLAYS.

Remember that the optimal strategy of 14/23 won't work for just a few games; it's best only in the long haul. For this reason we put a feature in the program which sets the amount needed to "win" for you. This goal is the starting $100, plus 11/23 dollars per play, *plus* a term which penalizes someone who chooses a small number of plays (the term 30/N in line 43). For 30 plays this only adds one extra point, but for someone who chooses 5 plays, it adds six points, for 3 plays 10 points, and so on.

Here's a listing of the program.

MORRA

```
LIST
1 RANDOMIZE
5 LET S1=100: LET S2=100
10 PRINT "RULES: YOU SHOW 2 OR 3 FINGERS; SO DOES THE COMPUTER"
20 PRINT "IF TOTAL # IS EVEN, COMPUTER PAYS YOU THE PRODUCT"
30 PRINT "IF TOTAL # IS ODD, YOU PAY COMPUTER THE SUM"
40 PRINT "HOW MANY PLAYS DO YOU WANT";
42 INPUT N
43 LET G=INT(100+N*11/23+30/N)
44 PRINT "YOU START WITH";S1;"POINTS"
45 PRINT "TO WIN YOU NEED";G+1;"POINTS"
50 PRINT "DO YOU WANT THE COMPUTER TO BE SMART";:INPUT A$
55 IF LEFT(A$,1)="Y" THEN LET B=14/23 ELSE LET B=9/23
90 PRINT TAB(30);"YOU";TAB(37);"COMPUTER"
100 FOR K=1 TO N
110 PRINT "YOUR PLAY(2 OR 3)";:INPUT Y
120 IF INT(Y)<>Y THEN 110
130 IF ABS(Y-2.5)>.6 THEN 110
150 GOTO 520
200 PRINT"    THE COMPUTER HAD";C
210 LET S1=S1+P:LET S2=S2-P
220 PRINT "****";N$;"****PAYOFF=";P;TAB(29);S1;TAB(38);S2
225 IF S1>G THEN 800
230 NEXT K
235 PRINT "THE COMPUTER WINS+*-/ FIE ON HUMANS"
236 PRINT"!#$%&()=@+*?,.<>#$%&()=+*"
240 STOP
510 REM-----COMPUTER CHOICE
520 LET X=RND(0)
530 IF X<B THEN 550
540 LET C=3:GOTO 610
550 LET C=2
600 REM-----CALCULATE PAYOFF
610 IF (C+Y)/2-INT((C+Y)/2)>.1 THEN 640
620 LET P=C*Y : LET N$=" EVEN"
630 GOTO 200
640 LET P=-(C+Y):LET N$="ODD"
650 GOTO 200
800 PRINT "!!!!!!!!!!!!!!!!!!"
810 PRINT"!!!!YOU WON!!!!"
815 PRINT"!!!!!!!!!!!!!!!!!!"
900 END
```

THIS "GOAL" CALCULATION IS EXPLAINED IN THE TEXT.

THE VALUE OF B IS USED IN LINE 530 TO DETERMINE HOW OFTEN THE COMPUTER PLAYS TWO FINGERS.

6.3   GRID GAMES; GAMES IN SPACE

Games can become more interesting when they are connected with the idea of movement through space. Classical board games like chess have this feature in the form of various board positions that the chess pieces can occupy. Maze games also depend on a geometrical "space" pattern that determines the various moves of the players trying to get out of the maze. Some recent sci-fi computer games rely on more complicated kinds of "boards" (called quadrant or sector maps) which show the relative positions of space ships, star bases, alien forces, and so on.

The idea of a game board can be made more useful for computer games by using something called a game grid instead. This is usually nothing more than an X-Y coordinate system for two dimensions, or an X-Y-Z coordinate system for three dimensions. An example of a three dimensional grid game would be 3-D Tictactoe where there are 27 positions in which plays can be made.

The picture below shows a two-dimensional board for a "sea battle" game on the left, and the corresponding grid form on the right.

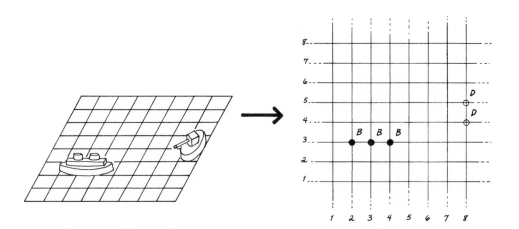

The grid form is useful because we can describe board positions with pairs of numbers. For example, our picture shows the ship "B" at positions (2,3),(3,3), and (4,3). The ship "D" is at positions (8,4) and (8,5). Numbers like this are needed if we wish to play computer games, since computers can't "see" the board. Let's illustrate how this all works with a game played on a 10 x 10 grid.

Spies on a Grid

The following program is a game that is a grid version of hide and seek. It's also a good way to become familiar with the X-Y or *Cartesian* Coordinate system. The program asks you to find four "spies" hidden at grid points on a ten by ten grid. Allowable grid points have the form (J,K) where J and K are integers between 0 and 9 inclusive. The player is given ten tries in which to find the positions of the spies. After each try, the player is told how close his or her guess was to each spy. At the end of the game, you can ask to see where the spies you didn't find were hidden. If you play another game, the spies move to new hidden locations.

After playing the game "in your head", you should also try it with the aid of graph paper and a compass. You will probably learn to find all the players in six or seven moves by using an approach that is similar to some radio navigational systems (e.g. LORAN). You'll also get some ideas on improving the game program.

A sample run of the program is shown at first. This is followed by a flow chart which explains the logic of the program. The numbers on the flow chart correspond to the statement numbers in the program listing, which is given after the flow chart.

```
RUN

THIS IS THE GAME OF SPIES ON A GRID
THE OBJECT IS TO FIND 4 SPIES HIDDEN ON A 10 X 10 GRID
YOUR SEARCH BASE IS AT (0,0).  ANY GUESS
YOU MAKE SHOULD CONTAIN TWO NUMBERS SEPARATED
BY COMMAS.  THE FIRST GIVES THE UNIT DISTANCE RIGHT
OF BASE AND THE SECOND IS THE UNIT DISTANCE ABOVE BASE.

LET'S BEGIN


TURN NUMBER 1 , WHAT IS YOUR GUESS?
? 4,5
YOUR DISTANCE FROM SPY 1 IS 5.8
YOUR DISTANCE FROM SPY 2 IS 4.2
YOUR DISTANCE FROM SPY 3 IS 3
YOUR DISTANCE FROM SPY 4 IS 3


TURN NUMBER 2 , WHAT IS YOUR GUESS?
? 4,2
YOUR DISTANCE FROM SPY 1 IS 3.6
YOUR DISTANCE FROM SPY 2 IS 3
YOUR DISTANCE FROM SPY 3 IS 4.2
YOU HAVE FOUND SPY 4


TURN NUMBER 3 , WHAT IS YOUR GUESS?
? 7,5
YOUR DISTANCE FROM SPY 1 IS 5
YOUR DISTANCE FROM SPY 2 IS 3
YOU HAVE FOUND SPY 3


TURN NUMBER 4 , WHAT IS YOUR GUESS?
? 7,0
YOU HAVE FOUND SPY 1
YOUR DISTANCE FROM SPY 2 IS 2


TURN NUMBER 5 , WHAT IS YOUR GUESS?
? 7,1
YOUR DISTANCE FROM SPY 2 IS 1


TURN NUMBER 6 , WHAT IS YOUR GUESS?
? 7,0
YOUR DISTANCE FROM SPY 2 IS 2


TURN NUMBER 7 , WHAT IS YOUR GUESS?
? 7,2
YOU HAVE FOUND SPY 2

YOU HAVE FOUND ALL THE SPIES IN  7  TURNS!

DO YOU WANT TO PLAY AGAIN?
? NO
GOOD DAY
```

TO FOLLOW THE REST OF THIS RUN, PUT X MARKS AT GUESSES, AND O MARKS AT PLACES WHERE SPIES ARE FOUND.

The logic of this game can be described by this flowchart:

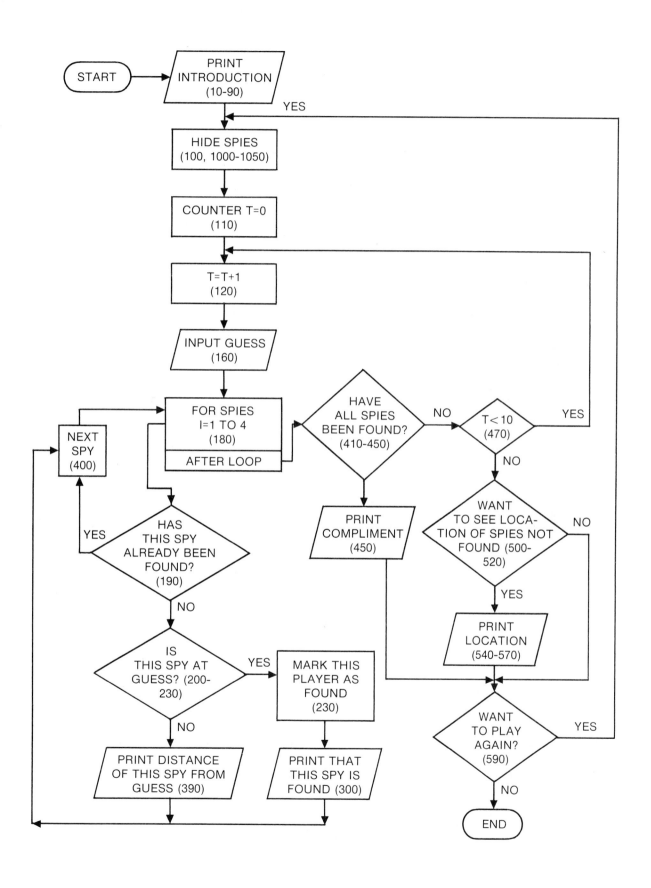

Here's a more normal RUN in which the user doesn't get all the spies in 10 guesses. Most of the guessing here was done by following "hunches". A better approach is to either use a compass on a grid to see where the spies might be, or to "calculate" where they are using the Pythagorean theorem. (This says that in a right triangle, the square of the hypotenuse equals the sum of the squares of the other two sides.)

```
RUN

THIS IS THE GAME OF SPIES ON A GRID
THE OBJECT IS TO FIND 4 SPIES HIDDEN ON A 10 X 10 GRID
YOUR SEARCH BASE IS AT (0,0).  ANY GUESS
YOU MAKE SHOULD CONTAIN TWO NUMBERS SEPARATED
BY COMMAS.  THE FIRST GIVES THE UNIT DISTANCE RIGHT
OF BASE AND THE SECOND IS THE UNIT DISTANCE ABOVE BASE.

LET'S BEGIN


TURN NUMBER 1 , WHAT IS YOUR GUESS?
? 5,6
YOUR DISTANCE FROM SPY 1 IS 1.4
YOUR DISTANCE FROM SPY 2 IS 3.1
YOUR DISTANCE FROM SPY 3 IS 4.1
YOUR DISTANCE FROM SPY 4 IS 2


TURN NUMBER 2 , WHAT IS YOUR GUESS?
? 5,8
YOUR DISTANCE FROM SPY 1 IS 1.4
YOUR DISTANCE FROM SPY 2 IS 1.4
YOUR DISTANCE FROM SPY 3 IS 5
YOUR DISTANCE FROM SPY 4 IS 2.8


TURN NUMBER 3 , WHAT IS YOUR GUESS?
? 4,7
YOU HAVE FOUND SPY 1
YOUR DISTANCE FROM SPY 2 IS 2.8
YOUR DISTANCE FROM SPY 3 IS 5.3
YOUR DISTANCE FROM SPY 4 IS 3.1


TURN NUMBER 4 , WHAT IS YOUR GUESS?
? 3,3
YOUR DISTANCE FROM SPY 2 IS 6.7
YOUR DISTANCE FROM SPY 3 IS 6.3
YOUR DISTANCE FROM SPY 4 IS 5
```

THIS PLAYER DIDN'T DO VERY WELL. FOLLOW THE RUN WITH A GRID DIAGRAM TO SEE WHERE HE WENT WRONG.

```
TURN NUMBER 5 , WHAT IS YOUR GUESS?
? 3,8
YOUR DISTANCE FROM SPY 2 IS 3.1
YOUR DISTANCE FROM SPY 3 IS 6.7
YOUR DISTANCE FROM SPY 4 IS 4.4


TURN NUMBER 6 , WHAT IS YOUR GUESS?
? 8,3
YOUR DISTANCE FROM SPY 2 IS 6.3
YOUR DISTANCE FROM SPY 3 IS 2.2
YOUR DISTANCE FROM SPY 4 IS 3.1


TURN NUMBER 7 , WHAT IS YOUR GUESS?
? 3,0
YOUR DISTANCE FROM SPY 2 IS 9.4
YOUR DISTANCE FROM SPY 3 IS 7.8
YOUR DISTANCE FROM SPY 4 IS 7.2


TURN NUMBER 8 , WHAT IS YOUR GUESS?
? 7,6
YOUR DISTANCE FROM SPY 2 IS 3.1
YOUR DISTANCE FROM SPY 3 IS 2.2
YOU HAVE FOUND SPY 4


TURN NUMBER 9 , WHAT IS YOUR GUESS?
? 4,8
YOUR DISTANCE FROM SPY 2 IS 2.2
YOUR DISTANCE FROM SPY 3 IS 5.8


TURN NUMBER 10 , WHAT IS YOUR GUESS?
? 6,8
YOUR DISTANCE FROM SPY 2 IS 1
YOUR DISTANCE FROM SPY 3 IS 4.2

YOU DIDN'T FIND ALL THE SPIES IN TEN TRIES.
DO YOU WANT TO KNOW WHERE THE SPIES YOU DIDN'T
FIND WERE HIDDEN?
? YES
SPY 2 HID AT ( 6 , 9 ).
SPY 3 HID AT ( 9 , 5 ).

DO YOU WANT TO PLAY AGAIN?
? NO
GOOD DAY
```

Here's a listing of the spies program. It should be studied in conjunction with the flowchart just given. For example, to see how the block HIDE SPIES works, study line 100, and the subroutine in lines 1000 to 1050.

SPIES
ON A GRID

```
LIST

10 DIM P(4,2)
20 PRINT "THIS IS THE GAME OF SPIES ON A GRID"
30 PRINT "THE OBJECT IS TO FIND 4 SPIES HIDDEN ON A 10 X 10 GRID"
40 PRINT "YOUR SEARCH BASE IS AT (0,0).  ANY GUESS"
50 PRINT "YOU MAKE SHOULD CONTAIN TWO NUMBERS SEPARATED"
60 PRINT "BY COMMAS.  THE FIRST GIVES THE UNIT DISTANCE RIGHT"
70 PRINT "OF BASE AND THE SECOND IS THE UNIT DISTANCE ABOVE BASE."
80 PRINT
90 PRINT "LET'S BEGIN"
100 GOSUB 1000
110 LET T=0
120 LET T=T+1
130 PRINT
140 PRINT
150 PRINT "TURN NUMBER";T;", WHAT IS YOUR GUESS?"
160 INPUT M,N
180 FOR I=1 TO 4
190 IF P(I,1)=-1 THEN 400
200 IF P(I,1)<>M THEN 380
220 IF P(I,2)<>N THEN 380
230 LET P(I,1)=-1
300 PRINT "YOU HAVE FOUND SPY";I
310 GOTO 400
380 LET D=SQR((P(I,1)-M)^2 + (P(I,2)-N)^2)
390 PRINT "YOUR DISTANCE FROM SPY";I;"IS";INT(D*100+.5)/100
400 NEXT I
410 FOR J=1 TO 4
420 IF P(J,1)<>-1 GOTO 470
430 NEXT J
440 PRINT
450 PRINT "YOU HAVE FOUND ALL THE SPIES IN ";T;" TURNS!"
460 GOTO 580
470 IF T<10 GOTO 120
480 PRINT
490 PRINT "YOU DIDN'T FIND ALL THE SPIES IN TEN TRIES."
500 PRINT "DO YOU WANT TO KNOW WHERE THE SPIES YOU DIDN'T"
510 PRINT "FIND WERE HIDDEN?"
520 INPUT B$
530 IF B$="NO" GOTO 580
540 FOR I=1 TO 4
550 IF P(I,1)=-1 GOTO 570
560 PRINT "SPY";I;"HID AT (";P(I,1);",";P(I,2);")."
570 NEXT I
580 PRINT
590 PRINT "DO YOU WANT TO PLAY AGAIN?"
600 INPUT C$
610 IF C$="YES" GOTO 100
620 PRINT "GOOD DAY"
630 GOTO 9999
1000 FOR J=1 TO 2
1010 FOR I=1 TO 4
1020 P(I,J)=INT(10*RND(1))
1030 NEXT I
1040 NEXT J
1050 RETURN
3990 PRINT
9999 END
```

6.4 GAMES OF CHANCE

The lure of the gambling casino is often connected with a belief that something called "luck" is just around the corner. Playing strategies are usually so simple (bet or not bet on some random event), that very little skill is involved. Such games are appropriately called "games of chance".

An exception to this situation is found in card games, which have both elements of chance and elements of skill. The game of "blackjack", for example, is one of the few casino games where a skillful player can influence the outcome. More complicated card games give a clever player even better odds, which is why they are usually not found in casinos.

A new idea for casino games (suggested by the advent of small computers), would be to have a "player vs. machine" contest. If the machine had a known playing strategy, the game could be practiced on one's own computer. Presumably the human player has a greater ability to learn, and could therefore, develop a counter-strategy for outfoxing the machine down at the casino. (We will not consider programs where the computer's strategy improves with time. This is a rather advanced subject, and the literature on chess playing games gives some indication of what's involved.)

We'll illustrate the player vs. machine idea by looking at a card-playing program called Crazy Eights. Before doing this, let's first look at a sub-problem common to all computer card playing simulations, namely the problem of writing a card-shuffling, card-dealing program.

A Poker Hand Shuffling and Dealing Program

Math books tell us that the number of different ways a poker hand can be dealt is given by the expression

$$C(52,5) = \frac{52!}{47!\ 5!} = 2,589,960$$

where the symbol 52! means "52 factorial", that is, 52*51*50*49* ... *3*2*1 (which is a very large number). The notation C(52,5) is shorthand for "combinations of 52 things taken 5 at a time", and the formula with the 3 factorials calculates how many such "combinations" can be formed. A *combination* is a grouping that does not allow repetitions (you can't have two aces of spades), and in which the order of the objects is not important (a pair followed by three of a kind is the same hand as three of a kind followed by a pair).

We won't use this formula, or write a program to systematically generate all these hands—it would take far too long. Instead, we'll use the RND function to simulate the way people "randomly" deal cards in a game.

Let's first look at a program that illustrates an "obvious" approach to the card-dealing problem, but which is actually a bad solution. We'll designate the possible cards by the numbers 1 to 52 (later we'll get fancier and use names like "3 of hearts" or "ace of spades"). Our program will first create a deck of cards by loading the numbers 1 to 52 into an array C(K) which can be thought of as holding the entire deck of cards.

```
10 DIM C(52)
20 FOR K = 1 TO 52
30 LET C(K) = K
40 NEXT K
```

Next we'll make a poker hand by randomly choosing five cards from this deck, and putting them in a "hand" array H(I)

```
50 FOR I= 1 TO 5
60 LET X=INT(52*RND+1)
70 IF C(X)<0 THEN 60
80 LET H(I)=C(X)
90 LET C(X)=-1
100 NEXT I
110 PRINT "CARDS IN HAND ARE"
120 FOR I=1 TO 5
130 PRINT H(I)
140 NEXT I
150 END
```

In line 80 a card C(X) (which was randomly picked) is placed in the Ith card of the hand. Then, to make sure this card is never used again, line 90 changes its value to -1. In this way, the test in line 70 can make sure previously used cards are never used.

What's wrong with this program? While it will work, it will take very long to run as more and more cards are dealt, or in a game where several hands are needed. This is because more and more cards will be marked -1 (already used). So the test in 70 will be "true" more and more, which means the program will have to try again and again to get an unused card.

A much better approach will be to move the "used" cards out of the way, and not even look at them. Here's how this can be done:

```
45 LET D=53
50 FOR I=1 TO 5
60 LET D=D-1
70 LET X=INT(D*RND+1)
80 LET H(I)=C(X)
90 LET C(X)=C(D)
100 NEXT I
```

Line 80 puts a randomly chosen card C(X) in the hand. So C(X) should not be used again. In this program, a card that is "used" is replaced by an unused card from the "bottom" of the deck (see line 90). When the next card is randomly picked, we only look at *unused* cards, because line 70 only generates random numbers from 1 to D (*not* from 1 to 52). Although D starts out as 52, it gets reduced by 1 each time a card is dealt.

Let's put all these ideas together in a card-dealing program that gives N poker players 5 cards each. To make it more useful, we'll print the cards in a more conventional notation, that is, a "1" will print as ACE OF HEARTS, a "2" will print as TWO OF HEARTS, etc., with "52" printing as KING OF SPADES.

The technique for doing this will be to break a number like H(I)=52 into two parts:

$$Q = INT((H(I)-1)/13) \qquad \text{and} \qquad Y = H(I)-Q*13$$

For   H(I)=52,

$$Q = INT(51/13) = 3 \qquad \text{and} \qquad Y=52-3*13=13$$

In general, the number Y will be 1,2,3,...,13
while Q+1 will be 1,2,3, or 4.

The numbers 1 to 13 can be translated into names like "ACE OF", "TWO OF",..., "KING OF", while the numbers 1 to 4 can become "HEARTS", "CLUBS", "DIAMONDS", and "SPADES".

Here's a listing of a complete program that incorporates all of these ideas, followed by two runs showing the deals to four players for two successive hands.

POKER DEALER

```
LIST

1 RANDOMIZE
5 DIM A$(13),C(52)
10  A$(1)="ACE OF "
11  A$(2)="TWO OF "
12  A$(3)="THREE OF "
13  A$(4)="FOUR OF "
14  A$(5)="FIVE OF "
15  A$(6)="SIX OF "
16  A$(7)="SEVEN OF "
17  A$(8)="EIGHT OF "
18  A$(9)="NINE OF "
19  A$(10)="TEN OF "
20  A$(11)="JACK OF "
21  A$(12)="QUEEN OF "
22  A$(13)="KING OF "
23  B$(1)="HEARTS"
24  B$(2)="CLUBS"
25  B$(3)="DIAMONDS"
26  B$(4)="SPADES"
30  FOR I=1 TO 52:C(I)=I:NEXT I
35  D=53
90  PRINT "HOW MANY PLAYERS";:INPUT N
95  FOR K=1 TO N
100 FOR I=1 TO 5
110 D=D-1
120 X=INT(D*RND(0)+1)
130 H(I)=C(X)
135 C(X)=C(D)
140 Q=INT((H(I)-1)/13)
150 Y=H(I)-1-Q*13
160 H$(I)=A$(Y+1)+B$(Q+1)
170 NEXT I
190 PRINT
200 PRINT "THE CARDS FOR PLAYER #";K;" ARE:"
210 FOR J=1 TO 5
220 PRINT H$(J)
230 NEXT J
235 NEXT K
240 END
```

```
RUN

HOW MANY PLAYERS? 4

THE CARDS FOR PLAYER # 1  ARE:
JACK OF HEARTS
FIVE OF SPADES
KING OF SPADES
FOUR OF DIAMONDS
EIGHT OF DIAMONDS

THE CARDS FOR PLAYER # 2  ARE:
QUEEN OF DIAMONDS
KING OF CLUBS
SEVEN OF HEARTS
TEN OF DIAMONDS
TWO OF DIAMONDS

THE CARDS FOR PLAYER # 3  ARE:
SEVEN OF SPADES
SIX OF DIAMONDS
EIGHT OF HEARTS
JACK OF SPADES
JACK OF DIAMONDS

THE CARDS FOR PLAYER # 4  ARE:
KING OF HEARTS
THREE OF CLUBS
SIX OF CLUBS
TEN OF HEARTS
THREE OF SPADES



RUN

HOW MANY PLAYERS? 4

THE CARDS FOR PLAYER # 1  ARE:
QUEEN OF DIAMONDS
KING OF HEARTS
ACE OF HEARTS
FIVE OF SPADES
NINE OF HEARTS

THE CARDS FOR PLAYER # 2  ARE:
SEVEN OF HEARTS
EIGHT OF HEARTS
KING OF SPADES
QUEEN OF CLUBS
SEVEN OF DIAMONDS

THE CARDS FOR PLAYER # 3  ARE:
TEN OF CLUBS
SEVEN OF CLUBS
KING OF DIAMONDS
TWO OF SPADES
JACK OF HEARTS

THE CARDS FOR PLAYER # 4  ARE:
EIGHT OF SPADES
ACE OF SPADES
KING OF CLUBS
FOUR OF CLUBS
TEN OF HEARTS
```

Crazy Eights

The rules for playing the Crazy Eights game are as follows. A standard 52 card deck is used, with both the computer and the human player being dealt a hand of seven cards. The rest of the deck is placed face down to form the stack. The top card of the stack is turned face up and placed beside it to form the starter. The first player must place on the starter a card that matches it either in suit or in rank. Each in turn must thus place one card on the starter pile, matching the last played.

If unable to play in turn, a player must draw cards one by one from the top of the stack until he is able and willing to play, or until he exhausts the stack. After the stack is exhausted, a hand must play in turn if it can; when it cannot, the turn passes.

All eights are wild. An eight may be played regardless of the last previous card, and regardless of whether the hand is able to play a natural card at that time. In playing an eight, the owner must name a suit, and the next card played must be of that suit (or another eight). No limitation as to rank may be made in playing an eight.

The player first to get rid of all his cards wins. If the stack is exhausted and no hand can play, the game ends as a block.

In scoring, the winner collects for all cards remaining in the other hand: 50 for each eight, 10 for each face card, 1 for each ace, and the index value for each other card. If the deal ends in a block, the player with the lowest count collects the difference of counts.

Here's a run of a program which simulates the playing of Crazy Eights. The program is interactive, continually matching the computer's strategy against the human player. A good way to follow the program is to use an actual deck of cards, playing the cards for both players as shown in the run:

```
RUN

CRAZY EIGHTS PROGRAM

ENTER CARD NAMES AS VALUE FOLLOWED BY A SUIT
THE CARD VALUES ARE: 2=2,3=3,4=4,5=5,6=6,7=7,8=8,9=9,10=10,
                     JACK=J,QUEEN=Q,KING=K,ACE=A
THE SUITS ARE: C=CLUB,D=DIAMOND,H=HEART,S=SPADE
IF YOU WANT TO PICK A CARD ANSWER 'NO' WHEN ASKED FOR YOUR PLAY


THE FIRST CARD DOWN IS AS

YOUR HAND IS: AH  3H  4D  5D  6S  7C  JD
DO YOU WISH TO PLAY A CARD? AH

WITH 7 CARD(S) LEFT, I PLAY A AD

YOUR HAND IS: 3H  4D  5D  6S  7C  JD
DO YOU WISH TO PLAY A CARD? 5D

WITH 6 CARD(S) LEFT, I PLAY A 6D
```

```
YOUR HAND IS: 3H  4D  6S  7C   JD
DO YOU WISH TO PLAY A CARD? 4D

WITH 5 CARD(S) LEFT, I PLAY A KD

YOUR HAND IS: 3H  6S  7C  JD
DO YOU WISH TO PLAY A CARD? JD

WITH 4 CARD(S) LEFT, I PLAY A JC

YOUR HAND IS: 3H  6S  7C
DO YOU WISH TO PLAY A CARD? 7C

WITH 3 CARD(S) LEFT, I PLAY A 2C

YOUR HAND IS: 3H  6S
DO YOU WISH TO PLAY A CARD? 3C
YOU DO NOT HAVE THIS CARD
DO YOU WISH TO PLAY A CARD? NO

YOUR HAND IS: 3H  6S  QS
DO YOU WISH TO PLAY A CARD? NO

YOUR HAND IS: 3H  6S  QS  KC
DO YOU WISH TO PLAY A CARD? KC

WITH 3 CARD(S) LEFT, I PLAY A 4C

YOUR HAND IS: 3H  6S  QS
DO YOU WISH TO PLAY A CARD? 3H
THAT IS NOT A LEGAL PLAY
DO YOU WISH TO PLAY A CARD? NO

YOUR HAND IS: 2D  3H  6S  QS
DO YOU WISH TO PLAY A CARD? NO

YOUR HAND IS: 2D  3H  6S  7S  QS
DO YOU WISH TO PLAY A CARD? NO

YOUR HAND IS: 2D  3H  4H  6S  7S   QS
DO YOU WISH TO PLAY A CARD? 4K
4K IS NOT A CARD
DO YOU WISH TO PLAY A CARD? NO

YOUR HAND IS: 2D  3H  4H  6S  7S  10H   QS
DO YOU WISH TO PLAY A CARD? 4H

WITH 2 CARD(S) LEFT, I PLAY A 7H

YOUR HAND IS: 2D  3H  6S  7S  10H   QS
DO YOU WISH TO PLAY A CARD? 7S

WITH 1 CARD(S) LEFT, I PLAY A 10S

YOUR SCORE IS  0
MY SCORE IS   31
I WON THAT HAND

DO YOU WISH TO PLAY AGAIN? NO

OUT OF 1 HAND(S) YOU WON 0 . YOUR TOTAL SCORE IS 0  ; MINE IS 31
LOOKS LIKE I AM HIGH SCORER
```

Explanation of How Crazy Eights Works

Crazy Eights was written in BASIC-PLUS. A project at the end of this chapter suggests you write it in minimal BASIC, using only the main ideas in our version. The key to understanding the program is to understand the data structures used. In particular, you need to know how we used some arrays to point to cards in hands, or in the deck of unused cards.

There are three "logical" arrays* D%,G%, and H% used in conjunction with a string array D$. Array D$ contains an ordered list of card names, D$(1) = "Ace of Clubs," D$(2) = "Ace of Diamonds" etc. (The order is Ace (considered a 1) of clubs, Ace of diamonds, Ace of hearts, Ace of spades, then 2 of clubs, 2 of diamonds, 2 of hearts, 2 of spades, then 3 of clubs, etc. The Jack is considered 11, Queen is 12, and King is 13).

Array D% tells us whether it is "true" or "false" that a given card is left in the deck. We agree that "true" in position I of D% is represented by making D%(I)=-1. So if D%(I)=-1, then D$(5) (2 of clubs) is still left in the deck. Similarly "false" is represented by making D%(I)=0. So if D%(18)=0, this means that the D$(18) card (the 5 of diamonds) is no longer in the deck.

The array G% is used to describe the human player's hand. Elements with value "true" in array G% point to cards in the human's hand. Finally, elements with value "true" in array H% indicate which cards are in the computer's hands.

Variables D1, H1, and H2 remember the total number of cards in the deck, the human's hand, and the computer's hand respectively. String variable C$ contains the name of the last card played. If C$ has no card value but is just a suit, this indicates that the last card played was an 8. In this case, C$ is the suit called for.

Logical variable B% is used to indicate if any player has been blocked yet. Variable B keeps count of the number of blocked plays in a row. Two blocked plays in a row ends the game.

---

*NOTE: If your version of BASIC doesn't have logical variables, just use ordinary variables. Instead of D%(52) use D(52), instead of G%(52) use G(52), and instead of H%(52) use H(52). Then change statements like IF G%(K) THEN 100 (which means "IF G%(K) is true then go to 100") to the form: IF G(K)=-1 THEN 100. You'll also have to change a statement like "IF NOT B% THEN 500" (which means "IF B% is not true then 500") to IF B=0 THEN 500. Logical variables are actually integer variables which take on only one of two values: 0(zero) which is taken to mean "false", and -1 which is taken to mean "true". (Chapter 10 explains integer variables.)

Finally, arrays U$ and C$ are just lists of the suit* and card values respectively. Array Z parallels array D$. Array Z contains the point value for scoring each card in the deck. Variables N1, N2, and N3 store the number of games the human won, the computer won, and total number of games respectively. Variables S1 and S2 store the total score for the human and computer respectively. Variables C1 and C2 store the point scores of the current game for the human and the computer.

We'll next show a listing of the program, and then follow this with an explanation of the lines in this listing.

CRAZY EIGHTS

```
LIST

10 RANDOMIZE
50 PRINT "CRAZY EIGHTS PROGRAM": PRINT
100 DIM D%(52),G%(52),H%(52),D$(52),Z(52),U$(4),C$(13)
130 MAT READ U$: MAT READ C$: MAT READ Z
200 DATA C,D,H,S
210 DATA A,2,3,4,5,6,7,8,9,10,J,Q,K
220 DATA 1,1,1,1,2,2,2,2,3,3,3,3,4,4,4,4,5,5,5,5,6,6,6,6,7,7,7,7
230 DATA 50,50,50,50,9,9,9,9,10,10,10,10,10,10,10,10,10,10,10,10
240 DATA 10,10,10,10
300 PRINT "ENTER CARD NAMES AS VALUE FOLLOWED BY A SUIT"
301 PRINT "THE CARD VALUES ARE: 2=2,3=3,4=4,5=5,6=6,7=7,8=8,9=9,10=10,"
302 PRINT "                     JACK=J,QUEEN=Q,KING=K,ACE=A"
303 PRINT "THE SUITS ARE: C=CLUB,D=DIAMOND,H=HEART,S=SPADE"
304 PRINT "IF YOU WANT TO PICK A CARD ANSWER 'NO' WHEN ASKED FOR YOUR PLAY"
305 PRINT
350 D$(I+J*4)=C$(J+1)+U$(I) FOR J=0 TO 12 FOR I=1 TO 4
450 MAT G%=ZER: MAT H%=ZER
510 MAT D%=CON : MAT D%=(-1%)*D%: D1=52: G%(FND(0)),H%(FND(0))=-1% FOR I=1 TO 7:
        C$=D$(FND(0)): H1,H2=7 : B=0: B%=0%:
        PRINT: PRINT "THE FIRST CARD DOWN IS ";C$
520 PRINT
750 IF H2=0 OR B=2 THEN 800 ELSE GOSUB 3000: PRINT
780 IF NOT(H1=0 OR B=2) THEN GOSUB 6000: PRINT: GOTO 750
800 C1,C2=0
810 IF H2<>0 THEN PRINT: PRINT "CARD(S) LEFT IN MY HAND: ";:
        FOR I=1 TO 52:
        PRINT D$(I);" "; IF H%(I):
        C1=C1+Z(I) IF H%(I): NEXT I: PRINT
820 C2=C2+Z(I) IF G%(I) FOR I=1 TO 52
830 IF C1=0 THEN 850 ELSE IF C1>=C2 THEN C1=C1-C2: C2=0: GOTO 850
840 C2=C2-C1: C1=0
850 S1=S1+C1: S2=S2+C2
870 PRINT "YOUR SCORE IS ";C1: PRINT "MY SCORE IS ";C2
890 IF C2<C1 THEN PRINT "YOU WON THAT HAND": N1=N1+1: GOTO 950
930 PRINT "I WON THAT HAND": N2=N2+1
950 PRINT: N3=N3+1: INPUT "DO YOU WISH TO PLAY AGAIN"; Z9$:
        IF Z9$="YES" THEN 450 ELSE PRINT: PRINT "OUT OF";N3;"HAND(S) YOU ";
        "WON";N1;". YOUR TOTAL SCORE IS";S1;" ; MINE IS";S2;".":
        IF S1>S2 THEN PRINT "LOOKS LIKE YOU ARE HIGH SCORER." ELSE
        PRINT "LOOKS LIKE I AM HIGH SCORER"
999 GOTO 6410
```

*The order of suits varies with games. You've probably noticed that in the card-dealing program we used the order HEARTS, CLUBS, DIAMONDS, SPADES. In the Crazy Eights program we used CLUBS, DIAMONDS, HEARTS, SPADES. All that matters is that you *know* the order, and do scoring according to the game's rules.

```
3000 PRINT "YOUR HAND IS: ";:
        PRINT D$(I);"  "; IF G%(I) FOR I=1 TO 52: PRINT
5000 INPUT "DO YOU WISH TO PLAY A CARD";Z9$
5020 IF Z9$<>"NO" THEN 5080
5025 IF D1>0 THEN 5030 ELSE IF NOT B% THEN PRINT "ALL THE CARDS ARE DEALT":
        B%=-1%: GOTO 5000
5028 PRINT "YOU ARE BLOCKED": B=B+1: RETURN
5030 I=FND(0): H1=H1+1: G%(I)=-1%: PRINT: GOTO 3000
5080 GOTO 5100 IF D$(I)=Z9$ FOR I=1 TO 52:
        PRINT Z9$;" IS NOT A CARD": GOTO 5000
5100 IF INSTR(1,C$,U$(I-INT((I-1)/4)*4))=0 AND INSTR(1,D$(I),"8")=0 AND
        INSTR(1,C$,C$(INT((I-1)/4)+1))=0 THEN
        PRINT "THAT IS NOT A LEGAL PLAY": GOTO 5000
5150 IF NOT G%(I) THEN PRINT "YOU DO NOT HAVE THIS CARD": GOTO 5000
5220 G%(I)=0: C$=D$(I): H1=H1-1: IF INSTR(1,C$,"8")=0 THEN
        B=0: RETURN
5230 INPUT "WHAT SUIT DO YOU WISH";S9$
5235 FOR I=1 TO 4: IF S9$=U$(I) THEN C$=U$(I):
        B=0: RETURN
5240 NEXT I: PRINT S9$;" IS NOT A SUIT": GOTO 5230
6000 GOTO 6160 IF H%(I) AND INSTR(1,D$(I),"8")=0 AND
        (INSTR(1,C$,U$(I-INT((I-1)/4)*4)) OR INSTR(1,C$,C$(INT((I-1)/4)+1)))
        FOR I=1 TO 52
6061 GOTO 6160 IF H%(I) FOR I=29 TO 32
6070 IF D1>0 THEN 6080 ELSE IF NOT B% THEN PRINT "ALL THE CARDS HAVE BEEN DEALT":
        B%=-1%
6075 PRINT "I AM BLOCKED": B=B+1: RETURN
6080 H%(FND(0))=-1%: H2=H2+1: GOTO 6000
6160 C$=D$(I): B=0: H%(I)=0%: H2=H2-1: PRINT "WITH";H2+1;"CARD(S) LEFT, ";:
        IF INSTR(1,C$,"8")=0 THEN PRINT "I PLAY A ";C$:
        RETURN
6210 MAT Y=ZER: Y(J)=Y(J)+1 IF H%(K) FOR K=J TO 52 STEP 4 FOR J=1 TO 4:
        P=1: P=J IF Y(J)>Y(P) FOR J=2 TO 4: C$=U$(P):
        PRINT "I CALL THE SUIT ";C$: RETURN
6300 DEF FND(X)
6310 K=INT(RND*52+1):
        GOTO 6320 IF D%(K1) FOR K1=K TO 52:
        GOTO 6320 IF D%(K1) FOR K1=1 TO K-1: STOP
6320 D%(K1)=0%: FND=K1: D1=D1-1: FNEND
6410 END
```

Explanation of Major Program Segments

Line	Explanation
10—350	This initializes arrays U$, C$ and D$, and prints out the rules of the game. Each MAT READ will have to be replaced with a FOR loop READ in minimal BASIC.
450—520	This initializes arrays D%, G%, and H% for a game. It puts 7 cards in both the computer's and the human's hand and picks the first card to be played. Also variables H1, H2, D1, B, B1%, and B2% are initialized.
750—780	Here is the heart of the game. The play alternates between the human (subroutine 3000) and the computer (subroutine 6000) until one of the players runs out of cards, or both players are blocked.
800—999	The score is computed and printed. The human is asked if another game is wanted.

3000—5240	These lines correspond to the human's turn. Let's break it down a bit further:
3000	The human is asked for his or her play.
5025—5030	A card is picked from the deck.
5080—5150	The card that the human plays is checked to make sure it is a real card, and a legal play, and that the human has the card.
5220	The card is removed from the human's hand.
5230—5240	When the card is an eight, the human calls a suit. This suit is checked to make sure it is legal.
6000—6210	The computer's move is created here.
6000	First, the computer checks to see if it has a card with either a similar suit or value equal to the one the human played. It skips over eights at this point.
6061	If it doesn't find a useable card at line 6000, it then checks for eights.
6070—6080	If it doesn't have a card to play, it picks a card from the deck and starts the search all over again.
6160	The computer removes the card played from its hand, prints the number of cards left in its hand, and the name of the card it played.
6210	If an eight was played, the computer looks for the best suit to call. It does this by choosing the most numerous suit in its hand.
6300—6320	Here's where cards are drawn from the deck, both for dealing, and for later play. The function FND returns a number between 1 and 52. This value is used as an index to a card. Also, the card is removed from the deck, because array D% and variable D1 are changed.
	These lines use a "multi-line" function called FND. (If your BASIC doesn't permit multi-line functions, then use a subroutine instead). What FND does is to randomly choose a number between 1 and 52. If that card is not in the deck, the deck is then searched sequentially from that point until a card in the deck is found. (This is much more efficient than picking numbers randomly until a card still in the deck is found. It's an idea borrowed from the technique called "hash coding". Another approach to dealing cards is to use the technique shown earlier in the Poker Hand Dealing program.)

6.5 DYNAMIC GAMES; HORSE RACE

The next three sections will discuss games that involve motion. They'll also introduce a few formulas from physics that will be helpful in writing other motion games. Books on "classical mechanics" are a good source of further information. These usually include sections called "statics" and "dynamics".

Both sections are concerned with the study of forces applied to mechanical systems, but dynamics also investigates the *motion* that results from applying force.

Games that involve motion can be very intriguing. We'll take a look at three examples, each of which progressively uses more know-how from the field of dynamics. A fourth type of "outer space" dynamic game will be outlined in the Project Ideas section.

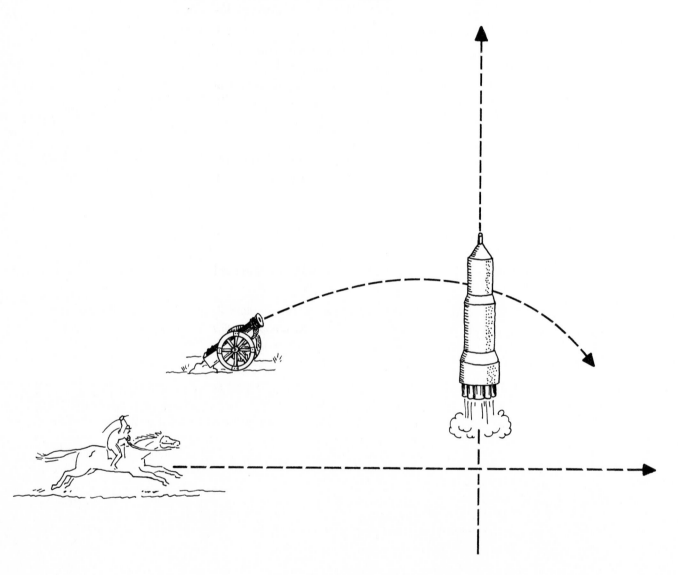

Our first game is called Horse Race, and all you have to know about dynamics is the familiar grade-school formula, distance = velocity * time. The game simulates the running of a race with horses that you enter by name. It then assigns odds to these horses, and asks for your bets. At the end of the race, the program calculates your winnings based on your bets, the posted odds, and whether your horse(s) came in first (win), second (place), or third (show). These calculations are handled by some simple multiplications (see lines 420-440, and lines 600-650).

Our program is organized around seven modules as follows:

1. The initialization module (lines 100-290) prints instructions, accepts the number and names of horses, randomly assigns odds, and asks how many bets will be made.
2. The bets are actually placed in subroutine 750-790.
3. The running of the race takes place in a sequence of four time-periods which are set up in lines 300-380.
4. The "dynamics" of the running (to determine how much each horse moves in each time period) is handled in subroutine 800-890.
5. The determination of winners and payoffs is done in subroutine 400-480.
6. The calculation of how much you win based on your bets is handled in subroutine 500-655.
7. We've called the game "Interrupt Downs" because you can change your bets at the end of the first, second, and third time periods. This is handled by subroutine 700-740.

The important arrays and variables used are the following:

Q(I)	holds the posted odds for horse #I.
D(I)	holds the distance horse #I has moved.
A(I)	holds the position of horse #I relative to the others. For example, A(5) = 3 would mean that horse #5 is in third place.
A$(I)	holds the name of horse #I.
H$(J),B(J), R$(J)	hold the horse name, bet and place for the Jth bet.
W1,P1,S1	hold the amounts paid for win, place, and show for the horse that came in first.
P2,S2	hold the amounts paid for place, and show for the horse that came in second.
S3	holds the amount paid for show for the third-place horse.

Subroutine 800 determines how far the horses move in each of the four time periods. For each period, the loop 810-811 calculates the distance D(I) for horse #I as follows:

(a) We assume that the time for each period is 10 seconds.
(b) We assume that each horse has a "basic" speed of 100 feet per second, but that it will vary by an amount that is higher for the better horses (that is, for horses with *lower* odds). This extra speed is calculated with the formula $100/Q(I)$. So for a horse with 5:1 odds, $Q(I) = 5$ and the increase is 20 feet per second. But for a horse with 2:1 odds, the increase is 50 feet per second.

(c) Now to add an element of chance, we subtract the number 50*RND from each horse's speed. This is a kind of "bad luck" term, and it represents a loss in speed that varies from 0 to 49 feet per second.

(d) Thus the net speed of horse #I is 100 + 100/Q(I)−50*RND. For a time period of 10 seconds, the distance D travelled is D=10*(100+100/Q(I)-50*RND) so D=1000+1000/Q(I)-500*RND. The *total* distance horse #I travels for the entire race is accumulated by taking the previous distance travelled (stored in the D(I) array) and adding the new distance D to it as follows:

D(I) = D(I)+D
So D(I) = D(I)+1000+1000/Q(I)-500*RND.

After these distances have been calculated for each horse in a given time period, they are printed in line 813. Then the loop 820 to 860 determines which horse is first, which is second and so on, using a sorting technique similar to that explained in Section 5.5. These positions are stored in A(I), and printed in line 870.

Here's a listing of the program followed by a run. You'll notice that you get a chance to change your bets each time period. What makes the race interesting is the random "bad luck" factor, since it can counteract the advantage of a horse with low odds. So though it is not likely, it is still possible for a long shot to win. To increase the chances for the long shots, you can try changing the -500*RND at the end of line 810 to -1000*RND.

NOTE: RND is legal in Standard BASIC, but in other versions you must use RND(1). On the TRS-80, use RND(0).

HORSE RACE

```
LIST
100 REM-----INITIALIZATION-----
160 PRINT "WELCOME TO INTERRUPT DOWNS, THE TRACK WHERE"
170 PRINT "YOU CAN CHANGE YOUR BETS DURING THE RACE"
200 PRINT "HOW MANY HORSES DO YOU WISH IN THE RACE";:INPUT N
210 PRINT "TYPE THE NAMES OF THE HORSES"
220 FOR I=1 TO N:INPUT A$(I):NEXT I
230 PRINT "YOUR ENTRIES HAVE BEEN EVALUATED. HERE ARE THE ODDS"
240 IF N>5 THEN LET A=15 ELSE LET A=7
250 FOR I=1 TO N: LET Q(I)=INT(A*RND)+2
260 PRINT A$(I);TAB(10);"----------";TAB(25);Q(I);" TO 1"
270 NEXT I:PRINT
280 PRINT "HOW MANY BETS DO YOU WISH TO PLACE";:INPUT M:PRINT
285 IF ABS(M-(N+1)/2)>(N-1)/2 THEN 280
290 GOSUB 750:PRINT
300 REM-----RUNNING OF THE RACE-----
305 PRINT "THE HORSES ARE AT THE STARTING GATE--AND"
310 PRINT "---THEY'RE OFF!!!"
320 GOSUB 800:GOSUB 700
330 PRINT "AT THE HALF THE TOTAL"
340 GOSUB 800:GOSUB 700
350 PRINT "INTO THE STRETCH THE"
360 GOSUB 800:GOSUB 700
370 PRINT "AND AT THE FINISH THE FINAL"
380 GOSUB 800
```

```
400 REM-----CALCULATION OF WINNERS & PAYOFFS-----
410 FOR I=1 TO N
420 IF A(I)=1 THEN W1$=A$(I):W1=2*Q(I):P1=1.1*Q(I):S1=.75*Q(I)
430 IF A(I)=2 THEN W2$=A$(I):P2=1.1*Q(I):S2=.75*Q(I)
440 IF A(I)=3 THEN W3$=A$(I):S3=.75*Q(I)
450 NEXT I
460 PRINT "HERE ARE THE RACE RESULTS:"
465 PRINT "HORSE";TAB(20);"WIN";TAB(30);"PLACE";TAB(40);"SHOW"
470 PRINT W1$;TAB(20);W1;TAB(30);P1;TAB(40);S1
475 PRINT W2$;TAB(30);P2;TAB(40);S2
480 PRINT W3$;TAB(40);S3:PRINT
500 REM-----BETTING RESULTS-----
505 PRINT:PRINT "HERE ARE THE RESULTS OF YOUR BETTING"
510 FOR J=1 TO M
515 IF H$(J)=W1$ THEN 535
520 IF H$(J)=W2$ THEN 555
525 IF H$(J)=W3$ THEN 570
530 GOTO 580
535 IF R$(J)="WIN" THEN 600
540 IF R$(J)="PLACE" THEN 610
545 IF R$(J)="SHOW" THEN 620
550 GOTO 580
555 IF R$(J)="PLACE" THEN 630
560 IF R$(J)="SHOW" THEN 640
565 GOTO 580
570 IF R$(J)="SHOW" THEN 650
580 NEXT J
585 STOP
600 PRINT H$(J);" PAYS $";W1*B(J)/2;" TO WIN "
605 GOTO 540
610 PRINT H$(J);" PAYS $";P1*B(J)/2;" TO PLACE"
615 GOTO 545
620 PRINT H$(J);" PAYS $";S1*B(J)/2;"TO SHOW"
625 GOTO 580
630 PRINT H$(J);" PAYS $";P2*B(J)/2;" TO PLACE"
635 GOTO 560
640 PRINT H$(J);" PAYS $";S2*B(J)/2;" TO SHOW"
645 GOTO 580
650 PRINT H$(J);" PAYS $";S3*B(J)/2;" TO SHOW"
655 GOTO 580
700 REM-----SUBROUTINE FOR CHANGING BETS-----
710 PRINT "WANT TO CHANGE BETS";:INPUT Z$
720 IF LEFT (Z$,1)="N" THEN 740
730 GOSUB 750
740 RETURN
750 REM-----SUBROUTINE FOR PLACING BETS-----
755 PRINT "TYPE NAME OF HORSE, BET, AND WIN PLACE OR SHOW"
760 FOR J=1 TO M
765 INPUT H$(J),B(J),R$(J)
770 NEXT J
775 PRINT
790 RETURN
800 REM-----SUBROUTINE FOR MOVING HORSES-----
810 FOR I=1 TO N:D(I)=D(I)+1000+1000/Q(I)-500*RND
811 NEXT I
812 PRINT "DISTANCES TRAVELLED ARE"
813 FOR I=1 TO N:PRINT D(I);:NEXT I:PRINT
820 FOR I=1 TO N
825 P=1
830 FOR K=1 TO N
835 IF D(I)<D(K) THEN P=P+1
850 NEXT K
852 A(I)=P
860 NEXT I
865 FOR I=1 TO N
870 PRINT A$(I); " IS #"; TAB(20); A(I)
875 NEXT I: PRINT
890 RETURN
999 END
```

```
RUN

WELCOME TO INTERRUPT DOWNS, THE TRACK WHERE
YOU CAN CHANGE YOUR BETS DURING THE RACE
HOW MANY HORSES DO YOU WISH IN THE RACE? 5
TYPE THE NAMES OF THE HORSES
? BALI HAI
? CONNIES CHOICE
? SCROOGE
? CHARLIES AUNT
? WILLIAM G.
YOUR ENTRIES HAVE BEEN EVALUATED. HERE ARE THE ODDS
BALI HAI   ----------      7 TO 1
CONNIES CHOICE----------   7 TO 1
SCROOGE    ----------      7 TO 1
CHARLIES AUNT----------    5 TO 1
WILLIAM G.----------       2 TO 1

HOW MANY BETS DO YOU WISH TO PLACE? 3

TYPE NAME OF HORSE, BET, AND WIN PLACE OR SHOW
? BALI HAI,100,WIN
? WILLIAM G.,50,PLACE
? SCROOGE,75,SHOW


THE HORSES ARE AT THE STARTING GATE--AND
---THEY'RE OFF!!!
DISTANCES TRAVELLED ARE
 1041.25   884.907  1009.63  722.202  1332.23
BALI HAI IS #          2
CONNIES CHOICE IS #    4
SCROOGE IS #           3
CHARLIES AUNT IS #     5
WILLIAM G. IS #        1

WANT TO CHANGE BETS? YES
TYPE NAME OF HORSE, BET, AND WIN PLACE OR SHOW
? SCROOGE,100,WIN
? WILLIAM G.,100,PLACE
? CHARLIES AUNT,50,SHOW

AT THE HALF THE TOTAL
DISTANCES TRAVELLED ARE
 1977.67  1799.08  2138.31  1895.3  2798.4
BALI HAI IS #          3
CONNIES CHOICE IS #    5
SCROOGE IS #           2
CHARLIES AUNT IS #     4
WILLIAM G. IS #        1

WANT TO CHANGE BETS? NO
INTO THE STRETCH THE
DISTANCES TRAVELLED ARE
 2659.67  2481.23  3164.67  3042.67  4031.14
BALI HAI IS #          4
CONNIES CHOICE IS #    5
SCROOGE IS #           2
CHARLIES AUNT IS #     3
WILLIAM G. IS #        1
```

```
WANT TO CHANGE BETS? NO
AND AT THE FINISH THE FINAL
DISTANCES TRAVELLED ARE
 3672.62   3250.02   4232.2   4157.3   5196.9
BALI HAI IS #         4
CONNIES CHOICE IS #   5
SCROOGE IS #          2
CHARLIES AUNT IS #    3
WILLIAM G. IS #       1

HERE ARE THE RACE RESULTS:
HORSE                 WIN       PLACE       SHOW
WILLIAM G.             4         2.2         1.5
SCROOGE                         7.7         5.25
CHARLIES AUNT                               3.75


HERE ARE THE RESULTS OF YOUR BETTING
WILLIAM G. PAYS $ 110   TO PLACE
CHARLIES AUNT PAYS $ 93.75   TO SHOW
STOP at line 585
```

6.6   PLOTTING TRAJECTORIES; THE ARCHERY GAME

Our second dynamic game is based on the physics of motion in 2-dimensions. It's a variation on the classical projectile problem. The player shoots some object (an arrow in our game) into the air. The player is allowed to specify an initial velocity and an initial angle with respect to the ground. The path (or "trajectory") of the object is then determined by the laws of motion for an object moving under the force of gravity, but with negligible air resistance. The object of the game is to hit a randomly selected target.

The player can ask for several arrows, but the greater the number requested, the less the score for a "hit". So the higher scores go to hits made by players who dared to play the game with only 1 or 2 arrows. On the other hand, asking for more arrows increases one's chance of making a hit (because you can learn how to choose A and V by studying the trajectories that missed). A table printed at the end of the program shows the relative payoff for each of these strategies.

To explain the formulas used in the program, a picture will be helpful. Imagine that the archer is at the left (marked "YOU"), and the target is at the right. Here's what a trajectory might look like.

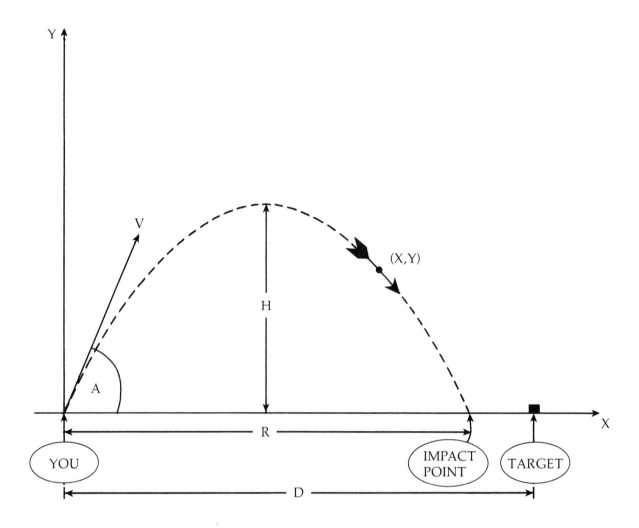

The arrow is shot with an initial angle A that you select. The player's choice must be less than 90 degrees (to avoid a hole in the head). The player must also give the arrow an initial velocity V. In our game this is limited to 100 feet per second maximum. Here are the formulas for each of the quantities shown on our diagram (to see how these formulas are derived you'll have to consult a physics book).

The position of the arrow at any time T after shooting is given by its (X,Y) coordinates

    X = V*COS(A)*T
    Y = T*(V*SIN(A)-G*T/2)

(The letter G represents the acceleration due to gravity on earth = 32.2 FT/SEC↑2.)

The maximum height reached (H), and range (R) of the arrow are given by

    H=(V*SIN(A))↑2/(2*G)
    R=V*V*SIN(2*A)/G

These last two formulas are used in our program in lines 110 and 120. Before they can be used, however, the angle A (which is supplied in degrees by the player in line 70) must be converted from degrees to radians. This is what line 100 does. The distance to the target D is calculated randomly in line 32.

To show what happens for each shot, our program prints a picture. Lines 130, 140, and 145 calculate *scale factors* which make sure the picture will fit on a terminal with 60 columns. If you only have 40 columns, change line 140 to LET S1=40/S. (Note: Scale factors were explained in Section 3.4).

The actual trajectory of the arrow is calculated in lines 200 to 290. This part of the program uses another formula derived in dynamics T1 = 2*V*SIN(A)/G. This is the total time the arrow will be in the air. Line 220 is a loop that goes from time 0 to T1, but in small clock "ticks" of T1/50. So if T1 is 100 seconds, each tick will be 2 seconds. Inside the loop, we take "snapshots" of our arrow by calculating X and Y for each tick of the clock (it's like making a time-lapse movie). When we're finished, the arrays X(M) and Y(M) will hold the position coordinates of the arrow for each one of these snapshots.

The next part of the program (lines 300 to 390) prints a picture of the trajectory. The technique used is the same as that explained in Section 7.2, so we won't go into any detail here. Then a picture of the ground line is printed in lines 400 to 450 with the positions of the archer, impact point, and target indicated by special symbols.

If the arrow misses the target, but the player still has some arrows left, the program branches from line 495 back to line 35. When an arrow hits the target, the program branches to line 515, and calculates the player's score with the formula in line 520. In this formula, N is the number of arrows requested, while K is the number actually used. Some of the possible scores this formula could give are printed in line 560. This will help competing players see how "daring" a strategy they might try on the next round.

Here's a program listing, followed by a run in which N=4 arrows were requested, and in which K=3 shots were required for a hit.

ARROW
TRAJECTORY

```
LIST

5 DIM X(100),Y(100),A$(72)
10 RANDOMIZE
15 LET G=32.2
20 PRINT "HOW MANY ARROWS DO YOU WANT";
30 INPUT N
32 LET D=INT(100*RND+50)
33 LET D=68
35 FOR K=1 TO N
50 PRINT "YOUR TARGET IS ";D"YARDS AWAY"
60 PRINT"WHAT ANGLE, VELOCITY WILL YOU USE (E;G. 35,50):";
70 INPUT A,V
80 IF A>89 THEN PRINT "MAX ANGLE=89": GOTO 60
90 IF V>100 THEN PRINT "MAX VELOCITY=100":GOTO 60
```

THIS LINE MAKES D=68 (FOR DEBUGGING). IT SHOULD BE REMOVED WHEN YOU'RE READY TO PLAY THE GAME.

```
100  LET A=A*3.14159265/180
110  LET R=V*V*SIN(2*A)/G
120  LET H=(V*SIN(A))^2/(2*G)
125  IF K>1 THEN 205
130  LET S=D:IF D<R THEN LET S=R
140  LET S1=60/S
145  LET S2=.8*S1
200  REM-----CALCULATE TRAJECTORY POINTS-----
205  T1=2*V*SIN(A)/G
210  IF T1=0 THEN LET T1=1
215  LET M=0:LET Z=0
220  FOR T=0 TO T1 STEP T1/50
225  LET M=M+1
230  LET X(M)=INT(S1*V*COS(A)*T)
240  LET Y(M)=INT(S2*(V*SIN(A)-G*T/2)*T)
245  IF Y(M)<Z THEN 290
250  LET Z=Y(M)
290  NEXT T
300  REM-----FILL & PRINT LINE IMAGE-----
305  A$(1)="I"
310  FOR I=2 TO 70:A$(I)=" ":NEXT I
320  FOR I=1 TO M
330  IF Y(I)<Z THEN 360
340  IF X(I)<63 THEN A$(X(I))="*"
350  LET Y(I)=-9
360  NEXT I
370  LET Z=Z-1
380  FOR I=1 TO 70:PRINT A$(I);:NEXT I:PRINT
390  IF Z >= 0 THEN 305
400  REM-----PRINT GROUND LINE-----
410  FOR I=1 TO 70: LET A$(I)="-": NEXT I
420  LET A$(1)="0"
425  LET A$(S1*R)="X"
430  LET A$(S1*D)="T"
440  FOR I=1 TO 70:PRINT A$(I);:NEXT I:PRINT
450  PRINT"0=YOU";TAB(S1*D-10);"T=TARGET=";D;"YARDS"
460  IF ABS(R-D)<3 THEN 480
470  PRINT "YOU MISSED BY ";R-D;"YARDS":GOTO 485
480  PRINT "HIT!!!!!!!!!!!!!!":GOTO 515
485  PRINT
490  PRINT "-------YOU HAVE";N-K;"ARROWS LEFT-------"
495  NEXT K
497  PRINT "YOU'RE OUT OF ARROWS--SCORE =0"
498  PRINT "IF YOU WANT TO TRY AGAIN TYPE RUN"
500  STOP:  REM---NEXT SECTION CALCULATES SCORES FOR HITS
515  PRINT "YOU USED";K;"OUT OF YOUR";N;"ARROWS"
517  PRINT "YOUR FINAL SCORE IS";
520  PRINT 100*(12-K)/(K*N)
530  PRINT "POSSIBLE SCORES FOR SOME CHOICES OF ARROWS ARE:"
535  PRINT "  1-ARROW 2-ARROWS 3-ARROWS 4-ARROWS 5-ARROWS 6-ARROWS"
540  FOR K=1 TO 6
550  FOR N=K TO 6
560  PRINT TAB(8*(N-1)+3);100*(12-K)/(K*N);
570  NEXT N
580  PRINT
590  NEXT K
900  END
```

```
RUN

HOW MANY ARROWS DO YOU WANT? 4
YOUR TARGET IS  68 YARDS AWAY
```

```
WHAT ANGLE, VELOCITY WILL YOU USE (E.G. 35,50):? 60,40
I                    ****
I           ****         ****
I         **               **
I       **                   **
I       **                   **
I      **                     *
I     *                       *
I     **                       *
I    *                         **
I   *                           *
I  *                             *
I  *                             *
**                               **
I                                 *
I                                 *
0-------------------------------X----------------------T---------
0=YOU                                    T=TARGET= 68 YARDS
YOU MISSED BY -24.9677 YARDS

-------YOU HAVE 3 ARROWS LEFT-------
YOUR TARGET IS  68 YARDS AWAY
WHAT ANGLE, VELOCITY WILL YOU USE (E.G. 35,50):? 45,50
I                        ** *** *** ** *
I                   ** *              ** *
I                 ***                    ** *
I               *                          *
I             **                            ** 
I           **                               * *
I          *                                  *
I          **                                  *
I         **                                    * *
I        **                                      *
I      **                                         *
I     *                                            *
I*                                                  *
*                                                    *
I
0-----------------------------------------------------T-------X--
0=YOU                                    T=TARGET= 68 YARDS
YOU MISSED BY  9.63975 YARDS

-------YOU HAVE 2 ARROWS LEFT-------
YOUR TARGET IS  68 YARDS AWAY
WHAT ANGLE, VELOCITY WILL YOU USE (E.G. 35,50):? 45,47
I                     * ****
I               * ****    * ****
I             ***           * **
I          **                 **
I        **                     **
I      * *                       **
I      *                          *
I    **                            **
I    *                              *
I   *                                *
I*                                    *
*                                      **
0------------------------------------------T----------
0=YOU                                    T=TARGET= 68 YARDS
HIT!!!!!!!!!!!!!
YOU USED 3 OUT OF YOUR 4 ARROWS
YOUR FINAL SCORE IS 75
POSSIBLE SCORES FOR SOME CHOICES OF ARROWS ARE:
```

1-ARROW	2-ARROWS	3-ARROWS	4-ARROWS	5-ARROWS	6-ARROWS
1100	550	366.667	275	220	183.333
	250	166.667	125	100	83.3333
		100	75	60	50
		50	50	40	33.3333
				28	23.3333
					16.6667

6.7   PLANET-X LANDER

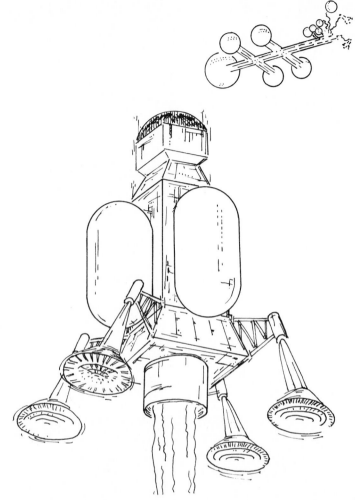

This is a simulation-game program in which you control the vertical descent of a spacecraft landing on a strange planet (or moon). As pilot-in-command you have control of a single rocket thruster. Using the computer's keyboard you can input a new throttle (thrust) setting for each 10 seconds of "mission-time".

Your ship is being pulled down by the gravitational force of Planet-X, so unless you use your rocket, the ship will descend faster and faster, that is, there will be downward acceleration. This will increase velocity and eventually lead to a disasterous impact.

On the other hand, if you try to counteract this downward acceleration with too much rocket thrust, you may go up! Even worse, you'll run out of fuel, and then fall helplessly with increasing speed. Your goal is to use just enough rocket thrust so that you land gently (which means with a small vertical speed—less than five meters per second which is about 10 mph), and preferably with some reserve fuel on board.

The simulation program has eight principal sections.

1. Initialization (lines 20 to 230)—The ship starts 100 kilometers (about 60 miles) up, so H=100. The ship has a mass of 5,000 kilograms (S=5000). There are 15,000 kilograms of fuel on board (E=15000). Initial velocity is 100 meters per second *down* (V=-100). Mission time starts at time zero (T=0). The acceleration due to gravity on Planet-X is G=2.4 meters per second per second. (about 1/4 of that on earth).

2. Line 240 prints a Progress Report showing mission time (T), velocity (V), altitude above the planet (H), and fuel remaining (E).

3. Lines 250 to 320 input and check your throttle command. You are allowed to type in a throttle "thrust" setting of 0 to 500 units. Each unit is 200 Newtons of force (about 900 pounds of thrust).

4. The fuel supply is decreased in line 330 at the rate of 1 kilogram of fuel for every unit of thrust.

5. The new velocity V and altitude H are calculated in lines 340 to 380. From Newton's second law we have:

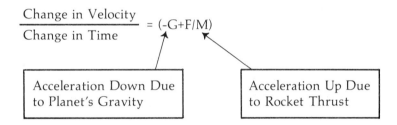

$$\frac{\text{Change in Velocity}}{\text{Change in Time}} = (-G+F/M)$$

| Acceleration Down Due to Planet's Gravity | Acceleration Up Due to Rocket Thrust |

F is the rocket thrust. Each unit of thrust is 200 Newtons, so the actual force is 200*F Newtons. In this simulation we'll do an update every 10 seconds, so the change in time is 10.Thus if we call the change in velocity V2 we have in line 350:

```
    V2 = 10*(-G+200*F/(S+E))
 or V2 = 2000*F/(S+E)-10*G
```

You'll notice that the mass is made up of two parts: the ship S, and the fuel E, so mass will decrease as you use up fuel. With a *change* of V2, the new velocity at the end of 10 seconds is found in line 355 as V=V+V2. The *change* in altitude is given in line 360 as D=(V1+V2/2)*10, where V1 is the velocity at the start of the ten second period, and V2/2 is the *average increase* (midway between 0 and 10 seconds). So the new altitude in kilometers is H=H-D/1000 (line 370).

6. Line 390 checks for an impact, and line 400 checks for an "out of fuel" condition. If neither is true, the mission clock is advanced in line 410, and we go back for another control input.

7. Lines 430 to 500 handle the out-of-fuel situation. The same formulas are used except calculations are done every .1 second. The variable K counts the tenths of a second until impact.

8. Line 510 decides whether you made a soft landing (less than 5 meters per second which is about 10 miles per hour), line 515 checks for a poor but safe landing (between 5 and 15 meters per second), and line 520 catches the disasters. Here's a listing and four runs showing each of these situations.

PLANET-X
LANDER

```
LIST

 20 PRINT "YOU HAVE JUST DEPARTED YOUR MOTHER SHIP"
 30 PRINT "AND ARE DESCENDING TO PLANET X."
 40 PRINT "AFTER EACH ? TYPE IN A ROCKET THRUST"
 50 PRINT "COMMAND AS A NUMBER BETWEEN 0 AND 500"
 60 PRINT "UNITS (EACH UNIT=200 NEWTONS=900 LBS. OF THRUST)
 70 PRINT "---------GOOD LUCK---------"
 80 PRINT
 90 PRINT "TIME:    VELOCITY: ALTITUDE:   FUEL:       THRUST:"
100 PRINT "SECONDS METERS/SEC KILOMETERS KILOGRAMS NEWTONS/100"
110 PRINT
200 LET H=100
210 LET S=5000
215 LET E=15000
220 LET T=0
225 LET G=2.4
230 LET V=-100
240 PRINT T;TAB(8);V;TAB(19);H;TAB(30);E;TAB(38);"F=";
250 INPUT F
260 IF ABS(F-250)>251 THEN 310
270 IF F>E THEN 325
280 GOTO 330
290 REM-----ILLEGAL THRUST MESSAGES-----
310 PRINT "ILLEGAL THRUST--PLEASE REPEAT"
320 GOTO 240
325 PRINT "ONLY";E;"UNITS OF FUEL LEFT--PLEASE REPEAT"
326 GOTO 240
330 LET E=E-F
340 LET V1=V
350 LET V2=2000*F/(S+E)-10*G
355 LET V=V+V2
360 LET D=(V1+V2/2)*10
370 LET H=H+D/1000
390 IF H<=.01 THEN 440
400 IF E<=0 THEN 430
410 LET T=T+10
420 GOTO 240
430 PRINT "YOU'RE OUT OF FUEL";H;"KILOMETERS UP"
435 LET F=0
440 LET K=0
450 LET K=K+.1
460 LET V1=V
470 LET V2=20*F/(S+E)-.1*G
480 LET V=V+V2
485 LET H=H+(V1+V2/2)/1000
490 IF H>0 THEN 450
500 PRINT "IMPACT IN APPROXIMATELY";K;"SECONDS"
505 PRINT "STANDBY":PRINT:PRINT
510 IF V>=-5 THEN 570
515 IF V>=-15 THEN 590
```

WE'LL USE -100 TO MEAN AN INITIAL VELOCITY OF 100 METERS PER SECOND DOWN.

THIS IS THE MAIN SIMULATION LOOP.

```
520 PRINT "CRUNCH!!! VELOCITY=";V;"M/SEC"
530 PRINT "THAT´S";V*3.2*3600/5280;"MPH--OH BOY!"
550 PRINT "TURN IN YOUR LICENSE AT ONCE"
560 GOTO 999
570 PRINT "BEAUTIFUL LANDING-- V=";V*3.2*3600/5280;"MPH"
575 PRINT "YOU HAD";E;"KILOGRAMS OF FUEL LEFT"
577 GOTO 999
590 PRINT"CLUNK--RATTLE-RATTLE--SQUINCH"
595 PRINT"V= ";V*3.2*3600/5280;"MPH: ROUGH, BUT YOU SURVIVED"
999 END
```

```
RUN

YOU HAVE JUST DEPARTED YOUR MOTHER SHIP
AND ARE DESCENDING TO PLANET X.
AFTER EACH ? TYPE IN A ROCKET THRUST
COMMAND AS A NUMBER BETWEEN 0 AND 500
UNITS (EACH UNIT=200 NEWTONS=900 LBS. OF THRUST)
----------GOOD LUCK----------

TIME:    VELOCITY:  ALTITUDE:   FUEL:      THRUST:
SECONDS  METERS/SEC KILOMETERS KILOGRAMS NEWTONS/100

 0       -100        100        15000   F=? 0
 10      -124        98.88      15000   F=? 0
 20      -148        97.52      15000   F=? 0
 30      -172        95.92      15000   F=? 0
 40      -196        94.08      15000   F=? 0
 50      -220        92         15000   F=? 0
 60      -244        89.68      15000   F=? 0
 70      -268        87.12      15000   F=? 0
 80      -292        84.32      15000   F=? 0
 90      -316        81.28      15000   F=? 0
 100     -340        78         15000   F=? 0
 110     -364        74.48      15000   F=? 0
 120     -388        70.72      15000   F=? 0
 130     -412        66.72      15000   F=? 0
 140     -436        62.48      15000   F=? 0
 150     -460        58         15000   F=? 0
 160     -484        53.28      15000   F=? 0
 170     -508        48.32      15000   F=? 0
 180     -532        43.12      15000   F=? 0
 190     -556        37.68      15000   F=? 500
 200     -528.718    32.2564    14500   F=? 500
 210     -500.086    27.1124    14000   F=? 500
 220     -470.032    22.2618    13500   F=? 500
 230     -438.477    17.7192    13000   F=? 500
 240     -405.334    13.5002    12500   F=? 500
 250     -370.51     9.62098    12000   F=? 500
 260     -333.904    6.0989     11500   F=? 500
 270     -295.404    2.95236    11000   F=? 500
 280     -254.888    .200896    10500   F=? 500
IMPACT IN APPROXIMATELY .1 SECONDS
STANDBY


CRUNCH!!! VELOCITY=-211.795 M/SEC
THAT´S-462.098 MPH--OH BOY!
TURN IN YOUR LICENSE AT ONCE
```

A REALLY BAD LANDING.

```
RUN

YOU HAVE JUST DEPARTED YOUR MOTHER SHIP
AND ARE DESCENDING TO PLANET X.
AFTER EACH ? TYPE IN A ROCKET THRUST
COMMAND AS A NUMBER BETWEEN 0 AND 500
UNITS (EACH UNIT=200 NEWTONS=900 LBS. OF THRUST)
----------GOOD LUCK----------

TIME:      VELOCITY:   ALTITUDE:   FUEL:       THRUST:
SECONDS    METERS/SEC  KILOMETERS  KILOGRAMS   NEWTONS/100

0          -100        100         15000    F=?  0
10         -124        98.88       15000    F=?  0
20         -148        97.52       15000    F=?  0
30         -172        95.92       15000    F=?  500
40         -144.718    94.3364     14500    F=?  500
50         -116.086    93.0324     14000    F=?  500
60         -86.0323    92.0218     13500    F=?  500
70         -54.4768    91.3192     13000    F=?  500
80         -21.3339    90.9402     12500    F=?  500
90          13.4896    90.901      12000    F=?  500
100         50.0957    91.2189     11500    F=?  500
110         88.5957    91.9124     11000    F=?  500
120         129.112    93.0009     10500    F=?  500
130         171.778    94.5053     10000    F=?  500
140         216.744    96.448      9500     F=?  500
150         264.173    98.8525     9000     F=?  500
160         314.247    101.745     8500     F=?  500
170         367.17     105.152     8000     F=?  500
180         423.17     109.103     7500     F=?  500
190         482.503    113.632     7000     F=?  500
200         545.46     118.772     6500     F=?  500
210         612.369    124.561     6000     F=?  500
220         683.607    131.041     5500     F=?  500
230         759.607    138.257     5000     F=?  500
240         840.87     146.259     4500     F=?  500
250         927.981    155.103     4000     F=?  500
260         1021.63    164.851     3500     F=?  500
270         1122.63    175.573     3000     F=?  500
280         1231.96    187.346     2500     F=?  500
290         1350.82    200.259     2000     F=?  500
300         1480.66    214.417     1500     F=?  500
310         1623.33    229.937     1000     F=?  500
320         1781.15    246.959     500      F=?  500
YOU'RE OUT OF FUEL 265.651 KILOMETERS UP
IMPACT IN APPROXIMATELY 1644.5 SECONDS
STANDBY


CRUNCH!!! VELOCITY=-1989.65 M/SEC
THAT'S-4341.06 MPH--OH BOY!
TURN IN YOUR LICENSE AT ONCE
```

THIS PILOT WENT THE WRONG WAY AND RAN OUT OF FUEL WAY UP.

NOW HE'S GOT TO FALL FOR 27.4 MINUTES, GOING FASTER & FASTER.

```
RUN

YOU HAVE JUST DEPARTED YOUR MOTHER SHIP
AND ARE DESCENDING TO PLANET X.
AFTER EACH ? TYPE IN A ROCKET THRUST
COMMAND AS A NUMBER BETWEEN 0 AND 500
UNITS (EACH UNIT=200 NEWTONS=900 LBS. OF THRUST)
----------GOOD LUCK----------

TIME:     VELOCITY:   ALTITUDE:    FUEL:        THRUST:
SECONDS   METERS/SEC  KILOMETERS   KILOGRAMS    NEWTONS/100

 0        -100        100          15000    F=? 0
 10       -124        98.88        15000    F=? 0
 20       -148        97.52        15000    F=? 0
 30       -172        95.92        15000    F=? 0
 40       -196        94.08        15000    F=? 0
 50       -220        92           15000    F=? 0
 60       -244        89.68        15000    F=? 0
 70       -268        87.12        15000    F=? 0
 80       -292        84.32        15000    F=? 0
 90       -316        81.28        15000    F=? 0
 100      -340        78           15000    F=? 0
 110      -364        74.48        15000    F=? 0
 120      -388        70.72        15000    F=? 0
 130      -412        66.72        15000    F=? 0
 140      -436        62.48        15000    F=? 0
 150      -460        58           15000    F=? 0
 160      -484        53.28        15000    F=? 0
 170      -508        48.32        15000    F=? 500
 180      -480.718    43.3764      14500    F=? 500
 190      -452.086    38.7124      14000    F=? 500
 200      -422.032    34.3418      13500    F=? 500
 210      -390.477    30.2792      13000    F=? 500
 220      -357.334    26.5402      12500    F=? 500
 230      -322.51     23.141       12000    F=? 500
 240      -285.904    20.0989      11500    F=? 500
 250      -247.404    17.4324      11000    F=? 500
 260      -206.888    15.1609      10500    F=? 500
 270      -164.222    13.3053      10000    F=? 100
 280      -174.799    11.6102      9900     F=? 100
 290      -185.285    9.80983      9800     F=? 200
 300      -181.888    7.97396      9600     F=? 200
 310      -178.11     6.17397      9400     F=? 200
 320      -173.941    4.41371      9200     F=? 500
 330      -124.948    2.91927      8700     F=? 500
 340      -73.1909    1.92857      8200     F=? 500
 350      -18.4507    1.47036      7700     F=? 200
 360      -10.4507    1.32586      7500     F=? 100
 370      -18.3217    1.18199      7400     F=? 100
 380      -26.0615    .960078      7300     F=? 200
 390      -17.0037    .744752      7100     F=? 200
 400      -7.39021    .622783      6900     F=? 100
 410      -14.4411    .513627      6800     F=? 150
 420      -12.69      .377972      6650     F=? 150
 430      -10.603     .261506      6500     F=? 130
 440      -11.7358    .149812      6370     F=? 140
 450      -10.8026    .03712       6230     F=? 150
IMPACT IN APPROXIMATELY .1 SECONDS
STANDBY


CLUNK--RATTLE-RATTLE--SQUINCH
V= -16.7914 MPH: ROUGH, BUT YOU SURVIVED
```

NOT GREAT,
BUT NOT FATAL.

```
RUN

YOU HAVE JUST DEPARTED YOUR MOTHER SHIP
AND ARE DESCENDING TO PLANET X.
AFTER EACH ? TYPE IN A ROCKET THRUST
COMMAND AS A NUMBER BETWEEN 0 AND 500
UNITS (EACH UNIT=200 NEWTONS=900 LBS. OF THRUST)
----------GOOD LUCK----------

TIME:      VELOCITY:   ALTITUDE:    FUEL:       THRUST:
SECONDS    METERS/SEC  KILOMETERS   KILOGRAMS   NEWTONS/100

0          -100        100          15000    F=?  0
10         -124        98.88        15000    F=?  0
20         -148        97.52        15000    F=?  0
30         -172        95.92        15000    F=?  0
40         -196        94.08        15000    F=?  0
50         -220        92           15000    F=?  0
60         -244        89.68        15000    F=?  0
70         -268        87.12        15000    F=?  0
80         -292        84.32        15000    F=?  0
90         -316        81.28        15000    F=?  0
100        -340        78           15000    F=?  0
110        -364        74.48        15000    F=?  0
120        -388        70.72        15000    F=?  0
130        -412        66.72        15000    F=?  0
140        -436        62.48        15000    F=?  0
150        -460        58           15000    F=?  0
160        -484        53.28        15000    F=?  0
170        -508        48.32        15000    F=?  0
180        -532        43.12        15000    F=?  500
190        -504.718    37.9364      14500    F=?  500
200        -476.086    33.0324      14000    F=?  500
210        -446.032    28.42.8      13500    F=?  500
220        -414.477    24.1192      13000    F=?  500
230        -381.334    20.1402      12500    F=?  500
240        -346.51     16.501       12000    F=?  500
250        -309.904    13.2189      11500    F=?  500
260        -271.404    10.3124      11000    F=?  500
270        -230.888    7.8009       10500    F=?  500
280        -188.222    5.70535      10000    F=?  500
290        -143.256    4.04796      9500     F=?  500
300        -95.8274    2.85254      9000     F=?  500
310        -45.7534    2.14464      8500     F=?  0
320        -69.7534    1.56711      8500     F=?  100
330        -78.828     .824199      8400     F=?  300
340        -57.0265    .144927      8100     F=?  500
IMPACT IN APPROXIMATELY .1 SECONDS
STANDBY



BEAUTIFUL LANDING-- V=-2.41685 MPH  ◄──
YOU HAD 7600 KILOGRAMS OF FUEL LEFT
```

A REALLY "SOFT" LANDING.

6.8   PROJECT IDEAS

1. The main timing loop in the Planet-X lander is between lines 240 and 420. Line 410 increments the "system clock" by 10 seconds each time around the loop. One way to get more accurate values for H and V would be to do the calculations in lines 340 to 400 with an inner loop based on 1 second updates. Do this by adding the statements:

   ```
   345 FOR I=1 TO 10
   395 NEXT I
   ```

   to your program. You'll also have to modify statements 350 and 360 because the time increment for this part of the program is no longer 10 seconds. For a hint on what changes to make, see lines 470 and 485.

2. Add new statements to the Planet-X program to make it a "two-way" lander program. First, the user must land safely on Planet-X. Then the problem is to get back up to the mother ship, using the fuel remaining on board. The clock should be reset to zero at this second blast-off. The conditions for making a safe docking are that ABS(100-H)<1, *and* ABS(V)<30. Here's what the second half of a run might look like:

```
BEAUTIFUL LANDING-- V=-2.70545 MPH ←
YOU HAD 7600 KILOGRAMS OF FUEL LEFT
WANT TO GO BACK TO MOTHER? YES
YOU'RE CLEARED FOR TAKEOFF.  HAVE A GOOD FLIGHT
TIME:     VELOCITY:    ALTITUDE:    FUEL:      THRUST:
  0         0            0           7600    F=? 500 ←
 10        58.6446      .293223      7100    F=? 500 ←
 20       120.852      1.1907        6600    F=? 500
 30       186.942      2.72967       6100    F=? 500
 40       257.281      4.95078       5600    F=? 500
 50       332.291      7.89865       5100    F=? 500
 60       412.458     11.6224        4600    F=? 500
 70       498.348     16.1764        4100    F=? 500
 80       590.627     21.6213        3600    F=? 0
 90       566.627     27.4076        3600    F=? 0
100       542.627     32.9538        3600    F=? 0
110       518.627     38.2601        3600    F=? 0
120       494.627     43.3264        3600    F=? 0
130       470.627     48.1526        3600    F=? 0
140       446.627     52.7389        3600    F=? 0
150       422.627     57.0852        3600    F=? 0
160       398.627     61.1915        3600    F=? 0
170       374.627     65.0577        3600    F=? 0
180       350.627     68.684         3600    F=? 0
190       326.627     72.0703        3600    F=? 0
200       302.627     75.2165        3600    F=? 0
210       278.627     78.1228        3600    F=? 0
220       254.627     80.7891        3600    F=? 0
230       230.627     83.2153        3600    F=? 0
240       206.627     85.4016        3600    F=? 0
250       182.627     87.3479        3600    F=? 0
260       158.627     89.0542        3600    F=? 0
270       134.627     90.5204        3600    F=? 0
280       110.627     91.7467        3600    F=? 0
290        86.627     92.733         3600    F=? 0
300        62.627     93.4792        3600    F=? 0
310        38.627     93.9855        3600    F=? 100
320        38.1564    94.3694        3500    F=? 90
330        35.5595    94.738         3410    F=? 70
340        28.3461    95.0575        3340    F=? 70
350        21.2747    95.3056        3270    F=? 75
360        15.5786    95.4899        3195    F=? 80
370        11.2951    95.6243        3115    F=? 85
380         8.46574   95.7231        3030    F=? 90
390         7.13577   95.8011        2940    F=? 100
400         8.64597   95.88          2840    F=? 120
410        15.7341    96.0019        2720    F=? 100
420        17.9808    96.1705        2620    F=? 100
430        20.5765    96.3632        2520    F=? 100
440        23.5307    96.5838        2420    F=? 100
450        26.8531    96.8357        2320    F=? 100
460        30.5539    97.1227        2220    F=? 100
470        34.6438    97.4487        2120    F=? 90
480        36.2484    97.8032        2030    F=? 80
490         5.27      98.1608        1950    F=? 70
500        31.6188    98.4952        1880    F=? 70
510        28.1768    98.7942        1810    F=? 80
CONGRATULATIONS -- YOU MADE IT.  YOU'RE NOW WITHIN ←
REACH OF THE AUTOMATIC DOCKING SYSTEM. WELCOME BACK
STOP at line 384
```

THIS IS THE END OF THE FIRST HALF OF A RUN.

THE CLOCK IS RESET, AND NOW WE TRY TO GO BACK UP TO THE MOTHER SHIP.

NOTICE HOW LITTLE THE SHIP MOVES AT FIRST, EVEN WITH FULL POWER.

BUT ONCE GOING, IT'S HARD TO SLOW DOWN!

THE CONDITIONS NEEDED FOR DOCKING ARE:
1. $99 < H < 101$
AND 2. $-30 < V < 30$

3. Sci-fi space games are very popular on computers . Study one of these, and then design your own version. Try to be different—there's little to be learned in just copying an existing version. Suggestion: After you get a simple version working, try adding accelerating forces based on "gravitational" pull from alien ships, starbases, etc. Use the Planet-X lander program for ideas.

4. Write the Crazy Eights program using minimal BASIC. It's best to do this from "scratch". This means *not* trying to translate the BASIC-PLUS statements we have shown, but rather developing your own program segments. Also consider modifying the rules of the game to take advantage of the things a computer can do (e.g., making the wild card a variable).

5. Modify the Horse Race program to allow several players. Give each a starting bankroll, and have the computer keep track of each person's wealth.

6. Write a two-way Archery program where the computer (located at the target) shoots back at you.

7. Rewrite one of the programs from this chapter in minimal BASIC, using remarks and indentations to clarify the program's structure. An example showing some techniques that can be used is given in the "style corner".

THE STYLE

CORNER

```
100 REM      SPIES      28 SEPTEMBER 1977      JOHN M. NEVISON
105
110 REM      THIS PROGRAM IS A STYLED VERSION OF AN ORIGINAL
115 REM      PROGRAM BY T. DWYER AND M. CRITCHFIELD.
120
125 REM      REFERENCE:  DWYER, T. AND CRITCHFIELD, M., "BASIC AND
130 REM                  THE PERSONAL COMPUTER," READING, MASS:
135 REM                  ADDISON-WESLEY PUBLISHING COMPANY, 1978.
140
145 REM      VARIABLES:
150 REM         A$....ANSWER TO A QUESTION
155 REM         D.....DISTANCE FROM GUESS TO A SPY
160 REM         G$....GAME STATE
165 REM         I.....INDEX VARIABLE
170 REM         T.....TURN COUNTER
175 REM         X.....THE X GUESS
180 REM         X(I)..THE X COORDINATE OF SPY I
185 REM         Y.....THE Y GUESS
190 REM         Y(I)..THE Y COORDINATE OF SPY I
195
200
205 REM      MAIN ROUTINE
210
215      PRINT "THIS IS THE GAME OF SPIES ON A GRID"
220      PRINT "THE OBJECT IS TO FIND 4 SPIES HIDDEN ON A 10 X 10 GRID"
225      PRINT "YOUR SEARCH BASE IS AT (0,0).  ANY GUESS"
230      PRINT "YOU MAKE SHOULD CONTAIN TWO NUMBERS SEPARATED"
235      PRINT "BY COMMAS.  THE FIRST GIVES THE UNIT DISTANCE RIGHT"
240      PRINT "OF BASE AND THE SECOND IS THE UNIT DISTANCE ABOVE BASE."
245      PRINT
250      PRINT "LET'S BEGIN"
255
260      GO SUB 355                     '*HIDE SPIES
265        FOR T = 1 TO 10
270           GO SUB 410                'TAKE A TURN
275           GO SUB 530                'WIN CHECK
280           IF G$ = "WIN" THEN 295
285        NEXT T
290        GO SUB 610                    'LOST GAME
295
300        PRINT
305        PRINT "DO YOU WANT TO PLAY AGAIN?"
310        INPUT A$
315        IF A$ <> "YES" THEN 325
320      GO TO 260                       '*
325
330      PRINT "GOOD DAY"
335
340      STOP
345
350
355 REM      SUBROUTINE:  HIDE SPIES
360 REM      IN:
365 REM      OUT: X(),Y()
370
375      FOR I = 1 TO 4
380         LET X(I) = INT(10 * RND)
385         LET Y(I) = INT(10 * RND)
390      NEXT I
395
400 RETURN
405
```

```
410 REM     SUBROUTINE:  TAKE A TURN
415 REM       IN: T, X(), Y()
420 REM      OUT: X()
425
430      PRINT
435      PRINT
440      PRINT "TURN NUMBER"; T; ", WHAT IS YOUR GUESS?"
445      INPUT X, Y
450      FOR I = 1 TO 4
455         IF X(I) = -1 THEN 505
460          IF X(I) <> X THEN 485
465           IF Y(I) <> Y THEN 485
470            PRINT "YOU HAVE FOUND SPY"; I
475            LET X(I) = -1
480            GO TO 510                    'NEXT I
485
490           LET D = SQR((X(I)-X)^2 + (Y(I)-Y)^2)
495           PRINT "YOUR DISTANCE FROM SPY"; I;
500           PRINT "IS"; INT(D*10)/10; "UNITS."
505
510      NEXT I
515
520 RETURN
525
530 REM     SUBROUTINE:  WIN CHECK
535 REM       IN : X()
540 REM      OUT:  G$
545
550      LET G$ = " "
555      FOR I = 1 TO 4
560         IF X(I) = -1 THEN 570
565          GO TO 600                   'RETURN
570
575      NEXT I
580      PRINT
585      PRINT "YOU HAVE FOUND ALL THE SPIES IN "; T; " TURNS!"
590      LET G$ = "WIN"
595
600 RETURN
605
610 REM     SUBROUTINE:  LOST GAME
615 REM       IN:  X()
620 REM      OUT:
625
630      PRINT
635      PRINT "YOU DIDN'T FIND ALL THE SPIES IN TEN TRIES."
640      PRINT "DO YOU WANT TO KNOW WHERE THE SPIES YOU DIDN'T"
645      PRINT "FIND WERE HIDDEN?"
650      INPUT A$
655      IF A$ = "NO" THEN 685
660       FOR I = 1 TO 4
665          IF X(I) = -1 THEN 675
670           PRINT "SPY"; I; "HID AT ("; X(I); ","; Y(I); ")."
675
680      NEXT I
685
690 RETURN
695
700      END
```

7

COMPUTER ART; MORE ON COMPUTER GRAPHICS

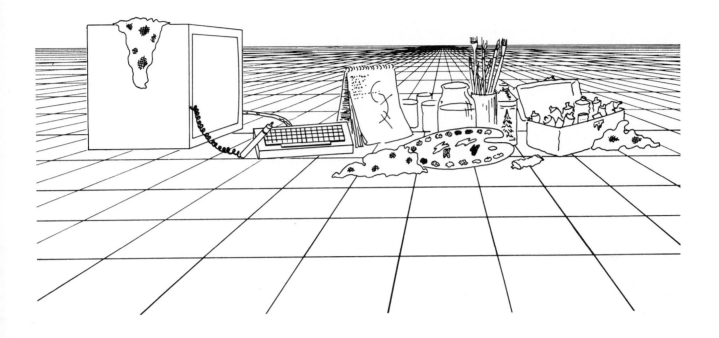

7.0   INTRODUCTION; THE ALPHANUMERIC CHARACTER SET

In Chapter 3 we emphasized graphic displays that can be produced on an alphanumeric terminal. These are of general interest because most personal computer systems have (or will have) this kind of output device. In this section we'll continue to emphasize graphics based on alphanumeric characters, and show that the results can be quite impressive. However we'll also introduce ideas that can easily be adapted to more expensive graphical displays.

To get a better feel for what potential alphanumeric chacters have as the basic elements in graphical patterns, it's helpful to print a reference sheet with blocks of each character. This way you can see both the patterns they produce, and the shades of gray the eye perceives when looking at a given group of characters from a distance.

SELF-TEST

1. Write a program that produces blocks of all the characters available on your terminal.

    Here's a solution to this problem done on a terminal which has both upper and lower case letters. The program uses the string function CHR$(X) to select the characters. The argument X in this function is the so-called ASCII code (American Standard Code for Information Interchange), given in decimal form. The value of the function is the character for that code. The decimal codes for the usable characters go from 32 to 126. You can see what value (character) is printed for each code from the run of the program. The variables in the program written as I%, J%, K%, and L% are *integer* variables. If your BASIC doesn't have these, simply use ordinary variables (I,J,K,L). If your BASIC doesn't have the CHR$ function, then use the GOSUB technique shown back in Section 4.3.

ASCII CHARACTERS

```
LIST

10  FOR I%=32% TO 126% STEP 4%
15  PRINT I%,I%+1%,I%+2%,I%+3%
18  FOR K%=1% TO 5%
20  FOR L%=0% TO 3%
25  FOR J%=1% TO 10%
30  PRINT CHR$(I%+L%);
35  NEXT J%
38  PRINT "      ";
40  NEXT L%
45  PRINT
48  NEXT K%
49  PRINT:PRINT
50  NEXT I%
60  END

RUN

    32              33              34              35
                !!!!!!!!!!      ----------      ##########
                !!!!!!!!!!      ----------      ##########
                !!!!!!!!!!      ----------      ##########
                !!!!!!!!!!      ----------      ##########
                !!!!!!!!!!      ----------      ##########


    36              37              38              39
$$$$$$$$$$      %%%%%%%%%%      &&&&&&&&&&      ----------
$$$$$$$$$$      %%%%%%%%%%      &&&&&&&&&&      ----------
$$$$$$$$$$      %%%%%%%%%%      &&&&&&&&&&      ----------
$$$$$$$$$$      %%%%%%%%%%      &&&&&&&&&&      ----------
$$$$$$$$$$      %%%%%%%%%%      &&&&&&&&&&      ----------


    40              41              42              43
((((((((((      ))))))))))      **********      ++++++++++
((((((((((      ))))))))))      **********      ++++++++++
((((((((((      ))))))))))      **********      ++++++++++
((((((((((      ))))))))))      **********      ++++++++++
((((((((((      ))))))))))      **********      ++++++++++
```

```
44              45              46              47
,,,,,,,,,,      ----------      ..........      //////////
,,,,,,,,,,      ----------      ..........      //////////
,,,,,,,,,,      ----------      ..........      //////////
,,,,,,,,,,      ----------      ..........      //////////
,,,,,,,,,,      ----------      ..........      //////////


48              49              50              51
0000000000      1111111111      2222222222      3333333333
0000000000      1111111111      2222222222      3333333333
0000000000      1111111111      2222222222      3333333333
0000000000      1111111111      2222222222      3333333333
0000000000      1111111111      2222222222      3333333333


52              53              54              55
4444444444      5555555555      6666666666      7777777777
4444444444      5555555555      6666666666      7777777777
4444444444      5555555555      6666666666      7777777777
4444444444      5555555555      6666666666      7777777777
4444444444      5555555555      6666666666      7777777777


56              57              58              59
8888888888      9999999999      ::::::::::      ;;;;;;;;;;
8888888888      9999999999      ::::::::::      ;;;;;;;;;;
8888888888      9999999999      ::::::::::      ;;;;;;;;;;
8888888888      9999999999      ::::::::::      ;;;;;;;;;;
8888888888      9999999999      ::::::::::      ;;;;;;;;;;


60              61              62              63
<<<<<<<<<<      ==========      >>>>>>>>>>      ??????????
<<<<<<<<<<      ==========      >>>>>>>>>>      ??????????
<<<<<<<<<<      ==========      >>>>>>>>>>      ??????????
<<<<<<<<<<      ==========      >>>>>>>>>>      ??????????
<<<<<<<<<<      ==========      >>>>>>>>>>      ??????????


64              65              66              67
@@@@@@@@@@      AAAAAAAAAA      BBBBBBBBBB      CCCCCCCCCC
@@@@@@@@@@      AAAAAAAAAA      BBBBBBBBBB      CCCCCCCCCC
@@@@@@@@@@      AAAAAAAAAA      BBBBBBBBBB      CCCCCCCCCC
@@@@@@@@@@      AAAAAAAAAA      BBBBBBBBBB      CCCCCCCCCC
@@@@@@@@@@      AAAAAAAAAA      BBBBBBBBBB      CCCCCCCCCC


68              69              70              71
DDDDDDDDDD      EEEEEEEEEE      FFFFFFFFFF      GGGGGGGGGG
DDDDDDDDDD      EEEEEEEEEE      FFFFFFFFFF      GGGGGGGGGG
DDDDDDDDDD      EEEEEEEEEE      FFFFFFFFFF      GGGGGGGGGG
DDDDDDDDDD      EEEEEEEEEE      FFFFFFFFFF      GGGGGGGGGG
DDDDDDDDDD      EEEEEEEEEE      FFFFFFFFFF      GGGGGGGGGG


72              73              74              75
HHHHHHHHHH      IIIIIIIIII      JJJJJJJJJJ      KKKKKKKKKK
HHHHHHHHHH      IIIIIIIIII      JJJJJJJJJJ      KKKKKKKKKK
HHHHHHHHHH      IIIIIIIIII      JJJJJJJJJJ      KKKKKKKKKK
HHHHHHHHHH      IIIIIIIIII      JJJJJJJJJJ      KKKKKKKKKK
HHHHHHHHHH      IIIIIIIIII      JJJJJJJJJJ      KKKKKKKKKK
```

```
   76            77            78            79
LLLLLLLLLL    MMMMMMMMMM    NNNNNNNNNN    OOOOOOOOOO
LLLLLLLLLL    MMMMMMMMMM    NNNNNNNNNN    OOOOOOOOOO
LLLLLLLLLL    MMMMMMMMMM    NNNNNNNNNN    OOOOOOOOOO
LLLLLLLLLL    MMMMMMMMMM    NNNNNNNNNN    OOOOOOOOOO
LLLLLLLLLL    MMMMMMMMMM    NNNNNNNNNN    OOOOOOOOOO


   80            81            82            83
PPPPPPPPPP    QQQQQQQQQQ    RRRRRRRRRR    SSSSSSSSSS
PPPPPPPPPP    QQQQQQQQQQ    RRRRRRRRRR    SSSSSSSSSS
PPPPPPPPPP    QQQQQQQQQQ    RRRRRRRRRR    SSSSSSSSSS
PPPPPPPPPP    QQQQQQQQQQ    RRRRRRRRRR    SSSSSSSSSS
PPPPPPPPPP    QQQQQQQQQQ    RRRRRRRRRR    SSSSSSSSSS


   84            85            86            87
TTTTTTTTTT    UUUUUUUUUU    VVVVVVVVVV    WWWWWWWWWW
TTTTTTTTTT    UUUUUUUUUU    VVVVVVVVVV    WWWWWWWWWW
TTTTTTTTTT    UUUUUUUUUU    VVVVVVVVVV    WWWWWWWWWW
TTTTTTTTTT    UUUUUUUUUU    VVVVVVVVVV    WWWWWWWWWW
TTTTTTTTTT    UUUUUUUUUU    VVVVVVVVVV    WWWWWWWWWW


   88            89            90            91
XXXXXXXXXX    YYYYYYYYYY    ZZZZZZZZZZ    [[[[[[[[[[
XXXXXXXXXX    YYYYYYYYYY    ZZZZZZZZZZ    [[[[[[[[[[
XXXXXXXXXX    YYYYYYYYYY    ZZZZZZZZZZ    [[[[[[[[[[
XXXXXXXXXX    YYYYYYYYYY    ZZZZZZZZZZ    [[[[[[[[[[
XXXXXXXXXX    YYYYYYYYYY    ZZZZZZZZZZ    [[[[[[[[[[


   92            93            94            95
\\\\\\\\\\    ]]]]]]]]]]    ^^^^^^^^^^    _____
\\\\\\\\\\    ]]]]]]]]]]    ^^^^^^^^^^    _____
\\\\\\\\\\    ]]]]]]]]]]    ^^^^^^^^^^    _____
\\\\\\\\\\    ]]]]]]]]]]    ^^^^^^^^^^    _____
\\\\\\\\\\    ]]]]]]]]]]    ^^^^^^^^^^    _____


   96            97            98            99
..........    aaaaaaaaaa    bbbbbbbbbb    cccccccccc
..........    aaaaaaaaaa    bbbbbbbbbb    cccccccccc
..........    aaaaaaaaaa    bbbbbbbbbb    cccccccccc
..........    aaaaaaaaaa    bbbbbbbbbb    cccccccccc
..........    aaaaaaaaaa    bbbbbbbbbb    cccccccccc


  100           101           102           103
dddddddddd    eeeeeeeeee    ffffffffff    gggggggggg
dddddddddd    eeeeeeeeee    ffffffffff    gggggggggg
dddddddddd    eeeeeeeeee    ffffffffff    gggggggggg
dddddddddd    eeeeeeeeee    ffffffffff    gggggggggg
dddddddddd    eeeeeeeeee    ffffffffff    gggggggggg


  104           105           106           107
hhhhhhhhhh    iiiiiiiiii    jjjjjjjjjj    kkkkkkkkkk
hhhhhhhhhh    iiiiiiiiii    jjjjjjjjjj    kkkkkkkkkk
hhhhhhhhhh    iiiiiiiiii    jjjjjjjjjj    kkkkkkkkkk
hhhhhhhhhh    iiiiiiiiii    jjjjjjjjjj    kkkkkkkkkk
hhhhhhhhhh    iiiiiiiiii    jjjjjjjjjj    kkkkkkkkkk
```

```
   108            109            110            111
1111111111     mmmmmmmmmm     nnnnnnnnnn     0000000000
1111111111     mmmmmmmmmm     nnnnnnnnnn     0000000000
1111111111     mmmmmmmmmm     nnnnnnnnnn     0000000000
1111111111     mmmmmmmmmm     nnnnnnnnnn     0000000000
1111111111     mmmmmmmmmm     nnnnnnnnnn     0000000000


   112            113            114            115
pppppppppp     qqqqqqqqqq     rrrrrrrrrr     ssssssssss
pppppppppp     qqqqqqqqqq     rrrrrrrrrr     ssssssssss
pppppppppp     qqqqqqqqqq     rrrrrrrrrr     ssssssssss
pppppppppp     qqqqqqqqqq     rrrrrrrrrr     ssssssssss
pppppppppp     qqqqqqqqqq     rrrrrrrrrr     ssssssssss


   116            117            118            119
tttttttttt     uuuuuuuuuu     vvvvvvvvvv     wwwwwwwwww
tttttttttt     uuuuuuuuuu     vvvvvvvvvv     wwwwwwwwww
tttttttttt     uuuuuuuuuu     vvvvvvvvvv     wwwwwwwwww
tttttttttt     uuuuuuuuuu     vvvvvvvvvv     wwwwwwwwww
tttttttttt     uuuuuuuuuu     vvvvvvvvvv     wwwwwwwwww


   120            121            122            123
xxxxxxxxxx     yyyyyyyyyy     zzzzzzzzzz     {{{{{{{{{{
xxxxxxxxxx     yyyyyyyyyy     zzzzzzzzzz     {{{{{{{{{{
xxxxxxxxxx     yyyyyyyyyy     zzzzzzzzzz     {{{{{{{{{{
xxxxxxxxxx     yyyyyyyyyy     zzzzzzzzzz     {{{{{{{{{{
xxxxxxxxxx     yyyyyyyyyy     zzzzzzzzzz     {{{{{{{{{{


   124            125            126            127
||||||||||     }}}}}}}}}}     ~~~~~~~~~~
||||||||||     }}}}}}}}}}     ~~~~~~~~~~
||||||||||     }}}}}}}}}}     ~~~~~~~~~~
||||||||||     }}}}}}}}}}     ~~~~~~~~~~
||||||||||     }}}}}}}}}}     ~~~~~~~~~~
```

7.1   COMPUTER FOLK ART

Human artists have used the technique of "repetitive design" throughout the ages. It's a timeless idea that has produced art that is intriguing, and often quite beautiful. The motivation has also been practical—it's pretty hard to imagine a textile or wallpaper design that doesn't involve some element of repetition.

The very word "repetition" suggests using a computer as an experimental tool for developing new patterns of this kind. The ability of computers to do nested looping is one of their strong points. Let's see if we can write some programs that make this capability available to an amateur artist who wants to explore the world of repetitive design.

The Repeat-A-Design Program

This program allows the artist to specify a rectangular pattern as the basic element of a design. The pattern is made up of 80 alphanumeric characters (this number can easily be changed of course). Then the creator can ask to see the effect of repeating this design six times across, and down as many teletype lines as desired.

The program puts each row of the artist's design in the string variable S\$ (see line 130). Then it transfers this string to the first row of the picture array P\$, repeating it six times across. For example, if the user first inputs the string ABCDEFGHIJ we have:

S\$ = | ABCDEFGHIJ |

and P\$(1) = | ABCDEFGHIJABCDEFGHIJABC . . . etc. six times . . . FGHIJ |

The next S\$ is placed in P\$(2) six times, and so on. The feature used in this program for "adding" six strings together across P\$(1) is the "+" or CONCATENATION operator for strings. For example, "CAT" + "DOG" gives CATDOG. So line 150 concatenates six copies of S\$.

```
150 FOR J=1 TO 6:P$(I)=P$(I)+S$:NEXT J
```

Here's a listing and run of the Repeat-A-Design program:

REPEAT-A-DESIGN

```
LIST

1 RANDOMIZE
5 A=8:B=10
6 DIM P$(8)
10 PRINT"REPEAT-A-DESIGN PROGRAM"
20 FOR I=1 TO 2
30 PRINT"XXXXXXXXXX"
40 IF I=2 THEN 90
50 FOR J=1 TO 6: PRINT"X          X": NEXT J
60 NEXT I
90 PRINT:PRINT"TYPE IN YOUR DESIGN."
100 PRINT"IT SHOULD BE";A;"STRINGS, EACH";B;"CHARACTERS LONG."
110 PRINT"FOLLOW EACH STRING WITH A CARRIAGE RETURN."
115 PRINT"IF YOU MAKE A MISTAKE, TYPE STOP."
120 PRINT"DESIGN--"
125 FOR I=1 TO 8
126 P$(I)=""        ◄──────────────
130 INPUT S$
140 IF S$="STOP" THEN 120
150 FOR J=1 TO 6: P$(I)=P$(I)+S$: NEXT J
160 NEXT I              ◄──────────
170 PRINT"HOW MANY LINES";:INPUT C
```

"" IS A NULL (EMPTY) STRING. S\$ IS ADDED TO IT REPEATEDLY IN LINE 150 TO MAKE ONE LONG STRING.

```
175 N=0
180 FOR I=1 TO 99
190 FOR J=1 TO 8
195 N=N+1
200 IF N>C THEN 250
210 PRINT P$(J)
220 NEXT J
230 NEXT I
250 PRINT"WANT MORE OF THIS DESIGN";:INPUT A$
260 IF A$="YES" THEN 170
999 END
```

```
RUN
REPEAT-A-DESIGN PROGRAM
XXXXXXXXXX
X        X
X        X
X        X
X        X
X        X
X        X
XXXXXXXXXX

TYPE IN YOUR DESIGN.
IT SHOULD BE 8 STRINGS, EACH 10 CHARACTERS LONG.
FOLLOW EACH STRING WITH A CARRIAGE RETURN.
IF YOU MAKE A MISTAKE, TYPE STOP.
DESIGN--
? ///****///
? /*      */
? *  *  *  *
? *   0%   *
? *   %0   *
? *  *  *  *
? /*      */
? ///****///
HOW MANY LINES? 24
///****/////////****/////////****/////////****/////////****/////////****///
/*      *//*      *//*      *//*      *//*      *//*      */
*  *  *  **  *  *  **  *  *  **  *  *  **  *  *  **  *  *  *
*   0%   **   0%   **   0%   **   0%   **   0%   **   0%   *
*   %0   **   %0   **   %0   **   %0   **   %0   **   %0   *
*  *  *  **  *  *  **  *  *  **  *  *  **  *  *  **  *  *  *
/*      *//*      *//*      *//*      *//*      *//*      */
///****/////////****/////////****/////////****/////////****/////////****///
///****/////////****/////////****/////////****/////////****/////////****///
/*      *//*      *//*      *//*      *//*      *//*      */
*  *  *  **  *  *  **  *  *  **  *  *  **  *  *  **  *  *  *
*   0%   **   0%   **   0%   **   0%   **   0%   **   0%   *
*   %0   **   %0   **   %0   **   %0   **   %0   **   %0   *
*  *  *  **  *  *  **  *  *  **  *  *  **  *  *  **  *  *  *
/*      *//*      *//*      *//*      *//*      *//*      */
///****/////////****/////////****/////////****/////////****/////////****///
///****/////////****/////////****/////////****/////////****/////////****///
/*      *//*      *//*      *//*      *//*      *//*      */
*  *  *  **  *  *  **  *  *  **  *  *  **  *  *  **  *  *  *
*   0%   **   0%   **   0%   **   0%   **   0%   **   0%   *
*   %0   **   %0   **   %0   **   %0   **   %0   **   %0   *
*  *  *  **  *  *  **  *  *  **  *  *  **  *  *  **  *  *  *
/*      *//*      *//*      *//*      *//*      *//*      */
///****/////////****/////////****/////////****/////////****/////////****///
WANT MORE OF THIS DESIGN? NO
```

Other Approaches to this Program

1. If your BASIC doesn't have the "+" concatenation operator, another approach is to make P$ an 8 x 6 array P$(J,K) and load up the repetitions across as follows:

```
6 DIM P$(8,6)
150 FOR K=1 TO 6
151 LET P$(J,K) = S$
152 NEXT J
```

The print statement 210 will have to be modified accordingly as follows:

```
210 FOR K=1 TO 6
211 PRINT P$(J,K);
212 NEXT K
213 PRINT
```

2. Here's an even simpler approach which uses a 1-dimensional string array. You'll notice that the printing is controlled by three loops; one to control repetition across the page, one to select the lines of the pattern, and one to control the number of lines of patterns.

SIMPLE
REPEAT-A-DESIGN

```
LIST

10 DIM P$(10)
20 PRINT "HOW MANY CHARACTERS PER LINE"
25 INPUT C
30 PRINT "HOW MANY LINES PER BLOCK"
35 INPUT L
36 PRINT "HOW MANY ROWS OF BLOCKS";
37 INPUT R
40 FOR J=1 TO L
50 PRINT "TYPE";C;"CHARACTERS FOR LINE #";J
60 INPUT P$(J)
70 NEXT J
100 PRINT "HOW MANY BLOCKS ACROSS";
105 INPUT B
110 PRINT "YOU NEED A TERMINAL WITH";B*C;"COLUMNS"
120 PRINT "WANT TO CHANGE # OF BLOCKS(0=NO)";
125 INPUT A
130 IF A>0 THEN 100
200 FOR I=1 TO R
210 FOR J=1 TO L
220 FOR K=1 TO B
230 PRINT P$(J);
240 NEXT K
250 PRINT
260 NEXT J
270 NEXT I
280 END
```

THESE 3 LOOPS PRINT THE PATTERN. R CONTROLS THE NUMBER OF ROWS OF BLOCKS, L THE NUMBER OF LINES PER BLOCK, AND B THE NUMBER OF BLOCKS PER ROW.

```
RUN

HOW MANY CHARACTERS PER LINE
? 7
HOW MANY LINES PER BLOCK
? 5
HOW MANY ROWS OF BLOCKS? 8
TYPE 7 CHARACTERS FOR LINE # 1
? !!!!!!!
TYPE 7 CHARACTERS FOR LINE # 2
? !     !
TYPE 7 CHARACTERS FOR LINE # 3
? !  #  !
TYPE 7 CHARACTERS FOR LINE # 4
? !     !
TYPE 7 CHARACTERS FOR LINE # 5
? !!!!!!!
HOW MANY BLOCKS ACROSS? 10
YOU NEED A TERMINAL WITH 70 COLUMNS
WANT TO CHANGE # OF BLOCKS(0=NO)? 0
!!!!!!!!!!!!!!!!!!!!!!!!!!!!!!!!!!!!!!!!!!!!!!!!!!!!!!!!!!!!!!!!!!!!!!!!
!       !!       !!       !!       !!       !!       !!       !!       !!       !!       !
!   #   !!   #   !!   #   !!   #   !!   #   !!   #   !!   #   !!   #   !!   #   !!   #   !
!       !!       !!       !!       !!       !!       !!       !!       !!       !!       !
!!!!!!!!!!!!!!!!!!!!!!!!!!!!!!!!!!!!!!!!!!!!!!!!!!!!!!!!!!!!!!!!!!!!!!!!
!!!!!!!!!!!!!!!!!!!!!!!!!!!!!!!!!!!!!!!!!!!!!!!!!!!!!!!!!!!!!!!!!!!!!!!!
!       !!       !!       !!       !!       !!       !!       !!       !!       !!       !
!   #   !!   #   !!   #   !!   #   !!   #   !!   #   !!   #   !!   #   !!   #   !!   #   !
!       !!       !!       !!       !!       !!       !!       !!       !!       !!       !
!!!!!!!!!!!!!!!!!!!!!!!!!!!!!!!!!!!!!!!!!!!!!!!!!!!!!!!!!!!!!!!!!!!!!!!!
!!!!!!!!!!!!!!!!!!!!!!!!!!!!!!!!!!!!!!!!!!!!!!!!!!!!!!!!!!!!!!!!!!!!!!!!
!       !!       !!       !!       !!       !!       !!       !!       !!       !!       !
!   #   !!   #   !!   #   !!   #   !!   #   !!   #   !!   #   !!   #   !!   #   !!   #   !
!       !!       !!       !!       !!       !!       !!       !!       !!       !!       !
!!!!!!!!!!!!!!!!!!!!!!!!!!!!!!!!!!!!!!!!!!!!!!!!!!!!!!!!!!!!!!!!!!!!!!!!
!!!!!!!!!!!!!!!!!!!!!!!!!!!!!!!!!!!!!!!!!!!!!!!!!!!!!!!!!!!!!!!!!!!!!!!!
!       !!       !!       !!       !!       !!       !!       !!       !!       !!       !
!   #   !!   #   !!   #   !!   #   !!   #   !!   #   !!   #   !!   #   !!   #   !!   #   !
!       !!       !!       !!       !!       !!       !!       !!       !!       !!       !
!!!!!!!!!!!!!!!!!!!!!!!!!!!!!!!!!!!!!!!!!!!!!!!!!!!!!!!!!!!!!!!!!!!!!!!!
!!!!!!!!!!!!!!!!!!!!!!!!!!!!!!!!!!!!!!!!!!!!!!!!!!!!!!!!!!!!!!!!!!!!!!!!
!       !!       !!       !!       !!       !!       !!       !!       !!       !!       !
!   #   !!   #   !!   #   !!   #   !!   #   !!   #   !!   #   !!   #   !!   #   !!   #   !
!       !!       !!       !!       !!       !!       !!       !!       !!       !!       !
!!!!!!!!!!!!!!!!!!!!!!!!!!!!!!!!!!!!!!!!!!!!!!!!!!!!!!!!!!!!!!!!!!!!!!!!
!!!!!!!!!!!!!!!!!!!!!!!!!!!!!!!!!!!!!!!!!!!!!!!!!!!!!!!!!!!!!!!!!!!!!!!!
!       !!       !!       !!       !!       !!       !!       !!       !!       !!       !
!   #   !!   #   !!   #   !!   #   !!   #   !!   #   !!   #   !!   #   !!   #   !!   #   !
!       !!       !!       !!       !!       !!       !!       !!       !!       !!       !
!!!!!!!!!!!!!!!!!!!!!!!!!!!!!!!!!!!!!!!!!!!!!!!!!!!!!!!!!!!!!!!!!!!!!!!!
!!!!!!!!!!!!!!!!!!!!!!!!!!!!!!!!!!!!!!!!!!!!!!!!!!!!!!!!!!!!!!!!!!!!!!!!
!       !!       !!       !!       !!       !!       !!       !!       !!       !!       !
!   #   !!   #   !!   #   !!   #   !!   #   !!   #   !!   #   !!   #   !!   #   !!   #   !
!       !!       !!       !!       !!       !!       !!       !!       !!       !!       !
!!!!!!!!!!!!!!!!!!!!!!!!!!!!!!!!!!!!!!!!!!!!!!!!!!!!!!!!!!!!!!!!!!!!!!!!
!!!!!!!!!!!!!!!!!!!!!!!!!!!!!!!!!!!!!!!!!!!!!!!!!!!!!!!!!!!!!!!!!!!!!!!!
!       !!       !!       !!       !!       !!       !!       !!       !!       !!       !
!   #   !!   #   !!   #   !!   #   !!   #   !!   #   !!   #   !!   #   !!   #   !!   #   !
!       !!       !!       !!       !!       !!       !!       !!       !!       !!       !
!!!!!!!!!!!!!!!!!!!!!!!!!!!!!!!!!!!!!!!!!!!!!!!!!!!!!!!!!!!!!!!!!!!!!!!!
```

> NOTE: While this approach is simpler, notice that it must repeat the same
> pattern across the page (lines 220 to 240). The previous two versions have the
> potential for using different patterns across because they use string arrays, and
> different patterns could be loaded in different parts of the array.

3. If you don't have string arrays, the approach shown in the following
   photographs can be tried.

```
LIST
   10 DIM A$(60),B$(8)
   20 FOR J=1 TO 5
   30 PRINT "TYPE 8 CHARACTERS";

   40 INPUT B$
   50 LET A$((J-1)*8+1)=B$
   60 NEXT J
   70 PRINT "HOW MANY ROWS DO YOU WAN
T PRINTED";
   80 INPUT R
   90 FOR I=1 TO R
  100 FOR J=1 TO 5
  110 FOR K=1 TO 5
  120 PRINT A$((J-1)*8+1,J*8);
  130 NEXT K
  150 NEXT J
  160 NEXT I
  200 END

>R
```

Simplified Repeat-A-Design program for a BASIC without
string arrays.

Output from the Simplified Repeat-A-Design program.

Randomized Patterns

The next interesting thing we can do is to let the computer vary the size of the blocks in a rectangular pattern. Here's a program that shows the possibilities. The number 72 in lines 50 and 70 is used to keep the pattern from going off the edge of a 72 column terminal (it will have to be changed for other sizes, of course). If you don't have the "+" concatenation operator, then use an array as shown in the previous section.

Here's a listing and run.

RANDOM PLAID

```
LIST

1 RANDOMIZE
2 PRINT"HOW MANY LINES";:INPUT A
5 PRINT"WHAT CHARACTERS (TYPE IN 2)";:INPUT A$,B$
10 T=0
15 REM-----SET RANDOM 'COLUMNS'----------
20 FOR I=1 TO 7
30 X(I)=INT(20*RND(0)+1)
40 T=T+X(I)
50 IF T>=72 THEN 70
60 NEXT I
70 X(I)=72-(T-X(I))
75 N=I
80 REM-----PRINT PICTURE----------
85 C=0
90 FOR I=1 TO 99
100 REM----- MAKE LINE STRING-----
105 X$=""
110 FOR I=1 TO N
120 FOR J=1 TO X(I)
130 X$=X$+A$
160 NEXT J
165 T$=A$:A$=B$:B$=T$
170 NEXT I
187 REM-----Z = RAND.ROW----------
190 Z=INT(10*RND(0)+1)
200 FOR J=1 TO Z
210 IF C > A THEN 999
230 PRINT X$
245 C=C+1
250 NEXT J
290 NEXT I
999 END
```

THE COLUMNS CAN BE FROM 1 TO 20 CHARACTERS WIDE.

T = TOTAL NUMBER OF CHARACTERS ACROSS. T MAY BE >, =, OR < 72 AFTER THE LOOP.

LINE 70 ADJUSTS THE LAST COLUMN, X(I), TO MAKE TOTAL CHARACTERS = 72. (IF TOTAL T WAS ALREADY 72, IT DOES NO HARM.)

THIS IS A "CIRCULAR SHIFT" WHICH CAUSES THE VALUES OF A$ AND B$ TO ALTERNATE AS THEY ARE ADDED TO X$.

1.   A$ 2.

T$ B$

3.

```
RUN

HOW MANY LINES? 50
WHAT CHARACTERS (TYPE IN 2)? .,$
.................$$$$$$$$$$$$$$................$$$$$$$$$$..$$$$$.......
.................$$$$$$$$$$$$$$................$$$$$$$$$$..$$$$$.......
.................$$$$$$$$$$$$$$................$$$$$$$$$$..$$$$$.......
$$$$$$$$$$$$$$$$$................$$$$$$$$$$$$$$$$..........$$.....$$$$$$$$
$$$$$$$$$$$$$$$$$................$$$$$$$$$$$$$$$$..........$$.....$$$$$$$$
$$$$$$$$$$$$$$$$$................$$$$$$$$$$$$$$$$..........$$.....$$$$$$$$
$$$$$$$$$$$$$$$$$................$$$$$$$$$$$$$$$$..........$$.....$$$$$$$$
$$$$$$$$$$$$$$$$$................$$$$$$$$$$$$$$$$..........$$.....$$$$$$$$
$$$$$$$$$$$$$$$$$................$$$$$$$$$$$$$$$$..........$$.....$$$$$$$$
$$$$$$$$$$$$$$$$$................$$$$$$$$$$$$$$$$..........$$.....$$$$$$$$
$$$$$$$$$$$$$$$$$................$$$$$$$$$$$$$$$$..........$$.....$$$$$$$$
$$$$$$$$$$$$$$$$$................$$$$$$$$$$$$$$$$..........$$.....$$$$$$$$
$$$$$$$$$$$$$$$$$................$$$$$$$$$$$$$$$$..........$$.....$$$$$$$$
................$$$$$$$$$$$$$$$.................$$$$$$$$$$..$$$$$.......
................$$$$$$$$$$$$$$$.................$$$$$$$$$$..$$$$$.......
................$$$$$$$$$$$$$$$.................$$$$$$$$$$..$$$$$.......
................$$$$$$$$$$$$$$$.................$$$$$$$$$$..$$$$$.......
$$$$$$$$$$$$$$$$$................$$$$$$$$$$$$$$$$..........$$.....$$$$$$$$
$$$$$$$$$$$$$$$$$................$$$$$$$$$$$$$$$$..........$$.....$$$$$$$$
$$$$$$$$$$$$$$$$$................$$$$$$$$$$$$$$$$..........$$.....$$$$$$$$
$$$$$$$$$$$$$$$$$................$$$$$$$$$$$$$$$$..........$$.....$$$$$$$$
$$$$$$$$$$$$$$$$$................$$$$$$$$$$$$$$$$..........$$.....$$$$$$$$
................$$$$$$$$$$$$$$$.................$$$$$$$$$$..$$$$$.......
................$$$$$$$$$$$$$$$.................$$$$$$$$$$..$$$$$.......
................$$$$$$$$$$$$$$$.................$$$$$$$$$$..$$$$$.......
................$$$$$$$$$$$$$$$.................$$$$$$$$$$..$$$$$.......
................$$$$$$$$$$$$$$$.................$$$$$$$$$$..$$$$$.......
$$$$$$$$$$$$$$$$$................$$$$$$$$$$$$$$$$..........$$.....$$$$$$$$
................$$$$$$$$$$$$$$$.................$$$$$$$$$$..$$$$$.......
$$$$$$$$$$$$$$$$$................$$$$$$$$$$$$$$$$..........$$.....$$$$$$$$
................$$$$$$$$$$$$$$$.................$$$$$$$$$$..$$$$$.......
................$$$$$$$$$$$$$$$.................$$$$$$$$$$..$$$$$.......
................$$$$$$$$$$$$$$$.................$$$$$$$$$$..$$$$$.......
................$$$$$$$$$$$$$$$.................$$$$$$$$$$..$$$$$.......
................$$$$$$$$$$$$$$$.................$$$$$$$$$$..$$$$$.......
................$$$$$$$$$$$$$$$.................$$$$$$$$$$..$$$$$.......
................$$$$$$$$$$$$$$$.................$$$$$$$$$$..$$$$$.......
................$$$$$$$$$$$$$$$.................$$$$$$$$$$..$$$$$.......
................$$$$$$$$$$$$$$$.................$$$$$$$$$$..$$$$$.......
$$$$$$$$$$$$$$$$$................$$$$$$$$$$$$$$$$..........$$.....$$$$$$$$
$$$$$$$$$$$$$$$$$................$$$$$$$$$$$$$$$$..........$$.....$$$$$$$$
$$$$$$$$$$$$$$$$$................$$$$$$$$$$$$$$$$..........$$.....$$$$$$$$
$$$$$$$$$$$$$$$$$................$$$$$$$$$$$$$$$$..........$$.....$$$$$$$$
$$$$$$$$$$$$$$$$$................$$$$$$$$$$$$$$$$..........$$.....$$$$$$$$
$$$$$$$$$$$$$$$$$................$$$$$$$$$$$$$$$$..........$$.....$$$$$$$$
$$$$$$$$$$$$$$$$$................$$$$$$$$$$$$$$$$..........$$.....$$$$$$$$
$$$$$$$$$$$$$$$$$................$$$$$$$$$$$$$$$$..........$$.....$$$$$$$$
$$$$$$$$$$$$$$$$$................$$$$$$$$$$$$$$$$..........$$.....$$$$$$$$
................$$$$$$$$$$$$$$$.................$$$$$$$$$$..$$$$$.......
```

There is no need to limit the patterns to just two kinds of characters. Here's a version using three characters, and as you can see the pattern starts to get a lot more interesting.

TRIPLE RANDOM PLAID

```
LIST

1 RANDOMIZE
2 PRINT"HOW MANY LINES";:INPUT A
4 PRINT"WHAT CHARACTERS (TYPE IN 3)";:INPUT A$,B$,C$
10 T=0
15 REM-----SET RANDOM "COLUMNS"----------
20 FOR I=1 TO 7
30 X(I)=INT(20*RND(0)+1)
40 T=T+X(I)
50 IF T>=72 THEN 70
60 NEXT I
70 X(I)=72-(T-X(I))
75 N=I
80 REM-----PRINT PICTURE----------
85 C=0
90 FOR I=1 TO 99
100 REM----- MAKE LINE STRING-----
105 X$=""
110 FOR I=1 TO N
120 FOR J=1 TO X(I)
130 X$=X$+A$
160 NEXT J
165 T$=A$:A$=B$:B$=C$:C$=T$  ←
170 NEXT I
187 REM-----Z = RAND.ROW----------
190 Z=INT(10*RND(0)+1)
200 FOR J=1 TO Z
210 IF C > A THEN 999
230 PRINT X$
245 C=C+1
250 NEXT J
290 NEXT I
999 END
```

AN EVEN BIGGER CIRCULAR SHIFT!

1.   A$ 2.

T$ B$

4.   C$ 3.

```
RUN

HOW MANY LINES? 50
WHAT CHARACTERS (TYPE IN 3)? .,$,/
..................$$$$$$$$$$$$$$$$$//////////////////...........$$/////........
..................$$$$$$$$$$$$$$$$$//////////////////.........$$/////........
..................$$$$$$$$$$$$$$$$$//////////////////........$$/////........
$$$$$$$$$$$$$$$$$//////////////////...................$$$$$$$$$$$//.....$$$$$$$
$$$$$$$$$$$$$$$$$//////////////////...................$$$$$$$$$$$//.....$$$$$$$
$$$$$$$$$$$$$$$$$//////////////////...................$$$$$$$$$$$//.....$$$$$$$
$$$$$$$$$$$$$$$$$//////////////////...................$$$$$$$$$$$//.....$$$$$$$
$$$$$$$$$$$$$$$$$//////////////////...................$$$$$$$$$$$//.....$$$$$$$
$$$$$$$$$$$$$$$$$//////////////////...................$$$$$$$$$$$//.....$$$$$$$
$$$$$$$$$$$$$$$$$//////////////////...................$$$$$$$$$$$//.....$$$$$$$
$$$$$$$$$$$$$$$$$//////////////////...................$$$$$$$$$$$//.....$$$$$$$
$$$$$$$$$$$$$$$$$//////////////////...................$$$$$$$$$$$//.....$$$$$$$
$$$$$$$$$$$$$$$$$//////////////////...................$$$$$$$$$$$//.....$$$$$$$
//////////////.................$$$$$$$$$$$$$$$$$//////////..$$$$$///////
//////////////.................$$$$$$$$$$$$$$$$$//////////..$$$$$///////
//////////////.................$$$$$$$$$$$$$$$$$//////////..$$$$$///////
//////////////.................$$$$$$$$$$$$$$$$$//////////..$$$$$///////
.................$$$$$$$$$$$$$$$$$//////////////////...........$$/////........
.................$$$$$$$$$$$$$$$$$//////////////////...........$$/////........
.................$$$$$$$$$$$$$$$$$//////////////////...........$$/////........
.................$$$$$$$$$$$$$$$$$//////////////////...........$$/////........
$$$$$$$$$$$$$$$$$//////////////////...................$$$$$$$$$$$//.....$$$$$$$
$$$$$$$$$$$$$$$$$//////////////////...................$$$$$$$$$$$//.....$$$$$$$
$$$$$$$$$$$$$$$$$//////////////////...................$$$$$$$$$$$//.....$$$$$$$
$$$$$$$$$$$$$$$$$//////////////////...................$$$$$$$$$$$//.....$$$$$$$
$$$$$$$$$$$$$$$$$//////////////////...................$$$$$$$$$$$//.....$$$$$$$
//////////////.................$$$$$$$$$$$$$$$$$//////////..$$$$$///////
.................$$$$$$$$$$$$$$$$$//////////////////...........$$/////........
$$$$$$$$$$$$$$$$$//////////////////...................$$$$$$$$$$$//.....$$$$$$$
//////////////.................$$$$$$$$$$$$$$$$$//////////..$$$$$///////
//////////////.................$$$$$$$$$$$$$$$$$//////////..$$$$$///////
//////////////.................$$$$$$$$$$$$$$$$$//////////..$$$$$///////
//////////////.................$$$$$$$$$$$$$$$$$//////////..$$$$$///////
//////////////.................$$$$$$$$$$$$$$$$$//////////..$$$$$///////
//////////////.................$$$$$$$$$$$$$$$$$//////////..$$$$$///////
//////////////.................$$$$$$$$$$$$$$$$$//////////..$$$$$///////
//////////////.................$$$$$$$$$$$$$$$$$//////////..$$$$$///////
//////////////.................$$$$$$$$$$$$$$$$$//////////..$$$$$///////
.................$$$$$$$$$$$$$$$$$//////////////////...........$$/////........
.................$$$$$$$$$$$$$$$$$//////////////////...........$$/////........
.................$$$$$$$$$$$$$$$$$//////////////////...........$$/////........
.................$$$$$$$$$$$$$$$$$//////////////////...........$$/////........
.................$$$$$$$$$$$$$$$$$//////////////////...........$$/////........
.................$$$$$$$$$$$$$$$$$//////////////////...........$$/////........
.................$$$$$$$$$$$$$$$$$//////////////////...........$$/////........
.................$$$$$$$$$$$$$$$$$//////////////////...........$$/////........
.................$$$$$$$$$$$$$$$$$//////////////////...........$$/////........
$$$$$$$$$$$$$$$$$//////////////////...................$$$$$$$$$$$//.....$$$$$$$
```

7.2   PAINT BY NUMBERS
(COMPUTER INSTIGATED ART)

You've probably already gotten the idea that the patterns used in the previous section would look great in color. This suggests using a scheme where the human artist (aged 4?) takes over and uses crayons or paints to finish the job "instigated" by the computer. To make it easier, you could print characters like R, G, B to mean Red, Green, Blue, and so on.

Here's another pattern program to use as a paint-by-character template. This time, the random generator is used to vary the width of the basic patterns. The effect is one of curved lines. One use of this program is to generate a supply of patterns that can be used for cut-and-paste projects.

```
RUN

HOW MANY LINES? 25
WHAT CHARACTERS (TYPE IN 2)? .,$


                  ..........................$$$$$$$$$$$$$$$$$$$$$$$$$$
                  ..........................$$$$$$$$$$$$$$$$$$$$$$$$$
                  ...........................$$$$$$$$$$$$$$$$$$$$$$$$$$$$
                  ...........................$$$$$$$$$$$$$$$$$$$$$$$$$$$$
                   ..........................$$$$$$$$$$$$$$$$$$$$$$$$$$
                   ..........................$$$$$$$$$$$$$$$$$$$$$$$$$$
                    .........................$$$$$$$$$$$$$$$$$$$$$$$$$$$$$$
                    ..........................$$$$$$$$$$$$$$$$$$$$$$$$$$$$$
                     ........................$$$$$$$$$$$$$$$$$$$$$$$$$$$$$
                     ........................$$$$$$$$$$$$$$$$$$$$$$$$$$$$$$$$
                      ......................$$$$$$$$$$$$$$$$$$$$$$$$$$$$
                      ......................$$$$$$$$$$$$$$$$$$$$$$$$$$
                       .....................$$$$$$$$$$$$$$$$$$$$$$$$$$
                       .....................$$$$$$$$$$$$$$$$$$$$$$$$$$
                    ........................$$$$$$$$$$$$$$$$$$$$$$$
                    ........................$$$$$$$$$$$$$$$$$$$$$$$
                      ......................$$$$$$$$$$$$$$$$$$$$$$$
                      ......................$$$$$$$$$$$$$$$$$$$$$$$
                        ....................$$$$$$$$$$$$$$$$$$$$$$$$
                        ....................$$$$$$$$$$$$$$$$$$$$$$$$
                         ...................$$$$$$$$$$$$$$$$$$$$$$$$
                         ...................$$$$$$$$$$$$$$$$$$$$$$$$
                          .................$$$$$$$$$$$$$$$$$$$$$$$
                          .................$$$$$$$$$$$$$$$$$$$$$$$
```

```
LIST

1 RANDOMIZE
10 PRINT"HOW MANY LINES";:INPUT L
20 PRINT"WHAT CHARACTERS (TYPE IN 2)";:INPUT A$,B$
25 PRINT:PRINT
30 C=35: X1=25: X2=25
50 FOR I=1 TO INT(L/2)
55 X$=""
60 FOR J=1 TO C-X1: X$=X$+" ": NEXT J
70 FOR J=1 TO X1: X$=X$+A$: NEXT J
90 FOR J=1 TO X2: X$=X$+B$: NEXT J
100 FOR J=1 TO 2: PRINT X$: NEXT J
110 C=C+INT(7*RND(0)-3)
120 X1=X1+INT(7*RND(0)-3)
130 X2=X2+INT(7*RND(0)-3)
140 NEXT I
999 END
```

VARIABLE STREAM

Here's a variation on the previous program that allows three symbols to be used. It also forces the pattern to be symmetrical about a vertical axis drawn through the middle of the pattern. This symmetry is brought about by multiplying X2 by 2 in line 60. This makes the number of characters in the middle (periods in our example) always change by 2, giving one for the left, and one for the right. Then line 75 creates enough blanks for the left margin to keep the entire line centered about column 30.5.

```
RUN

HOW MANY LINES? 35
WHAT CHARACTERS (TYPE 3)? <,.,>
              <<<<<<<<<<.............>>>>>>>>>>
  <<<<<<<<<<<<<<<<<<<................>>>>>>>>>>>>>>>>>>>
        <<<<<<<<<<<<<...............>>>>>>>>>>>>>
          <<<<<<<<<<<..............>>>>>>>>>>>
          <<<<<<<<<<<..............>>>>>>>>>>>
      <<<<<<<<<<<<<<<<..............>>>>>>>>>>>>>>>>
          <<<<<<<<<<<<.............>>>>>>>>>>>>
  <<<<<<<<<<<<<<<<<<<<.............>>>>>>>>>>>>>>>>>>>>
            <<<<<<<<<<<..........>>>>>>>>>>>
          <<<<<<<<<.............>>>>>>>>>
        <<<<<<<<<<<<<<<..........>>>>>>>>>>>>>>>
        <<<<<<<<<<<<<<...........>>>>>>>>>>>>>>
        <<<<<<<<<<<<<<...........>>>>>>>>>>>>>>
          <<<<<<<<<<<<<..........>>>>>>>>>>>>>
      <<<<<<<<<<<<<<<<<..........>>>>>>>>>>>>>>>>>
          <<<<<<<<<<.............>>>>>>>>>>
        <<<<<<<<<<<<<<...........>>>>>>>>>>>>>>
          <<<<<<<<<<<.............>>>>>>>>>>>
          <<<<<<<<<<<<<<..........>>>>>>>>>>>>>>
          <<<<<<<<<<<<.............>>>>>>>>>>>>
  <<<<<<<<<<<<<<<<<<<<..............>>>>>>>>>>>>>>>>>>>>
          <<<<<<<<<<<..............>>>>>>>>>>>
        <<<<<<<<<<<<<<............>>>>>>>>>>>>>>
        <<<<<<<<<<<<<...........>>>>>>>>>>>>>
          <<<<<<<<<<<.............>>>>>>>>>>>
        <<<<<<<<<<<<<<<..........>>>>>>>>>>>>>>>
          <<<<<<<<<<<<<..........>>>>>>>>>>>>>
            <<<<<<<<<<..........>>>>>>>>>>
          <<<<<<<<<<<<.............>>>>>>>>>>>>
            <<<<<<<<<<..........>>>>>>>>>>
      <<<<<<<<<<<<<<...........>>>>>>>>>>>>>>
    <<<<<<<<<<<<<<<<<..............>>>>>>>>>>>>>>>>>
      <<<<<<<<<<<<<<<<...........>>>>>>>>>>>>>>>>
  <<<<<<<<<<<<<<<<<<<<..............>>>>>>>>>>>>>>>>>>>>
          <<<<<<<<<<<..............>>>>>>>>>>>
```

**SYMMETRIC
STREAM**

```
LIST

5 RANDOMIZE
10 PRINT "HOW MANY LINES";:INPUT L
20 PRINT "WHAT CHARACTERS (TYPE 3)";:INPUT A$,B$,C$
40 FOR I=1 TO L
50 X1=INT(11*RND(0)+10)
60 X2=2*INT(6*RND(0)+5)
75 LET X=30-(2*X1+X2)/2
77 LETX$=""
80 FOR J=1 TO X:X$=X$+" ":NEXT J
90 FOR J=1 TO X1:X$=X$+A$:NEXT J
110 FOR J=1 TO X2:X$=X$+B$:NEXT J
130 FOR J=1 TO X1:X$=X$+C$:NEXT J
140 PRINT X$
150 NEXT I
160 END
```

Permutations and Patterns

The following program gives more than permutations. Technically, it generates all possible "3-samples of five strings". You could easily get permutations if you wished by eliminating the repetitions (see the BOB&TED&ALICE&CAROL program in Section 4.2).* However, for a pattern program, the repetitions are interesting, so we let the program print all the 3-samples of five things (there are 5*5*5=125). The output is reduced, and shown sideways. With some imagination you may see it as an abstract version of a big city skyline. Experimenting with different string lengths will produce other effects. Incidentally, this program was written for a BASIC without subscripted string variables:

---

*NOTE: The words sample, permutation, selection, and combination all refer to groupings of objects, but with the following technical distinctions (which are not always used in non-mathematical writing):

Samples include both rearrangements and repetitions. For two objects A and B, the 2-samples are

    AA, AB, BA, and BB

Permutations exclude repetitions. The 2-permutations of A and B are

    AB and BA

Selections exclude rearrangements. The 2-selections of A and B are

    AB, AA, and BB

Combinations exclude both repetitions and rearrangements. The 2-combinations of A and B are

    AB

SKYLINE SAMPLES

```
LIST

10 REM-----3-SAMPLES OF N ITEMS (UP TO 5) -----
20 PRINT"MAKE A PICTURE"
30 PRINT"PLEASE TYPE IN FIVE STRINGS"
40 INPUT A$,B$,C$,D$,E$
50 PRINT"HOW MANY STRINGS DO YOU WANT";:INPUT N
60 FOR I=1 TO N
70 FOR J=1 TO N
80 FOR K=1 TO N
90 ON I GOSUB 200,210,220,230,240
100 ON J GOSUB 200,210,220,230,240
110 ON K GOSUB 200,210,220,230,240
120 PRINT
130 NEXT K
140 NEXT J
150 NEXT I
160 GOTO 999
200 PRINT A$;: RETURN
210 PRINT B$;: RETURN
220 PRINT C$;: RETURN
230 PRINT D$;: RETURN
240 PRINT E$;: RETURN
999 END
```

```
MAKE A PICTURE
PLEASE TYPE IN FIVE STRINGS
? /////
? $$$$$$$$$
? 000000000000
? IIIIIIIIIIII
? ........
HOW MANY STRINGS DO YOU WANT? 5
```

7.3   ELECTRIC FIELD ART

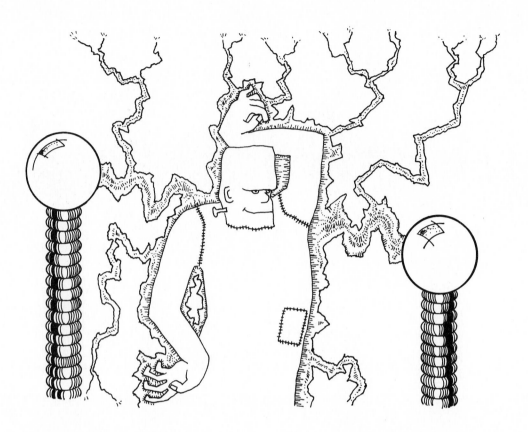

New ideas for "computer art" are often suggested by graphing patterns that arise from mathematical or scientific computations. In this section we'll show how to generate some striking patterns by using the mathematical formulas that describe the potential of an electric field due to several point charges.

The basic formula says that electric field potential V is proportional to the charge causing the field, but inversely proportional to the distance R from the charge. With several charges C(I), a sum of field potentials must be taken.

If you look at the listing of our program, you'll see that this is done in line 95 which is controlled by the I loop.

```
80 FOR I=1 TO N
95 V=V+C(I)/R
```

R is the distance from any point (X,Y) to charge C(I), and it's calculated in line 85 by the good old Pythagorean formula. In our program, all these calculations are done as part of what's called a multi-line function (in lines 60 to 120). If your BASIC doesn't have multi-line functions, you can use a subroutine instead. In this case,

make line 60 GOTO 130
make line 110 RETURN
make line 120 STOP
make line 150 GOSUB 70
and make line 151 LET Z=V

The technique for plotting different characters for different field strengths is to scale Z (the field strength) with line 155. This scaling makes most of the values fall in the range 32 to 126. Any values that stray out of this range are pushed back in by lines 156 and 158. Then line 160 converts the scaled Z into an ASCII character (see Section 7.0). Line 165 is used to create some blank spaces between adjacent regions which makes the pattern more striking. For example, line 165 would make all Z values from 88.6 to 88.9 blanks, while all Z values from 88.0 to 88.5 would produce the character "X" (from line 160).

Our plot is for 78 Y values (line 140), and 60 X values (line 130). The factor $\sqrt{3}/2$ used to scale X (lines 35 and 135) is arbitrary. You can experiment with other values. Here's the program listing and a run.

ELECTRIC FIELDS

```
LIST

10 PRINT "HOW MANY CHARGES DO YOU HAVE";
20 INPUT N
30 FOR I=1 TO N
32 PRINT "TYPE IN THE X AND Y POSITIONS OF CHARGE ";I;:INPUT A(I),B(I)
34 NEXT I
35 FOR I=1 TO N:A(I)=A(I)*SQR(3)/2:NEXT I
40 PRINT "TYPE IN THE SIZE OF EACH CHARGE. USE 3 FOR A CHARGE OF 3Q"
50 FOR I=1 TO N:PRINT "CHARGE ";I;:INPUT C(I):NEXT I
60  DEF FNP(X,Y)
70 V=0
80 FOR I=1 TO N
85 R=SQR((X-A(I))**2+(Y-B(I))**2)
90 IF R=0 THEN 100
95 V=V+C(I)/R:GOTO 105
100 V=99999:GOTO 110
105 NEXT I
110 FNP=V
120 FNEND
130 FOR J=1 TO 121 STEP 2
135 X=J*SQR(3)/2
140 FOR Y=1 TO 78
150 Z=FNP(X,Y)
155 Z=(Z+1)*50
156 IF Z<32 THEN Z=32
158 IF Z>126 THEN Z=126
160 B$=CHR$(Z)
165 IF Z>INT(Z)+0.5 THEN B$=" "
170 PRINT B$;
250 NEXT Y
260 PRINT :NEXT J
9000 END
```

THIS IS A MULTILINE FUNCTION. IT CAN BE REPLACED BY A SUBROUTINE AS EXPLAINED IN THE TEXT.

```
RUN

HOW MANY CHARGES DO YOU HAVE? 5
TYPE IN THE X AND Y POSITIONS OF CHARGE  1 ? 20,20
TYPE IN THE X AND Y POSITIONS OF CHARGE  2 ? 20,60
TYPE IN THE X AND Y POSITIONS OF CHARGE  3 ? 60,50
TYPE IN THE X AND Y POSITIONS OF CHARGE  4 ? 90,20
TYPE IN THE X AND Y POSITIONS OF CHARGE  5 ? 90,60
TYPE IN THE SIZE OF EACH CHARGE. USE 3 FOR A CHARGE OF 3Q
CHARGE  1 ? 1
CHARGE  2 ? 1
CHARGE  3 ? -2
CHARGE  4 ? -1
CHARGE  5 ? 1
```

```
 3333          4444444444444444444444444            44444444444444444444444            3333
 333       44444          444444444444444444444444444                444444           333
 33      4444     555555555        444444444444444444         55555        4444         33
 3      444    555          5555     44444444444444     5555         5555    4444         3
       444   55  666666666     555      444444444     555  66666666    555    4444
      444   55  6  77    77  66  555    44444444    555  6  777777  66  55    444
     444   55 6  78  9999 8 7 6  55     444444    55  6  7 8 999 8 7 6  5    444
     444   5 67      <  <     7 6  55    444444    55 6 7  9:;<<<;:98  6 55    44
    44  55 6    ; @ DC@      7 6  55    444444    5  6     ;=@ D @=;  87 6 5    44
    44  55 6789 =       A= 987 6 55    44444444    5  67 9    VJV       6 5    44
    444 55 67 9 =       = 987 6 5    4444444444   55 6    :     VJVG   :    6 5    44
      44  56  8 ;=@ D @=;      6 55    44444    4444  55 6789 = B B = 9876 5    44      3
 3    444 55 6  89:;  <  ;:98  6 55   444          444 55 67          76 55 44     33
 33    444 55 6 7 88    88  66 5  444      333      44  5  6 7 888  7 6 5   44     333
 333    444   55 66      6  5  444   333333333333   44  5  66666   55 44       3333
 33333     444    55      555  44   33333        333    444           444    33333
  333333     444        444   333   222222222      333     3333333333       33333
    333333      444444    3333   222222        22222     3333333333
       333333333      333333    22222     1111111111      222222                22222
           333333333     3333    22222    11111        11111    2222222222222   22222
 2222              222222    1111     00000      00000   11111             22222
 2222222222222222222222222    111     000   //////////   000    11111
 222222222222222222         1111    000   ///    ....   ....  ///   000   11111
            11111     00   //   ..  --       --  ..  //   000   111111
         111111      000   // . - , ++      ++ , -- . /  000   111111
       111111111      0000  //  . - , * )   ( ) + ,- .. //  00   11111
    1111111111111      0000  //  . - , *)('&%     &   +, - . //  00   1111
 111111111111111       0000  ///  .. - ,      ´$´      "$& )*+, - . /  000   1111
 11111111111       000000   ///  . - ,      #     #  ) ,- . //  00   111
 1111111      0000000   ///  . - ,+  ( $!    ! ´ *+, . /  00   111
 111      0000000    ////  .. -- ,+*)(&$!   ! ´ *+, . /  00   111
 1       00000000    ////  .. -- ,+   ´%       #  ) ,- . //  00   111
     00000000    /////  ... -- , +*)(´  "$& )*+, . /  00   1111
     0000000    //////    ... - , +*   &%    &   +, . /  000   11111
   000000    ////////    ... -- , + *) ((((( )  +,- . //  00   111111
  000000     //////     .....    -- , ++    ++ , - . /  00   111111
 00000    ////     .............   ---   ,,,,,  -- .. //  00   111111
 0000    /////    ..................    ---    .. /  00  11111
 00    /////  ...    .................  //  00  11    2222222
 0    ///  ... --    ----  .......    ///  00  1 22       222222222
 0    ///  .. -- --     ,, --  ....   ////  00  1 22 3  4444    333    22222
     ///  .. - , + **  *  + ,, - ...   ///    00  1 2 3 4  66  5 44  33    22
     //  .. - ,        *+ , - ..   ///   00  1 23 456789    76  44 333      2
     //  . . - , )      )*+, - ..  //  000 11 2 3      =@ @ ;9   5 4 333
     ///  . - ,+*(&"     ( + - .  ///  00 11 2  4568 >EThT ; 765 4 333
     ///  . - ,+*(&"    "&( + - . //  000  1  2 3 45 8    Th   ; 76  44 333
     //  . -, )  #   #  )  , - . //  00  11  2 3 45679;> B >  8 65 44 333
     //  .. - , )     ´ ´      , - .. //  00   11 22 3 4 56789: :    6 5 4  333
     ///  .. - ,+  ***  + - ..  //  000  111 22  3 4 5 6 7777 6 5  4    333
     ///  .. -- ,,, ,,, -- .  ///  000  11  22 33 44 55    55 44  333
 0    ///   ..  -------   .. ///  0000  11  22 33  444     444   3333
 00    ///  .....   ....  ///  0000  111  222  33           33333
 000    /////           ////  0000  111  222     333333333333333
 00000    //////////////  0000  11111  2222     333333333            2
 0000000    ///////   00000  11111  22222                      222
  000000000        0000000   111111   2222222           222222
   000000000000    00000000   111111   22222222222    222222222
    00000000000000000000000  1111111  22222222222222222222222
     00000000000000000000  1111111   2222222222222222222222
       00000  1111111111   2222222222222222222
           00000  1111111111   22222222222222222222
               11111111111   2222222222222222222
```

The Lissajous Christmas Tree

The next two programs are presented just for fun, and we'll not try to explain them. They were developed by a science teacher (Mike Shore) for his students, and if you want to figure out how they work grab your old physics textbook and look up the subject of Lissajous figures. Then throw in the information that the coefficient of the COS function in line 50 is variable, and so is the translation of the SIN function in line 60. As to how the plotting is done—well, there will be an explanation of a more structured general plotting program in Section 7.4 which will be a better one to study. Incidentally, the reason the second program was written to produce an "upside-down" tree was to use the letter "V" as a pointed star on top of the tree.

LISSAJOUS TREE 1

```
LIST

10  W=.0314159265
20  D=3.14159265/4
30  DIM A$(1,61),Z$(100),X(100),Y(100)
40  FOR I=1 TO 100:T=I*8.6
50  X(I)=(100-T/10)*COS(W*T+D)+125
60  Y(I)=20*SIN(2*W*T)+20+T/5
70  NEXT I
90  J=29:GOSUB 300
100 FOR I=1 TO 61:A$(1,I)=" ":NEXT I
105 J=J-1
110 FOR I=1 TO 100
120 IF Y(I)>(J+.5)*256/36 THEN 200
130 NEXT I
135 IF J<6 THEN A$(1,30)="H"
140 FOR I=1 TO 61:PRINT A$(1,I);:NEXT I:PRINT
150 IF J<1 THEN 500
160 GOTO 100
200 K=INT(X(I)/256*60+0.5):A$(1,K)="*":Y(I)=Y(I)-300
220 GOTO 130
300 PRINT TAB(28)"*"
310 PRINT TAB(27)"* *"
320 PRINT TAB(25)"*        *"
330 PRINT TAB(27)"* *"
340 PRINT TAB(28)"*"
350 RETURN
500 END
```

**LISSAJOUS
TREE 2**

```
RUN

                                    H
                                    H
              00                    H
                 00                 H
                   O                H                O              00
                 O         O        O        O                  O
                                    O                      O
              00                 O                    O O
              O     O                      O     O          O
                O     O                                   O
                    O                                   O
                 00     O                 O         O O
                 00     O             O         O
                   O         O     O     O        00
                    O     O     O     O
                      O     O     O        00
                      O     O     O O  00
                      O         O O 00
                        O
                        O           00
                      O   O O  00
                        O     O
                      000 000
                       O  O
                      00 O
                        O
                        ^
                      /   \
                     <     >
                      \   /
                        V
```

```
LIST

100 W=.0314159265
110 DIM A$(1,61),Z$(100),X(100),Y(100)
120 A=1:B=1:J=0:D=3.14159265/4
130 FOR I=1 TO 100
140 X=(100-I*9/10)*COS(W*I*9+D)+125
145 Y=20*SIN(2*W*I*9)+20+I*9/5
147 Z$(I)="O"
150 X(I)=X/125-1:Y(I)=Y/125
155 NEXT I
210 GOSUB 250
215 IF J>5 GOTO 220
218 A$(1,30)="H"
220 FOR I=1 TO 61:PRINT A$(1,I);:NEXT I:PRINT
230 IF J<26 GOTO 210
240 GOTO 330
250 FOR I=1 TO 61:LET A$(1,I)=" ":NEXT I
260 J=J+1:FOR I=1 TO 100
270 IF Y(I)<(J-.5)/15 THEN 300
280 NEXT I
290 GOTO 320
300 LET K=INT((X(I)+1)*30+1.5):LET A$(1,K)=Z$(I):Y(I)=Y(I)+2*B+1
310 GOTO 280
320 RETURN
330 FOR I=1 TO 61:LET A$(1,I)=" ":NEXT I
340 LET A$(1,31)="^"
345 GOSUB 500
350 LET A$(1,30)="/":A$(1,31)=" ":A$(1,32)="\"
355 GOSUB 500
360 A$(1,29)="<":A$(1,30)=" ":A$(1,32)=" ":A$(1,33)=">"
365 GOSUB 500
370 A$(1,29)=" ":A$(1,30)="\":A$(1,32)="/":A$(1,33)=" "
375 GOSUB 500
380 A$(1,30)=" ":A$(1,31)="V":A$(1,32)=" "
385 GOSUB 500
399 GOTO 520
500 FOR I=1 TO 61 :PRINT A$(1,I);:NEXT I:PRINT
510 RETURN
520 END
```

7.4   PLOTTING MULTIPLE-VALUED FUNCTIONS;
AUTOMATIC SCALING

Many interesting mathematical functions are multiple-valued. This means that for a given argument, there can be several functional values. For example, for X=4, SQR(X) has values of both +2 and -2. The SQR(X) function on computers usually just gives the +2 value, and ignores the -2 possibility. But for other functions invented by programmers (like those used in the Lissajous Christmas tree programs), being able to find and graph several values on the same line is important.

Let's first look at a simple way of graphing two values on the same line, and then go to a much more powerful program which can handle any number of values. The general program will also include such nice features an automatic scaling, and automatic placing and printing of axes.

First, A Simple Approach to "Double" Graphs

Suppose we we want to plot both the SIN and COS functions on the same graph. We know from trigonometry that the picture should look something like that in our sketch.

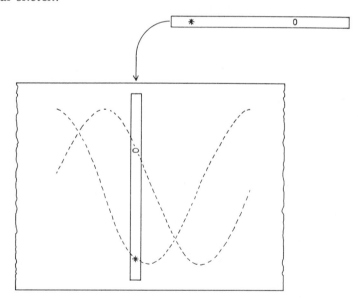

Imagine this to be the paper from a terminal rotated 90 degrees. So the arrow points to one line on the terminal. This means we want to print two characters on that line as shown in the horizontal rectangle. The 0 is for the cosine, and the * is for the sine. The problem is that a terminal usually can't backup, so our program has to know ahead of time which symbol to print first. Here's a program that does this by comparing the two functions (in line 80), and printing the symbol for the smaller value first. In case they are equal (line 90) it would print a "+" sign. A better test for line 90 would be: IF ABS(Y1-Y2)<.01 THEN 120 which means print "+" if they are "practically" equal.

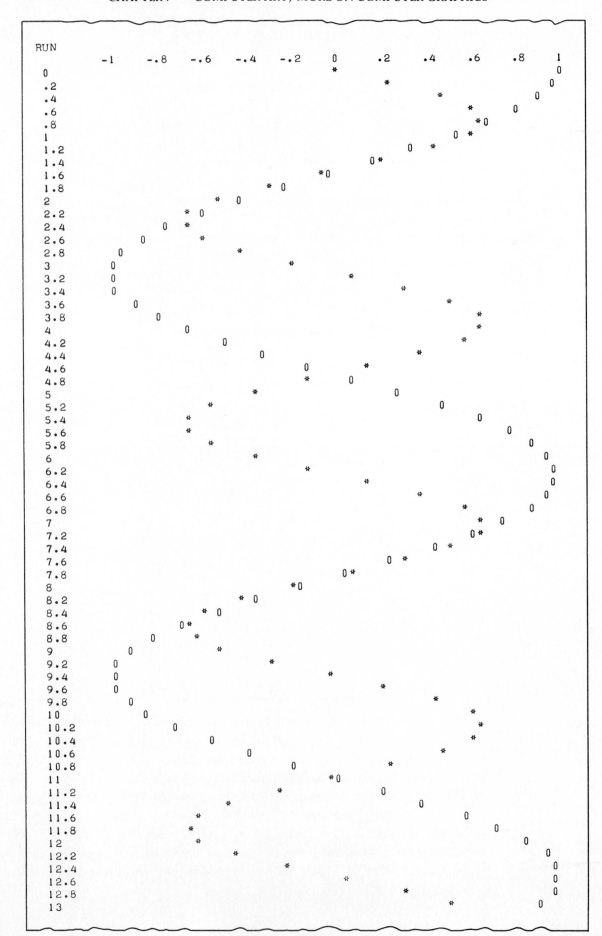

DOUBLE GRAPH

```
LIST

10 FOR F = -1 TO 1.1 STEP .2
20 PRINT TAB (9 + 30 * (F + 1)); INT (F * 100)/100;
30 NEXT F
40 PRINT
50 FOR A = 0 TO 13 STEP .2
60 LET Y1 =20*(SIN(2*A)+1)+20
70 LET Y2 = 30 * (COS (A) + 1) +10
75 PRINT INT (100 * A + .5)/100;
80 IF Y2 < Y1 THEN 140
90 IF Y2 = Y1 THEN 120
100 PRINT TAB (Y1); "*" ; TAB (Y2); "0"
110 GOTO 150
120 PRINT TAB (Y1); "+"
130 GOTO 150
140 PRINT TAB (Y2); "0"; TAB (Y1); "*"
150 NEXT A
160 END
```

A General Plotting Program with Automatic
Scaling and Automatic Axes

This program uses a 1-dimensional string array A$ which is "loaded" with all
the symbols needed for one line of printing. For example, it may look like
this:

We can call A$ a "line image". It holds the symbols for one line of a graph as
follows:

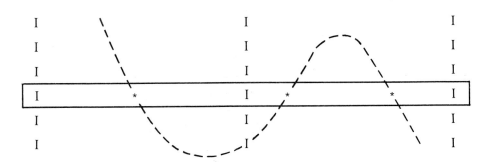

Our graphing program will have to figure out ahead of time exactly how many asterisks go in the line image, and at what positions. It should also calculate where the Y axis "I" symbol goes, and put in the left and right border symbols (if desired).

We've decided to scale our graph so it fills a space 60 characters wide and 36 lines high. This makes the space a square, since terminals usually print 10 horizontal characters per inch, but only six vertical lines per inch. In order to do scaling, our program will generate a table of X and Y values, and while doing so "remember" what the smallest (MIN) and largest (MAX) values are.

Then the difference between MAX and MIN values of X divided into 60 gives the X scale factor (# of terminal spaces per X unit). Similarly, the differences between the MAX and MIN of Y divided into 36 will give the Y scale factor (number of terminal lines per Y unit). Of course the numbers 60 and 36 can be modified for other terminals.

The heart of our plotting program is in lines 600 to 650. J is the row number for the line image we are about to fill. The FOR loop in 600 searches through the table of X and Y values, and tests for which Y values should *not* have "*" symbols put in the line image for row J (see line 610). When it finds one which *should* go in this row, then it must calculate in which column position the "*" goes. This is done in line 620, while line 630 does the actual insertion of the "*" in A\$. Line 640 then changes this Y value to a negative number as a signal that it's been taken care of, and should be skipped the next time around the loop. The functions of the other parts of the program are explained in the balloons on the listing.

To use this program, you must put the function you want plotted in lines 60 and 70 using what's called parametric form. Our listing contains the two parametric equations

```
60 X(M) = COS(A)↑3
70 Y(M) = SIN(A)↑3
```

The idea is that you let some third quantity called a *parameter* change, and then calculate each X and Y in terms of this quantity. The parameter we are using is A, which can be thought of as an angle. (Amateur Radio buffs will recognize A as w*t, that is, as angular frequency * time). The parameter is changed in line 40. In our example we are generating 63 values of A (0,.1,.2,.3,...,6.0,6.1,6.2). This is because we want the angle A to go through 360 degrees, which is from 0 to 6.2 (2*π) radians.

SUPER PLOT

```
10    DIM A$(61),B$(62),X(100),Y(100)
20  LET M = 0
30  LET J=36
40  FOR A=0 TO 6.2 STEP .1
50  LET M = M + 1
60  LET X(M) =COS(A)^3
70  LET Y(M)=SIN(A)^3
80  REM FIND MIN AND MAX
90  IF M<>1 THEN 150
100 LET X9 = X(1)
110 LET X1 = X(1)
120 LET Y9 = Y(1)
130 LET Y1 = Y(1)
140 GOTO 230
150 IF X9> = X(M) THEN 170
160 LET X9 = X(M)
170 IF X1 <X(M) THEN 190
180 LET X1 = X(M)
190 IF Y9> = Y(M) THEN 210
200 LET Y9 = Y(M)
210 IF Y1<Y(M) THEN 230
220 LET Y1 = Y(M)
230 NEXT A
240 FOR I = 1 TO M
250 LET Y(I) = Y(I) - Y1
260 LET X(I) = X(I) - X1
270 NEXT I
280 LET S1 = 59/(X9 - X1)
290 LET S2 = 36/(Y9 - Y1)
300 LET A1=36-INT(.5+Y9*S2)
310 LET A2=INT(1.5-X1*S1)
320 LET A$(61)="I"
420 PRINT
430 GOSUB 900
490 FOR I = 1 TO 60
500 IF I<>A2 THEN 530
510 LET A$(I)="I"
520 GOTO 540
530 LET A$(I)=" "
540 NEXT I
550 IF J<>A1 THEN 600
560 FOR I = 1 TO 60
570 LET A$(I) = "-"
580 NEXT I
590 A$(A2) = "+"
600 FOR I = 1 TO M
610 IF Y(I)<=(J-.5)/S2 THEN 650
620 LET K=INT(X(I)*S1+1.5)
630 LET A$(K) = "*"
640 LET Y(I) = -Y(I)
650 NEXT I
660 LET V=Y1+J/S2
680 PRINT TAB(10); "I";
690 FOR I = 1 TO 61
700 PRINT A$(I);
710 NEXT I
720 PRINT
730 LET J = J - 1
740 IF J>=0 THEN 490
750 GOSUB 900
880 GOTO 999
900 B$(1)="      I"
910 FOR I=2 TO 61:B$(I)="-":NEXT I
920 B$(62)="I"
930 FOR I=1 TO 62:PRINT B$(I);:NEXT I
940 PRINT
950 RETURN
999 END
```

THIS LOOP CALCULATES THE TABLE OF X AND Y VALUES.

X9 AND Y9 WILL HOLD MAX. X1 AND Y1 WILL HOLD MIN.

HERE'S WHERE THE MAXIMUM AND MINIMUM VALUES OF X AND Y ARE FOUND.

THIS LOOP TRANSLATES ALL THE X AND Y VALUES (TO AVOID NEGATIVE NUMBERS).

THE X AND Y SCALE FACTORS ARE CALCULATED HERE.

A1 AND A2 LOCATE THE X AND Y AXES...

WHICH ARE INSERTED IN A$ HERE...

AND HERE.

THIS LOOP FILLS UP ONE LINE IMAGE WITH "" SYMBOLS.*

AND THIS LOOP PRINTS IT.

SUBROUTINE 900 FILLS AND PRINTS THE TOP (OR BOTTOM) BORDER.

NOTE: If you're running this program on a 16 line terminal you'll need all the room for plotting, so omit the top and bottom borders by taking out the subroutine in lines 900 to 950. Also change the number 36 to 15 in lines 30, 290, and 300. You'll also want to take out the TAB(10) in line 680. If you have less than 60 columns, you'll have to reduce the numbers 59 (or 60 or 61) in lines 280, 440, 490, 560, and 690 by 14 (or maybe by 22).

Here's a run of the program on an 80 column terminal:

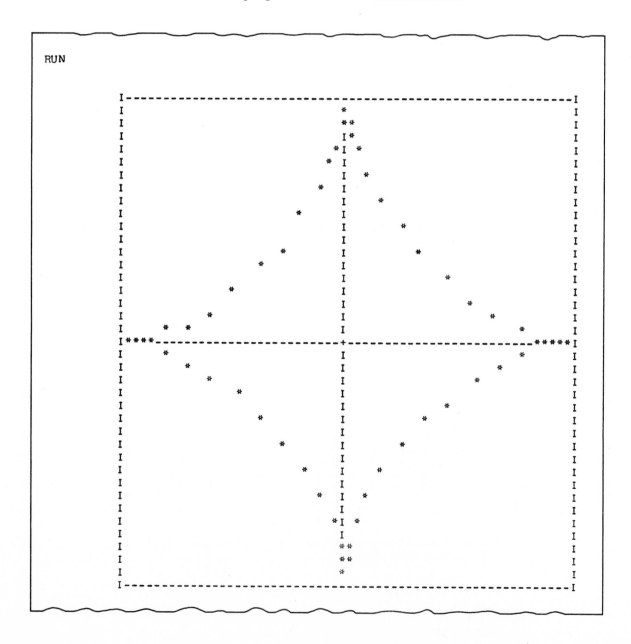

7.5   ULTRA PLOT: AUTOMATIC SCALING AND AXIS LABELING

In this program we'll add an automatic axis labeling feature to the previous program. This is found in subroutine 770 to 870. This routine prints the axis labels as 3 or 4 digit decimal numbers if they are within a range that doesn't take more than 4 places (e.g. .0005 or 2326). Otherwise (line 860), it converts to the E notation explained in Section 2.6. Just for variety, this version of the program generates the top and bottom borders by using the string concatenation operator "+". If you don't have this, get rid of lines 430 to 470, add subroutine 900 to 950 from the previous program, and change lines 480 and 750 to read GOSUB 900. Notice that using "+" avoids the need for an array B$. So if you don't have "+" for strings, you'll also have to include a dimension statement DIM B$(62).

Here's a listing of the Ultra Plot program:

ULTRA PLOT

```
LIST
10 DIM A$(61), X(100), Y(100)
20 LET M=0
30 LET J=36
40 FOR A=0 TO 6.2 STEP .1
50 LET M = M + 1
60 LET X(M)=COS(A)-.5*COS(2*A)-.5
70 LET Y(M)=SIN(A)-.5*SIN(2*A)
80 REM FIND MIN AND MAX
90 IF M<>1 THEN 150
100 LET X9 = X(1)
110 LET X1 = X(1)
120 LET Y9 = Y(1)
130 LET Y1 = Y(1)
140 GOTO 230
150 IF X9> = X(M) THEN 170
160 LET X9 = X(M)
170 IF X1 <X(M) THEN 190
180 LET X1 = X(M)
190 IF Y9> = Y(M) THEN 210
200 LET Y9 = Y(M)
210 IF Y1<Y(M) THEN 230
220 LET Y1 = Y(M)
230 NEXT A
240 FOR I = 1 TO M
250 LET Y(I) = Y(I) - Y1
260 LET X(I) = X(I) - X1
270 NEXT I
280 LET S1 = 59/(X9 - X1)
290 LET S2 = 36/(Y9 - Y1)
300 LET A1=36-INT(.5+Y9*S2)
310 LET A2=INT(1.5-X1*S1)
320 LET A$(61)="I"
330 FOR I = 1 TO 6
340 LET V=X1+I*10/S1
350 PRINT TAB(I*10+6);
360 GOSUB 770
370 NEXT I
```

```
380 PRINT
390 FOR I = 1 TO 6
400 PRINT TAB(I*10+10);"^";
410 NEXT I
420 PRINT
430 LET B$ = TAB(10) + "I"
440 FOR I = 1 TO 60
450 LET B$ = B$ + "-"
460 NEXT I
470 LET B$ = B$ + "I"
480 PRINT B$
490 FOR I = 1 TO 60
500 IF I<>A2 THEN 530
510 LET A$(I)="I"
520 GOTO 540
530 LET A$(I)=" "
540 NEXT I
550 IF J<>A1 THEN 600
560 FOR I = 1 TO 60
570 LET A$(I) = "-"
580 NEXT I
590 A$(A2) = "+"
600 FOR I = 1 TO M
610 IF Y(I)<=(J-.5)/S2 THEN 650
620 LET K=INT(X(I)*S1+1.5)
630 LET A$(K) = "*"
640 LET Y(I) = -Y(I)
650 NEXT I
660 LET V=Y1+J/S2
670 GOSUB 770
680 PRINT TAB(10); "I";
690 FOR I = 1 TO 61
700 PRINT A$(I);
710 NEXT I
720 PRINT
730 LET J = J - 1
740 IF J>=0 THEN 490
750 PRINT B$
760 GOTO 880
770 REM SUBROUTINE
780 IF V<>0 THEN 810
790 PRINT V;
800 GOTO 870
810 LET E = INT(LOG(ABS(V))/2.303 + .5)
820 IF E>2 THEN 860
830 IF E<-2 THEN 860
840 PRINT INT(V * 10^(2-E) + .5)/ 10^(2-E);
850 GOTO 870
860 PRINT INT(V*10^(1-E)+.5)/10;"E";E;
870 RETURN
880 END
```

THIS METHOD OF CREATING THE TOP AND BOTTOM BORDERS DOESN'T USE A STRING ARRAY.

THIS IS THE AXIS LABELING SUBROUTINE.

Here's a run of this program as shown, followed by several other runs in which the function (lines 60 and 70) and parameter choice (line 40) are changed. The first run uses the parametric equations for a curve called the "cardioid" so it might make a nice enclosure for your next mailing of Valentine letters. In our example, the parameter is A and it varies from 0 to 6.2 in line 40. The values of X and Y are calculated in lines 60 and 70.

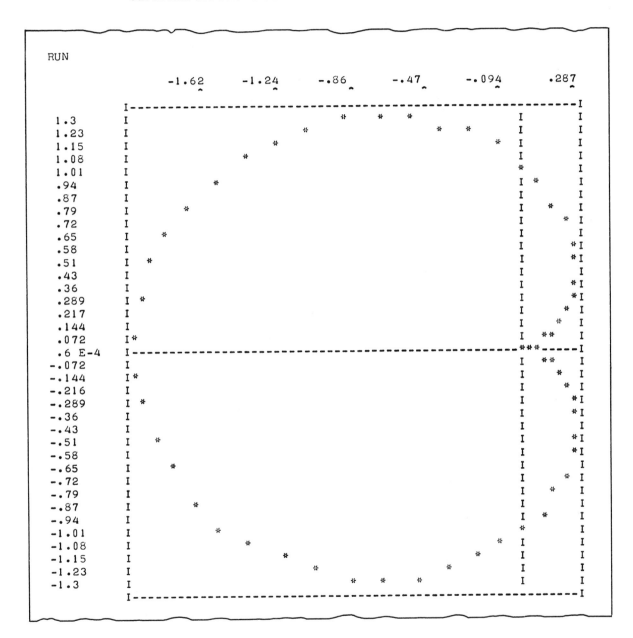

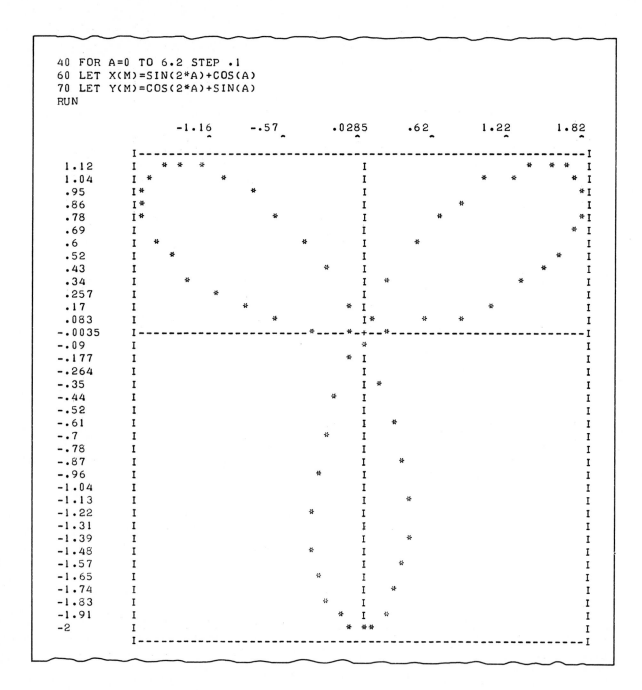

```
40 FOR A=-2.9 TO 2.9 STEP 0.075
60 LET X(M)=A
70 LET Y(M)=A*A*(A*A-8)+10

RUN
```

```
              -1.92        -.94        .036        1.02        1.99        2.97
                 ^            ^           ^           ^           ^           ^
        I----------------------------------------------------------------------I
  13.4  I*                                        I                             I
  12.9  I                                         I                             I
  12.4  I                                         I                           * I
  11.8  I                                         I                             I
  11.3  I                                         I                             I
  10.7  I                                         I                             I
  10.2  I                                       **I                             I
   9.7  I *                                  ** I**                             I
   9.1  I                                   *    I  *                           I
   8.6  I                                *   I     *                       *    I
   8    I                                *   I      *                            I
   7.5  I                              *     I       *                          I
   7    I                            *       I                                   I
   6.4  I  *                                 I        *                         I
   5.9  I                          *         I                          *     I
   5.3  I                        *           I         *                       I
   4.8  I                                    I         *                       I
   4.3  I                        *           I                                  I
   3.7  I  *                   *             I           *                 *   I
   3.2  I                                    I          *                 *    I
  2.64  I                    *               I                                  I
   2.1  I                                    I           *                     I
  1.56  I   *              *                 I                                  I
  1.02  I                *                   I          *               *      I
   .48  I                                    I         *                       I
 -.058  I---------------*--------------------+------------------------------------I
  -.6   I   *                                I         *                        I
 -1.14  I                 *                  I                        *         I
 -1.68  I                *                   I          *                       I
 -2.22  I           *                        I         *            *          I
 -2.76  I                *                   I                                  I
  -3.3  I       *          *                 I                         *       I
  -3.8  I                                    I          *         *            I
  -4.4  I       *        *                   I          *       *             I
  -4.9  I        *      *                    I         *                      I
  -5.5  I         **   *                     I         *   *                  I
   -6   I         ***                        I                ***             I
        I----------------------------------------------------------------------I
```

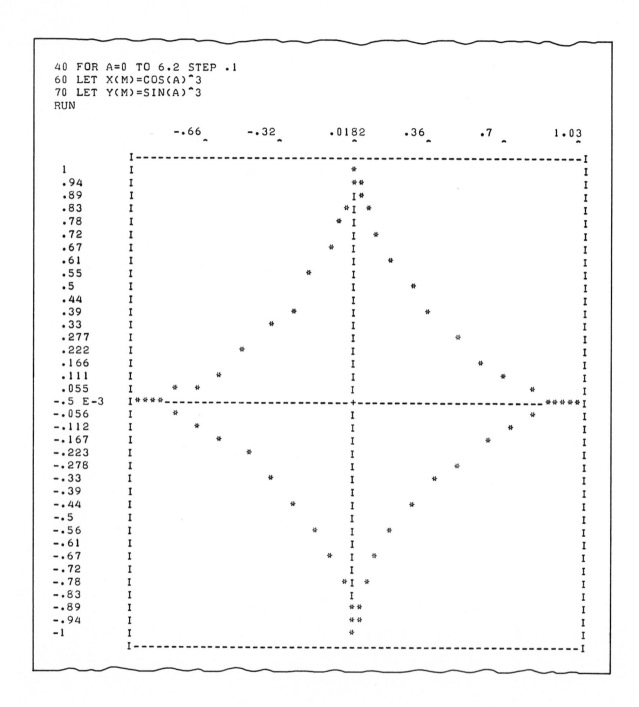

```
40 FOR A=-4.9 TO 5 STEP .1
60 LET X(M)=A
70 LET Y(M)=1/(2*PI)*EXP(-A^2/2)
RUN
```

7.6 PROJECTS

1. Write a program which will allow a non-programmer to experiment with the effect of different coefficients on a plot of a polynomial of the form $Y(X) = A * X * X + B * X + C$. The user should be able to set the coefficients through an INPUT statement. The program should ask the user to set the range for the X values, and suggested ranges should be given in a PRINT statement for the inexperienced user. Y values should be scaled automatically to fit on the output screen or paper.

2. Using the program in Section 7.4 as your model generate four or five different values for each line using a separate formula for each one similar to the zigzag in Section 3.2. Different sized zigzags should cross and re-cross each other producing a macrame-like effect.

3. Write a program that allows the user to input a design motif. Then have the program distort the design. A classical example of such distortion is what is called 'anamorphic art'. (see *Creative Computing* for July-August, 1977 (Vol. 3, No. 4.)

4. Adapt the idea behind the "electric field art" program to simulate a three-dimensional graph. The X and Y axes should have their usual meaning, but Z axis information should be coded by selecting alphanumeric symbols that get progressively lighter in tone as Z increases. The effect should be like looking down on a terrain from an airplane, where the mountain tops are light in tone (printed with, say, the "."), while the valleys are darkest(printed with @). A sample function to use is $Z(X,Y) = X^2 - Y^2 + 10$ where X goes from -3 to +3 and Y goes from -3 to +3.

5. Rewrite one of the programs from this chapter in minimal BASIC, using remarks and indentations to clarify the program's structure. An example showing some techniques that can be used is given in the "style corner".

THE STYLE CORNER

```
100 REM      ELECTRIC    1 OCTOBER 1977    JOHN M. NEVISON
110
120 REM      THIS IS A STYLED VERSION OF AN ORIGINAL
130 REM      BASIC-PLUS PROGRAM BY M. SHORE
140
150 REM      REFERENCE:  DWYER, T. AND CRITCHFIELD, M., "BASIC AND
160 REM                  THE PERSONAL COMPUTER," READING, MASS:
170 REM                  ADDISON-WESLEY PUBLISHING COMPANY, 1978.
180
190 REM      VARIABLES:
200 REM          C(I)...SIZE OF CHARGE I
210 REM          D......DISTANCE FROM POINT  TO CHARGE
220 REM          I,J....INDEX VARIABLES
230 REM          N......NUMBER OF CHARGES
240 REM          V......VALUE OF THE FIELD AT X,Y
250 REM          X,Y....X AND Y  POSITION IN THE FIELD
260 REM          X(I)...X POSITION OF  CHARGE I
270 REM          Y(I)...Y POSITION OF CHARGE I
280
290
```

```
300 REM     MAIN PROGRAM
310
320 REM     PLOT THE ELECTRIC FIELD THAT SURROUNDS A
330 REM     SET OF POINT CHARGES.
340
350     PRINT "HOW MANY CHARGES DO YOU HAVE";
360     INPUT N
370     FOR I = 1 TO N
380        PRINT "TYPE IN THE X AN Y POSITIONS OF CHARGE "; I;
390        INPUT X(I), Y(I)
400     NEXT I
410     FOR I = 1 TO N
420        LET X(I) = X(I) * SQR(3)/2
430     NEXT I
440     PRINT "TYPE IN THE SIZE OF EACH CHARGE.";
450     PRINT "  USE 3 FOR A CHARGE OF 3Q."
460     FOR I = 1 TO N
470        PRINT "CHARGE ";I;
480        INPUT C(I)
490     NEXT I
500
510     FOR J = 1 TO 121 STEP 2
520        LET X = J * SQR(3)/2
530        FOR Y = 1 TO 72
540           GO SUB 740                    'CHARGE AT POINT
550           LET V = (V+1) * 50
560           IF V >= 32 THEN 580
570            LET V = 32
580
590            IF V <= 126 THEN 610
600            LET V = 126
610
620            LET B$ = CHR$(V)
630            IF V <= INT(V) + 0.5 THEN 650
640            LET B$ =" "
650
660           PRINT B$;
670        NEXT Y
680        PRINT
690     NEXT J
700
710     STOP
720
730
740 REM     SUBROUTINE:  CHARGE AT POINT
750 REM       IN:  X, Y, X(), Y(), C()
760 REM      OUT:  V
770
780 REM     CALCULATE THE TOTAL CHARGE, V, AT A POINT, (X,Y),
790 REM     IN THE FIELD.
800
810     LET V = 0
820     FOR I = 1 TO N
830        LET D = SQR((X-X(I))^2 + (Y-Y(I))^2)
840        IF D = 0 THEN 870
850         LET V = V + C(I)/D
860         GO TO 900                   'THEN BOTTOM
870
880         LET V = 99999
890         GO TO 920                   'LOOP EXIT
900
910     NEXT I
920
930 RETURN
940     END
```

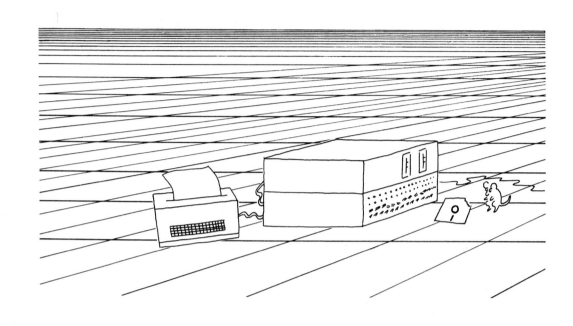

DATA BASES FOR FUN AND
PROFIT; COMPUTER FILES

8.0 INTRODUCTION

Most computer programs can be thought of as "data processing machines." You feed them data (for example, the raw data about each down in a football game), and they then "process" this data, extracting new information from it (for example, statistics about player performance). In this chapter we'll look at some programs where there is a *lot* of data (often called a data base), and see that DATA statements are not always the best way to store all this information. This will then lead to a discussion of what are called "computer files." It will be seen that these provide a more sophisticated means of storing data.

Not all versions of BASIC have computer files, so some of our sample programs will show how to get along with only DATA statements. By comparing the programs that use DATA statements with the programs that use files, you can probably get a clearer picture of how the file statements in BASIC work, and decide if you want a system with these features.

8.1   A DIET INFORMATION PROGRAM USING DATA STATEMENTS

This program uses three kinds of data to create reports at the request of the user. The first kind of data is information about the user that affects nutritional needs—in this case the number of calories eaten each day. The second kind of data is information about what an "average person" requires each day for good nutrition. The third kind of data is information about particular foods.

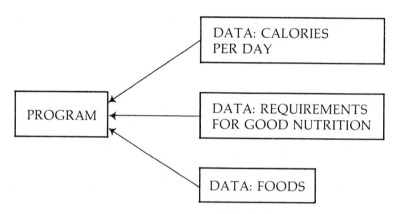

The data about the user's calories per day is obtained from an INPUT statement. The data on requirements for good nutrition is contained in assignment statements or in some cases is calculated from the user's calories. The data on foods is in the form of DATA statements, with two DATA statements for each food.

The arrangement of these DATA statements is worth commenting on. The first line contains the food name and portion stored as one string, followed by the weight in grams, and the calories. The second line contains values for protein, carbohydrate, fiber, fat, polyunsaturates, salt, potassium, calcium, magnesium, phosphorus, iron, thiamine, riboflavin, niacin, vitamin C, vitamin A, and vitamin D—in that order.

These are not the only components of food that are important, but a decision was made when constructing this data to limit the size of the task (all this data was entered by hand). If you decide to create a system of this kind you may wish to include the eight essential amino acids and more vitamins and minerals, or on the other hand you may prefer a more limited selection of food components such as protein, fat, and carbohydrate. However you decide, the basic sources of data are listed in Section 8.6.

The other alteration you may wish to make is to add more food items. This program contains only twenty-eight foods. It would be more interesting to have more foods, but the program could get rather cumbersome. The use of files would make a big difference here.

The program itself prints out several different things at the request of the user. That is—it generates different kinds of *reports* by using the same data in different ways. The following flowchart shows how it does this.

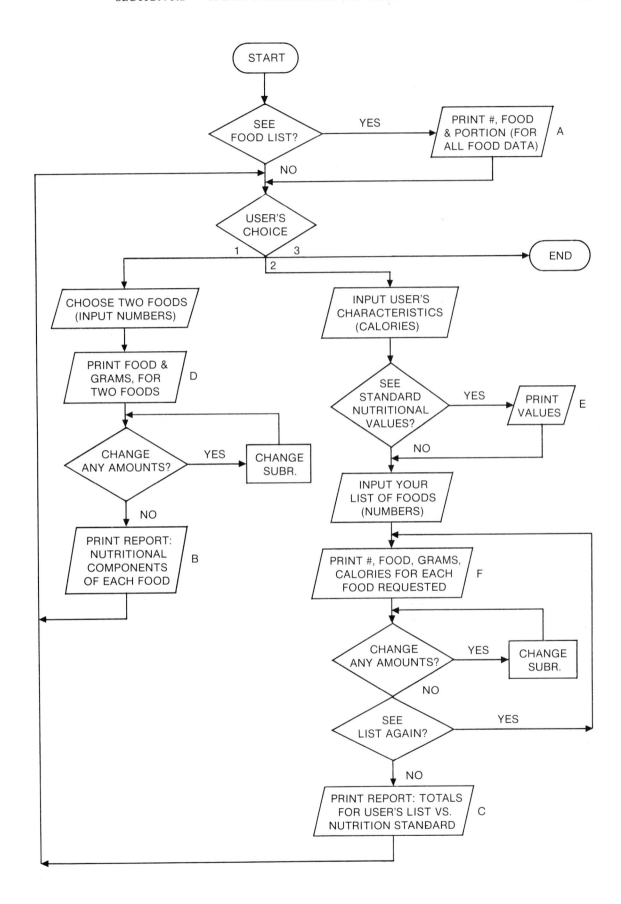

First, the user can request the program to print out the number, name and portion for each food. This is a handy reference for the user. Next, the user makes a three-way choice: he can compare two foods, he can ask to input a list of foods and compare the total with his daily needs, or he can end the program. The program will always return to this point after generating a report. The change subroutine allows the user to have the amounts of a food changed before a report is calculated. These reports (labeled A, B, and C on the flowchart) are the major reports produced by the program. The other print routines (labeled D, E, and F) could be considered reports too. They help the user make decisions about the inputs given to the program. It's a matter of degree.

Here is an example showing reports A, D, and B.

```
RUN

DIET INFORMATION PROGRAM

DO YOU WISH TO SEE THE FOOD LIST? YES
   1 .   MILK WHOLE,1 CUP
   2 .   BRUSSELS SPR.,1/2 CUP
   3 .   COLLARDS,1/2 CUP
   4 .   MUSHROOMS,1/2 CUP
   5 .   TOMATO,1 MED.
```

```
6 .    ONIONS, 1 TBLSPN.
7 .    BEAN SPRTS., 1 CUP
8 .    PICKLES,SOUR, 1 SL.
9 .    OREO COOKIE,1
10 .    COFFEE,BLACK, 6 OZ.
11 .    APRICOTS,CANNED, 2 MED.HLFS.
12 .    CANTALOUPE, 1/4 MED.
13 .    GRAPEFRUIT JU., 1/2 CUP
14 .    ORANGE JU., 1/2 CUP
15 .    PLUM, 1 MED.
16 .    BISCUIT, 1
17 .    RICE,COOKED,1/2 CUP
18 .    BREAD,WHITE, 1 SL.
19 .    JAM, 1 TBLSPN.
20 .    CORN, 1/3 CUP
21 .    PORK CHOP,COOKED, 1 OZ.
22 .    CHICKEN COOKED, 1.3 OZ.
23 .    HALIBUT, BROILED, 1 OZ.
24 .    BACON, 1 SL.
25 .    MAYONNAISE, 1 TBLSPN.
26 .    EGG,WHOLE, 1 LARGE
27 .    FIG BAR, 1 SML.
28 .    CHEESE,CHEDDAR, 1 OZ.

DO YOU WANT A REPORT ON:
    1. A COMPARISON OF TWO FOODS
    2. A LIST OF FOODS
OR--3. EXIT FROM THIS PROGRAM.
TYPE 1, 2, OR 3? 1
TYPE THE NUMBERS OF TWO FOODS? 13,16

            GRAPEFRUIT JU., 1/2 CUP 100 GRAMS
            BISCUIT, 1            35 GRAMS

WANT TO CHANGE THE AMOUNT OF A FOOD? YES
TYPE THE # OF FOOD YOU WISH TO CHANGE? 13
DO YOU WANT TO MULTIPLY IT, OR TYPE IN
A NEW GRAM WT.(TYPE M OR G)? G
GRAMS? 300

            GRAPEFRUIT JU., 1/2 CUP 300 GRAMS
            BISCUIT, 1            35 GRAMS

WANT TO CHANGE THE AMOUNT OF A FOOD? NO

    FOOD # 13
    FOOD # 16
```

THE USER KNOWS THAT THE GRAPEFRUIT HAS 43 CALORIES AND THE BISCUIT HAS 129, SO...

THE USER TRIPLES THE AMOUNT OF GRAPEFRUIT.

G = GRAMS (1 OZ.=27.35 G)
MG = MILLIGRAMS = G * .001
MCG = MICROGRAMS = G * .000001
IU = INTERNATIONAL UNITS

ENERGY CALORIES	CARBO. G	FAT G	SALT MG	CALCIUM MG	PHOS. MG	THIAMINE MCG	NIACIN MG	VIT. A IU
129.00	30.30	0.60	3.00	30.00	45.00	150.00	0.60	300.00
129.00	16.00	6.00	219.00	42.00	61.00	74.00	0.60	0.00

PROTEIN G	FIBER G	POLYUN. G	POTAS. MG	MAGNES. MG	IRON MG	RIBO. MCG	VIT. C MG	VIT. D IU
1.80	0.30	0.00	552.00	36.00	0.90	60.00	102.00	0.00
2.60	0.10	0.70	41.00	7.00	0.60	74.00	0.0p	0.00

In this example, by changing the amount of grapefruit juice to 300 grams, the user obtained a comparison of amounts with an equal number of calories for the two foods. In the next example, again report B, the user multiplies the amount of onions by 10 to compare equal weights of the two foods.

```
DO YOU WANT A REPORT ON:
    1. A COMPARISON OF TWO FOODS
    2. A LIST OF FOODS
OR--3. EXIT FROM THIS PROGRAM.
TYPE 1, 2, OR 3? 1
TYPE THE NUMBERS OF TWO FOODS? 5,6

        TOMATO,1 MED.        100 GRAMS
        ONIONS, 1 TBLSPN.     10 GRAMS

WANT TO CHANGE THE AMOUNT OF A FOOD? YES
TYPE THE # OF FOOD YOU WISH TO CHANGE? 6
DO YOU WANT TO MULTIPLY IT, OR TYPE IN
A NEW GRAM WT.(TYPE M OR G)? M
MULTIPLIER? 10

        TOMATO,1 MED.        100 GRAMS
        ONIONS, 1 TBLSPN.    100 GRAMS

WANT TO CHANGE THE AMOUNT OF A FOOD? NO

    FOOD # 5
    FOOD # 6
```

NOTICE: THE PORTION DOES NOT CHANGE; PROJECT #5 SUGGESTS A CURE FOR THIS.

ENERGY CALORIES	CARBO. G	FAT G	SALT MG	CALCIUM MG	PHOS. MG	THIAMINE MCG	NIACIN MG	VIT. A IU
22.00	4.70	0.20	3.00	13.00	27.00	60.00	0.70	900.00
40.00	9.00	0.00	10.00	30.00	40.00	30.00	0.20	40.00

PROTEIN G	FIBER G	POLYUN. G	POTAS. MG	MAGNES. MG	IRON MG	RIBO. MCG	VIT. C MG	VIT. D IU
1.10	0.50	0.00	244.00	14.00	0.50	40.00	23.00	0.00
2.00	1.00	0.00	160.00	10.00	1.00	40.00	10.00	0.00

The following is an example of report C, a list of foods totalled and compared to daily needs. In this example, the user types in that he will eat 2000 calories a day. The user also chooses to see report E, the standard nutritional requirements, before inputting a list of foods.

```
DO YOU WANT A REPORT ON:
    1. A COMPARISON OF TWO FOODS
    2. A LIST OF FOODS
OR--3. EXIT FROM THIS PROGRAM.
TYPE 1, 2, OR 3? 2
HOW MANY CALORIES DO YOU NEED EACH DAY
(REFER TO A TABLE OR MULTIPLY
YOUR WEIGHT BY APPROX. 16.5)? 2000

WANT TO SEE THE VALUES USED AS
AN APPROX. STANDARD BY THIS PROGRAM? YES

THIS PROGRAM USES THESE FOOD VALUES FROM THE
U.S. RECOMMENDED DAILY ALLOWANCES (U.S. RDA)
AND OTHER SOURCES AS AN APPROX. STANDARD OF GOOD
DAILY NUTRITION.  (ZERO MEANS REQUIREMENT NOT SET.)

  ENERGY  CARBO.    FAT   SALT CALCIUM  PHOS. THIAMINE  NIACIN   VIT. A
 CALORIES     G      G     MG      MG     MG     MCG       MG       IU
--------:-------:-------:-------:-------:-------:-------:-------:-------:
 2000.00  275.00  66.67 1000.00 1000.00 1000.00 1500.00   20.00 5000.00


  PROTEIN   FIBER POLYUN.  POTAS. MAGNES.    IRON   RIBO.  VIT. C   VIT. D
      G       G      G      MG      MG       MG     MCG      MG       IU
--------:-------:-------:-------:-------:-------:-------:-------:-------:
   75.00    5.00   24.00    0.00  400.00   18.00 1700.00   60.00  400.00


READY TO TYPE A LIST OF FOODS? YES
PLEASE TYPE THE NUMBER OF EACH FOOD, AND A CARRIAGE RETURN.
TYPE ZERO WHEN FINISHED (LIMIT IS 20).

? 25
? 24
? 22
? 18
? 8
? 6
? 5
? 1
? 0

 #   FOOD                          GRAMS   CALORIES
 25   MAYONNAISE, 1 TBLSPN.         14      101
 24   BACON, 1 SL.                  10       61
 22   CHICKEN COOKED, 1.3 OZ.       40       55
 18   BREAD,WHITE, 1 SL.            23       62
 8    PICKLES,SOUR, 1 SL.           30        3
 6    ONIONS, 1 TBLSPN.            100       40
 5    TOMATO,1 MED.                100       22
 1    MILK WHOLE,1 CUP             244      159
WANT TO CHANGE ANY AMOUNTS? YES
TYPE THE # OF FOOD YOU WISH TO CHANGE? 6
DO YOU WANT TO MULTIPLY IT, OR TYPE IN
A NEW GRAM WT.(TYPE M OR G)? G
GRAMS? 10
```

CALORIES VARY BY AGE, SEX, WEIGHT, ACTIVITY, AND META-BOLISM. TABLES ARE FOUND IN MANY DIET BOOKS.

100 G IS THE VALUE LEFT BY THE CHANGE SUBROUTINE IN THE PREVIOUS EXAMPLE.

USER CHANGES IT BACK AGAIN.

```
WANT TO CHANGE ANY AMOUNTS? YES
TYPE THE # OF FOOD YOU WISH TO CHANGE? 25
DO YOU WANT TO MULTIPLY IT, OR TYPE IN
A NEW GRAM WT.(TYPE M OR G)? M
MULTIPLIER? 2
WANT TO CHANGE ANY AMOUNTS? YES
TYPE THE # OF FOOD YOU WISH TO CHANGE? 24
DO YOU WANT TO MULTIPLY IT, OR TYPE IN
A NEW GRAM WT.(TYPE M OR G)? M
MULTIPLIER? 4
WANT TO CHANGE ANY AMOUNTS? YES
TYPE THE # OF FOOD YOU WISH TO CHANGE? 22
DO YOU WANT TO MULTIPLY IT, OR TYPE IN
A NEW GRAM WT.(TYPE M OR G)? M
MULTIPLIER? 2
WANT TO CHANGE ANY AMOUNTS? YES
TYPE THE # OF FOOD YOU WISH TO CHANGE? 18
DO YOU WANT TO MULTIPLY IT, OR TYPE IN
A NEW GRAM WT.(TYPE M OR G)? M
MULTIPLIER? 2
WANT TO CHANGE ANY AMOUNTS? 5
TYPE THE # OF FOOD YOU WISH TO CHANGE? 5
DO YOU WANT TO MULTIPLY IT, OR TYPE IN
A NEW GRAM WT.(TYPE M OR G)? M
MULTIPLIER? .5
WANT TO CHANGE ANY AMOUNTS? NO
WANT TO SEE YOUR LIST AGAIN? YES
```

USER CAN CHECK THE CHANGES:

```
 #   FOOD                            GRAMS      CALORIES
25   MAYONNAISE, 1 TBLSPN.            28          202
24   BACON, 1 SL.                     40          244
22   CHICKEN COOKED, 1.3 OZ.          80          110
18   BREAD,WHITE, 1 SL.               46          124
 8   PICKLES,SOUR, 1 SL.              30            3
 6   ONIONS, 1 TBLSPN.                10            4
 5   TOMATO,1 MED.                    50           11
 1   MILK WHOLE,1 CUP                244          159
WANT TO CHANGE ANY AMOUNTS? NO
WANT TO SEE YOUR LIST AGAIN? NO
```

= *2 TABLESPOONS* ✓
= *4 SLICES* ✓
= *2.6 OZ.* ✓
= *2 SLICES* ✓
= *SAME* ✓
= *BACK TO 1 TBLSPN.* ✓
= *½ TOMATO* ✓
= *SAME* ✓

NO MORE CHANGES ARE NEEDED.

```
—— STANDARD
—— YOUR TOTALS
```

ENERGY CALORIES	CARBO. G	FAT G	SALT MG	CALCIUM MG	PHOS. MG	THIAMINE MCG	NIACIN MG	VIT. A IU
2000.00	275.00	66.67	1000.00	1000.00	1000.00	1500.00	20.00	5000.00
857.00	40.95	56.40	986.50	361.50	550.50	473.00	10.77	1037.00

PROTEIN G	FIBER G	POLYUN. G	POTAS. MG	MAGNES. MG	IRON MG	RIBO. MCG	VIT. C MG	VIT. D IU
75.00	5.00	24.00	0.00	400.00	18.00	1700.00	60.00	400.00
44.95	0.45	2.80	864.00	76.00	4.57	862.00	16.50	0.00

Here the user has changed the amounts to agree with what he has eaten,
apparently a generous sandwich and a glass of milk. (This report option
could also be used to total an entire day's food intake, the ingredients of a
recipe, or a single food.)

In the next example, the user types in 1200 for the daily calories (evidently planning a reducing diet). Notice how the values for protein, carbohydrate, fat, and polyunsaturates change in accordance with this new amount. Very low calorie diets are not considered healthy but this is only moderately low. (The program will, however, calculate 'standards' for low calorie levels without complaint.). A report is requested for 4 cups (1 quart) of milk. The user was perhaps contemplating a diet of milk alone. From the report, we can see that even if the amount of milk we're doubled to 2 quarts to equal the calorie amount, the requirements for carbohydrate, fiber, polyunsaturates, magnesium, iron, thiamine, niacin, vitamin C, vitamin A, and vitamin D would not be filled.

```
DO YOU WANT A REPORT ON:
     1. A COMPARISON OF TWO FOODS
     2. A LIST OF FOODS
OR--3. EXIT FROM THIS PROGRAM.
TYPE 1, 2, OR 3? 2
HOW MANY CALORIES DO YOU NEED EACH DAY
(REFER TO A TABLE OR MULTIPLY
YOUR WEIGHT BY APPROX. 16.5)? 1200

WANT TO SEE THE VALUES USED AS
AN APPROX. STANDARD BY THIS PROGRAM? YES

THIS PROGRAM USES THESE FOOD VALUES FROM THE
U.S. RECOMMENDED DAILY ALLOWANCES (U.S. RDA)
AND OTHER SOURCES AS AN APPROX. STANDARD OF GOOD
DAILY NUTRITION.  (ZERO MEANS REQUIREMENT NOT SET.)

  ENERGY  CARBO.     FAT    SALT CALCIUM  PHOS. THIAMINE  NIACIN   VIT. A
 CALORIES     G       G      MG      MG     MG     MCG       MG      IU
 -------:------:-------:-------:-------:-------:-------:-------:-------:
 1200.00  165.00   40.00 1000.00 1000.00 1000.00 1500.00   20.00 5000.00


 PROTEIN   FIBER POLYUN.  POTAS. MAGNES.    IRON   RIBO.  VIT. C  VIT. D
     G       G       G      MG      MG      MG     MCG       MG      IU
 ------:------:-------:-------:-------:-------:-------:-------:-------:
   45.00    5.00   14.40    0.00  400.00   18.00 1700.00   60.00  400.00


READY TO TYPE A LIST OF FOODS? YES
PLEASE TYPE THE NUMBER OF EACH FOOD, AND A CARRIAGE RETURN.
TYPE ZERO WHEN FINISHED (LIMIT IS 20).

? 1
? 0
```

```
 #   FOOD                                GRAMS    CALORIES
 1   MILK WHOLE,1 CUP                      244       159
WANT TO CHANGE ANY AMOUNTS? YES
TYPE THE # OF FOOD YOU WISH TO CHANGE? 1
DO YOU WANT TO MULTIPLY IT, OR TYPE IN
A NEW GRAM WT.(TYPE M OR G)? M
MULTIPLIER? 4
WANT TO CHANGE ANY AMOUNTS? NO
WANT TO SEE YOUR LIST AGAIN? NO

     STANDARD
     YOUR TOTALS

  ENERGY   CARBO.     FAT     SALT CALCIUM   PHOS. THIAMINE  NIACIN   VIT. A
 CALORIES      G       G       MG      MG      MG     MCG      MG       IU
--------:-------:-------:-------:-------:-------:-------:-------:-------:
 1200.00  165.00   40.00 1000.00 1000.00 1000.00 1500.00   20.00 5000.00
  636.00   48.00   34.40  488.00 1152.00  908.00  280.00    0.80 1360.00

 PROTEIN    FIBER POLYUN.  POTAS. MAGNES.    IRON    RIBO.  VIT. C  VIT. D
      G        G       G      MG      MG      MG     MCG      MG       IU
--------:-------:-------:-------:-------:-------:-------:-------:-------:
   45.00    5.00   14.40    0.00  400.00   18.00 1700.00   60.00  400.00
   34.00    0.00    0.00 1408.00  128.00    0.00 1680.00    8.00    0.00


DO YOU WANT A REPORT ON:
   1. A COMPARISON OF TWO FOODS
   2. A LIST OF FOODS
OR--3. EXIT FROM THIS PROGRAM.
TYPE 1, 2, OR 3? 3
```

Before looking at the listing of this program, it should be made clear that the "standards of good nutrition" contained in it are not permanent or absolute. The various sources of these values are noted on page 363.

Some Variables Used in the Diet Information Program

F$ =	Food name and portion are read and stored in this array.
F =	Components of foods. There are 19 components for each food.
P1 =	In the print subroutine, this array is used to print the first food of a two-food comparison, or the standard values for good nutrition.
P2 =	In the print subroutine, this array is used to print the second food of a two-food comparison, or the totals of the user's food list--if flag F1=1.
V =	Values for the standard of good nutrition: V(1) not used.
V(2) = B =	Calories per day, input by user.
V(3) =	Protein, calculated to be 15% of calories. (The average number of calories in 1 gram of protein is 4, so the calculation is (B * .15)/4.) The source for this percentage, and those for carbohydrate, fat, and polyunsaturates is reference book 3 in Section 8.6.
V(4) =	Carbohydrate, calculated to be 55% of calories.
V(5) =	Fiber, 5 grams. This is a guess! Four to six servings of fruit, vegetables, or cereal would provide this amount. It is agreed by experts that we need some. NOTE: In the printouts, the

value for fiber should be subtracted from carbohydrate to get the "real" value for carbohydrate (fiber is indigestable carbohydrate).

$V(6) =$ Fat, 30% of calories.

$V(7) =$ Polyunsaturated fat, 35% of total fat ($V(6)$).

$V(8) =$ Salt, 1000 milligrams, an estimated average need.

$V(9) =$ Potassium, no standard is known for this important mineral yet, so a zero is used. Zeros must often be used in food data also when no value is known.

$V(10) =$ Calcium, 1000 milligrams. Source for this and the following vitamins and minerals is the U.S. Recommended Daily Allowance, reprinted in many diet books, including those listed in 8.6.

$V(11) =$ Magnesium, 400 milligrams.

$V(12) =$ Phosphorus, 1000 milligrams.

$V(13) =$ Iron, 18 milligrams.

$V(14) =$ Thiamine, 1500 micrograms.

$V(15) =$ Riboflavin, 1700 micrograms.

$V(16) =$ Niacin, 20 milligrams.

$V(17) =$ Vitamin C, 60 milligrams.

$V(18) =$ Vitamin A, 5000 International Units.

$V(19) =$ Vitamin D, 400 International Units.

DIET INFORMATION $X =$ Numbers for users food list, input by user.

```
LIST
1 PRINT "DIET INFORMATION PROGRAM":PRINT
10 DIM F$(28),F(28,19),P1(19),P2(19),V(19),X(20)
20 FOR I=1 TO 19:F(0,I)=0:NEXT I
24 FOR I=1 TO 28
26 READ F$(I)
30 FOR J=1 TO 19:READ F(I,J):NEXT J
34 NEXT I
35 PRINT"DO YOU WISH TO SEE THE FOOD LIST";:INPUT A$
36 IF A$="NO" THEN 155
40 FOR I=1 TO 28:PRINT I;".   ";F$(I):NEXT I
150 REM-----CHOICE----------
155 PRINT:PRINT"DO YOU WANT A REPORT ON:"
160 PRINT "    1. A COMPARISON OF TWO FOODS"
165 PRINT "    2. A LIST OF FOODS"
170 PRINT "OR--3. EXIT FROM THIS PROGRAM."
180 PRINT"TYPE 1, 2, OR 3";:INPUT A
185 FOR I=1 TO 19:P1(I)=0:P2(I)=0:X(I+1)=0:NEXT I
190 ON A GOTO 330, 610, 9999
330 REM-----COMPARES----------
340 PRINT"TYPE THE NUMBERS OF TWO FOODS";:INPUT A,B
405 PRINT:PRINT TAB(10);F$(A);TAB(30);F(A,1);"GRAMS"
415 PRINT TAB(10);F$(B);TAB(30);F(B,1);"GRAMS"
420 PRINT:PRINT"WANT TO CHANGE THE AMOUNT OF A FOOD";
425 INPUT A$:IF A$="NO" THEN 465
430 GOSUB 9000
460 GOTO 405
465 PRINT:PRINT TAB(5);"FOOD #";A:PRINT TAB(5);"FOOD #";B:PRINT
470 FOR I=1 TO 19:P1(I)=F(A,I):P2(I)=F(B,I):NEXT I:F1=1
480 GOSUB 8000
490 GOTO 155
610 REM-----ANALYSIS----------
620 PRINT"HOW MANY CALORIES DO YOU NEED EACH DAY"
625 PRINT"(REFER TO A TABLE OR MULTIPLY"
630 PRINT"YOUR WEIGHT BY APPROX. 16.5)";:INPUT B
```

```
640 V(2)=B: V(3)=(B*.15)/4
645 V(4)=(B*.55)/4: V(5)=5
650 V(6)=(B*.30)/9: V(7)=.36*V(6)
655 V(8)=1000: V(10)=1000
660 V(11)=400: V(12)=1000
665 V(13)=18: V(14)=1500
670 V(15)=1700: V(16)=20
675 V(17)=60: V(18)=5000: V(19)=400
677 FOR I=1 TO 19:P1(I)=V(I):NEXT I:F1=0
680 PRINT:PRINT"WANT TO SEE THE VALUES USED AS"
685 PRINT"AN APPROX. STANDARD BY THIS PROGRAM";:INPUT A$
690 IF A$="NO" THEN 785
695 PRINT:PRINT"THIS PROGRAM USES THESE FOOD VALUES FROM THE"
700 PRINT"U.S. RECOMMENDED DAILY ALLOWANCES (U.S. RDA)"
705 PRINT"AND OTHER SOURCES AS AN APPROX. STANDARD OF GOOD"
710 PRINT"DAILY NUTRITION.  (ZERO MEANS REQUIREMENT NOT SET.)":PRINT
780 GOSUB 8000
785 PRINT"READY TO TYPE A LIST OF FOODS";:INPUT A$:IF A$="NO" THEN 155
800 PRINT"PLEASE TYPE THE NUMBER OF EACH FOOD, AND A CARRIAGE RETURN."
805 PRINT"TYPE ZERO WHEN FINISHED (LIMIT IS 20).":PRINT
810 FOR I=1 TO 20
820 INPUT X(I)
830 IF X(I)=0 THEN 840
835 NEXT I
840 PRINT:PRINT" #  FOOD";TAB(35);"GRAMS    CALORIES"
850 FOR J=1 TO I-1
860 PRINT X(J);TAB(5);F$(X(J));TAB(35);F(X(J),1);TAB(44);F(X(J),2)
870 NEXT J
880 PRINT"WANT TO CHANGE ANY AMOUNTS";:INPUT A$
890 IF A$="NO" THEN 920
900 GOSUB 9000
910 GOTO 880
920 PRINT"WANT TO SEE YOUR LIST AGAIN";:INPUT A$
921 IF A$="YES" THEN 840
925 FOR K=1 TO 19
930 FOR J=1 TO I-1
940 F(0,K)=F(0,K)+F(X(J),K)
950 NEXT J
960 NEXT K
970 FOR I=1 TO 19:P2(I)=F(0,I):NEXT I:F1=1
980 PRINT:PRINT TAB(5);"STANDARD":PRINT TAB(5);"YOUR TOTALS":PRINT
990 GOSUB 8000
1000 GOTO 155
5000 DATA "MILK WHOLE,1 CUP",244,159
5001 DATA 8.5,12,0,8.6,0,122,352,288,32,227,0,70,420,.2,2,340,0
5002 DATA "BRUSSELS SPR.,1/2 CUP",70,25
5003 DATA 2.9,4.5,1.1,.3,0,7,191,22,20,50,.8,56,98,.6,61,364,0
5004 DATA "COLLARDS,1/2 CUP",100,29
5005 DATA 2.7,4.9,.8,.6,0,25,234,152,57,39,.6,140,200,1.2,46,5400,0
5006 DATA "MUSHROOMS,1/2 CUP",100,17
5007 DATA 1.9,2.4,.6,.1,0,400,197,6,13,68,.5,20,250,2,2,0,0
5008 DATA "TOMATO,1 MED.",100,22
5009 DATA 1.1,4.7,.5,.2,0,3,244,13,14,27,.5,60,40,.7,23,900,0
5010 DATA "ONIONS, 1 TBLSPN.",10,4
5011 DATA .2,.9,.1,0,0,1,16,3,1,4,.1,3,4,.02,1,4,0
5012 DATA "BEAN SPRTS., 1 CUP",100,28
5013 DATA 3.2,5.2,.7,.2,0,4,156,17,0,48,.9,90,100,.7,6,20,0
5014 DATA "PICKLES,SOUR, 1 SL.",30,3
5015 DATA .2,.7,.1,.1,0,0,0,8,0,6,.4,0,18,0,2,93,0
5016 DATA "OREO COOKIE,1",11.6,40
5017 DATA .59,8.46,0,2.06,0,0,0,0,0,0,0,0,0,0,0,0,0
5018 DATA "COFFEE,BLACK, 6 OZ.",170,5
5019 DATA .3,.8,0,.1,0,0,0,5,0,5,.2,10,10,.9,0,0,0
5020 DATA "APRICOTS,CANNED, 2 MED.HLFS.",60,40
5021 DATA .4,10,0,.1,0,1,145,7,4,9,.2,12,12,.2,2,1070,0
5022 DATA "CANTALOUPE, 1/4 MED.",150,45
5023 DATA 1,11.2,.4,.2,0,18,376,21,24,24,.6,60,45,.9,50,5100,0
5024 DATA "GRAPEFRUIT JU., 1/2 CUP",100,43
5025 DATA .6,10.1,.1,.2,0,1,184,10,12,15,.3,50,20,.2,34,100,0
5026 DATA "ORANGE JU., 1/2 CUP",100,45
```

```
5027 DATA .7,10.4,.1,.2,0,1,200,11,11,17,.2,90,30,.4,50,200,0
5028 DATA "PLUM, 1 MED.",60,45
5029 DATA .5,11.8,.2,.1,0,1,102,7,5,11,.3,18,18,.3,2,180,0
5030 DATA "BISCUIT, 1",35,129
5031 DATA 2.6,16,.1,6,.7,219,41,42,7,61,.6,74,74,.6,0,0,0
5032 DATA "RICE,COOKED,1/2 CUP",100,109
5033 DATA 2,24.2,.1,.1,0,374,28,10,8,28,.9,110,0,1,0,0,0
5034 DATA "BREAD,WHITE, 1 SL.",23,62
5035 DATA 2,11.6,0,.7,0,117,24,19,5,22,.6,60,50,.6,0,0,0
5036 DATA "JAM, 1 TBLSPN.",20,55
5037 DATA .1,14.2,.1,.1,0,0,0,2,0,2,.1,4,4,.04,1,2,0
5038 DATA "CORN, 1/3 CUP",100,91
5039 DATA 3.3,21,.7,1,0,0,196,3,48,89,.6,120,100,1.4,9,400,0
5040 DATA "PORK CHOP,COOKED, 1 OZ.",30,117
5041 DATA 7.4,0,0,9.5,.7,20,127,4,8,80,1,288,84,1.7,0,0,0
5042 DATA "CHICKEN COOKED, 1.3 OZ.",40,55
5043 DATA 9.6,0,0,1.5,.4,26,110,4,9,80,.7,20,76,3.5,0,36,0
5044 DATA "HALIBUT, BROILED, 1 OZ.",30,51
5045 DATA 7.6,0,0,2.1,0,40,157,5,8,75,.2,15,21,2.5,0,204,0
5046 DATA "BACON, 1 SL.",10,61
5047 DATA 3,.3,0,5.2,.5,102,24,1,2,22,.3,51,34,.5,0,0,0
5048 DATA "MAYONNAISE, 1 TBLSPN.",14,101
5049 DATA .15,.3,0,11.2,0,84,5,3,0,4,.01,3,6,0,0,39,0
5050 DATA "EGG,WHOLE, 1 LARGE",54,88
5051 DATA 7,.5,0,6.2,.5,66,70,29,6,110,1.2,60,160,.1,0,640,27
5052 DATA "FIG BAR, 1 SML.",16,56
5053 DATA .7,12.1,.3,.8,0,0,0,11,0,11,.2,3,10,.1,0,0,0
5054 DATA "CHEESE,CHEDDAR, 1 OZ.",28,112
5055 DATA 7,.6,0,9.1,.3,197,23,211,13,134,.3,8,130,0,0,370,0
7999 REM-----PRINT SUBR----------
8000 PRINT" ENERGY CARBO.     FAT    SALT CALCIUM";
8015 PRINT" PHOS. THIAMINE  NIACIN  VIT. A"
8020 PRINT"CALORIES      G      G      MG      MG";
8025 PRINT"      MG     MCG     MG     IU"
8030 PRINT"-------:-------:-------:-------:-------:";
8035 PRINT"-------:-------:-------:-------:"
8040 FOR J=2 TO 18 STEP 2
8044 PRINT USING"#####.##",P1(J);
8045 NEXT J
8046 PRINT:IF F1=0 THEN 8051
8047 FOR J=2 TO 18 STEP 2
8048 PRINT USING"#####.##",P2(J);
8050 NEXT J
8051 PRINT:PRINT
8055 PRINT" PROTEIN    FIBER POLYUN.   POTAS. MAGNES.";
8060 PRINT"    IRON     RIBO.  VIT. C  VIT. D"
8065 PRINT"      G      G      G      MG      MG";
8070 PRINT"      MG     MCG     MG     IU"
8075 PRINT"-------:-------:-------:-------:-------:";
8080 PRINT"-------:-------:-------:-------:"
8085 FOR J=3 TO 19 STEP 2
8090 PRINT USING"#####.##",P1(J);
8091 NEXT J
8092 PRINT:IF F1=0 THEN 8110
8094 FOR J=3 TO 19 STEP 2
8095 PRINT USING"#####.##",P2(J);
8100 NEXT J
8110 PRINT:PRINT
8120 RETURN
9000 REM-----AMOUNT CHANGE SUBR.----------
9010 PRINT"TYPE THE # OF FOOD YOU WISH TO CHANGE";:INPUT C
9020 PRINT"DO YOU WANT TO MULTIPLY IT, OR TYPE IN"
9030 PRINT"A NEW GRAM WT.(TYPE M OR G)";:INPUT A$
9040 IF A$="G" THEN 9080
9050 PRINT"MULTIPLIER";:INPUT M:GOTO 9090
9080 PRINT"GRAMS";:INPUT G: M=G/F(C,1)
9090 FOR J=1 TO 19: F(C,J)=F(C,J)*M: NEXT J
9100 RETURN
9999 END
```

8.2   USING FILES INSTEAD OF DATA STATEMENTS

The diet information program just shown saved its data about foods in DATA statements. If you decide to add additional food data (see project idea #1 at the end of this chapter), the program could become too large for the RAM memory in your computer. This suggests finding a way to store data on an external memory device (like tape or disk), and having the program read it in as needed.

The simplest way to do this is by using what are called "sequential files." The word sequential means that the data on these files must be read in sequence, starting from the beginning. There is no way to jump to the middle of the data.

This should be a familiar idea, since the DATA statements in BASIC store data sequentially. Recall that when a program is RUN, there is a pointer that is set to the beginning of this data. Then the pointer is moved sequentially by use of the READ statement.

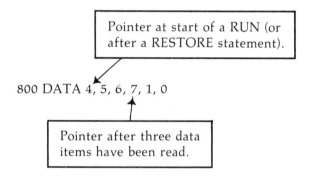

The order in which this data is stored is obviously very important, and the programmer must know what it is.

Sequential files are a similar means of storing ordered data, not inside the program, but externally on tape or disk. Again, the programmer must take care of ordering the data so it can be read in the right sequence.

To *store* data in a sequential file, you usually use three statements. Here's what these are in Altair Disk Extended BASIC:

```
6 OPEN "O", 1, "AGE", 0
7 PRINT #1,A,B,C
8 CLOSE 1
```

Line 6 says OPEN (or activate) for "O"utput on channel 1 a file called "AGE", using disk drive #0. Line 7 says PRINT (which really means magnetically record) on the channel 1 file the data stored in variables A, B, and C *in that order*. Line 8 says CLOSE (or deactivate) the file on channel 1.

As you can see, files have a name (like "AGE") which is used for later retrieval from *external* storage, and a channel number which is used for working on the file from *within* a program. The programmer invents both the name and channel number, following the rules set down in his system reference manual.

To later read this data from the file back into program variables, the following statements are used:

```
10 OPEN "I",1,"AGE",0
20 INPUT #1,X,Y,Z
30 CLOSE 1
```

Line 10 means OPEN for "I"nput using channel #1 the file called "AGE", which is stored on the disk drive 0 (if your computer has several disk drives, these are numbered 0,1,2,etc.). Line 20 says INPUT three pieces of data from the file on channel #1, and store them in sequence in the variables X, Y, and Z. 30 says CLOSE (or deactivate) the file using channel #1.

Here's a little demonstration program that shows how these statements can be used within a BASIC program. The program first stores the three numbers A, B, and C on the sequential file "AGE" (line 7). Then it reads them back into X, Y, and Z (line 20). Next it stores the numbers 65-X, 65-Y, and 65-Z on a different file called "RETIRE" (line 80). Finally, it reads back these retirement figures into the variables D, E, and F (line 110). The ordinary PRINT statements (9, 35, 95, and 130) were inserted to help you see what actually happened (since file operations are "invisible" to the user).

FILE DEMO

```
LIST

5 A=55: B=48: C=33
6 OPEN "O",1,"AGE",0
7 PRINT #1,A,B,C
8 CLOSE 1
9 PRINT "AT LINE 9 X,Y,Z=";X;Y;Z
10 OPEN "I",#1,"AGE",0
20 INPUT #1,X,Y,Z
30 CLOSE 1
35 PRINT "AT LINE 35 X,Y,Z=";X;Y;Z
40 OPEN"O",2,"RETIRE",0
80 PRINT #2,65-X,65-Y,65-Z
90 CLOSE 2
95 PRINT "AT LINE 95 D,E,F=";D;E;F
100 OPEN "I",1,"RETIRE",0
110 INPUT #1,D,E,F
120 CLOSE 1
130 PRINT "AT LINE 130 D,E,F=";D;E;F
999 END
OK
RUN
AT LINE 9 X,Y,Z= 0   0   0
AT LINE 35 X,Y,Z= 55   48   33
AT LINE 95 D,E,F= 0   0   0
AT LINE 130 D,E,F= 10   17   32
OK
```

8.3   MORE ON FILES: SEQUENTIAL FILES VERSUS RANDOM ACCESS FILES

There are many applications where it is wasteful to have to go through all the data in sequence just to find one particular item. It would be nice to be able to skip over data and go directly to the needed information. An example would be a program to find credit information about one particular customer chosen at random from a file that has thousands of records. We need "random access" files.

The idea behind random access files can be partly simulated in ordinary BASIC by using a two-dimensional array. We'll illustrate this in the next section, where a charge-card type program is shown. The simulated random access file is the daily transaction file which is stored in the array T(N,I).

More advanced versions of BASIC have disk random file capabilities. These go under such names as "direct access files", "random access files", and "record I/O files". A full discussion of such files is outside the scope of this first volume. What we will do is describe some of the special BASIC statements needed, and then show an example of their use. (Our example is a solution to project 3 at the end of this chapter. It uses what are called "record I/O files" in BASIC-PLUS, or simply "random files" in Altair Disk Extended BASIC. It's presented as a listing without explanation, and recommended only to the brave.)

The GET, PUT and FIELD Statements; MKS$, CVS, and LSET

The idea behind random files is to organize the data as a set of records which can be accessed by number. A set of records is called a file, and it can be pictured like this:

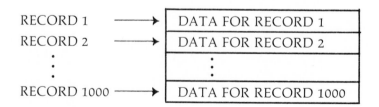

RANDOM ACCESS FILE OPENED ON CHANNEL #1

Our picture shows a file organized as 1000 records. A program can retrieve the data in any record of this file, say record 400, with a statement of the type:

230 GET #1, 400 (where #1 is the file channel number)

There is no need to search through all the records sequentially. Similarly, data can be stored in any record, say record 25, with a statement of the type:

380 PUT #1, 25

(Note: If you just say GET #1, or PUT #1, then the record right after the last one used is accessed.)

The programmer must also assign "fields" within the records to the BASIC variables he will be using. The size of these fields depends on the data. Data is always stored in these fields in the form of strings, that is, as ASCII characters. Each record can hold up to 128 characters. So we have to tell our program how we wish to group these characters. For example, suppose we decide to store the name, address, and zipcode of an account in each record of the file on channel #1 as follows:

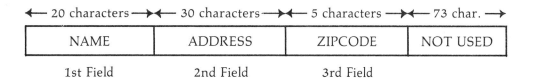

NAME	ADDRESS	ZIPCODE	NOT USED
1st Field	2nd Field	3rd Field	

←— 20 characters —→←— 30 characters —→←— 5 characters —→←— 73 char. —→

(Note: Since we are not, in this example planning to convert any of this data to integers or decimal numbers, length of field = # of characters to be printed.)

We would tell our program this with the statement:

198 FIELD #1, 20 AS N$, 30 AS P$, 5 AS Z$

where N$, P$, and Z$ are the BASIC variables we'll use to hold the name, address and zipcode.

In this example, the last 73 characters aren't used. In order not to waste space at the end of our records, the following trick can be used to squeeze two 64-character subrecords into one record:

193 FIELD #1, 64*(I-1) AS D$, 20 AS N$, 30 AS P$, 5 AS Z$

When I=1, this statement is the same as the one above since zero characters go into the dummy variable D$. But when I is 2, the first 64 characters are skipped over before the actual variables N$, P$, and Z$ are used. So I indicates whether the first or second half of the record is being used.

Since only ASCII characters can be stored in random file records, a special function MKI\$ is provided to 'make an integer' into a two-character string. Conversely, there is a function CVI which 'converts to integer' a two-character string. Similar functions called MKS\$ and CVS are used to make single precision decimal numbers (like 3.1416) into four-character strings, and convert such strings back into decimal numbers. For example, an assignment statement for making a numerical variable B into a field variable A\$ looks like this:

```
90 A$=MKS$(B)
```

The assignment statement for storing the contents of a string variable into a fielded string variable is a little different, too

```
290 LSET C$=X$
```

This means "set C\$=X\$, and if X\$ is shorter than C\$, *left*-justify it and fill up the remaining space in C\$ with blanks.". (If X\$ is longer than C\$, extra characters will be ignored.)

One additional thing: random access files are opened for *both* input and output with one statement. For example, to open a random file on channel #1, with the file name "FOODDAT", stored on a disk in drive 1 for both input (PUT) and output (GET), you write:

```
25 OPEN "R", 1, "FOODDAT", 1
```

This file is closed with the statement

```
999 CLOSE 1
```

If instead you use the statement

```
999 CLOSE
```

this will close all open files. It's a good idea to put such a statement near the end of a program.

Here's a solution to project 3 which shows how all these ideas go together.

FOOD DATA EDITOR

```
LIST

1 CLEAR 10000
10 PRINT"FOOD DATA EDITOR"
20 DIM P1(19),T$(19)
25 OPEN "R",1,"FOODDAT",1
30 FIELD #1,26 AS F$(1), 26 AS F$(2)
40 FOR J=1 TO 19
50 FIELD #1,( 48+4*J) AS D$, 4 AS T$(J)
60 NEXT J
70 REM-----CHOICE-----
75 F1=0
80 PRINT"1. PRINT WHOLE FILE"
90 PRINT"2. EDIT A FOOD"
95 PRINT"3. EXIT FROM PROGRAM  --TYPE 1,2, OR 3";:INPUT A
100 ON A GOTO 110,300,9000
105 REM-----PRINT WHOLE FILE-----
110 F1=1:GOSUB 8000
```

```
125 FOR I=1 TO 249
130 GET #1
140 PRINT I;".   ";F$(1);F$(2);CVS(T$(1));"GRAMS"
150 FOR J=2 TO 18 STEP 2
160 PRINT USING"#####.##";CVS(T$(J));
170 NEXT J
175 PRINT
180 FOR J=3 TO 19 STEP 2
190 PRINT USING"#####.##";CVS(T$(J));
200 NEXT J
210 PRINT
220 NEXT I
230 GOTO 75
299 REM-----EDIT A FOOD-----
300 PRINT"TYPE INDEX NO. OF FOOD YOU WISH TO CHANGE";
305 INPUT X
310 GET #1,X
320 FOR J=1 TO 19:P1(J)=CVS(T$(J)):NEXT J
330 PRINT F$(1),F$(2),P1(1);"GRAMS"
340 GOSUB 8000
345 PRINT"READY TO CHANGE";:INPUT A$
346 IF A$="NO" THEN 490
350 PRINT"NEW FOOD NAME";:INPUT G$(1)
360 PRINT"NEW PORTION";:INPUT G$(2)
370 PRINT"TYPE NEW VALUES IN ORDER"
380 PRINT"IF YOU MAKE A MISTAKE TYPE 9999"
390 FOR J=1 TO 19
400 INPUT P1(J)
410 IF P1(J)=9999 THEN 350
420 NEXT J
430 LSET F$(1)=G$(1)
440 LSET F$(2)=G$(2)
450 FOR J=1 TO 19:T$(J)=MKS$(P1(J)): NEXT J
460 PUT #1,X
470 PRINT"WANT TO SEE FOOD #";X;: INPUT A$
480 IF A$="YES" THEN 310
490 PRINT"ANOTHER FOOD";:INPUT A$
500 IF A$="YES" THEN 300
510 GOTO 75
7999 REM-----PRINT SUBR----------
8000 PRINT"  ENERGY  CARBO.     FAT     SALT CALCIUM";
8015 PRINT"  PHOS. THIAMINE  NIACIN  VIT. A"
8020 PRINT"CALORIES       G        G        MG       MG";
8025 PRINT"     MG      MCG       MG       IU"
8030 PRINT"------:------:-------:-------:-------:";
8035 PRINT"------:------:-------:-------:"
8036 IF F1=1 THEN 8051
8040 FOR J=2 TO 18 STEP 2
8044 PRINT USING"#####.##";P1(J);
8045 NEXT J
8046 PRINT
8051 PRINT:PRINT
8055 PRINT" PROTEIN    FIBER POLYUN.  POTAS. MAGNES.";
8060 PRINT"     IRON     RIBO.  VIT. C  VIT. D"
8065 PRINT"        G        G        G       MG       MG";
8070 PRINT"     MG      MCG       MG       IU"
8075 PRANT"------:-------:-------:-------:-------:";
8080 PRINT"------:-------:-------:-------:"
8082 IF F1=1 THEN 8102
8085 FOR J=3 TO 19 STEP 2
8090 PRINT USING"#####.##";P1(J);
8091 NEXT J
8092 PRINT
8102 PRINT:PRINT
8120 RETURN
9000 CLOSE
9999 END
OK
```

```
RUN
FOOD DATA EDITOR
1. PRINT WHOLE FILE
2. EDIT A FOOD
3. EXIT FROM PROGRAM  --TYPE 1,2, OR 3? 1
   ENERGY   CARBO.     FAT   SALT CALCIUM  PHOS. THIAMINE  NIACIN  VIT. A
  CALORIES      G       G     MG     MG     MG      MCG       MG      IU
  -------:-------:-------:-------:-------:-------:-------:-------:-------:


  PROTEIN    FIBER POLYUN.  POTAS. MAGNES.    IRON   RIBO.   VIT. C  VIT. D
       G        G       G      MG     MG       MG     MCG       MG      IU
  -------:-------:-------:-------:-------:-------:-------:-------:-------:


  1 .   MILK WHOLE              1 CUP(8 FL. OZ.)            244 GRAMS
    159.00   12.00    8.60  122.00  288.00  227.00   70.00    0.20  340.00
      8.50    0.00    0.00  352.00   32.00    0.00  420.00    2.00    0.00
  2 .   MILK EVAPORATED         1/2 CUP                    120 GRAMS
    165.00   11.60    9.50  142.00  300.00  246.00   48.00    0.20  384.00
      8.40    0.00    0.00  364.00   30.00    0.12  408.00    1.00    0.00
  3 .   MILK POWDERED WHOLE     1/4 CUP                     30 GRAMS
    150.00   11.50    8.30  121.00  272.00  212.00   87.00    0.20  340.00
      7.90    0.00    0.30  400.00   29.00    0.15  438.00    2.00    0.00
  4 .   BUTTERMILK WHOLE        1 CUP (8 FL. OZ.)          244 GRAMS
    102.00   12.00    2.40  212.00  293.00  220.00  100.00    0.20  100.00
      8.10    0.00    0.00  388.00   33.00    0.00  410.00    2.00    0.00
  5 .   BUTTERMILK SKIM         1 CUP (8 FL. OZ.)          244 GRAMS
     88.00   12.40    0.20  318.00  296.00  232.00  100.00    0.20    0.00
      8.80    0.00    0.00  342.00   34.00    0.00  440.00    2.00    0.00
  6 .   ASPARAGUS COOKED        2/3 CUP CUT PIECES         100 GRAMS
     20.00    3.60    0.20    1.00   21.00   50.00  160.00    1.40  900.00
      2.20    0.70    0.00  183.00   20.00    0.60  180.00   26.00    0.00
  7 .   BEET GREENS COOKED      1/2 CUP                    100 GRAMS
     18.00    3.30    0.20   76.00   99.00   25.00   70.00    0.30 5100.00
      1.70    1.10    0.00  332.00  106.00    1.90  150.00   15.00    0.00
  8 .   BROCCOLI COOKED         1 LRG. STALK(2/3 CUP)      100 GRAMS
     26.00    4.50    0.30   10.00   88.00   62.00   90.00    0.80 2500.00
      3.10    1.50    0.00  267.00   24.00    0.80  200.00   90.00    0.00
  9 .   BRUSSELS SPROUTS COOKED 1/2 CUP(5 TO 6)             70 GRAMS
     25.00    4.50    0.30    7.00   22.00   50.00   56.00    0.60  364.00
      2.90    1.10    0.00  191.00   20.00    0.80   98.00   61.00    0.00
 10 .   CABBAGE RAW             1 CUP SHREDDED             100 GRAMS
     24.00    5.40    0.20   20.00   49.00   29.00   50.00    0.30  130.00
      1.30    0.80    0.00  233.00   13.00    0.40   50.00   47.00    0.00
```

```
  ⋮
```

```
1. PRINT WHOLE FILE
2. EDIT A FOOD
3. EXIT FROM PROGRAM  --TYPE 1,2, OR 3? 3
OK
```

```
RUN
FOOD DATA EDITOR
1. PRINT WHOLE FILE
2. EDIT A FOOD
3. EXIT FROM PROGRAM  --TYPE 1,2, OR 3? 2
TYPE INDEX NO. OF FOOD YOU WISH TO CHANGE? 42
CARROTS COOKED                    1/2 CUP DICED                   100 GRAMS
   ENERGY   CARBO.      FAT    SALT CALCIUM   PHOS. THIAMINE   NIACIN  VIT. A
 CALORIES        G        G      MG      MG      MG     MCG       MG      IU
 -------:-------:-------:-------:-------:-------:-------:-------:-------:
    31.00     7.10     0.20   33.00   33.00   31.00   50.00     0.5010500.00


   PROTEIN    FIBER POLYUN.   POTAS. MAGNES.    IRON    RIBO.  VIT. C  VIT. D
        G        G        G      MG      MG      MG     MCG       MG      IU
 -------:-------:-------:-------:-------:-------:-------:-------:-------:
     0.90     1.00     0.00  222.00   23.00    0.60   50.00    6.00    0.00


READY TO CHANGE? YES
NEW FOOD NAME? CHEERIOS CEREAL
NEW PORTION? 1 CUP
TYPE NEW VALUES IN ORDER
IF YOU MAKE A MISTAKE TYPE 9999
? 25
? 102
? 3.4
? 17.7
? .3
? 1.8
? 0
? 275
? 0
? 42
? 0
? 100
? 1.1
? 302
? 49
? .5
? 0
? 0
? 0
WANT TO SEE FOOD # 42 ? YES
CHEERIOS CEREAL                    1 CUP                         25 GRAMS
   ENERGY   CARBO.      FAT    SALT CALCIUM   PHOS. THIAMINE   NIACIN  VIT. A
 CALORIES        G        G      MG      MG      MG     MCG       MG      IU
 -------:-------:-------:-------:-------:-------:-------:-------:-------:
   102.00    17.70     1.80  275.00   42.00  100.00  302.00    0.50    0.00


   PROTEIN    FIBER POLYUN.    PTAS. MAGNES.    IRON    RIBO.  VIT. C  VIT. D
        G        G        G      MG      MG      MG     MCG       MG      IU
 -------:-------:-------:-------:-------:-------:-------:-------:-------:
     3.40     0.30     0.00    0.00    0.00    1.10   49.00    0.00    0.00


READY TO CHANGE? NO
ANOTHER FOOD? NO
1. PRINT WHOLE FILE
2. EDIT A FOOD
3. EXIT FROM PROGRAM  --TYPE 1,2, OR 3? 3
OK
```

SOMEONE WHO WAS SICK OF CARROTS DECIDED TO CHANGE #42 TO CHEERIOS

WITH THESE VALUES.

8.4   BUSINESS APPLICATIONS

One of the earliest applications of computers was to the business world. The term "data processing" was coined at that time, which is why that phrase is often used to mean business programs (obviously the words themselves are really much more general). The range of business applications has continued to grow, and it now includes much more than "dollars and cents" type accounting programs. In fact, as the following list shows, several ideas of value to business can be found in other chapters where they appear in "unbusiness like" disguise. We can lump business applications into four big categories:

1.   Planning and Prediction; Management Information

      The football scouting program of Chapter 5 was a form of management information system. It summarized and interpreted raw data for the chief "executive" (the coach) of the operation. The graphing techniques of Chapters 3 and 7 are often used to show data trends more clearly in such management reports. The diet program in this chapter is also a form of management report meant for the consumer. The computer systems used by airlines and hotels to make reservations are another form of information system.

2.   Training and Education

      The business world also uses computers for training. Examples range from simple CAI (computer assisted instruction) programs of the arithmetic drill type shown in Chapter 2, to simulation-games of the kind shown in Chapters 6 and 9.

3.   Word Processing

      The "letter-writing" program of Chapter 4 illustrates how computers can be used to prepare documents from stored information, functioning something like an automated secretary. Word processing systems also include editing features which make it easy to update text.

4.   Record Keeping

      Fiscal and inventory record-keeping programs are at the heart of most business operations. These include such things as payroll, accounting, invoicing, and inventory systems. The operations at a bank are also large record- keeping systems, and the new idea of "electronic funds transfer" really amounts to swapping computer data between banks (a somewhat frightening prospect!). And of course tax and credit information systems involve the same operations.

In this section we'll illustrate part of the fourth area by showing how to design and write a credit-card type accounting system. This might be a national system, or (more likely) a local one for something like a department store. The ideas also apply to other business situations where the accounting is based on the following two operations:

(1) Transactions—either sales or payments

If gathered at the time of sale (say at the cash register), these are called point of sale (POS) transactions. Of course transactions can also be made by phone or mail.

(2) Master File Operations

The function of these operations is to take all the transactions for some period (say one day), and use them to update a master file that contains data about each customer account. Bills and other kinds of documents are then produced from this file, usually on a monthly basis.

A Charge Account Program

In this section, we'll illustrate how these two operations work together in a program that stores the master file in DATA statements. Then in the next section, we'll show how to use "sequential files" instead of DATA statements. As we'll see, the second method has the important advantage that the computer program can automatically update the master file, so there is no need to type in new DATA statements at the end of each day.

The Problem

The Ace Widget Co. allows its customers to buy merchandise on account, that is, they can say "charge it". This means that the customers must be sent monthly bills (or invoices). For our example, the bill will contain the customer's account number, name, and address. Then it will show the charges accumulated in the last month, the previous balance (which should be old charges *minus* any payments made), the interest charged on the unpaid balance (we'll use 1.5% per month), and the total amount due. For example, if R. Jones charged $45.99 during the past month, and had an unpaid balance of $180.00, his bill would be the following:

Charges this month		$ 45.99
Previous balance		180.00
Interest on previous balance		2.70
	Total due	$ 228.69

If the same Mr. Jones had also sent in a payment of $150.00 during the month, then this would have been subtracted from his balance, and the billing would be as follows:

Charges this month		$ 45.99
Previous balance		30.00
Interest on previous balance		.45
	Total due	$ 76.44

To spread the billing out, each customer will be assigned a billing day "number". If Jones has the number 3, this means he gets billed on the third day of each month. However transactions are recorded *every* day on his master file record. The word "record" means a collection of such data. For our problem, we'll put six pieces of data in each record: Account #, name, address, balance, charges this month, and billing day. If we put this information in a DATA statement, here's what Mr. Jones' old master file record would look like if he had account #001:

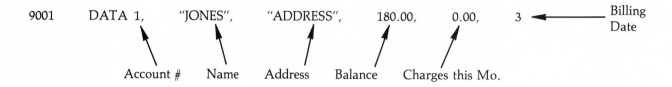

9001   DATA 1,   "JONES",   "ADDRESS",   180.00,   0.00,   3 ←——— Billing Date

Account #   Name   Address   Balance   Charges this Mo.

Of course the address would actually be split further into street, city, zipcode, etc. In our example, this is the record *before* he charged the $45.99 this month. On the day after he charged it, the 0.00 should be changed to $45.99 because the master file is to be updated each night.

When the date happens to be a 3, something different happens that night. A *bill* is printed, and the 45.99 is added to the balance along with interest. this means that Jones' master file record would then look like the following:

1, "R. JONES", "ADDRESS", 228.69, 0.00, 3

If DATA statements are used then a new data statement would have to be typed in for Jones. This is obviously not desirable, and we'll find a way around this in the next section. But for now it will be easier to follow what's going on if we first develop a program that uses DATA statements for the master file.

In addition to a master file, we'll also need a transaction file to record the charges and payments for one day. We'll use a 100 by 2 array for this, and use the subscript (or index) on the array to also mean account number as follows:

TRANSACTION CODE	TRANSACTION AMOUNT
$T(1,1) = 1$	$T(1,2) = 45.99$
$T(2,1) = 3$	$T(2,2) = 0$
$T(3,1) = 2$	$T(3,2) = 4.98$
.	.
.	.
.	.
$T(99,1) = 1$	$T(99,2) = 8.75$

$P = 1 \longrightarrow$ (points to first row of table above)

The codes are 1 for charge, 2 for payment on account, and 3 for "close account request". The pointer P is used to select account numbers. If Jones is account #1 (P = 1), then the first row in this array says that Jones charged (code 1) a \$45.99 purchase today.

We'll explain how these ideas go together by first presenting a general flowchart. This will be followed by a BASIC listing and run. Study the listing by comparing the line numbers with those shown for the various blocks in the flowchart. Notice that at the end the program prints out a "dump" (a kind of listing) of what new DATA would have to be entered in the master file for the next day's business.

The variables used in the program are as follows:

$M_1, D_1, Y_1 =$	Current Date (Month, Day, Year)
$N, C, A =$	Transaction Record Account *Number*, *Code*, and *Amount*
Codes are	1 = Charge
	2 = Payment
	3 = Request to close account
$T(N,1)$	stores the code for account #N after a transaction
$T(N,2)$	stores the amount for account #N after a transaction
$M =$	Master file record account #
$N\$ =$	Name on MFR
$A\$ =$	Address on MFR
$B =$	Balance on MFR
$L =$	Latest month's charges on MFR
$D =$	Billing day for this MFR
$P =$	Pointer to the transaction file record which is being compared to a MFR
$T_1 =$	Total charges today
$T_2 =$	Total payments today
$T_3 =$	Total number of accounts closed today

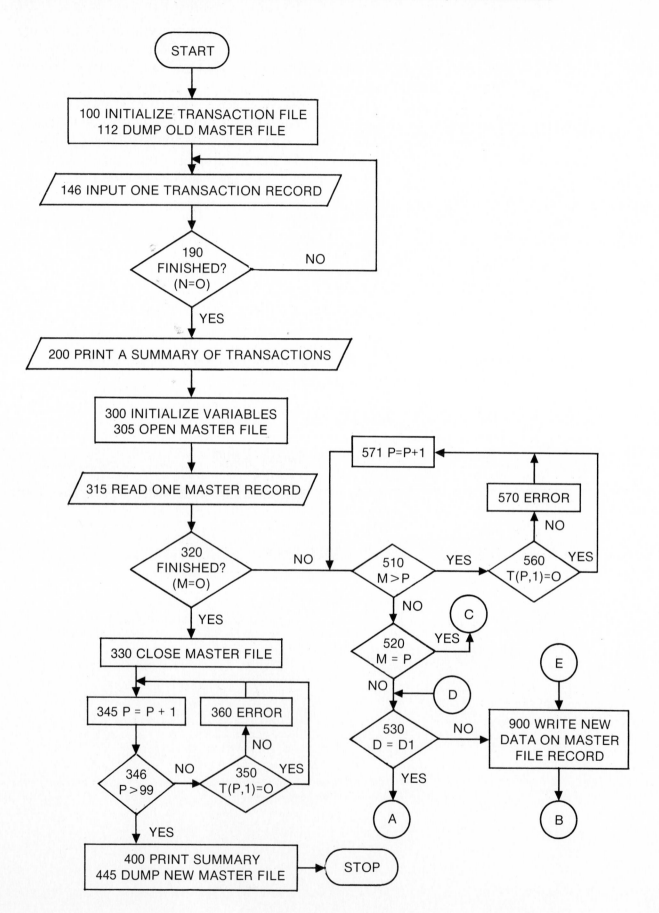

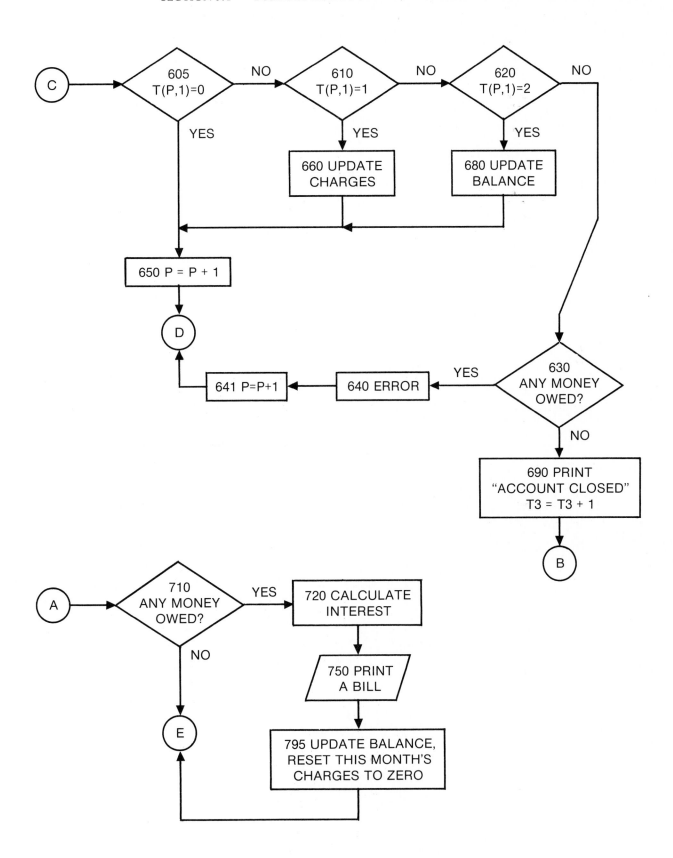

Note: the letters A, B, C, D, and E show how these flowcharts fit together.

CHARGE
ACCOUNT

```
LIST
100 DIM T(100,2),M(20),N$(20),A$(20),L(20)
110 DIM B(20),D(20)
112 PRINT"DUMP OF OLD MASTER FILE"
114 FOR Z=1 TO 99
116 READ M,N$,A$,B,L,D: IF M=0 THEN 119
117 PRINT M;TAB(5);N$;TAB(15);A$;TAB(28);B;TAB(37);L;TAB(45);D
118 NEXT Z
119 GOSUB 8000: RESTORE
120 PRINT"TYPE DATE IN FORM 1,8,77";:INPUT M1,D1,Y1
130 REM----TRANSACTION DATA NOW PLACED IN RAM-----
140 PRINT"INPUT TRANSACTIONS. TYPE 0,0,0 WHEN FINISHED"
145 PRINT"TYPE ACCT.#,CODE,AMT."
146 INPUT N,C,A
147 IF N=0 THEN 200
150 IF C=0 THEN 175
160 IF ABS(C-2)>1 THEN PRINT"ILLEGAL CODE":GOTO 140
170 IF ABS(N-50)>49 THEN PRINT"ILLEGAL ACCT.#":GOTO 140
172 GOTO 180
175 A=0: PRINT"TRANS. FOR ACCT.#";N;" VOIDED."
180 T(N,1)=C: T(N,2)=A
190 IF N<>0 THEN 146
200 PRINT"SUMMARY OF TRANSACTIONS TODAY:"
205 GOSUB 8000
220 PRINT"ACCOUNT","CODE","AMOUNT"
230 FOR N=1 TO 99
240 IF T(N,1)=0 THEN 260
250 PRINT N,T(N,1),T(N,2)
260 NEXT N
270 GOSUB 8000
300 P=1: T1=0: T2=0: T3=0
305 REM-----OPEN MASTER FILE-----
310 REM-----READ IN ONE MFR-----
315 READ M,N$,A$,B,L,D
320 IF M>.1 THEN 500
330 REM-----CLOSE MASTER FILE-----
340 REM-----CHECK FOR TRANS.NOT MATCHED TO A MFR-----
345 P=P+1
346 IF P>99 THEN 400
350 IF T(P,1)=0 THEN 345
360 PRINT"ERROR: NO MFR FOR ACCT.#";P
365 PRINT "WARNING******THIS TRANSACTION HAS NOT BEEN RECORDED"
370 GOTO 340
399 REM-----FINAL SUMMARY-----
400 GOSUB 8000
410 PRINT"TOTAL CHARGES TODAY = ";T1
420 PRINT"TOTAL PAYMENTS TODAY = ";T2
430 PRINT T3;"ACCOUNTS WERE CLOSED TODAY."
440 GOSUB 8000
445 PRINT"DUMP OF NEW MASTER FILE":GOSUB 8000
450 FOR J=1 TO K
455 PRINT M(J);TAB(5);N$(J);TAB(15);A$(J);
456 PRINT TAB(28);B(J);TAB(37);L(J);TAB(45);D(J)
460 NEXT J
465 GOSUB 8000
470 STOP
```

```
500  REM-----PROCESS THE MFR JUST READ-----
510  IF M>P THEN 560
520  IF M=P THEN 600
530  IF D=D1 THEN 700
540  GOTO 900
560  IF T(P,1)<>0THEN 570
565  P=P+1:GOTO 510
570  GOSUB 8000: PRINT"ERROR: NO MASTER RECORD FOR ACCT.#";P
571  GOSUB 8000: P=P+1: GOTO 510
600  REM-----UPDATING OF MFR-----
605  IF T(P,1)=0 THEN 650
610  IF T(P,1)=1 THEN 660
620  IF T(P,1)=2 THEN 680
630  IF B+L=0 THEN 690
640  GOSUB 8000: PRINT"ERROR: TRIED TO CLOSE ACTIVE ACCT.#";M
641  GOSUB 8000:P=P+1:GOTO 530
650  P=P+1: GOTO 530
660  L=L+T(P,2)
670  T1=T1+T(P,2): GOTO 650
680  B=B-T(P,2)
685  T2=T2+T(P,2): GOTO 650
690  PRINT"ACCT.#";M;" CLOSED.":T3=T3+1: GOTO 315
700  REM-----CALC.INTEREST & PRINT BILL-----
710  IF B+L=0 THEN 900
720  I=B*.015
730  IF I<0 THEN I=0
740  GOSUB 8000
750  PRINT TAB(30);M1;"/";D1;"/";Y1
755  PRINT"ACE WIDGET CO."
760  PRINT"FERNWOOD,OHIO":PRINT
765  PRINT N$: PRINT A$: PRINT"U.S.A"
770  PRINT:PRINT"FRIENDLY CHARGE ACCT.#";M:PRINT
775  PRINT"CHARGES THIS MONTH: $";L
780  PRINT"PREVIOUS BALANCE:    $";B
790  PRINT"INTEREST:            $";I
791  GOSUB 8000
792  PRINT"TOTAL DUE:           $";INT(100*(L+B+I))/100
793  PRINT: GOSUB 8000
795  B=L+B+I: L=0
900  REM-----SIMULATE WRITING A NEW MFR-----
910  K=K+1
920  M(K)=M: N$(K)=N$: A$(K)=A$: B(K)=B: L(K)=L: D(K)=D
930  GOTO 310
8000 FOR J=1 TO 40: PRINT"-";: NEXT J: PRINT: RETURN
9001 DATA 1,"R.JONES","ADDRESS 1",180.00,0.00,3
9003 DATA 3,"J.KING","ADDRESS 3",0.00,30.99,18
9004 DATA 4,"S.ADAMS","ADDRESS 4",17.38,92.46,3
9006 DATA 6,"F.JOSHUA","ADDRESS 6",846.45,25.78,27
9007 DATA 7,"B.WALTERS","ADDRESS 7",15.08,0.00,3
9008 DATA 8,"F.WALLER","ADDRESS 8",-15.65,230.99,17
9010 DATA 10,"M.MORTON","ADDRESS 10",18.26,39.95,3
9015 DATA 15,"O.DUPONT","ADDRESS 15",83.57,39.50,5
9020 DATA 20,"U.TELLUM","ADDRESS 20",0.00,0.00,3
9034 DATA 34,"U.UPDIKE","ADDRESS 34",0.00,0.00,25
9998 DATA 0,"","",0,0,0
9999 END
```

```
RUN
DUMP OF OLD MASTER FILE
   1    R.JONES     ADDRESS  1       180        0          3
   3    J.KING      ADDRESS  3       0          30.99      18
   4    S.ADAMS     ADDRESS  4       17.38      92.46      3
   6    F.JOSHUA    ADDRESS  6       846.45     25.78      27
   7    B.WALTERS   ADDRESS  7       15.08      0          3
   8    F.WALLER    ADDRESS  8       -15.65     230.99     17
  10    M.MORTON    ADDRESS 10       18.26      39.95      3
  15    O.DUPONT    ADDRESS 15       83.57      39.5       5
  20    U.TELLUM    ADDRESS 20       0          0          3
  34    U.UPDIKE    ADDRESS 34       0          0          25
--------------------------------------------
TYPE DATE IN FORM 1,8,77? 12,3,77
INPUT TRANSACTIONS.  TYPE 0,0,0 WHEN FINISHED
TYPE ACCT.#,CODE,AMT.
? 34,3,0
? 1,1,45.99
? 88,1,16
? 88,0,0
TRANS. FOR ACCT.# 88  VOIDED.
? 8,1,16.00
? 77,1,25.99
? 3,3,0
? 6,2,800.00
? 15,2,100.00
? 0,0,0
SUMMARY OF TRANSACTIONS TODAY:
--------------------------------------------
ACCOUNT         CODE           AMOUNT
   1             1             45.99
   3             3             0
   6             2             800
   8             1             16
  15             2             100
  34             3             0
  77             1             25.99
--------------------------------------------
--------------------------------------------
                                 12 / 3 / 77
ACE WIDGET CO.
FERNWOOD,OHIO

R.JONES
ADDRESS 1
U.S.A

FRIENDLY CHARGE ACCT.# 1

CHARGES THIS MONTH: $ 45.99
PREVIOUS BALANCE:   $ 180
INTEREST:           $ 2.7
--------------------------------------------
TOTAL DUE:          $ 228.69

--------------------------------------------
--------------------------------------------
ERROR: TRIED TO CLOSE ACTIVE ACCT.# 3
--------------------------------------------
--------------------------------------------
                                 12 / 3 / 77
ACE WIDGET CO.
FERNWOOD,OHIO

S.ADAMS
ADDRESS 4
U.S.A
```

```
FRIENDLY CHARGE ACCT.# 4

CHARGES THIS MONTH: $ 92.46
PREVIOUS BALANCE:   $ 17.38
INTEREST:           $ .2607
-----------------------------------------------
TOTAL DUE:          $ 110.1


-----------------------------------------
-----------------------------------------
                             12 / 3 / 77
ACE WIDGET CO.
FERNWOOD,OHIO

B.WALTERS
ADDRESS 7
U.S.A

FRIENDLY CHARGE ACCT.# 7

CHARGES THIS MONTH: $ 0
PREVIOUS BALANCE:   $ 15.08
INTEREST:           $ .2262
-----------------------------------------
TOTAL DUE:          $ 15.3


-----------------------------------------
-----------------------------------------
                             12 / 3 / 77
ACE WIDGET CO.
FERNWOOD,OHIO

M.MORTON
ADDRESS 10
U.S.A

FRIENDLY CHARGE ACCT.# 10

CHARGES THIS MONTH: $ 39.95
PREVIOUS BALANCE:   $ 18.26
INTEREST:           $ .2739
-----------------------------------------
TOTAL DUE:          $ 58.48


-----------------------------------------
ACCT.# 34   CLOSED.
ERROR: NO MFR FOR ACCT.# 77
WARNING******THIS TRANSACTION HAS NOT BEEN RECORDED
-----------------------------------------
TOTAL CHARGES TODAY =  61.99
TOTAL PAYMENTS TODAY =  900
 1 ACCOUNTS WERE CLOSED TODAY.
-----------------------------------------
DUMP OF NEW MASTER FILE
-----------------------------------------
  1    R.JONES    ADDRESS 1     228.69    0        3
  3    J.KING     ADDRESS 3     0         30.99    18
  4    S.ADAMS    ADDRESS 4     110.101   0        3
  6    F.JOSHUA   ADDRESS 6     46.45     25.78    27
  7    B.WALTERS  ADDRESS 7     15.3062   0        3
  8    F.WALLER   ADDRESS 8     -15.65    246.99   17
 10    M.MORTON   ADDRESS 10    58.4839   -0       3
 15    O.DUPONT   ADDRESS 15    -16.43    39.5     5
 20    U.TELLUM   ADDRESS 20    0         0        3
-----------------------------------------
STOP at line 470
```

8.5   USING FILES IN THE CHARGE ACCOUNT PROGRAM

The master file for the charge account program shown in the previous section was stored in DATA statements. For a large customer base, several hundred (or even several thousand) DATA statements would be needed. This won't work because there will not be enough RAM memory to hold such a long program on most machines. An even more serious problem is that the master file must be updated every day which would mean typing in new DATA statements. Doing all that manual work would defeat the whole purpose of using a computer. It's time for a better way.

The answer will be to store the master file data on an external storage medium—either tape or disk. We'll show how to do this using the sequential disk file commands explained in Section 8.2. Sequential files will be adequate for our purposes. (Random files would have the advantage of direct access to any customer account, but not all computer systems have random files.)

To convert the charge account program, three things will have to be done:

1. A program called CREATE will be written which allows the user to create the initial master file of customer records.
2. A program called UPDATE will be written so that the master file can be updated—new accounts added, old accounts removed, changes of address made, errors in data corrected. (Actually CREATE and UPDATE could be combined, but the ideas will be simpler to follow if they are treated separately.)
3. The program called CHARGE ACCOUNT in the previous section will be modified by removing the DATA statements (lines 9001 to 9998). Then the READ data statement (line 116) will be replaced with file INPUT statements that read master file data from disk. Most importantly, new statements that automatically update the master file will take the place of the old "simulated update" statements in lines 900 to 920. We'll call this revised program FILE CHARGE ACCOUNT.

Here are listings and sample runs for each of these programs. Normally, the CREATE program would only be used once to initialize the master file. UPDATE would be used occasionally to change or delete accounts. However the FILE CHARGE ACCOUNT program would normally be used every day. After all the day's transactions have been entered, it produces a sorted record of those transactions, invoices and special messages, and an automatically updated master file.

The trickiest part of FILE CHARGE ACCOUNT is the "writing" of the new master file. Records are read from the old file "MASTER" (line 315), but the updated records are written on a "scratch" file called "TEMP" (line 910). When the end of the old file "MASTER" is reached (line 920), the file "TEMP" is renamed as "MASTER" (line 442). Before this renaming is possible however, the old masterfile must be "killed" (line 441). Incidentally, the CHR$(34) in line 910 is a trick to put quotation marks around the string data being written on the new file.

We've left the feature of dumping old and new master files in the program so you can see how the file is changed. It is also good practice to have hard copy backup in case the magnetic files get erased. Of course this gets unwieldy for large files, so a more professional system would require that the operator always make extra copies of the master file disks (or tapes), and that these be be stored separately.

It would be best to study the listings and runs of CREATE and UPDATE in conjunction with Section 8.4, using the flowchart in that section.

CREATE

```
LOAD "CREATE
OK
LIST

110 OPEN "O",1,"MASTER",0
130 FOR M=1 TO 9
140 PRINT"IS THERE DATA FOR ACCT.#";M;:INPUT T$
145 IF T$="STOP" THEN 210
150 IF LEFT$(T$,1)="Y" THEN 170
160 N$="NONAME ": A$="NOADDRESS ": B=0: L=0: D=0
165 GOTO 190
170 PRINT"TYPE NAME,ADDRESS,BALANCE,LATEST CHARGES,BILLING DATE"
180 PRINT"ACCT.NO.";M: INPUT N$,A$,B,L,D
190 PRINT #1,M;CHR$(34);N$;CHR$(34);CHR$(34);A$;CHR$(34);B;L;D
200 NEXT M
210 CLOSE 1
220 OPEN "I",1,"MASTER",0
230 PRINT"ECHO CHECK OF MASTER FILE"
235 FOR K=1 TO 9
240 INPUT #1,M,N$,A$,B,L,D
250 PRINT M;N$;"   ";A$;"   ";B;L;D
255 IF EOF(1) THEN 270
260 NEXT K
270 PRINT"END OF FILE"
280 END
OK

RUN
IS THERE DATA FOR ACCT.# 1 ? N
IS THERE DATA FOR ACCT.# 2 ? Y
TYPE NAME,ADDRESS,BALANCE,LATEST CHARGES,BILLING DATE
ACCT.NO. 2
? JOHN SMITH,70 MAIN ST. MILTOWN PA,34.40,3.99,4
IS THERE DATA FOR ACCT.# 3 ? N
IS THERE DATA FOR ACCT.# 4 ? N
IS THERE DATA FOR ACCT.# 5 ? Y
TYPE NAME,ADDRESS,BALANCE,LATEST CHARGES,BILLING DATE
ACCT.NO. 5
? SAM SPADE,LOWER WHARF SAN FRANCISCO,980.90,0,13
IS THERE DATA FOR ACCT.# 6 ? N
IS THERE DATA FOR ACCT.# 7 ? N
IS THERE DATA FOR ACCT.# 8 ? N
IS THERE DATA FOR ACCT.# 9 ? Y
TYPE NAME,ADDRESS,BALANCE,LATEST CHARGES,BILLING DATE
ACCT.NO. 9
? ELROY SCRUGGS,MUSIC CNTR. NASHVILLE,56.65,34.43,10
ECHO CHECK OF MASTER FILE
 1 NONAME    NOADDRESS    0   0   0
 2 JOHN SMITH  70 MAIN ST. MILTOWN PA   34.4  3.99  4
 3 NONAME    NOADDRESS    0   0   0
 4 NONAME    NOADDRESS    0   0   0
 5 SAM SPADE  LOWER WHARF SAN FRANCISCO   980.9  0  13
 6 NONAME    NOADDRESS    0   0   0
 7 NONAME    NOADDRESS    0   0   0
 8 NONAME    NOADDRESS    0   0   0
 9 ELROY SCRUGGS  MUSIC CNTR. NASHVILLE   56.65  34.43  10
END OF FILE
OK
```

UPDATE

```
LOAD "UPDATE"
OK
LIST

100 OPEN"I",1,"MASTER",0
105 OPEN"O",2,"TEMP",0
110 INPUT"WHICH ACCT.# TO BE UPDATED";M1
120 INPUT #1,M,N$,A$,B,L,D
130 IF M<>M1 THEN 150
135 PRINT M;N$;" ";A$;" ";B;L;D
140 PRINT"TYPE NAME,ADDRESS,BALANCE,LATEST CHARGES,BILLING DATE"
145 PRINT"ACCT.#";M: INPUT N$,A$,B,L,D
150 PRINT #2,M;CHR$(34);N$;CHR$(34);CHR$(34);A$;CHR$(34);B;L;D
155 IF EOF(1) THEN 900
160 IF M=M1 THEN 110 ELSE 120
900 CLOSE
905 KILL"MASTER"
907 NAME"TEMP" AS "MASTER"
910 PRINT"END OF FILE"
930 PRINT"ECHO CHECK OF MASTER FILE"
932 OPEN "I",1,"MASTER",0
935 FOR K=1 TO 9
940 INPUT #1,M,N$,A$,B,L,D
950 PRINT M;N$;"   ";A$;"   ";B;L;D
955 IF EOF(1) THEN 970
960 NEXT K
970 CLOSE
980 END

OK


RUN
WHICH ACCT.# TO BE UPDATED? 5
 5 SAM SPADE LOWER WHARF SAN FRANCISCO 980.9  0  13
TYPE NAME,ADDRESS,BALANCE,LATEST CHARGES,BILLING DATE
ACCT.# 5
? SAM SPADE,UPPER WHARF SAN FRANCISCO,980.90,0,13
WHICH ACCT.# TO BE UPDATED? 7
 7 NONAME   NOADDRESS    0  0  0
TYPE NAME,ADDRESS,BALANCE,LATEST CHARGES,BILLING DATE
ACCT.# 7
? CARL SCHMIDT,OLD BREWERY RD. SUDSVILLE,100.50,50.75,13
WHICH ACCT.# TO BE UPDATED? 10
END OF FILE
ECHO CHECK OF MASTER FILE
 1 NONAME    NOADDRESS     0  0  0
 2 JOHN SMITH  70 MAIN ST. MILTOWN PA   34.4  3.99  4
 3 NONAME    NOADDRESS     0  0  0
 4 NONAME    NOADDRESS     0  0  0
 5 SAM SPADE   UPPER WHARF SAN FRANCISCO   980.9  0  13
 6 NONAME    NOADDRESS     0  0  0
 7 CARL SCHMIDT   OLD BREWERY RD. SUDSVILLE   100.5  50.75  13
 8 NONAME    NOADDRESS     0  0  0
 9 ELROY SCRUGGS   MUSIC CNTR. NASHVILLE    56.65  34.43  10
OK
```

FILE CHARGE
ACCOUNT

```
LOAD "CHARGF"
OK
LIST

100 DIM T(100,2):F=0
101 PRINT "DUMP OF OLD MASTER FILE"
102 OPEN "I",1,"MASTER",0
104 FOR Z=1 TO 99
106 INPUT #1,M,N$,A$,B,L,D
108 IF D=0 THEN 112
110 PRINT M;TAB(5);N$;TAB(19);A$;TAB(44);B;TAB(53);L;TAB(61);D
112 IF EOF(1) THEN 117
116 NEXT Z
117 IF F>0 THEN 9999
118 OPEN"O",2,"TEMP",0
119 CLOSE 1: GOSUB 8000
120 PRINT"TYPE DATE IN FORM 1,8,77";::INPUT M1,D1,Y1
130 REM-----TRANSACTION DATA NOW PLACED IN RAM-----
140 PRINT"INPUT TRANSACTIONS.  TYPE 0,0,0 WHEN FINISHED"
145 PRINT"TYPE ACCT.#,CODE,AMT."
146 INPUT N,C,A
147 IF N=0 THEN 200
150 IF C=0 THEN 175
160 IF ABS(C-2)>1 THEN PRINT"ILLEGAL CODE":GOTO 140
170 IF ABS(N-50)>49 THEN PRINT"ILLEGAL ACCT.#":GOTO 140
172 GOTO 180
175 A=0: PRINT"TRANS. FOR ACCT.#";N;" VOIDED."
180 T(N,1)=C: T(N,2)=A
190 IF N<>0 THEN 146
200 PRINT"SUMMARY OF TRANSACTIONS TODAY:"
205 GOSUB 8000
220 PRINT"ACCOUNT","CODE","AMOUNT"
230 FOR N=1 TO 99
240 IF T(N,1)=0 THEN 260
250 PRINT N,T(N,1),T(N,2)
260 NEXT N
270 GOSUB 8000
300 P=1: T1=0: T2=0: T3=0
305 OPEN "I",1,"MASTER",0
310 REM-----READ IN ONE MFR-----
315 INPUT #1,M,N$,A$,B,L,D
320 GOTO 500
330 CLOSE
340 REM-----CHECK FOR TRANS.NOT MATCHED TO A MFR-----
345 P=P+1
346 IF P>9 THEN 400
350 IF T(P,1)=0 THEN 345
360 PRINT"ERROR: NO MFR FOR ACCT.#";P
365 PRINT "WARNING******THIS TRANSACTION HAS NOT BEEN RECORDED"
370 GOTO 340
399 REM-----FINAL SUMMARY-----
400 GOSUB 8000
410 PRINT"TOTAL CHARGES TODAY = ";T1
420 PRINT"TOTAL PAYMENTS TODAY = ;T2
430 PRINT T3;"ACCOUNTS WERE CLOSED TODAY."
440 GOSUB 8000
441 CLOSE:KILL "MASTER"
442 NAME "TEMP" AS "MASTER"
445 PRINT"DUMP OF NEW MASTER FILE":GOSUB 8000
446 F=1: GOTO 102
470 STOP
500 REM-----PROCESS THE MFR JUST READ-----
510 IF M>P THEN 560
520 IF M=P THEN 600
530 IF D=D1 THEN 700
540 GOTO 900
560 IF T(P,1)<>0THEN 570
565 P=P+1:GOTO 510
```

```
570 GOSUB 8000: PRINT"ERROR: NO MASTER RECORD FOR ACCT.#";P
571 GOSUB 8000: P=P+1: GOTO 510
600 REM-----UPDATING OF MFR-----
605 IF T(P,1)=0 THEN 650
610 IF T(P,1)=1 THEN 660
620 IF T(P,1)=2 THEN 680
630 IF B+L=0 THEN 690
640 GOSUB 8000: PRINT"ERROR: TRIED TO CLOSE ACTIVE ACCT.#";M
641 GOSUB 8000:P=P+1:GOTO 530
650 P=P+1: GOTO 530
660 L=L+T(P,2)
670 T1=T1+T(P,2): GOTO 650
680 B=B-T(P,2)
685 T2=T2+T(P,2): GOTO 650
690 PRINT"ACCT.#";M;" CLOSED.":T3=T3+1: GOTO 315
700 REM-----CALC.INTEREST & PRINT BILL-----
710 IF B+L=0 THEN 900
720 I=B*.015
73  IF I<0 THEN I=0
74  GOSUB 8000
750 PRINT TAB(30);M1;"/";D1;"/";Y1
755 PRINT"ACE WIDGET CO."
760 PRINT"FERNWOOD,OHIO":PRINT
765 PRINT N$: PRINT A$: PRINT"U.S.A"
770 PRINT:PRINT"FRIENDLY CHARGE ACCT.#";M:PRINT
775 PRINT"CHARGES THIS MONTH: $";L
780 PRINT"PREVIOUS BALANCE:    $";B
790 PRINT"INTEREST:            $";I
791 GOSUB 8000
792 PRINT"TOTAL DUE:           $";INT(100*(L+B+I))/100
793 PRINT: GOSUB 8000
795 B=L+B+I: L=0
900 REM-----          WRITING A NEW MFR-----
910 PRINT #2,M;CHR$(34);N$;CHR$(34);CHR$(34);A$;CHR$(34);B;L;D
920 IF EOF(1) THEN 400
930 GOTO 310
8000 FOR J=1 TO 40: PRINT"-";: NEXT J: PRINT: RETURN
9999 END
OK
```

```
RUN
DUMP OF OLD MASTER FILE
    2    JOHN SMITH      70 MAIN ST. MILTOWN PA     34.4      3.99     4
    5    SAM SPADE       UPPER WHARF SAN FRANCISCO 980.9      0       13
    7    CARL SCHMIDT    OLD BREWERY RD. SUDSVILLE 100.5     50.75    13
    9    ELROY SCRUGGS   MUSIC CNTR. NASHVILLE      56.65    34.43    10
----------------------------------------
TYPE DATE IN FORM 1,8,77? 3,13,78
INPUT TRANSACTIONS.  TYPE 0,0,0 WHEN FINISHED
TYPE ACCT.#,CODE,AMT.
? 2,2,10.00
? 7,1,89.90
? 5,1,56.89
? 9,3,0
? 0,0,0
SUMMARY OF TRANSACTIONS TODAY:
----------------------------------------
ACCOUNT        CODE         AMOUNT
2              2            10
5              1            56.89
7              1            89.9
9              3            0
----------------------------------------
```

```
--------------------------------------------
                                 3 / 13 / 78
ACE WIDGET CO.
FERNWOOD,OHIO

SAM SPADE
UPPER WHARF  SAN FRANCISCO
U.S.A

FRIENDLY CHARGE ACCT.# 5

CHARGES THIS MONTH: $ 56.89
PREVIOUS BALANCE:   $ 980.9
INTEREST:           $ 14.7135
--------------------------------------------
TOTAL DUE:          $ 1052.5


--------------------------------------------
--------------------------------------------
                                 3 / 13 / 78
ACE WIDGET CO.
FERNWOOD,OHIO

CARL SCHMIDT
OLD BREWERY RD. SUDSVILLE
U.S.A

FRIENDLY CHARGE ACCT.# 7

CHARGES THIS MONTH: $ 140.65
PREVIOUS BALANCE:   $ 100.5
INTEREST:           $ 1.5075
--------------------------------------------
TOTAL DUE:          $ 242.65


--------------------------------------------
--------------------------------------------
ERROR: TRIED TO CLOSE ACTIVE ACCT.# 9
--------------------------------------------
--------------------------------------------
TOTAL CHARGES TODAY =  146.79
TOTAL PAYMENTS TODAY =  10
 0 ACCOUNTS WERE CLOSED TODAY.
--------------------------------------------
DUMP OF NEW MASTER FILE
--------------------------------------------
   2    JOHN SMITH    70 MAIN ST. MILTOWN PA      24.4     3.99    4
   5    SAM SPADE     UPPER WHARF SAN FRANCISCO 1052.5     0      13
   7    CARL SCHMIDT  OLD BREWERY RD. SUDSVILLE  242.658   0      13
   9    ELROY SCRUGGS MUSIC CNTR. NASHVILLE       54
```

8.6   PROJECTS

1. Write a diet information program with a larger number of food items, or differently chosen food components. Here are some references:

1. Bowes and Church, *Food Values of Portions Commonly Used, Twelfth Edition*, J. B. Lippincott Co. Philadelphia, 1975.
2. Bernice K. Watt, et al, *Handbook of Nutritional Contents of Foods*, Dover Publications, Inc., N. Y., 1975 (Republication of Agriculture Handbook No. 8, *Composition of Foods*, U. S. D. A., 1963.)
3. National Nutritional Consortium, Inc., *Nutrition Labeling How it Can Work for You*, N. N. C., Inc., 9650 Rockville Pike, Bethesda, MD, 20014, 1975.
4. U. S. Department of Agriculture, Home and Garden Bulletin #1, *Family Fare, a Guide to Good Nutrition*, U. S. Government Printing Office, 1974.
5. American Diabetes Association, *Exchange Lists for Meal Planning*, A. D. A., Inc., 1 West 48 Street, New York, NY, 10020, 1976.
6. Iva Bennett and Martha Simon, *The Prudent Diet*, D. White Company, 1972.

Suggestion: An additional value associated with each food could be a code—1 for Milk Exchanges, 2 for Vegetable Exchanges, etc. (see reference 5 above). This code could be used in a new program to plan menus.

2. If you have a BASIC that allows use of "random access" files, convert the diet information program to use such files instead of DATA statements.

3. (Continuation of project 2) Write a program that allows you to "edit" (change, delete, or add to) this random food file. A partial solution (changes only) is shown in Section 8.3. It is written in Altair Disk Extended BASIC. Your BASIC may be different.

4. Sometimes rather simple additions to or modifications of the user dialogue can make a program such as the diet program easier to use. Some changes of this type are suggested:

(a)   Have the program calculate a percentage of the daily needs which are filled by the user's food list and print this out with report C.

(b)   Have the program print a warning if the user types in a low number for calories per day. Low might be under 900.

(c)   Change the program to display food name, grams, and *calories* in report D before the comparison of two foods, so that the user can easily decide how to change the amount of a food.

5. Put the portion in a string separate from food name. When the amount is changed, change the portion string to a blank. Decide whether it would be worthwhile to store the portion as a number and a string and calculate a new portion whenever the amount is changed.

6. See if there is any way for a dishonest customer to outfox the charge account program. Then find a way to have the program guard against the loophole you found.

7. The invoices printed by the charge account program don't explicitly show payments made in the past month. Revise the program to make this possible . Also use the PRINT USING statement to make the decimal points line up, and to round all amounts to the nearest cent.

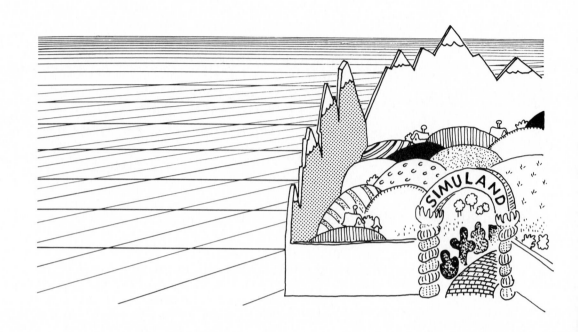

COMPUTER SIMULATIONS

9.0 INTRODUCTION

The dictionary defines a simulation as "an imitation; a feigning or pretending". Back in Chapter 6 we saw that many computer games are also simulations. For example, a program may "pretend" that cards have been dealt for some kind of game, or it may act "as if" you are an astronaut controlling the action of a space ship landing on Planet-X.

Simulations can make the learning of complicated skills a lot easier. Airline pilots regularly practice flying in jet simulators where they learn to cope with emergencies of all kinds. Even though these simulators have physical parts (like control wheels and flight instruments), a computer is used to handle most of the calculations. Much larger computer-controlled flight simulators are used by NASA for training pilots of new spacecraft. In general, simulations are used to model large *systems*, that is, collections of interacting parts. Other examples include business systems, economic systems, ecological systems, political systems, and distributed manufacturing systems.

Some of these systems are called *deterministic* because, given the same *input* and starting situation (called the initial *state*), the *output* will be uniquely determined. For example, one might simulate a large chemical manufacturing plant where (if all the input ingredients, temperatures, mixing ratios, etc. are the same) the output is supposed to be deterministic, that is, replicable day after day.

But there are also important systems where random, unpredictable events enter the picture. These are called *stochastic* systems. For example, a simulation of a social or business system is stochastic in nature because it involves people (who are not *individually* predictable), so statistical methods must be used.

For both deterministic and stochastic simulations, the idea is that one can experiment with different configurations before trying the real thing. Using a computer makes this a lot easier, especially in terms of handling the probabilistic calculations that stochastic models require. In fact, some writers define a simulation as *"a numerical technique for conducting experiments on a digital computer"*.

9.1   TO SIMULATE OR NOT TO SIMULATE: THAT SHOULD BE THE QUESTION

There are definite advantages to using simulations. For one thing, they allow dangerous experiments (like landing on the moon) to be first tried in safety. Simulations also permit untrained personnel to learn by making mistakes. The example of a simulation program that allows beginning medical students to prescribe treatment (based on computer generated symptoms and computer responses to student-requested lab tests) is an interesting one. When the program prints "WRONG TREATMENT-PATIENT JUST EXPIRED—WOULD YOU LIKE TO TRY AGAIN?", everybody is glad it was only a simulation.

On the other hand, we should also realize that the models underlying simulations are usually quite simplistic compared to reality. There are often critical factors not taken into account. Some of the assumptions that underlie a model may be just plain wrong. There are all kinds of subtleties to nature, social systems, and human behavior that are only dimly understood. Since a simulation can be no better than the model on which it's based, this means that the results should always be reviewed by human judgment, and checked against human experience.

Unfortunately, people are all too prone to accept anything that comes out of a computer as "perfect", and beyond questioning. Users of personal computers will know better. The same errors (or worse!) you've seen appear in your own work can (and will) appear in use of the "big" machines. As computer scientist Joseph Weizenbaum explains in his book *Computer Power and Human Reason*, there is undoubtedly a need to be thoughtfully critical of how computers are used, especially in areas where the subtleties of human judgment are needed. The simulation programs in this section — and in fact all the computer programs in this (and other) books — should be viewed in this light.

9.2   SOME SIMULATION TERMINOLOGY

Computer simulations have become useful in such a variety of fields that there are now entire books written on the subject. As a result, a fair amount of special "jargon" has been invented. It will be useful to know some of this terminology, so let's become text-bookish for a moment and look at some definitions.

We've already seen that simulations deal with *systems* (collections of interacting components like people, machines, data, and algorithms). Further, systems have *input* and *output*. At any given time we can talk about the configuration of all the variables in a system as its *state* (something like using the phrase "state of the nation" to describe all the things going on in a country at a particular time). The collection of data, equations, assumptions, and computer programs used to describe a system is called a *model* of the system. If a model contains elements that behave randomly (usually with time), it's called *stochastic*; otherwise it's called *deterministic*.

The Crazy Eights card game in Section 6.4 is an example of a partly stochastic simulation. The randomize statement in this program makes sure the hands being dealt each player are not predictable. On the other hand, the Planet-X Lander program of Section 6.8 is based on a deterministic model. It uses formulas derived from Newton's laws of motion, and if you always supply the same inputs to this program, the landing craft will always behave the same way.

Queuing Systems

There is a large class of simulations where something or other has to "wait on line" for service. Examples include the simulation of traffic at bridge toll booths, simulations of people going through checkout counters at a supermarket, the simulation of airplanes stacked up in an airport holding pattern, and simulations of computer program throughput in a large system where many users are waiting for service.

A waiting line (whether it has cars, people, airplanes, or programs) is called a queue (pronounced "kyoo"; the word queue is derived from the French language, and it originally meant tail, pigtail, or braid). The three main elements in a Queuing System are:

(1) A *source* of potential "customers"
(2) The waiting line (or *queue*)
(3) Some kind of *service facility* that processes the needs of the customers.

In order to study a queuing system, we need to know a number of parameters (variables which are fixed for a given problem). These are also called the *system specifications.*

A. Source Size - This is the potential number of customers. If the number is finite but very large, we usually call it infinite. For example, the number of potential customers for a bargain sale in a large city can be considered infinite. The simulations we will show are of this type. This means our program will never run out of customers.

B. Interarrival Time - This is the time between the arrival of one customer and the arrival of the next customer. The interarrival time can be more or less constant as in a dentist's office where the appointments are scheduled at half hour intervals. In other situations, the interarrival time between customers seems to vary randomly. Customers walking off the street and into a store don't follow a regular pattern. This kind of random arrival pattern can be modeled using a logarithmic random generator (more on this later).

C. Service Time - The service time is the time required by a server to handle a customer. This service time may be constant for each customer or vary randomly. A worker on an assembly line might take exactly five minutes to fasten a part onto each washing machine coming down the line. But the time needed by a teller at a bank will vary, depending upon the types of transactions required by each customer.

D. Maximum Queuing Capacity - In some queuing systems, the queue capacity is assumed to be infinite. Every customer is allowed to wait until service can be provided. Other systems, called loss systems, allow only finite queues or no queues at all. When the queue is filled in a loss system, any additional customers are turned away. An example is the queue of people waiting to get into a show that is already sold out. No new additions are allowed.

E Queue Discipline - The queue discipline is the rule for selecting the next customer to receive service. The most common queue discipline is first-come first-served (abbreviated as FCFS). Another queue discipline often used is last-come first-served (LCFS). An example of LCFS would be the queue of freight cars on a railroad siding. Random selection for service (RSS) is another queue discipline used. In RSS, the next customer is chosen randomly from among all the customers waiting. Radio shows that call people by randomly flipping phone book pages use RSS.

F. Number of Servers - The simplest queuing system is the single server system. An example is the small ice-cream truck with only one clerk. A multiserver system has many identical servers at the service facility. A bank with three tellers is an example of a multi-server system.

So What's the Problem?

There are many questions that arise in complicated queuing systems, especially when random events (like the arrival of a customer) are part of the system. Three examples of questions that one would like answered are the following:

1. What is the average (or "mean") waiting time a customer will have to wait on line?
2. What is the average (or "mean") number of customers waiting on line?
3. How busy will the servers be? Or to say it another way, (thinking like a boss), what percentage of the time will their service be utilized?

We'll look at these questions more closely in connection with a specific example in the next section, where we'll also describe a new kind of data structure.

9.3 DATA STRUCTURES FOR QUEUING SIMULATIONS; THE "DELI" PROBLEM

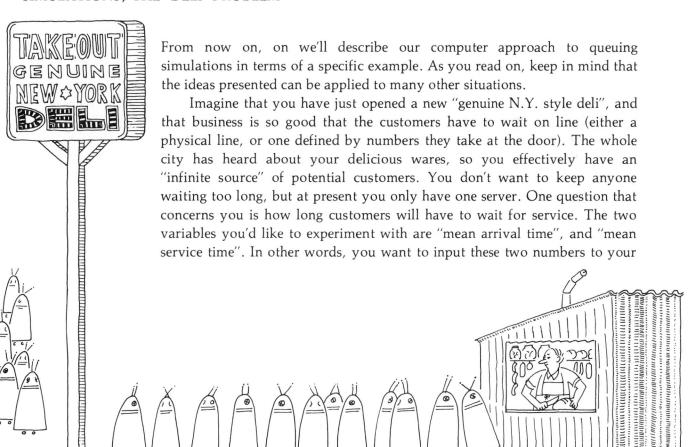

From now on, on we'll describe our computer approach to queuing simulations in terms of a specific example. As you read on, keep in mind that the ideas presented can be applied to many other situations.

Imagine that you have just opened a new "genuine N.Y. style deli", and that business is so good that the customers have to wait on line (either a physical line, or one defined by numbers they take at the door). The whole city has heard about your delicious wares, so you effectively have an "infinite source" of potential customers. You don't want to keep anyone waiting too long, but at present you only have one server. One question that concerns you is how long customers will have to wait for service. The two variables you'd like to experiment with are "mean arrival time", and "mean service time". In other words, you want to input these two numbers to your simulation program. As output, you want the program to tell you how large the waiting line will get, how long the average customer will have to wait, and how busy your clerk will be. If you find these answers unacceptable, then you'll want to write a multi-server simulation to find our what effect increasing the number of clerks has (this is discussed in Section 9.4).

To store information about customers waiting on line we'll use a data structure called a Queue. (It's also called a FIFO storage scheme since it's most often used for first-in-first-out type problems). This structure is nothing more than an array with two shifting pointers, one to keep track of the beginning of the line, and one for the end of the line. It can be pictured as follows, using B for the "beginning of line" pointer, and E for "end of line".

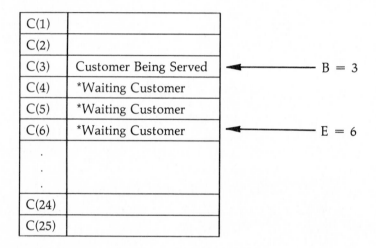

The starred sections represent data about customers who have *not yet* been served, that is, people in the waiting line. The pointer B shows the beginning of the line where customer #3 is already *being* served. When it's time to serve customer #4, B is changed to B+1. Similarly, when it's time to put a new customer on line , E is changed to E+1. So both pointers keep moving down. For a long simulation, this means that C would have to be a very large array even though only the part between B and E is needed at any given time. This structure is very wasteful of memory.

The simplest way to solve this difficulty is to use what's called a *circular queue*. Actually we'll still use an ordinary array, but we'll make it act as though it were circular. Also, to handle our small store problem, we'll need two storage locations for each customer, one to remember what time the customer entered the line, and the other to note how much service time the customer will require. If we allow a maximum of 25 people on line, this means dimensioning a 25x2 array C(25,2). Here's how we can picture this array:

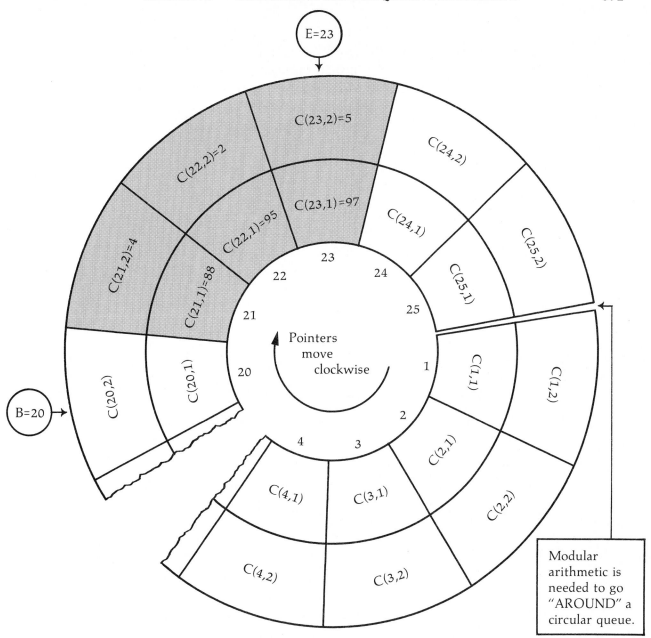

This is a circular queue with 25 locations. Our picture shows three customers (in positions 21,22,23) who have not yet been served. The data for customer 21 is C(21,1)=88 (which means the customer arrived 88 minutes past the start of the simulation), and C(21,2)=4 (which means this customer will require 4 minutes of service time).

When a customer enters the system our program will increment E and then put the customer where E is pointing. Similarly, when a server is free, we'll first increment B (it will then be pointing at the next customer), and then serve this customer, using data from row B. When B and E are equal, this means that the queue is empty.

To get the circular effect we'll use modular arithmetic. A familiar example of modular arithmetic is found on clocks, where although the hours actually keep increasing indefinitely, they are never counted higher than 12.

So instead of counting 10,11,12,13,14,15, etc., a clock counts 10,11,12,1,2,3,etc. We can say that it uses modulo 12 addition.

For the queue in our problem, we'll want both E and B to count 21, 22, 23, 24, 25, 1, 2, 3, etc. even though they are going 21, 22, 23, 24, 25, 26, 27, 28, etc. Here's a function that makes this happen:

DEF FNA(X)=X-INT((X-1)/25)*25

For example, when X=25, this function has the value

25-INT(24/25)*25=25-0*25=25

But when X=26, the value is

26-INT(25/25)*25=26-1*25=1

So we have defined a function which does modulo 25 arithmetic.

Inventing a New Kind of Random Number Generator

To simulate customers walking into the deli at unpredictable time intervals we'll need some kind of random number generator. Can we just go ahead and use RND? Let's see what's needed.

The RND function in BASIC is set up so that it has what's called *uniform* distribution. For some problems this is very desirable. For example, in a craps simulation we want X=INT(6*RND+1) to produce the numbers 1,2,3,4,5, and 6 with equal probability. This means that a graph showing *frequency* (that is, how many of each kind of die throw X appears in say 600 tries) would show the following *uniform* distribution:

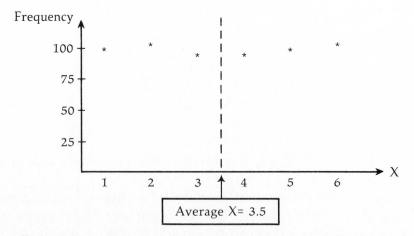

It's called uniform because all 6 values show up with about the same frequency (about 100 each). Also note that the average value of all 600 X's would be approximately 3.5.

Uniform distribution of random numbers is not suitable for queuing problems because the time between customers walking randomly into a store is anything but uniform. Experimental studies show that interarrival times vary greatly, *and* that more are "below average" than "above average". The same is true of service time required. In a business which averages say 10 minutes service per customer, there will be more customers requiring less than 10 minutes than more than 10 minutes. What this means is that a graph of the frequency of 1000 interarrival times with an *average* value of 3 minutes would look something like this:

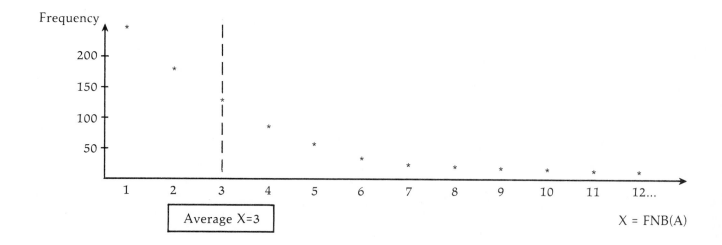

We say that these numbers are *exponentially* distributed because the frequency with which they appear is given by a formula that uses the exponential function. However, to generate such numbers randomly, the LOG function must be used as follows:

$$FNB(A)=INT(-A*LOG(RND)+.5)$$

The argument A is the average value about which other values are to be distributed exponentially. The term .5 is included for "roundoff". It makes the integer part of a number like 5.6 become 6, while 5.4 becomes 5.

SELF-TEST

1. Write a program that uses the FNB function just described to generate 1000 numbers and plot their distribution. The program should also calculate the *actual* average of all the numbers generated, and compare this with the value of A you used.

A Single-Server Simulation Program

We'll now show how to write a program that simulates what happens in a one-clerk store. Its purpose is to allow the user to experiment with the parameters in a single-server queuing system. The program will start by defining the modulo and exponential random number functions we just discussed.

```
110 DEF FNA(X)=X-INT((X-1)/25)*25
130 DEF FNB(X)=INT(-X*LOG(RND(1))+.5)
```

The data structures and variables used will be as follows:

C(25,2)	will be used as a circular queue
C(I,1)	will hold the arrival time of the customer in position #I
C(I,2)	will hold the required service time of the customer in position #I.
T	is the system *clock*. It's contents indicate how many time units have elapsed since the simulation started.
A	holds the clock time when the next customer will *arrive*.
S	holds the clock time when the *server* will be available.
B and E	are pointers to the *beginning* and *end* of the queue.
N	is the total *number* of time units for which the simulation will be run.
I	is the average *interarrival* time.
J	is the average *service time* required.
L1	is the *total* length of the waiting line.
S1	is the *total* time the server was busy.
W1	is the *total* time customers spent waiting.

The program has three sections:

(a)   An initialization and input section (lines 100 to 260)

(b)   The main simulation section which is a large loop that runs the simulation, with the clock T going from 1 to N. This loop is found in lines 300 to 800. Each time around the loop represents a step of one time unit (usually thought of as 1 minute).

(c)   A final output section (lines 900 to 960) which prints the statistics gathered for the simulation.

Let's take a closer look at part (b), the main simulation loop.

(b1) FIRST CHECK THE CLOCK

Line 320   See if it's time to put a new customer on line. If not, go to line 610; otherwise go to line 410.

(b2) IF IT'S OK, PUT A NEW CUSTOMER ON LINE

Line 410:   Make room for the new customer by incrementing the end-of-line pointer.

Line 420:   Make sure there's still room in the circular queue.

Lines 430-440:   Actually put the data about our new customer in the queue.

(b3) GET READY FOR THE NEXT TIME AROUND

Line 510:   Set A to the time when the next customer will arrive.

Line 520:   Go back and see if this customer should be put on line.

(b4) SEE IF IT'S POSSIBLE TO GIVE SERVICE

Line 610:   If the server is not available, go to line 710.

Line 620:   If the queue is empty, go to line 710.

(b5) ALL OK TO GIVE SERVICE

Line 630:   Fetch the customer from the waiting line by advancing the B pointer.

Line 640:   Post a "do not disturb the server" sign by resetting the server's clock S.

Lines 650, 660:   Figure out how much this last customer was waiting, and add it to W1 (the total waiting time).

Line 670:   Go back and see if server is still available.

(b6) GET READY FOR NEXT TIME AROUND THE LOOP

Lines 710-730:   Update the totaling counters for later use in statistics.

Line 800:   Go back, advance the system clock by 1, and repeat everything.

The listing that follows should be studied in conjunction with these explanations. Also look at the runs that follow, and you'll see how one can use the program as an experimental tool for evaluating different queuing situations.

SINGLE
SERVER
QUEUE

```
10   Q=RND(-1)
100  REM----DEFINE MODULO FUNCTION
110  DEF FNA(X)=X-INT((X-1)/25)*25
120  REM-----DEFINE RANDOM GENERATOR WITH EXPONENTIAL DISTRIBUTION
130  DEF FNB(X)=INT(-X*LOG(RND(1))+.5)
140  REM-----INITIALIZE VARIABLES
150  LET A=0:E=0:B=0:S=0
160  DIM C(25,2)
200  REM-----INPUT BLOCK
210  PRINT "TYPE # OF TIME UNITS FOR SIMULATION";
220  INPUT N
230  PRINT "TYPE AVERAGE INTERARRIVAL TIME";
240  INPUT I
250  PRINT "TYPE AVERAGE SERVICE TIME";
260  INPUT J
300  REM---------MAIN SIMULATION LOOP----------
310  FOR T=1 TO N
315  REM-----NEW CUSTOMER BLOCK-----
320  IF A>T THEN 610
410  LET E=E+1
420  IF E-B>25 THEN PRINT "QUEUE OVERFLOW":STOP
430  C(FNA(E),1)=T
440  C(FNA(E),2)=FNB(J)
500  REM-----RESET NEXT CUSTOMER CLOCK TIME
510  A=T+FNB(I)
520  GOTO 320
600  REM-----SERVICE BLOCK
610  IF S>T THEN 710
620  IF B=E THEN 710
630  LET B=B+1
640  LET S=C(FNA(B),2)+T
650  LET W=T-C(FNA(B),1)
660  LET W1=W+W1
670  GOTO 610
700  REM-----FINAL STATISTICS BLOCK
710  LET L=E-B
720  LET L1=L1+L
730  IF S>T THEN LET S1=S1+1
800  NEXT T
900  REM--------- OUTPUT BLOCK ---------------
910  PRINT "------------------"
920  PRINT "SERVER UTILIZATION =";S1/N*100;"%"
930  PRINT "AVERAGE LINE LENGTH =";L1/N
940  PRINT "AVERAGE CUSTOMER WAITING TIME =";W1/B
950  PRINT "NUMBER OF CUSTOMERS LEFT ON LINE =";E-B
960  PRINT "NUMBER OF CUSTOMERS WHO ENTERED STORE=";E
999  END
```

```
    RUN

    TYPE # OF TIME UNITS FOR SIMULATION? 420
    TYPE AVERAGE INTERARRIVAL TIME? 5
    TYPE AVERAGE SERVICE TIME? 3
    -----------------
    SERVER UTILIZATION = 52.1429 %
    AVERAGE LINE LENGTH = .321429
    AVERAGE CUSTOMER WAITING TIME = 1.6962
    NUMBER OF CUSTOMERS LEFT ON LINE = 1
    NUMBER OF CUSTOMERS WHO ENTERED STORE= 80

    Ready

    RUNNH
    TYPE # OF TIME UNITS FOR SIMULATION? 420
    TYPE AVERAGE INTERARRIVAL TIME? 2
    TYPE AVERAGE SERVICE TIME? 5
    QUEUE OVERFLOW
    STOP at line 420

    Ready

    RUNNH
    TYPE # OF TIME UNITS FOR SIMULATION? 420
    TYPE AVERAGE INTERARRIVAL TIME? 5
    TYPE AVERAGE SERVICE TIME? 5
    -----------------
    SERVER UTILIZATION = 82.1429 %
    AVERAGE LINE LENGTH = 1.37143
    AVERAGE CUSTOMER WAITING TIME = 7.07895
    NUMBER OF CUSTOMERS LEFT ON LINE = 4
    NUMBER OF CUSTOMERS WHO ENTERED STORE= 80

    Ready

    RUNNH
    TYPE # OF TIME UNITS FOR SIMULATION? 60
    TYPE AVERAGE INTERARRIVAL TIME? 10
    TYPE AVERAGE SERVICE TIME? 15
    -----------------
    SERVER UTILIZATION = 98.3333 %
    AVERAGE LINE LENGTH = .916667
    AVERAGE CUSTOMER WAITING TIME = 8.66667
    NUMBER OF CUSTOMERS LEFT ON LINE = 1
    NUMBER OF CUSTOMERS WHO ENTERED STORE= 7

    Ready

    RUNNH
    TYPE # OF TIME UNITS FOR SIMULATION? 120
    TYPE AVERAGE INTERARRIVAL TIME? 10
    TYPE AVERAGE SERVICE TIME? 30
    -----------------
    SERVER UTILIZATION = 100 %
    AVERAGE LINE LENGTH = 3.25833
    AVERAGE CUSTOMER WAITING TIME = 37
    NUMBER OF CUSTOMERS LEFT ON LINE = 6
    NUMBER OF CUSTOMERS WHO ENTERED STORE= 12
```

9.4   MULTI-SERVER QUEUING SIMULATIONS

The sample runs of the single-server queuing simulation shown in the last section indicate that "overflow" can occur. This means that there isn't enough room on the queue for all the customers. Another problem is that the customers may have to wait an unreasonably long time. The solution to both problems is to add more servers. The question is how many. A simulation will help answer that question.

There are two kinds of multi-server systems. One uses multiple servers, but each has their own queue. Supermarkets use such a system. The other approach is to have several servers but only one queue. When a server is free, he calls "next", and the person at the head of the line gets served. Some banks do this. Stores like bakeries (or our deli) that give customers numbers are also using a single queue, even though there may be several servers.

In this section we'll modify our previous program so it simulates a single-queue multi-server system. We'll allow up to 10 servers, and store the clock time when server #I will be free in S(I). So we'll have to dimension an array S(10). the user can experiment with different numbers of servers between 1 and 10. This number is input in line 280, and checked in line 290.

```
280 INPUT S5
290 IF ABS(S5-5.5)>4.6 THEN 270
```

Then, during each time unit, we check to see if a server is free as follows:

```
610 FOR M=1 TO S5
612 IF S(M)<=T THEN 620
614 NEXT M
616 GOTO 700
```

If the Mth server is free and a customer is waiting, the program assigns to S(M) the time when the Mth server will be finished serving his customer.

```
640 S(M)=C(FNA(B),2)+T
```

At the end of each time unit, the program checks to see how many servers are being utilized.

```
730 FOR M=1 TO S5
740 IF S(M)>T THEN S1=S1+1
750 NEXT M
```

At the end of the run, the total server utilization is printed.

```
920 PRINT "TOTAL SERVER UTILIZATION IS";S1/(N*S5)*100;"%"
```

All other lines of the single-server program remain unchanged. Here's a listing and some runs of this new program.

**MULTI-
SERVER
QUEUE**

```
 10   Q=RND(-1)
100   REM----DEFINE MODULO FUNCTION
110   DEF FNA(X)=X-INT((X-1)/25)*25
120   REM-----DEFINE RANDOM GENERATOR WITH EXPONENTIAL DISTRIBUTION
130   DE FNB(X)=INT(-X*LOG(RND(1))+.5)
140   REM-----INITIALIZE VARIABLES
150   LET A=0:E=0:B=0:S=0
160   DIM C(25,2)
170   DIM S(10)
200   REM-----INPUT BLOCK
210   PRINT "TYPE # OF TIME UNITS FOR SIMULATION";
220   INPUT N
230   PRINT "TYPE AVERAGE INTERARRIVAL TIME";
240   INPUT I
250   PRINT "TYPE AVERAGE SERVICE TIME";
260   INPUT J
270   PRINT "HOW MANY SERVERS";
280   INPUT S5
290   IF ABS(S5-5.5)>4.6 THEN 270
300   REM-----MAIN SIMULATION LOOP--------------
310   FOR T=1 TO N
315   REM-----PUT NEW CUSTOMER ON QUEUE---
320   IF A>T THEN 610
410   LET E=E+1
420   IF E-B>25 THEN PRINT "QUEUE OVERFLOW":STOP
430   C(FNA(E),1)=T
440   C(FNA(E),2)=FNB(J)
500   REM-----RESET NEXT CUSTOMER CLOCK TIME
510   A=T+FNB(I)
520   GOTO 320
600   REM-----SERVICE BLOCK
610   FOR M=1 TO S5
612   IF S(M)<=T THEN 620
614   NEXT M
616   GOTO 700
620   IF B=E THEN 710
630   LET B=B+1
640   LET S(M)=C(FNA(B),2)+T
650   LET W=T-C(FNA(B),1)
660   LET W1=W+W1
670   GOTO 610
700   REM-----FINAL STATISTICS BLOCK
710   LET L=E-B
720   LET L1=L1+L
730   FOR M=1 TO S5
740   IF S(M)>T THEN LET S1=S1+1
750   NEXT  M
800   NEXT T
900   REM-----OUTPUT BLOCK----------------------
910   PRINT "-----------------"
920   PRINT "TOTAL SERVER UTILIZATION IS";S1/(N*S5)*100;"%"
930   PRINT "AVERAGE LINE LENGTH =";L1/N
940   PRINT "AVERAGE CUSTOMER WAITING TIME =";W1/B
950   PRINT "NUMBER OF CUSTOMERS LEFT ON LINE =";E-B
960   PRINT "NUMBER OF CUSTOMERS WHO ENTERED STORE=";E
999   END
```

```
RUN

TYPE # OF TIME UNITS FOR SIMULATION? 420
TYPE AVERAGE INTERARRIVAL TIME? 2
TYPE AVERAGE SERVICE TIME? 5
HOW MANY SERVERS? 2
QUEUE OVERFLOW
STOP at line 420

Ready

RUN
SIM932  03:55 PM          21-Jan-77
TYPE # OF TIME UNITS FOR SIMULATION? 420
TYPE AVERAGE INTERARRIVAL TIME? 2
TYPE AVERAGE SERVICE TIME? 5
HOW MANY SERVERS? 3
-----------------
TOTAL SERVER UTILIZATION IS 70.873 %
AVERAGE LINE LENGTH = 1.36429
AVERAGE CUSTOMER WAITING TIME = 2.71429
NUMBER OF CUSTOMERS LEFT ON LINE = 4
NUMBER OF CUSTOMERS WHO ENTERED STORE= 207

Ready

RUN
SIM932  03:56 PM          21-Jan-77
TYPE # OF TIME UNITS FOR SIMULATION? 1000
TYPE AVERAGE INTERARRIVAL TIME? 2
TYPE AVERAGE SERVICE TIME? 5
HOW MANY SERVERS? 2
QUEUE OVERFLOW
STOP at line 420

Ready

RUN
SIM932  03:57 PM          21-Jan-77
TYPE # OF TIME UNITS FOR SIMULATION? 1000
TYPE AVERAGE INTERARRIVAL TIME? 2
TYPE AVERAGE SERVICE TIME? 5
HOW MANY SERVERS? 3
-----------------
TOTAL SERVER UTILIZATION IS 81.0333 %
AVERAGE LINE LENGTH = 5.035
AVERAGE CUSTOMER WAITING TIME = 9.56667
NUMBER OF CUSTOMERS LEFT ON LINE = 11
NUMBER OF CUSTOMERS WHO ENTERED STORE= 521

Ready

RUN
SIM932  03:59 PM          21-Jan-77
TYPE # OF TIME UNITS FOR SIMULATION? 1000
TYPE AVERAGE INTERARRIVAL TIME? 2
TYPE AVERAGE SERVICE TIME? 5
HOW MANY SERVERS? 4
-----------------
TOTAL SERVER UTILIZATION IS 62.475 %
AVERAGE LINE LENGTH = .85
AVERAGE CUSTOMER WAITING TIME = 1.63148
NUMBER OF CUSTOMERS LEFT ON LINE = 0
NUMBER OF CUSTOMERS WHO ENTERED STORE= 521
```

9.5   SIMULATION GAMES

It was mentioned earlier (in Chapter 6) that the notion of some kind of "payoff" of points is an essential feature of games. When there are several players in a game, this usually means that some will win points, and others will lose them. It is in this sense that the operations of the business world can be viewed as a game, where the "points" won and lost are dollars. The operations of a war also can be viewed as a game, except that the point system is a lot more grim.

Because the consequences of winning and losing such real-life games are very serious, it has been proposed that people practice them with simulations. This has in fact been done, with varying degrees of realism.

A more sophisticated type of simulation game is one that allows several players to interact with the simulation in "real time". This means that things happen just as fast as they would in real life—there are no noticeable delays due to computer processing.

Even when multi-terminal games deal with fantasy, they can serve as a tool for learning to deal with social or political systems. While the hardware for such simulations is beyond the means of individual amateurs, it is possible that several personal computers could be linked together for such games.

We'll not pursue the multi-terminal idea any further here. However we can perhaps stimulate some thinking by illustrating the idea of a social type simulation, but with only one human player. We'll do this in the next section.

9.6   THE SPACE COLONY GAME

The inhabitants of the Mayflower II Starship are on their way to colonize Argyle 88, one of the planets of Alpha G44-X3. They must decide what sort of government they will have when they get there and are determined to spend the time enroute playing simulation games to help them decide. They wish to achieve stable government so that they can become members of the Galactic Federation in good standing as soon as possible.

Drawing upon the ancient writings of some 20th century anthropologists, they begin building a rather simple model of government based on competing factions, shifting coalitions, and a few basic motivations. Later on they plan to increase the complexity of the game by adding more variables and more consequences for each possible move.

Playing the Game

You are a member of the planetary council, which consists of five administrators, each of whom controls at the outset a randomly chosen amount of wealth. The council is split into two opposing coalitions, each with 2 members—you must decide which side to join. This causes a "confrontation" between the two sides, resulting in a "win" for one of the coalitions, and a "loss" for the other.

Each coalition has a leader (called a chief) who may not have the most wealth under his control, but who has an unmeasurable quantity of prestige. It is therefore possible for the losing coalition to attract a member from the winning side by offering him the position of chief.

When conflict arises, the side with greater wealth wins and the opposing side suffers a corresponding loss. In this two-coalition system the 5th member often holds the balance of power. In the system modeled he *must* join one of the groups in order to wield power. Thus splinter groups are prevented from forming, and are not included in the program.

In a real government, coalitions may last many years. Our simulation accelerates time so that members change sides after each confrontation, according to their best advantage. "Advantage" is defined for this model in the following way.

In playing the game you will not really try to win—it's not that kind of game. You try not to lose, that is, not go bankrupt or find that there is only one member in the winning coalition (causing an impasse ending the program). You are considered a "winner" if you survive 15 confrontations. (Corresponding, perhaps, in a real government to retiring and becoming an "elder statesman".)

There are three moves at your disposal in this program to influence the course of events:

1. As chief of the winning coalition, you decide what percent (between 10 and 99) of their holdings the losers must forfeit, and what percent of this payment (10 to 50) you are paid by the members of your coalition as a bonus for being chief.
2. As a member of the losing coalition, you may invite a member of the opposition to join your side. You may have to offer him the chieftainship in order to get him.
3. As a member of the winning coalition, you may attempt to keep a particularly valuable member by offering him the chieftainship.

Some strategies which could be used to govern your moves are:

Strategy #1 - Play the game so as to accumulate as much wealth as possible, ignoring the effect on other members (only those with wealth may remain on the council.)

Strategy #2 - Accumulate wealth and ignore how many times you must change your allegiance to a coalition.

Strategy #3 - Accumulate wealth and always insist on being the chief.

Strategy #4 - Accumulate wealth and protect all players from bankruptcy, or at least your own coalition members.

Strategy #5 - Accumulate wealth but stay with one side and try to maintain your position in it at all costs.

Any combination of the above may be used and more.

Making it Better

After you've played the game a few times, you'll probably think of improvements you'd like to see in the program. For example, consider the implications of *always* making the wealthiest member the coalition chief. Among other things, this would restrict the user's ability to accumulate wealth and make it difficult to attract someone from the winning coalition. Some specific suggestions are contained in the projects section of this chapter.

How The Program Works

This general explanation of the program's logic is followed by a listing and a partial run. A brief look at the run will probably make this explanation more meaningful.

Line Number	*Explanation*
10—140	Initializes variables; prints heading; randomly sets the wealth of each member between 50 and 1,000; creates coalitions; calls subroutine at line 930 which prints out tables.
150—240	Prompts user to select a coalition to join and his role—chief or member; updates value of that coalition and the number of members in it.

Variables:	(Note: N% means N is integer variable.*)
X%	Counts confrontations.
V(I%)	Value of each member (I% can be 1—5).
M%(1), M%(2)	Number of members in each coalition.
T(1), T(2)	Total value of each coalition.

---

*If your BASIC doesn't have integer variables simply omit the % sign.

C(I%)	Checklist of which member is in which coalition. = 1% if member is in coalition 1 = 2% if member is in coalition 2 = 0% if member is not in the council (I% can be 1—5)
F%(1), F%(2) Y% O%	Number of whichever member is currently chief of coalition 1, 2. User's coalition number (1 or 2). Other side's coalition number (2 or 1).

250—259	Confrontation: coalition with greater total value wins; survivor is congratulated and program branches to end.
260—262, 265	User's side lost: sets payment and bonus percentages to default values and branches around calcualtions for winning side.
270—320	Users side lost: if user is chief, he inputs the percent of their total wealth which the losers must pay and the percentage of this payment which will be his bonus as chief.

B	"Bonus" to chief.
	    Winning chief gets 20% more (or percent he requests).
	    Losing chief pays 10% less.

B1	Each member's share of winnings or losses.
B2	Each member's share of "bonus".
B3	Actual amount each member gains or loses.
V1	Each losing member's share of remaining payment if the one member goes bankrupt.

530—540	Updates total for each side; types new tables.

K%	Flag used while shifting a member; if = 0, it signals that the chieftainship has already been promised to another to keep him.
N%	Loop control for cycling through membership to locate a member from the winning side to move over to the losers.

550—770 560—690	Moves one member from winning side to losing side; If user was on losing side, he may select a member of the opposition to request. If losing side will lose again despite this new member, he must be offered the chieftainship to convince him to shift sides.
700—770	User's coalition won: subroutine at 1065 selects a member to request for the losing coalition. User may give the selected member the chieftainship in order to keep him. If he does this, the next member in order is moved, beginning again at the top of the list when necessary. Chiefs are not requested to move.
780—900	Adjusts statistics for both sides:
790	Update # of losing side's chief if this has changed.
790	If shifted member was chief of winning coalition, selects a new chief (wealthiest member) using subroutine at 1120.
810	If user was shifted, updates flags.
820	Alters coalition # for shifted member.
830—840	Alters number of members in each coalition and updates total value of each side.
850	If either coalition has lost all of its members, the game ends; otherwise, goes to next confrontation.

860—900	If game ends, types messages; user may elect to play again or stop.
920—1050	Types coalition tables: types for each coalition: each member's number, his value, the total value of the coalition and identifies the chief.
1060—1110	Selects member to shift sides: This can only be done if the winning side has more than one member; otherwise, types error message and returns specifying member #0. The "next" (using a continuous loop through the membership) member from the winning side is chosen. The chief, however, is not considered.
1120—1170	Choses new chief for winners. If opposition successfully attracts chief of the winning coalition, this routine selects the wealthiest remaining member of the winning side to be chief.

SPACE
COLONY
GAME

```
LIST

10 !   SPACE COLONY GAME
15 !    A SIMULATION GAME OF SHIFTING COALITIONS
20 DIM V(5),M%(2),T(2),C%(5),F%(2)
30 PRINT "WELCOME TO ARGYLE 88!!": PRINT
40 PRINT "YOU ARE ABOUT TO JOIN THE ARGYLE 88 PLANETARY COUNCIL."
50 PRINT "THERE ARE FOUR OTHER MEMBERS - YOU ARE #5."
60 RANDOMIZE
65 X%=0%
70 V(I%)=1000.*RND+50. FOR I%=1% TO 5%
80 M%(1),M%(2)=2%: N%=0%
90 F%(1)=1%: F%(2)=3: P2=.2: R2=.3
100 T(1)=V(1)+V(2): T(2)=V(3)+V(4)
110 C%(1),C%(2)=1%: C%(3),C%(4)=2%
120 C%(5)=0%
130 PRINT: PRINT "YOU ARE WORTH" V(5)
140 GOSUB 930
145 !----------END INITIALIZATION----------------------------
150 PRINT: INPUT "WHICH COALITION DO YOU WISH TO JOIN: 1 OR 2";Y%
160 IF Y%=1% THEN O%=2%: GO TO 190
170 IF Y%<>2% THEN INPUT "REPLY 1 OR 2"; Y%: GO TO 160
180 O%=1%
190 INPUT "AS CHIEF (C) OR MEMBER (M)"; A$
200 IF A$="C" THEN F%(Y%)=5%: GO TO 220
210 IF A$<>"M" THEN INPUT "REPLY C OR M"; A$: GO TO 200
220 IF T(O%)=T(Y%)+V(5) THEN V(5)=1000.*RND+50.: GO TO 220
230 T(Y%)=T(Y%)+V(5): M%(Y%)=M%(Y%)+1%
240 C%(5)=Y%
245 !----------CONFRONTATION--------------------------------------
250 X%=X%+1%
251 IF X%<16% THEN 258
252 PRINT:PRINT"CONGRATULATIONS, YOU HAVE SURVIVED 15 CONFRONTATIONS."
253 PRINT"YOU MAY NOW RETIRE.":PRINT
254 PRINT"    XXXXXX":PRINT" XX        XX":PRINT" XX          XXX"
255 PRINT"X  XX    XX    X":PRINT"X   XX X        X":PRINT"X     XX        X"
256 PRINT" X               X":PRINT"  XX          XX":PRINT"    XXXXXX"
257 PRINT"ARGYLE 88":PRINT"PRIZE FOR PEACE":PRINT:GOTO 880
258 PRINT:PRINT"---------------CONFRONTATION NUMBER";X%;"---------------"
259 IF T(Y%) > T(O%) THEN GOTO 270
260 PRINT"YOU LOST THE GAMBLE.  OTHER SIDE NOW CONTROLS WEALTH."
262 R=R2:W%=O%
265 L%=Y%:P=P2:GOTO 330
```

```
270 PRINT"SUCCESS! YOUR SIDE NOW CONTROLS THE MAJORITY OF WEALTH."
272 W%=Y%:L%=O%
280 IF F%(Y%)<>5% THEN R=R2: P=P2: GO TO 330
290 INPUT "WHAT % DO YOU DEMAND FOR PAYMENT FROM LOSING COALITION"; R
300 IF R<10 OR R>90 THEN INPUT"RANGE IS 10 TO 90";R: GOTO 300
310 INPUT "WHAT BONUS % TO YOU AS CHIEF";P
320 IF P<10 OR P>50 THEN INPUT"RANGE IS 10 TO 50";P: GOTO 320
322 R=R/100: P=P/100
325 !---------CALC. WINNERS SHARE----------------------------------
330 R1=R*T(L%): B=P*R1
335 PRINT"TOTAL PAYMENT: ";R1;"  BONUS TO CHIEF: ";B
340 IF M%(W%)=1% THEN B2=R1: B=0: GO TO 380
350 B1=R1/M%(W%)
360 B2=B/(M%(W%)-1%): B3=B1-B2
370 V(I%)=V(I%) + B3 IF C%(I%)=W% FOR I%=1% TO  5%
380 I%=F%(W%): V(I%)=V(I%)+B2+B
385 !---------CALC. LOSERS PAYMENT----------------------------------
390 IF M%(L%)=1% THEN I%=F%(L%): V(I%)=V(I%)-R1: GO TO 530
400 B1=R1/M%(L%): B=.1*R1
410 B2=B/(M%(L%)-1%): B3=B1+B2
420 FOR I%=1% TO  5%: IF C%(I%)<>L% THEN GO TO 510
430 V(I%)=V(I%)-B3
440 IF V(I%)>0 THEN GO TO 510
450 IF I%=5% THEN 455
452 GOTO 460
455 PRINT"YOU HAVE LOST ALL WEALTH AND MUST LEAVE COUNCIL":GOTO 870
460 M%(L%)=M%(L%)-1%: C%(I%)=0%
470 PRINT I% "HAS LOST ALL WEALTH AND MUST LEAVE THE COUNCIL."
471 PRINT:PRINT"  XXXXX"
472 PRINT" X      X"
473 PRINT" X(O O)X"
474 PRINT"  X A X"
475 PRINT"  XIIIX           BYE, BYE";I%
476 PRINT"   XXX":PRINT
480 IF V(I%)=0 THEN GO TO 510
485 IF M%(L%)=0% THEN 510
490 V1=-V(I%)/M%(L%)
500 V(J%)=V(J%)-V1 IF C%(J%)=L% FOR J%=1% TO 5%
510 NEXT I%
520 I%=F%(L%): V(I%)=V(I%)+B2+B
530 T(W%)=T(W%)+R1: T(L%)=T(L%)-R1
540 GOSUB 930
545 !----------MOVE MEMBER TO LOSING SIDE------------------------
550 K%=0%
560 IF W%=Y% THEN GO TO 700
570 !-----USER'S COALITION LOST----------
580 INPUT "SPECIFY # OF OPPOSITION MEMBER YOU WANT"; J%
590 IF J%<1% OR J%>5% THEN INPUT "RANGE IS 1 TO 5"; J%: GO TO 590
600 IF C%(J%)=0% THEN INPUT "OUT OF COUNCIL--CHOOSE AGAIN";J%: GO TO 590
610 IF C%(J%)=Y% THEN PRINT "ALREADY IN YOUR COALITION": GO TO 580
620 INPUT "WILL YOU MAKE HIM CHIEF"; A$
630 IF A$="Y" THEN GO TO 790
640 IF A$<>"N" THEN INPUT "REPLY Y OR N"; A$: GO TO 620
650 IF T(W%)-V(J%)<T(L%)+V(J%) THEN GO TO 800
660 INPUT "HE WILL ONLY COME AS CHIEF - WILL YOU MAKE HIM CHIEF"; A$
670 IF A$="Y" THEN GO TO 790
680 IF A$<>"N" THEN INPUT "REPLY Y OR N"; A$: GO TO 670
690 GO TO 580
700 !-----USER'S COALITION WON-----------
710 GOSUB 1070: IF J%=0 THEN GO TO 870
720 PRINT "OPPOSITION WOULD LIKE" J% "TO JOIN THEM."
730 IF K%<>0 THEN GO TO 790
740 INPUT "WILL YOU MAKE HIM CHIEF TO KEEP HIM"; A$
750 IF A$="N" THEN GO TO 790
760 IF A$<>"Y" THEN INPUT "REPLY Y OR N"; A$: GO TO 750
770 IF K%=0% THEN K%,F%(W%)=J%: GO TO 710
```

```
780 !----------ADJUST STATISTICS, EACH SIDE-----------------------
790 F%(L%)=J%
800 IF F%(W%)=J% THEN GOSUB 1120
810 IF J%=5% THEN Y%=L%: O%=W%
820 C%(J%)=L%
830 M%(W%)=M%(W%)-1%: T(W%)=T(W%)-V(J%)
840 M%(L%)=M%(L%)+1%: T(L%)=T(L%)+V(J%)
850 IF M%(1)>0 AND M%(2)>0 THEN GO TO 250
860 PRINT "ALL MEMBERS ARE IN ONE COALITION!"
870 PRINT "SO LONG": PRINT : PRINT
880 INPUT "WOULD YOU LIKE TO PLAY AGAIN"; A$
890 IF A$="Y" THEN GO TO 40
900 IF A$<>"N" THEN INPUT "REPLY Y OR N";A$: GO TO 890
910 GOTO 1180
920 !----------PRINT COALITION TABLES-----------------------------
930 X$=" "
940 FOR I%=1% TO 2%
950 PRINT: PRINT "     COALITION   #" I%
960 C1%=F%(I%)
970 PRINT "MEMBER        VALUE"
980 FOR J%=1% TO 5%
990 IF C%(J%)<>I% THEN GO TO 1030
1000 IF J%=C1% THEN X$="CHIEF"
1010 PRINT J%,V(J%),X$
1020 X$=" "
1030 NEXT J%
1040 PRINT "TOTAL VALUE=" T(I%): J%=J%+1%: NEXT I%
1050 RETURN
1060 !---------SELECT MEMBER TO CHANGE SIDES-----------------------
1070 IF M%(W%)>1% THEN 1090
1080 PRINT"WINNING COALITION ONLY HAS ONE MEMBER--GAME MUST END"
1081 J%=0%: RETURN
1090 N%=N%+1%: IF N%=6% THEN N%=1%
1100 IF C%(N%)<>W% OR F%(W%)=N% THEN 1090
1110 J%=N%: RETURN
1120 !---------NEW CHIEF FOR WINNERS-------------------------------
1130 V1=0: I1%=0: FOR I%=1% TO 5%
1140 IF C%(I%)<>W% OR J%=I% THEN GO TO 1160
1150 IF V(I%)>V1 THEN I1%=I%: V1%=V(I%)
1160 NEXT I%: F%(W%)=I1%
1170 RETURN
1180 END
```

```
RUN

WELCOME TO ARGYLE 88!!

YOU ARE ABOUT TO JOIN THE ARGYLE 88 PLANETARY COUNCIL.
THERE ARE FOUR OTHER MEMBERS - YOU ARE #5.

YOU ARE WORTH 835.919

     COALITION   # 1
MEMBER        VALUE
  1           595.197        CHIEF
  2           404.34
TOTAL VALUE= 999.536
```

```
        COALITION   # 2
MEMBER          VALUE
  3             269.269        CHIEF
  4             176.556
TOTAL VALUE= 445.825

WHICH COALITION DO YOU WISH TO JOIN: 1 OR 2? 2
AS CHIEF (C) OR MEMBER (M)? C

---------------CONFRONTATION NUMBER 1 ---------------
SUCCESS! YOUR SIDE NOW CONTROLS THE MAJORITY OF WEALTH.
WHAT % DO YOU DEMAND FOR PAYMENT FROM LOSING COALITION? 20
WHAT BONUS % TO YOU AS CHIEF? 10
TOTAL PAYMENT:  199.907    BONUS TO CHIEF:  19.9907

        COALITION   # 1
MEMBER          VALUE
  1             515.234        CHIEF
  2             284.395
TOTAL VALUE= 799.629

        COALITION   # 2
MEMBER          VALUE
  3             325.909
  4             233.197
  5             922.546        CHIEF
TOTAL VALUE= 1481.65
OPPOSITION WOULD LIKE 3 TO JOIN THEM.
WILL YOU MAKE HIM CHIEF TO KEEP HIM? N

---------------CONFRONTATION NUMBER 2 ---------------
SUCCESS! YOUR SIDE NOW CONTROLS THE MAJORITY OF WEALTH.
WHAT % DO YOU DEMAND FOR PAYMENT FROM LOSING COALITION? 10
WHAT BONUS % TO YOU AS CHIEF? 10
TOTAL PAYMENT:  112.554    BONUS TO CHIEF:  11.2554

        COALITION   # 1
MEMBER          VALUE
  1             472.088
  2             241.25
  3             299.647        CHIEF
TOTAL VALUE= 1012.98

        COALITION   # 2
MEMBER          VALUE
  4             278.218
  5             990.078        CHIEF
TOTAL VALUE= 1268.3
OPPOSITION WOULD LIKE 4 TO JOIN THEM.
WILL YOU MAKE HIM CHIEF TO KEEP HIM? N

---------------CONFRONTATION NUMBER 3 ---------------
YOU LOST THE GAMBLE.  OTHER SIDE NOW CONTROLS WEALTH.
TOTAL PAYMENT:  297.023    BONUS TO CHIEF:  59.4047
```

We won't show all of this simulation since it goes on and on and on (like real politics!). Let's pick it up again at Confrontation #13. Notice that the sum of the wealth is still the same (about 2281 units) since our model is based on "zero-sum" game theory.

```
---------------CONFRONTATION NUMBER 13 ---------------
SUCCESS! YOUR SIDE NOW CONTROLS THE MAJORITY OF WEALTH.
WHAT % DO YOU DEMAND FOR PAYMENT FROM LOSING COALITION? 10
WHAT BONUS % TO YOU AS CHIEF? 50
TOTAL PAYMENT:  85.2952    BONUS TO CHIEF:  42.6476

        COALITION  # 1
MEMBER          VALUE
  4             963.858
  5             549.765         CHIEF
TOTAL VALUE= 1513.62

        COALITION  # 2
MEMBER          VALUE
  1             202.55
  2             191.757
  3             373.35          CHIEF
TOTAL VALUE= 767.657
OPPOSITION WOULD LIKE 4 TO JOIN THEM.
WILL YOU MAKE HIM CHIEF TO KEEP HIM? Y
OPPOSITION WOULD LIKE 5 TO JOIN THEM.

---------------CONFRONTATION NUMBER 14 ---------------
SUCCESS! YOUR SIDE NOW CONTROLS THE MAJORITY OF WEALTH.
WHAT % DO YOU DEMAND FOR PAYMENT FROM LOSING COALITION? 70
WHAT BONUS % TO YOU AS CHIEF? 10
TOTAL PAYMENT:  674.701    BONUS TO CHIEF:  67.4701

        COALITION  # 1
MEMBER          VALUE
  4             289.157         CHIEF
TOTAL VALUE= 289.157

        COALITION  # 2
MEMBER          VALUE
  1             348.735
  2             337.942
  3             519.535
  5             785.911         CHIEF
TOTAL VALUE= 1992.12
OPPOSITION WOULD LIKE 1 TO JOIN THEM.
WILL YOU MAKE HIM CHIEF TO KEEP HIM? N

---------------CONFRONTATION NUMBER 15 ---------------
SUCCESS! YOUR SIDE NOW CONTROLS THE MAJORITY OF WEALTH.
WHAT % DO YOU DEMAND FOR PAYMENT FROM LOSING COALITION? 10
WHAT BONUS % TO YOU AS CHIEF? 10
TOTAL PAYMENT:  63.7892    BONUS TO CHIEF:  6.37892

        COALITION  # 1
MEMBER          VALUE
  1             323.219         CHIEF
  4             250.884
TOTAL VALUE= 574.103
```

```
        COALITION    # 2
MEMBER          VALUE
  2             356.016
  3             537.609
  5             813.553        CHIEF
TOTAL VALUE= 1707.18
OPPOSITION WOULD LIKE 2 TO JOIN THEM.
WILL YOU MAKE HIM CHIEF TO KEEP HIM? N


CONGRATULATIONS, YOU HAVE SURVIVED 15 CONFRONTATIONS.
YOU MAY NOW RETIRE.


     XXXXX
   XX        XX
  XX         XXX
X  XX   XX    X
X   XX X      X
X    XX       X
 X            X
   XX      XX
     XXXXX
ARGYLE 88
PRIZE FOR PEACE

WOULD YOU LIKE TO PLAY AGAIN? NO
```

This game finally ends because 15 confrontations have been survived by the player, who is awarded the Argyle 88 Peace Prize.

Now let's look at a run where player #5 is very greedy. As a result, Player #4 is "wiped out" early in the game. This makes the game less stable, since losses can no longer be spread out as much as before. Whether or not this was a good strategy for #5 is open to debate. To find out, you'll have to finish the game.

```
   RUN
   WELCOME TO ARGYLE 88!!

   YOU ARE ABOUT TO JOIN THE ARGYLE 88 PLANETARY COUNCIL.
   THERE ARE FOUR OTHER MEMBERS - YOU ARE #5.

   YOU ARE WORTH 128.156

        COALITION    # 1
   MEMBER          VALUE
    1             821.027        CHIEF
    2             831.83
   TOTAL VALUE= 1652.86


        COALITION    # 2
   MEMBER          VALUE
    3             801.74         CHIEF
    4             523.969
   TOTAL VALUE= 1325.71

   WHICH COALITION DO YOU WISH TO JOIN: 1 OR 2? 1
   AS CHIEF (C) OR MEMBER (M)? C
```

```
--------------CONFRONTATION NUMBER 1 --------------
SUCCESS! YOUR SIDE NOW CONTROLS THE MAJORITY OF WEALTH.
WHAT % DO YOU DEMAND FOR PAYMENT FROM LOSING COALITION? 50
WHAT BONUS % TO YOU AS CHIEF? 50
TOTAL PAYMENT:  662.854    BONUS TO CHIEF:  331.427

     COALITION   # 1
MEMBER         VALUE
 1             876.264
 2             887.068
 5             680.534       CHIEF
TOTAL VALUE= 2443.87

     COALITION   # 2
MEMBER         VALUE
 3             536.598       CHIEF
 4             126.256
TOTAL VALUE= 662.854
OPPOSITION WOULD LIKE 1 TO JOIN THEM.
WILL YOU MAKE HIM CHIEF TO KEEP HIM? N

--------------CONFRONTATION NUMBER 2 --------------
SUCCESS! YOUR SIDE NOW CONTROLS THE MAJORITY OF WEALTH.
WHAT % DO YOU DEMAND FOR PAYMENT FROM LOSING COALITION? 30
WHAT BONUS % TO YOU AS CHIEF? 50
TOTAL PAYMENT:  461.736    BONUS TO CHIEF:  230.868
 4 HAS LOST ALL WEALTH AND MUST LEAVE THE COUNCIL.

  XXXXX
 X     X
 X(O O)X
  X A X
  XIIIX          BYE, BYE 4
   XXX


     COALITION   # 1
MEMBER         VALUE
 2             887.068
 5             1142.27       CHIEF
TOTAL VALUE= 2029.34

     COALITION   # 2
MEMBER         VALUE
 1             743.155       CHIEF
 3             334.228
TOTAL VALUE= 1077.38
OPPOSITION WOULD LIKE 2 TO JOIN THEM.
WILL YOU MAKE HIM CHIEF TO KEEP HIM? Y
OPPOSITION WOULD LIKE 5 TO JOIN THEM.
```

9.7 PROJECT IDEAS

1. Rewrite the Space Colony game in standard BASIC, making changes that reflect your own ideas.

2. Improve the Space Colony game as follows: a. Increase the number of members in the council. b. Permit a chief to give up his bonus if his followers are in financial straits. c. Come up with a shorter print format for the table information. How about a short version with an optional expanded one upon request?

3. In the Space Colony game a chief might spend some of his wealth on his followers in order to maintain their allegiance. Introduce "rebates" at periodic intervals (or at the chief's discretion). Decrease the chief's value by the amount he elects to spend, and increase the value of his followers proportionally. If the user is chief, he could select the occasion and percent of his wealth to spend. A message something like, "Members are restless and need encouragement. What will you do?" could remind him of his duties as patron. Include some lower limit, so that if he elects to spend below that amount, he receives a message of grievance from his coalition.

4. In the Space Colony game give the user a prestige score. Make it increase (or decrease) with every round. Make it entirely independent of wealth. For example:

    +2 for becoming chief
    +1 for winning a round (being on winning side)
    -1 for losing chieftainship
    +2 for being a good patron (as in project 3)
    -1 for giving a cheap "rebate"
    -1 for losing a round

    after earning a certain amount of prestige points the game could end and the user immediately retire.

5. Write a simulation program that allows several players to take turns in sequence. If you have joystick controls available, read ahead to Section 10.3, and see if your game could include this kind of input.

6. Adapt the "N.Y. Deli" simulation program to a supermarket simulation, with several checkout lines. Experiment with the value of having "express lines" for customers with a small number of items. Run simulations with and without this feature to see what effect it has on "customer throughput".

7. Rewrite one of the programs from this chapter in minimal BASIC, using remarks and indentations to clarify the program's structure. An example showing some techniques that can be used is given in the "style corner".

THE
STYLE
CORNER

```
100 REM     SERVER     1 OCTOBER 1977     JOHN M. NEVISON
105
110 REM     THIS PROGRAM IS A STYLED VERSION OF AN ORIGINAL
115 REM     PROGRAM BY T. DWYER AND M. CRITCHFIELD.
120
125 REM     REFERENCE:  DWYER, T. AND CRITCHFIELD, M., "BASIC AND
130 REM                 THE PERSONAL COMPUTER," READING, MASS:
135 REM                 ADDISON-WESLEY PUBLISHING COMPANY, 1978.
140
145 REM     VARIABLES:
150 REM         A......CLOCK TIME OF NEXT PERSON'S ARRIVAL
155 REM         A(I)...CLOCK  ARRIVAL TIME OF I'TH PERSON
160 REM         B......NUMBER OF THE PERSON AT BEGINNING OF QUEUE
165 REM         E......NUMBER OF THE PERSON AT END OF QUEUE
170 REM         I9.....AVERAGE INTERARRIVAL TIME
175 REM         L1.....CUMULATIVE LINE LENGTH
180 REM         N......NUMBER OF TIME UNITS IN SIMULATION
185 REM         S......CLOCK TIME OF NEXT PERSON'S SERVICE
190 REM         S1.....CUMULATIVE SERVER TIME
195 REM         S9.....AVERAGE SERVICE TIME
200 REM         T......CLOCK TIMER INDEX VARIABLE
205 REM         W1.....CUMULATIVE CUSTOMER WAITING TIME
210
215 REM     DIMENSIONS:
220     DIM A(25)
225
230 REM     FUNCTIONS:
235 REM     LOCATION (MODULO) FUNCTION
240     DEF FNL(X) = X-INT((X-1)/25)*25
245 REM     INTERVAL (EXPONENTIAL DISTRIBUTION) FUNCTION
250     DEF FNI(X) = INT(-X*LOG(RND)+.5)
255
260
265 REM     MAIN PROGRAM
270
275 REM     MODEL A SINGLE SERVER QUEUE FOR  N TIME UNITS.
280
285     GO SUB 395                 'INITIALIZE VARIABLES
290     FOR T = 1 TO N
295        IF T < A THEN 310       '*
300           GO SUB 475           'NEW CUSTOMER ARRIVES
305        GO TO 295               '*
310
315        IF T < S THEN 335       '*
320           IF B = E THEN 335
325           GO SUB 545           'CUSTOMER IS SERVED
330        GO TO 315               '*
335
340        LET L1 = L1 + (E - B)
345        IF T >= S THEN 355
350         LET S1 = S1+1
355
360     NEXT T
365
370     GO SUB 595                 'PRINT OUT
375
380     STOP
385
390
```

```
395 REM     SUBROUTINE:  INITIALIZE VARIABLES
400 REM        IN:
405 REM       OUT:  A, B, E, S, N, I9, S9
410
415     LET B = 0
420     LET E = 0
425     LET S = 0
430
435     PRINT "TYPE # OF TIME UNITS FOR SIMULATION";
440     INPUT N
445     PRINT "TYPE AVERAGE INTERARRIVAL TIME";
450     INPUT I9
455     PRINT "TYPE AVERAGE SERVICE TIME";
460     INPUT S9
465 RETURN
470
475 REM     SUBROUTINE:  NEW CUSTOMER ARRIVES
480 REM       IN:  B, E, T, I9
485 REM      OUT:  E, A, A()
490
495     LET E = E + 1
500     IF (E-B) <= 25 THEN 515
505      PRINT "QUEUE OVERFLOW"
510      STOP
515
520     LET A(FNL(E)) = T
525     LET A = T + FNI(I9)
530
535 RETURN
540
545 REM     SUBROUTINE:  CUSTOMER IS SERVED
550 REM       IN:  B, E, A(), W1, S9, T
555 REM      OUT:  B, W1, S
560
565     LET B = B+1
570     LET S = T + FNI(S9)
575     LET W1 = W1 + (T - A(FNL(B)))
580
585 RETURN
590
595 REM     SUBROUTINE:  PRINT OUT
600 REM       IN:  N, B, E, L1, S1, W1
605 REM      OUT:
610
615     PRINT "------------------------"
620     PRINT "SERVER UTILIZATION  = ";S1/N*100;"%"
625     PRINT "AVERAGE LINE LENGTH  = ";L1/N
630     PRINT "AVERAGE CUSTOMER WAITING TIME  = ";W1/B
635     PRINT "NUMBER OF CUSTOMERS LEFT ON LINE  = ";E-B
640     PRINT "NUMBER OF CUSTOMERS WHO ENTERED STORE  = ";E
645
650 RETURN
655
660     END
```

10

EXTENDING MICROCOMPUTERS

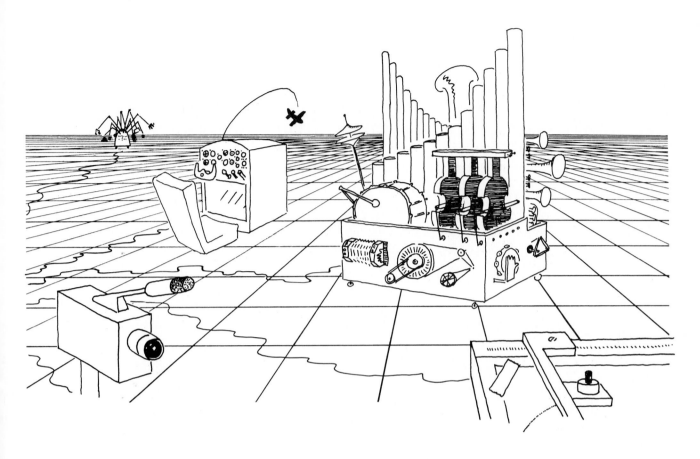

10.0 INTRODUCTION

The programs shown in the previous chapters have covered a lot of ground: graphs, word processing, games, information systems, sorting methods, computer art, data processing, and simulations. This range of ideas—all of which work on personal computers—is impressive, especially when compared to what the "big" computers do. And yet the answer to the question "Is there more?" is an unqualified "Yes.".

There are two directions one can follow in making microcomputers more useful. The first is to apply more sophisticated algorithms to the same application areas just listed. For example, algorithms from the field of numerical analysis can help one design dynamic games of greater complexity than those we've shown. New kinds of games and simulations can also be derived from the algorithms used in the study of networks. These same algorithms can be used to produce interesting computer art. And of course, advanced algorithms contribute to the practical application of computers in both the scientific and business worlds.

The second way to extend microcomputers is with hardware. The most humanly interesting hardware extensions are those that employ new kinds of I/O (Input/Output) devices. For example, on the input side, using a joystick instead of a keyboard can make a Planet-X lander program a great deal more realistic. On the output side, hardware to control motion, generate sounds, or display detailed color graphics makes for some very dramatic results.

In this last chapter there won't be space to discuss any new algorithms (that's another book). But we can take a brief look at what's possible with more humanly oriented I/O. Our goal will be to invite some blue-sky thinking about how personal computers might be used in the future. This may mean fantasying a bit, but that's where half the fun is. And as recent developments have shown, the chances that today's gleam in the eye will be tomorrow's real product are very good indeed.

10.1   COLOR GRAPHICS

One of the most dramatic ways to improve computer output is to add color. Color graphics conveys information to human viewers in a form that makes complex ideas much easier to assimilate. The change from black and white to color is at least as impressive as the change from monaural to full stereo sound.

Until a few years ago, the hardware for color graphics cost a small fortune. This situation is changing however, mainly through the efforts of manufacturers who have devised ingenious ways to use the technology of color TV in conjunction with computer technology. It now seems likely that the electronics for generating high resolution color signals will be made available as low-cost IC (integrated circuit) chips.

One of the first products designed for this purpose was the Cromemco TV Dazzler. It consists of two boards that plug into the slots on a standard 100-pin motherboard.

TV Dazzler boards (photograph courtesy of Cromemco, Mountain View CA 94043).

The output from the boards is a coaxial cable that goes to a color TV monitor. Photos of some color art produced with the TV Dazzler are shown on the color pages found later in this section. Color plates 1 and 2 were both produced with a Dazzler connected to a standard color TV set, using an X-Y digitizer for input. The programming of the Dazzler is a bit complicated, and the interested reader is referred to articles on the subject in the computer hobbyist magazines. (See for example, the article, *The Cybernetic Crayon* in BYTE, December, 1976).

COMPUCOLOR

A more recent example of a personal color system is the Compucolor 8051. It comes in the form of a complete computer system packaged in a cabinet not much bigger than a 19-inch color TV. That's impressive because the cabinet contains the CPU, memory, I/O, PROM's, the graphics controller, power supplies, and a 19-inch color display tube. The colors are of much greater purity than those usually seen on TV since the color system uses a very wide bandwidth (75 MHz) and the three color circuits (Red, Green, Blue) are kept separate. This is the same approach used in professional color monitors. Since any of these colors can be on or off, 8 colors (including black) are available.

The photo in color plate 3 shows a typical system which consists of the computer/color-display in the large cabinet, a keyboard for input, and a "light pen" for interactive computing (see Section 10.4).

The large screen holds 48 lines of 80 characters each, about four times as many as found on most TV displays. When characters are used for graphics, there are therefore 3840 plotting positions available. But a finer division of each character into a 4x2 array of "points" is also possible:

<table>
<tr><td>1 Character Mode
Block:</td><td></td><td>8 Point Plot Mode
Positions:</td></tr>
</table>

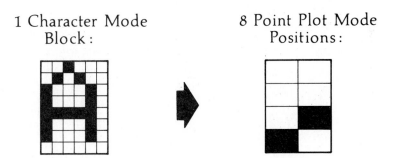

In point plot mode, one character block becomes 8 "point" positions. Each of these points (which is really a small rectangle) can be turned on or off separately. This means there are 160 point positions for the horizontal direction (X axis), and 192 points for the vertical direction (Y axis). So a total of 30,720 points can be plotted.

A special hardware feature called "vector graphics" is also available. This makes it possible for the computer to draw approximations to straight lines on the screen if you simply tell it where to start (X0,Y0), and where to finish (X1,Y1). The hardware figures out all the point positions in between, and plots them automatically.

The compucolor 8051 comes with a BASIC interpreter stored in ROM (read only memory). This means that you never have to load BASIC—you call for it by just pressing two keys (Escape, followed by W).

The BASIC has all the standard features and a few extra ones (including string arrays). It also has the special key word PLOT. This feature makes it quite easy to program graphics of all kinds in color. Let's look at some examples of how it works.

The word PLOT is used in BASIC statements of the form

25 PLOT I

where I is an integer from 0 to 255. When PLOT I is initially used, the value of I determines what *mode* you enter. There are quite a few modes. The main mode is "point plot" (PLOT 2). After you enter a "mode", the meaning of PLOT I is different, and it depends on what mode you're in.

Example 1. Suppose we want to plot the curve Y=X*X. We first use PLOT 2 to put the program in point plot mode. *After* saying PLOT 2, each *pair* of PLOT statements that follows will then give the X and Y positions of the point to be plotted. When finished plotting points, we use PLOT 255 to escape from the plot mode we're in. Here's a program that plots 100 points of our curve.

```
10 PLOT 2
20 FOR X = 0 TO 99
30 LET Y = INT(X*X/100)
40 PLOT X:PLOT Y
50 NEXT X
60 PLOT 255
```

To understand the output of this program you have to know that the "origin" for point plot mode is the point (0,0), and that it's located in the lower left corner of the screen. All points (X,Y) must be described by positive integers with X going from 0 to 159, and Y going from 0 to 191. To make Y=X*X fit on the screen, we divided by 100 (because when X=99, Y=9801 which would be way off the screen). Our graph will look something like this:

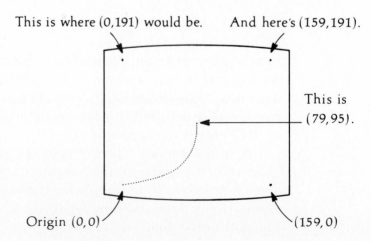

This is where (0,191) would be.   And here's (159,191).

This is (79,95).

Origin (0,0)   (159,0)

Example 2. Here's a program to plot a sine function. We'll let X go from 0 to 159, but actually plot SIN (X/13). This will make the argument of SIN go from 0 to a little over 12 radians which will give about two cycles of the function. Since the SIN function has values from -1 to 1, we'll multiply it by 95 and then add 95. This will make Y go from 0 to 190. We'll start the program with the command PLOT 12 which means "clear screen" of any previous stuff.

SINE WAVE

```
10 PLOT 12:PLOT 2              'Clear screen, go into plot mode
20 FOR X=0 TO 159             'Get X
30 Y=95*SIN(X/13)+95         'Calculate Y
40 PLOT X: PLOT Y            'Plot X,Y
50 NEXT X                     'Back to line 20
60 PLOT 255                   'Exit plot mode
```

Adding Color

The preceding programs will plot in whatever color the machine was using last. Color can be changed with either the PLOT 6 or the PLOT 29 modes. After entering the PLOT 6 mode, the statement PLOT I will produce various combinations of foreground colors, background colors, and "blink" states, all depending on what I is. For example, for I = 0 to 7, you'll get the eight possible foreground colors on a background of black with no blink.

The PLOT 29 mode is a little simpler. It only allows foreground (which means the actual point being plotted) color to be specified. It is followed by PLOT I, where I specifies color according to the codes 16=Black, 17=Red, 18=Green, 19=Yellow, 20=Blue, 21=Violet, 22=Cyan (light blue), and 23=White.

We'll illustrate this feature in a moment, but let's first look at an example of a sub-plot mode (this is a mode that follows the PLOT 2 main mode).

Bar Graph Mode

After you go into PLOT 2 mode, you can go into several sub-plot modes. For example, PLOT 250 means go into X (horizontal) bar graph mode. It's followed by three PLOT statements that tell where to put the bar graph, and how long to make it.

    PLOT 2: PLOT 250: PLOT 0: PLOT 96: PLOT 159

means draw a horizontal bar (line) from X=0 to X=159, but 96 units up on the screen (the Y position).

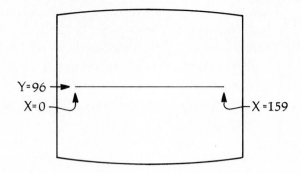

The code for Y (vertical) bar graphs is PLOT 246.

PLOT 2: PLOT 246: PLOT 0: PLOT 80: PLOT 190

means draw a vertical bar (line) from Y=0 to Y=190, but 80 units to the right (the X position).

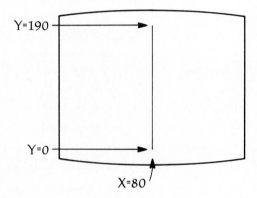

Bar graphs are also useful for drawing rectangles and grid patterns. Color plate 4 shows output that consists of parts of rectangles drawn with bar graph mode.

A Combined Program

Here's a program that graphs the sine function, using seven different colors (codes 17 to 23). It also uses bar-graph mode to plot the X and Y axes for the graph. The axes are drawn in yellow (code 19). A photo of the output is shown in color plate 5.

COLOR
SINEGRAPH

```
10 PLOT 12                                   'Erase screen
20 PLOT 29: PLOT 19                          'Set color=yellow
30 PLOT 2                                    'Go into main plot mode
40 PLOT 246: PLOT 0: PLOT 0: PLOT 190        'Plot Y bar graph
50 PLOT 250: PLOT 0: PLOT 95: PLOT 159       'Plot X bar graph
60 PLOT 255                                  'Exit plot mode
70 FOR X = 0 TO 159                          'Get X
80 PLOT 29: PLOT 17+X/22                      'Set a color depending on X
90 Y = 95*SIN(X/13)+95                       'Calculate Y
100 PLOT 2                                   'Point plot mode
110 PLOT X: PLOT Y                           'Plot one point
120 PLOT 255                                 'Exit plot mode
130 NEXT X                                   'Back to line 70
```

Notice in line 100 that going into main plot mode *also* puts you in point plot mode. So PLOT 2 is an exception. It puts you in general plot mode *and* in point plot mode.

Vector Mode

The bar graph modes are used to draw horizontal and vertical lines. Vector mode lets you draw lines (called vectors) between *any* two points. This means slanted lines can be drawn on the screen. You start with PLOT 253 and then give the coordinates of the starting position with PLOT X0:PLOT Y0. Then you say PLOT 242, followed by the coordinates of the end position with PLOT X1:PLOT Y1. (Any variable name can be used. We find these easy to remember.) Here's a program that let's you experiment with drawing vectors on the screen using seven colors in sequence (black is skipped because it would draw an "invisible" line).

INTERACTIVE VECTOR

```
10 PLOT 12:C=0                               'Erase screen
20 C=C+1                                     'Start with color code 1
30 IF C>7 THEN C=1                           'Only allow 7 color codes
40 PLOT 6:PLOT C                             'Set the color
50 PRINT "TYPE X0,Y0";
60 INPUT X0,Y0                               'Get starting point
70 PRINT "TYPE X1,Y1";
80 INPUT X1,Y1                               'Get end point
90 PLOT 2                                    'Go into plot mode
100 PLOT 253:PLOT X0:PLOT Y0                 'Draw vector starting at X0,Y0...
110 PLOT 242:PLOT X1,PLOT Y1                 '... to X1,Y1
120 PLOT 255                                 'Exit plot mode
130 GOTO 20
```

If you wish to draw a bunch of lines where the end point of one is the starting point of the next one (as in drawing polygons), then you only need to use PLOT 253 once. Here's an example that draws random vectors in this fashion, making an attractive abstract type of drawing. The output is shown in color plate 6.

RANDOM VECTOR

```
10 K=16                              'Initialize color selector
20 PLOT 12:PLOT 2                    'Enter plot mode
30 PLOT 253:PLOT 79:PLOT 91          'Start vector in center
40 K=K+1                             'Select color …
50 IF K>23 THEN K=17                 '…between 17 and 23
70 X=160*RND(1):Y=190*RND(1)         'Choose random point
80 PLOT 2:PLOT 242:PLOT X:PLOT Y     'Draw vector
90 GOTO 40
```

Incremental Plot

Another submode that can follow PLOT 2 is the PLOT 251 incremental plot. This allows you to move the graphic "point" element (which is really a small rectangle) a small "increment" (or step). There are eight directions in which you can move, as shown by the arrows in the following diagram:

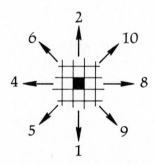

The numbers next to the arrow are "direction codes". A given direction is selected by using the proper direction code in a second PLOT statement. For example to plot a point in the middle of the screen and then move it one "increment" to the right, you'd say

```
10 PLOT 2:PLOT 80:PLOT 92
20 PLOT 251:PLOT 8
```

PLOT 251 means "increment (move) the point", and PLOT 8 means "to the right". The distance moved is very small (the width of one point).

Here's a program that uses this feature to produce what's called a random walk pattern. We'll only use direction codes 1, 2, 4, and 8. These will be generated by the formula

$$E = 2\uparrow INT(4*RND(1))$$

So we'll randomly get the numbers

$2^0=1$, $2^1=2$, $2^2=4$, and $2^3=8$.

This means our point will randomly "decide" to move down, up, left or right.

To make the pattern even more interesting, we'll use another random number (from 5 to 9) to decide how many increments (tiny steps) to take in each direction. We'll also change colors. The result is a rather striking weave-type color abstraction. (Actually random walk techniques originated for practical reasons. They are used in solving several types of mathematical and scientific problems that can't be handled by conventional methods.)

Here's our program:

RANDOM WALK

```
10 PLOT 12                          'Erase screen
15 PLOT 2:PLOT 80:PLOT92            'Plot a point in middle of screen
20 FOR C=17 TO 23                   'Select a color
30 PLOT 255:PLOT 29:PLOT C          'Activate color
40 PLOT 2:PLOT 251                  'Go into incremental plot mode
50 E = 2↑INT(4*RND(1))              'Choose direction
60 FOR K=1 TO 5*RND(1)+5            'Choose number of steps
70 PLOT E                           'Plot in direction E
80 NEXT K                           ' for K steps
90 NEXT C                           'Get next color and direction
100 GOTO 20                         'Repeat the whole cycle
```

Line 50 selects a random direction, while the loop 60-80 determines how many increments (steps) to take in that direction. The main loop 20-90 repeats the process for seven different colors. Line 100 makes the program go on and on, filling the screen to any density you wish. Color plate 7 shows the output of this program after 20 seconds. Color plate 8 shows the output after about 20 minutes. The plotting is very rapid, but paths are often retraced. When the plotting point "walks" off one edge of the screen, it reappears on the opposite side due to "wrap-around" in the display memory.

A game can be made out of this program by betting on which portions of black will be filled up next. This is easy to do because pressing the break key temporarily halts execution of the program. The players can then stick a small initialed piece of masking tape on the black area of their choice. Pressing the RETURN key resumes execution.

There are several other sub-plot modes available, including an incremental vector mode. This has the effect of shifting a vector to a new position very close to the starting position. Since vectors are drawn rapidly, this mode has interesting possiblilities for producing simple animation.

It is also possible to interact with color graphics using an input device called a "light pen". This will be explained in Section 10.4 where a program using the light pen will be described.

10.2   BINARY, HEXADECIMAL, AND OCTAL NUMBERS

When programming in a higher level language like BASIC, there is usually no need to know how the computer represents numbers or letters. Using an ASCII keyboard for input and a standard terminal for output, the programmer uses normal alphanumeric *symbols* (like A, B, C, 0, 1, 2, %, $, etc.). The ASCII codes for these alphanumeric symbols were discussed in Sections 1.2 and 3.8, and they're summarized in Appendix B.

But what about *numbers*? If a programmer uses a number like 97, how is it actually stored inside the computer? Are ASCII codes used? The answer is no. It's true that when you type 97 at the keyboard, the ASCII codes for 9 and 7 are sent to the computer. But if you want 97 to be used as a *number* (not as a *string* of two characters), then the computer has to use a different kind of "code" for storing the 97. It must be stored as a binary number.

Binary numbers may look like ASCII codes, but they're really structured more like the decimal numbers learned in school. Decimal 97 really means 9*10 + 7 * 1. In other words, it's a code where the *positions* of the digits are used as part of the representation. We associate powers of ten with each position because we have ten digits 0, 1, 2, 3, 4, 5, 6, 7, 8, 9 available. When we wish to write a number greater than 9, we use the same symbols but place them in different positions. For example, when we write 8902 we really mean

$$8 * 10^3 + 9 * 10^2 + 0 * 10^1 + 2 * 10^0$$

or $8 * 1000 + 9 * 100 + 0 * 10 + 2 * 1$

(Notice that 10^0 means 1.) The representation 8902 is called a decimal number, or more precisely a "base 10 numeral".

Computers aren't able to use this system because *internally* they are limited to two digits (usually called 0 and 1). It's as though they only had two fingers. Of course computers also must use a positional notation for larger numbers. The system used is based on powers of two. For example, the number 1100001 means

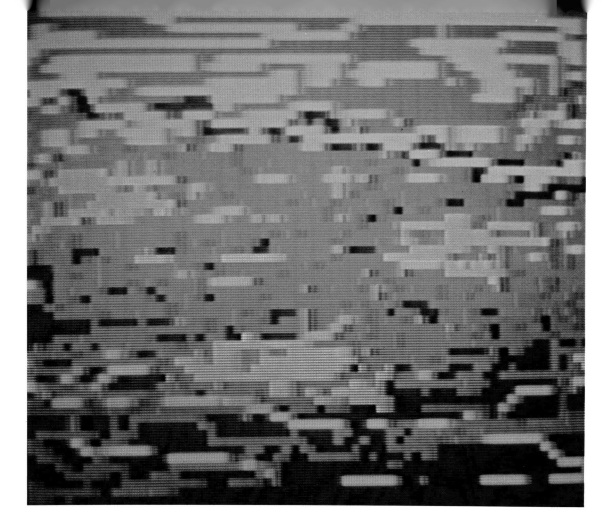

Plate 1
Lily Pond Produced with a Dazzler connected to a standard color TV set, using an X-Y digitizer for input. The attempt here was to approximate soft contours and an impressionist color scheme. See Section 10.1 for further information.

Plate 2
Windows and Spaces
Another design produced with the dazzler and digitizer. Makes use of the precise horizontal and vertical lines that are possible with this technology. It achieves a dreamlike quality, and an illusion of overlapping forms. See Section 10.1.

Plate 3
Bouquet of Flowers
Produced by the Compucolor 8051 computer, shown here with keyboard and light pen. Design was input with the light pen used somewhat like an artist's brush. Colors were chosen with the keyboard. See Sections 10.1 and 10.4.

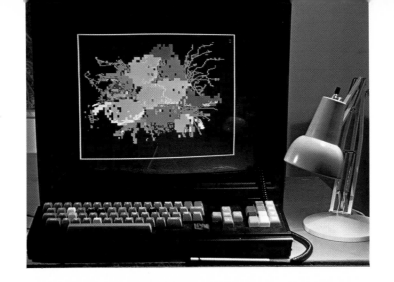

Plate 4
Temple This design was produced by a program using bar graph mode on the Compucolor. The subtle relationships that occur between the different areas of color are what makes it interesting. See Section 10.1.

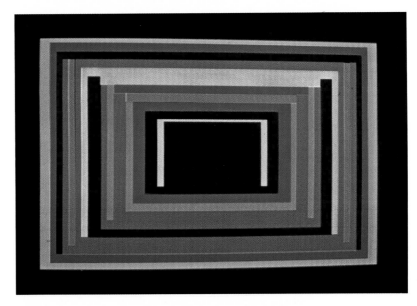

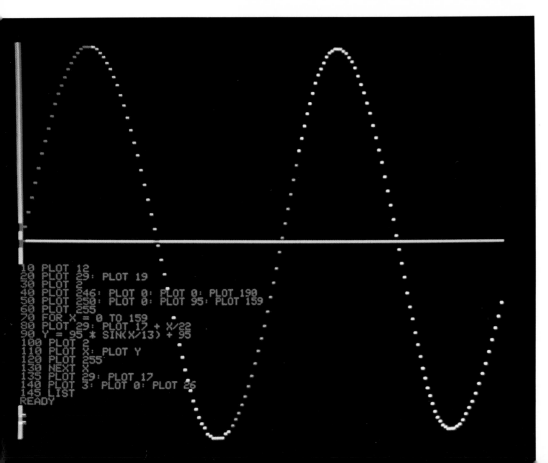

Plate 5
Sine Wave This is the output and listing of a Compucolor program using point plot and bar graph modes. See Section 10.1.

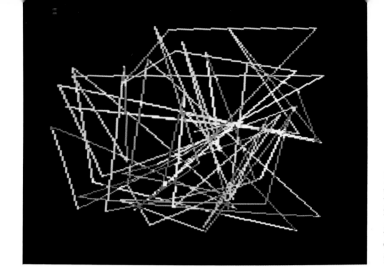

Plate 6
Random Vectors This is the output from a program on the Compucolor using vector mode. See Section 10.1.

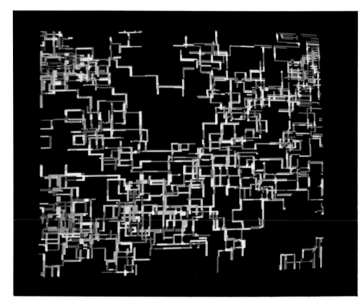

Plate 7
Random Walk: 20 Seconds This is output from a program on the Compucolor using incremental plot mode. It was halted after 20 seconds. See Section 10.1.

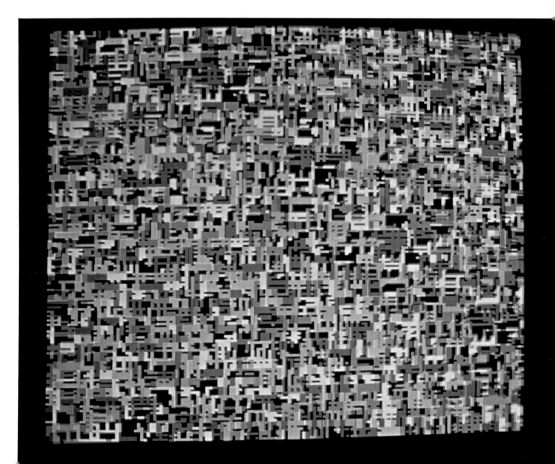

Plate 8
Random Walk: 20 Minutes Same program as shown in plate 7, but allowed to run for 20 minutes to fill the screen. See Section 10.1.

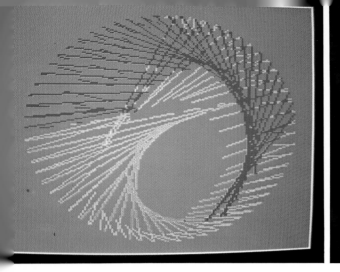
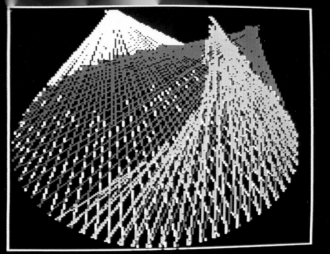

Plates 9 and 10
Spring Dance (left); **Circus** (right). Both of these pictures were produced by the Light Pen Crayon program explained in Section 10.4. The output is partially controlled by the computer program, and partially controlled by input from the human user.

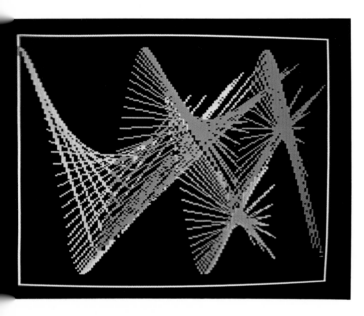

Plate 11
Melody The Light Pen Crayon program was modified here so that the program-determined points describe a sine wave instead of an ellipse, as in Plates 9 and 10. Again, human-input points make up part of the design. See Section 10.4.

Plate 13
Lissajous Butterfly Another variation on the Light Pen Crayon program. This time the computer drew a 3 by 2 Lissajous figure while the human user held the light pen in the central area of the picture. See Section 10.5.

Plate 12
Electric Fields This is the pattern generated by formulas describing the potential of an electric field with several point charges. See Section 10.5.

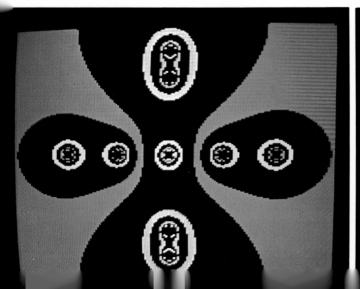

$$1 * 2^6 + 1 * 2^5 + 0 * 2^4 + 0 * 2^3 + 0 * 2^2 + 0 * 2^1 + 1 * 2^0$$

or $1 * 64 + 1 * 32 + 0 * 16 + 0 * 8 + 0 * 4 + 0 * 2 + 1 * 1$

In decimal notation, this would be written 97, since

$$64 + 32 + 0 + 0 + 0 + 0 + 1 = 97$$

The representation of the quantity 97 as 1100001 is called a binary number, or a "base 2 numeral". You can see that it uses only two digits. These are called binary digits, and each digit can be stored as one "bit" of information. In most microcomputers, memory is organized around groups of eight bits, each of which is called a *byte*. So this binary number would be stored inside the computer as the byte

0	1	1	0	0	0	0	1

SELF-TEST

What are the decimal equivalents of each of the following binary numbers
(a) 00011100   (b) 10000001   (c) 11111111
Solution: Associate the eight bits in each of these binary numbers with the decimal numbers for powers of two:
    128, 64, 32, 16, 8, 4, 2, 1.
Keep only the decimal numbers that are associated with 1 bits, and add them up. This gives
    (a) $16 + 8 + 4 = 28$ (b) $128 + 1 = 129$ (c) Your turn.

The answer to (c) is 255. This is the largest integer that a single byte can hold. Notice that another formula for the largest number one byte can hold is $2^8 - 1 = 256 - 1 = 255$.

To represent larger numbers, two bytes are used together. This gives 16 bits. The largest number that can be represented with 16 bits is $2^{16} - 1 = 65,535$. (Now you know why some versions of BASIC tell you that the largest line number permitted is 65,535. They obviously use two bytes to store line numbers.)

Hexadecimal Numbers

As we'll see in the next section, when you start using fancier I/O devices (like joysticks or digital to analog converters), you sometimes have to think in terms of binary numbers. This is difficult for humans. A long string of zeros and ones is hard to read, and it's very easy to make mistakes.

To make the contents of a byte easier to read, the bits are often grouped into fours, and the following hex (short for hexadecimal) symbols are used for these groups:

Binary	Hex	Decimal Equivalent
0000	0	00
0001	1	01
0010	2	02
0011	3	03
0100	4	04
0101	5	05
0110	6	06
0111	7	07
1000	8	08
1001	9	09
1010	A	10
1011	B	11
1100	C	12
1101	D	13
1110	E	14
1111	F	15

The hex symbols are what creatures with 16 fingers might use in doing what they would call hexadecimal arithmetic. This is based on powers of 16. For example, the number 2B3 means

$$2 * 16^2 + 11 * 16^1 + 3 * 16^0 =$$

$$2 * 256 + 11 * 16 + 3 * 1 =$$

$$512 + 176 + 3 = 691$$

Using hex notation, a byte can be represented with only two symbols. To do this, group the bits in two parts, and then replace each group by its corresponding hex digit. For example

$$\text{BINARY} \quad \text{HEX}$$
$$11000101 = \quad C5$$

To convert this number to decimal form, you can either work with the left side and get

$$2^7 + 2^6 + 2^2 + 2^0 = 128 + 64 + 4 + 1 = 197$$

or you can work with the right side and get

$$12 * 16^1 + 5 * 16^0 =$$

$$12 * 16 + 5 * 1 = 192 + 5 = 197$$

Octal Numbers

Another way to "condense" binary numbers is to organize the bits in groups of three, starting at the right. For the preceding example, we'd have

$$\overbrace{11}\,\overbrace{000}\,\overbrace{101}$$

The leftmost group is filled in with zeros as needed. Then a conversion to *octal* digits is done using the following table:

Binary	Octal
000	0
001	1
010	2
011	3
100	4
101	5
110	6
111	7

So for our example we have

BINARY	OCTAL
$\overbrace{011}\,\overbrace{000}\,\overbrace{101}$ =	305

Octal numbers are the kind creatures with eight fingers might use. For them,

$$305 \text{ octal} = 3 * 8^2 + 0 * 8^1 + 5 * 8^0$$

$$= 3 * 64 + 5 = 192 + 5 = 197$$

When reading in a computer book you have to make sure which system is being used. Binary numbers are usually easy to spot, but the others need to be distinguished. This is sometimes done with subscripts as follows:

$$00011001_2 \text{ means binary } 0001\,1001$$

$$31_8 \qquad \text{means octal 31}$$

$$25_{10} \qquad \text{means decimal 25}$$

$$19_{16} \qquad \text{means hex 19}$$

In BASIC, when you say something like

LET X=25

it's understood that this number is *decimal* notation. To show an octal number, you use the & sign in front of the digits.

LET X=&31

To show a hex number, you use the symbols &H in front of the digits.

LET X=&H19

In BASIC you can't use binary numbers directly. To store 00011001_2 in X, you must use one of the above statements.

Binary Arithmetic; Two's Complement Representation

Inside the computer, all arithmetic operations are done on binary numbers. The addition table for binary arithmetic is very simple:

```
0 + 0 = 0
0 + 1 = 1
1 + 0 = 1
1 + 1 = 10 (0, with a carry of 1)
```

Example:

Binary	Decimal
01101101	109
+00101010	+42
10010111	151

To avoid doing subtraction, many computers use a trick. They *add* the "two's complement" of the number being subtracted instead. To see how this works, let's first use a similar trick for decimal numbers. Here we'll add the "ten's complement". Problem:

$$
\begin{array}{cc}
\begin{array}{r} 109 \\ -042 \\ \hline 67 \end{array}
&
\begin{array}{r} a \\ -b \\ \hline c \end{array}
\end{array}
$$

Instead of subtracting 42, we'll first change to the "nine's complement". You do this by replacing each digit with its difference from 9. The nine's complement of 042 is 957. Then you add 1 to get the ten's complement. This will be 958. Finally, you add the ten's complement of 042 to the 109, and throw away the leftmost digit.

$$
\begin{array}{r} 109 \\ +958 \\ \hline \cancel{1}067 \end{array}
\qquad \text{This is } 109-42.
$$

Now let's do this in binary arithmetic, except that "nine's complement" becomes "one's complement" and "ten's complement" becomes "two's complement". We'll use 8-bit numbers for our example.

$$
\begin{array}{ccc}
\begin{array}{r} 01101101 \\ -00101010 \\ \hline ? \end{array}
&
\begin{array}{r} a \\ -b \\ \hline c \end{array}
&
\begin{array}{r} 109 \\ -\ \ 42 \\ \hline \end{array}
\end{array}
$$

First form the one's complement of the number being subtracted (this is easy—just change 0's to 1's and 1's to 0's). The one's complement of b = 11010101. Next form the two's complement by adding 1. The two's complement of b = 11010110. Finally, add the two's complement of b to a, keeping only the right-most 8 bits.

$$
\begin{array}{r} 01101101 \\ +11010110 \\ \hline 01000011 \end{array}
\qquad \text{This is } 67 = a - b.
$$

Handling Negative Numbers

We've seen that one byte of memory lets us represent decimal numbers from 0 to 255. But we'll also want to represent negative numbers. One way to do this is to "steal" the leftmost bit and use it for the sign of the number. If we use 0 to mean + and 1 to mean -, then the numbers from -127 to +127 can be represented as follows:

$$
\begin{array}{rcr}
01111111 & = & +127 \\
01111110 & = & +126 \\
\vdots & & \vdots \\
00000001 & = & +\ 1 \\
00000000 & = & +\ 0 \\
10000000 & = & -\ 0 \\
10000001 & = & -\ 1 \\
\vdots & & \vdots \\
11111110 & = & -126 \\
11111111 & = & -127
\end{array}
$$

One catch to this scheme is that it has two different ways of representing zero. Another is that the rules for two's complement arithmetic don't work when subtracting a larger number from a smaller one.

The solution to both these difficulties is to represent negative numbers by two's complements. This gives us the following scheme:

$$
\begin{array}{rcr}
01111111 & = & +127 \\
01111110 & = & +126 \\
\vdots & & \vdots \\
00000010 & = & +\ 2 \\
00000001 & = & +\ 1 \\
00000000 & = & 0 \\
11111111 & = & -\ 1 \\
11111110 & = & -\ 2 \\
\vdots & & \vdots \\
10000001 & = & -127 \\
10000000 & = & -128
\end{array}
$$

Notice that there is only one representation for zero. Also watch what happens when we subtract 109 from 42:

$$
\begin{array}{rcrcr}
00101010 & = & b & = & 42 \\
-01101101 & = & -a & = & -109
\end{array}
$$

One's complement of a = 10010010
Two's complement of a = 10010011

Adding this to b we get

$$
\begin{array}{r}
00101010 \\
+\,10010011 \\
\hline
10111101
\end{array}
$$

Because the first bit is a 1, we know this is a negative number in two's complement system. To see what it is in regular binary notation, form the two's complement of the last seven bits and put a minus sign in front of the result

Last seven bits	=	0111101
One's complement	=	1000010
Two's complement	=	1000011
b − a	=	−1000011
	=	−67

We'll see what all of the above has to do with BASIC programming in the next section where we show how to interface a digital computer to analog signals.

Floating Point Arithmetic; Integer Variables

So far all the numbers we've shown in binary form have been integers. But practical problems also involve what are called "real" numbers, expressed in a form that includes a decimal point. These are also called "floating point" numbers. Standard BASIC automatically takes care of moving the decimal point during arithmetic operations with floating point numbers. For example, a statement like

PRINT (4+1.25+0.0625)*.01

is perfectly legal in standard BASIC, and the answer will appear as

.053125

The decimal will be in the correct place, and the answer will be accurate to about 6 or 7 "significant digits" (our example has only 5 significant digits—leading zeros don't count).

The way this is done inside the machine is to represent numbers with the scientific notation explained back in Section 2.6. This is usually done by using 3 bytes of memory to store the significant digits, and an extra byte to store the exponent. For example, the above number could be written as

53125×10^{-6}

To store it, four bytes are used: three to hold the 53125 significant digit part, and an additional byte to hold the -6 exponent part. When arithmetic is done on floating point numbers, the exponent part is used to automatically keep track of the decimal point. Of course all of this is done in binary form.

Some versions of BASIC also allow what's called "double precision" arithmetic. They use more than three bytes to store the significant digits of floating point numbers. Double precision numbers usually have an accuracy of about 15 or 16 significant digits.

The process of keeping track of the decimal in floating point arithmetic takes time. If you are doing a problem where you know some of the variables will always be integers (which means the decimal is always on the right), you might not want to use floating point arithmetic. In some extended BASIC's you can arrange for this by using a % sign after the variable name. When you say

    10 LET N%=4893

the interpreter will store the number 4893 *without* an exponent, and use only two bytes for the significant digits. This means that N% is limited to integers from -32768 to +32767.

N% is called an integer variable. Integer variables are used to speed up arithmetic, decrease the memory required, and to make sure *exact* integer values are stored in certain variables.

10.3   ANALOG I/O; USING JOYSTICKS AND OSCILLOSCOPES WITH A COMPUTER

When you use an ASCII keyboard for input, pressing a key sends one 7-bit digital code to the computer. Pressing a sequence of keys sends a sequence of 7-bit codes. These go, one after the other, to what's called an *input port* of the machine.

For many applications, the keys can't be pressed fast enough to give a continual flow of information. It's too hard to find the keys, especially if you are also trying to do something else (like watching output). What's needed is a more human-oriented input device.

A good example of where this need arises is in flight simulator programs. The pilot must supply several kinds of input: thrust, bank, attitude, etc. To simulate an aircraft realistically, thrust should be input with a throttle. Similarly, aileron and elevator commands would feel more natural if they could be input from an aircraft control wheel as a continuous stream of data.

Some aircraft use a "joystick" for this purpose. Miniature joysticks are also used for controlling model aircraft. A joystick usually provides two output signals called X and Y. X corresponds to left-right (bank) input, while Y corresponds to up-down (elevator) input.

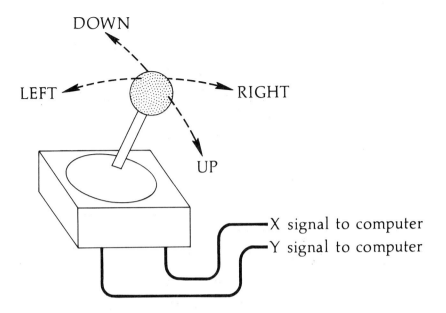

The easiest way to produce X and Y signals from a joystick is with two potentiometers. These are variable resistors which provide variable voltages that correspond to the joysticks's position. Here's how one of them could be connected (say for the Y axis).

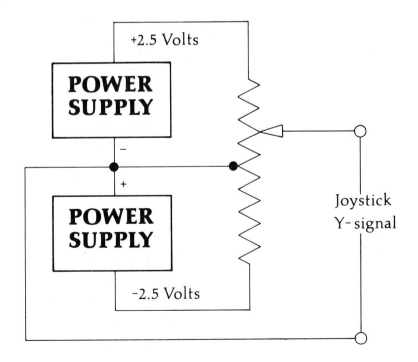

The Y motion of the joystick moves the slider on the potentiometer. With the power supplies shown in our diagram, the joystick can provide a signal from +2.5 volts to -2.5 volts. The middle "neutral" position gives a signal of 0 volts. A second potentiometer coupled to the same joystick could provide similar voltages for the X motion.

When an electrical signal like this is fed to a computer, it is called an *analog input*. Before the computer can use such an input, it must be converted to digital form. The device that does this is called an analog-to-digital (A/D) converter.

There are also output devices that require analog signals in the form of electrical voltages. Examples include electrical meters, oscilloscopes, and electric motors. To run such devices from a computer, a digital-to-analog (D/A) converter is needed.

Conversion is usually done with special circuitry. Here's a picture of a board that contains such circuitry. It's called the Cromemco D+7A converter.

D+7A digital to analog converter board (photograph courtesy of Cromemco, Mountain View CA 94043).

The board plugs into a standard 100-pin microcomputer bus, and provides seven A/D and D/A converter circuits. (It can also accept some simple digital inputs to sense the pushing of buttons on a joystick console.)

A Joystick/Oscilloscope Planet-X Lander

To illustrate use of this board, we'll show how to write a BASIC program similar to the Planet-X Lander shown in Chapter 6. However this will be a "real-time" version, where things happen as rapidly as they do in real life. The setup we'll use will be as follows:

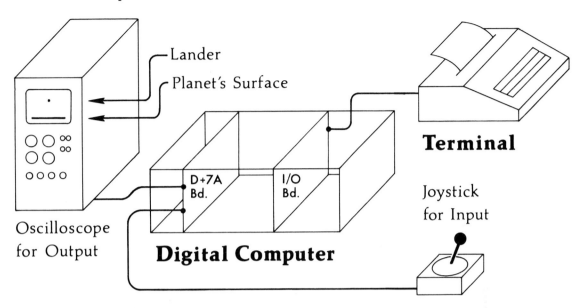

The program is entered and debugged from the terminal in the normal way. To use the program, you type RUN on the terminal keyboard. Then you move over to the joystick which acts as your rocket throttle. The descent of the lander will be pictured on the oscilloscope as a spot that starts at the top of the screen. To slow the lander down, you apply throttle using the joystick. (Our version only uses Y axis control. For a project, we suggest a 2-D version using both X and Y axes.) Apply too much throttle, and the lander goes back up. Apply too little, and it falls toward Planet-X with increasing speed. When the lander reaches the planet, the terminal takes over and prints a message telling what kind of landing you made. The terminal will also print a message if you run out of fuel.

A program to do this will have to use two new BASIC statements. The statement

I%=INP(26)

means accept input from port number 26 and store it in integer variable I%. This happens to be the port to which we connected the joystick *by way of* an analog-to-digital coverter. Other ports could have been used. The other new statement is

OUT 27, H

This means send the contents of variable H to output port number 27. Since we've got one of our D/A converters wired to port 27, the value of H then gets converted to an analog voltage which appears on the wire coming out of this converter. This wire is connected to the Y input terminal on the oscilloscope. The voltage on the wire then makes the electron "spot" on the oscilloscope screen move to a position corresponding to H.

The D/A and A/D converters on the Cromemco board use two's complement codes. Also, an increment of 1 digital unit corresponds to .02 volts. So the relation between digital and analog signals is as follows:

8-Bit Binary Code at Port	Corresponding Analog Voltage	Decimal Equivalent
0111111	+2.54	127
0111110	+2.52	126
.	.	.
.	.	.
.	.	.
00000010	+0.04	2
00000001	+0.02	1
00000000	±0.00	0
11111111	−0.02	255
11111110	−0.04	254
.	.	.
.	.	.
.	.	.
10000001	−2.54	129
10000000	−2.56	128

There are good reasons for using two's complement codes as was explained in the previous section. However the decimal equivalents are a bit strange. To make the decimal values match a scheme where voltage = .02 * decimal value, we can subtract 256 from all the decimal values below the zero. Then the numbers 255 to 128 become -1 to -128. This is easily done with the BASIC statements

```
225 I% = INP(26)
230 IF I%>=128 THEN I%=I%-256
```

A similar conversion needs to be done when data is output from the computer to a digital-to-analog converter. Suppose the digital values are stored in the variable H. If H has values that go from -128 to +127, these can be converted to voltages that go from -2.56 to +2.54, by the statement

```
190 IF H<0 THEN OUT 27,H+256 ELSE OUT 27,H
```

However in some applications (such as our Planet-X Lander) H may only have positive values. Suppose H goes from 0 to 255. Then we can use the statement

```
205 IF H>=128 THEN OUT 27,H-128 ELSE OUT 27,H+128
```

to convert H to the decimal equivalents shown in our table. Here's a lander program that uses these ideas.

JOYSTICK
PLANET-X

```
LIST

10  REM-----OSCILLOSCOPE PLANET X LANDER-----
40  T=.1              'TIME INCREMENT
50  T2=T*T/2          'CALC.TIME SQUARED/2
60  V=0               'INITIAL VELOCITY
70  H=250             'INITIAL HT.(KM)
80  G=2               'GRAVITY ON PLANET X
90  S=9000            'MASS OF LDR
95  N=1000            'NEWTONS PER UNIT OF INPUT
100 E%=13000          'MASS OF FUEL (KG)
200 REM-----SIMULATION LOOP-----
205 IF H>=128 THEN OUT 27,H-128 ELSE OUT 27,H+128
220 IF E%=0 THEN A=-G: GOTO 260
225 I%=INP(26)
230 IF I%>=128 THEN I%=I%-256
233 IF ABS(I%)>E% THEN I%=SGN(I%)*E%:PRINT "OUT OF FUEL"
234 E%=E%-ABS(I%)
235 F=N*I%
240 A=F/(S+E%)-G
260 H=H+V*T+A*T2
270 V=V+A*T
300 IF H+V*T>0 THEN 205
301 REM-----END OF LOOP-----
305 OUT 27,128
310 IF H+V*T<0 THEN V=V+A*H/V
320 PRINT "YOU'RE DOWN...LANDING VELOCITY=";V
330 IF V>-10 THEN PRINT"BEAUTIFUL LANDING":GOTO 360
340 IF V>-20 THEN PRINT"CRUNCH!!--BUMPY LANDING":GOTO 360
350 PRINT "KABOOM!!! TURN IN YOUR LICENSE"
360 IN@UT "WANT TO TRY AGAIN";A$
370 IF LEFT$(A$,1)="Y" THEN 10
999 END
OK
RUN
YOU'RE DOWN...LANDING VELOCITY=-30.8891  ←
KABOOM!!! TURN IN YOUR LICENSE
WANT TO TRY AGAIN? Y
YOU'RE DOWN...LANDING VELOCITY=-19.1287  ←
CRUNCH!!--BUMPY LANDING
WANT TO TRY AGAIN? Y
YOU'RE DOWN...LANDING VEOCITY=-8.50783  ←
BEAUTIFUL LANDING
WANT TO TRY AGAIN? Y
YOU'RE DOWN...LANDING VELOCITY=-9.80819  ←
BEAUTIFUL LANDING
WANT TO TRY AGAIN? Y
OUT OF FUEL
YOU'RE DOWN...LANDING VELOCITY=-24.6407  ←
KABOOM!!! TURN IN YOUR LICENSE
WANT TO TRY AGAIN? N
OK
```

THESE MESSAGES ONLY APPEAR AFTER THE ACTUAL DESCENT IS MADE, USING A JOYSTICK FOR INPUT AND AN OSCILLOSCOPE FOR OUTPUT.

The output statement in line 205 sends a voltage (through the D/A converter) to the oscilloscope every time around the loop. On a typical microcomputer this happens about 10 times per second. So if we let our time increment T = .1, the simulation will be very close to a "real time" situation.

The joystick throttle setting is also input to the program every time around the loop (see line 225). So it is "sampled" every 0.1 second and stored in I%. Line 230 converts I% to a number from -128 to +127. We did this so that the throttle will have zero thrust at its neutral middle setting. Thus it can be used for both up and down rocket thrust. (This is a little silly for a lander program, but it comes in handy for more general space game programs.) The force F is calculated as F=N*I% in line 235, where N is the number of Newtons of force per throttle unit.

The height of the lander is 250 kilometers to start with. It gets updated every 0.1 second with the formula in line 260:

$$H = H + V * T + 1/2 * (A * T * T)$$

To reduce calculation time, the last term is calculated as A * T2, where T2 has been made equal to 1/2 * T * T *before* going into the loop. The velocity V is updated in line 270. The letter A stands for acceleration, and it's made up of the acceleration due to the rocket force F (up), minus the acceleration due to the planet's gravity G (down). By Newton's law, the acceleration from the rocket force F is F/(S + E%), where S + E% is the mass of the lander *and* the fuel combined.

10.4   DOWN THE ROAD

One of the most obvious extensions of analog output is to use the voltage to drive a motor. Then computers can be used to control the motion of things (Robots, anyone?). An article describing how to run motors from analog signals appeared in *BYTE* for August, 1977.

Motors can also be controlled digitally. A kit with the parts for two digitally controlled motor mechanisms suitable for building an X-Y plotter is available from Sylvanhills Labs. The motors and a frame are mounted on a board as shown in the photograph.

Kit for building an X-Y plotter (photograph courtesy of Silvanhills Labs, Strafford MO 65757).

The pen in the middle is moved around to produce hard-copy graphics. The results can be very attractive. Here are a few examples of X-Y plotter output.

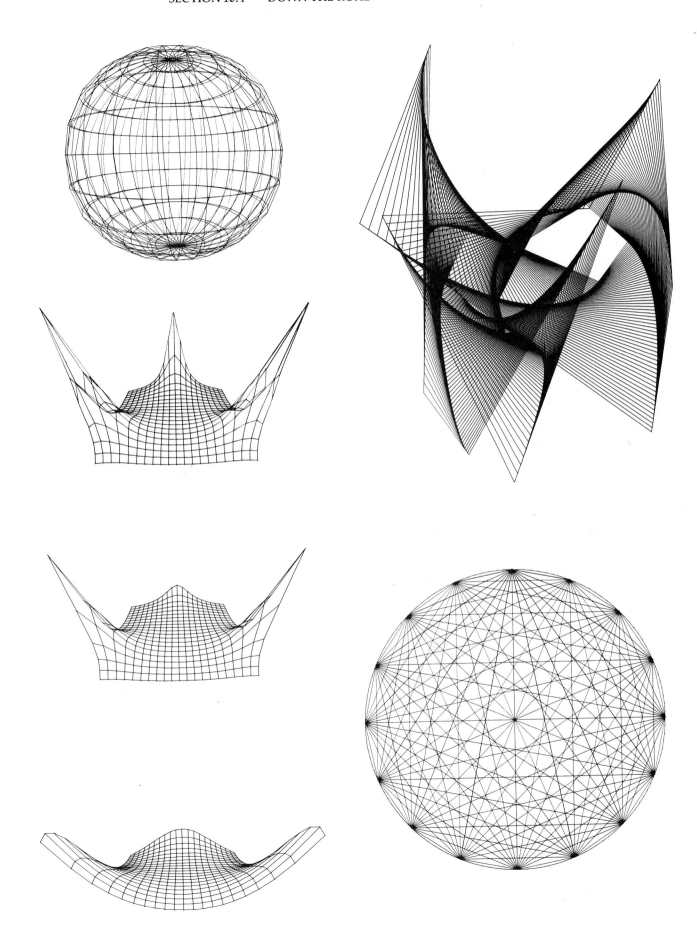

Using Light Pens as Input Devices

A light pen is a pen-like device with a photo-cell at the "tip", and a wired connection to the computer. When the photo-cell is held against the face of the CRT graphics display, the cell detects the light coming from a special "position-reporting pattern" on the screen. The X and Y coordinates of the position being touched by the pen are then sent to the computer.

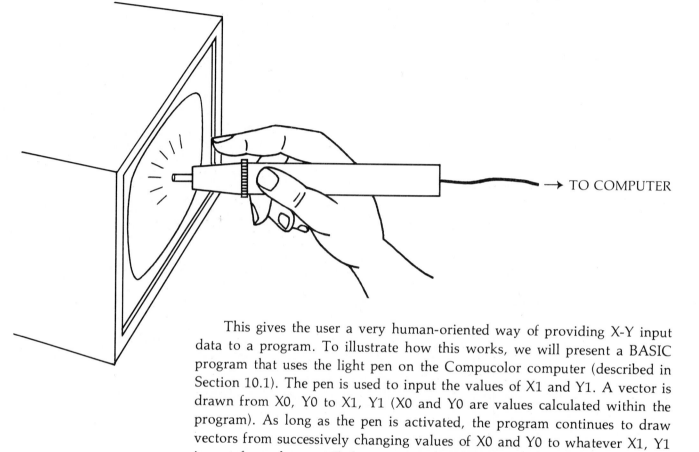

→ TO COMPUTER

This gives the user a very human-oriented way of providing X-Y input data to a program. To illustrate how this works, we will present a BASIC program that uses the light pen on the Compucolor computer (described in Section 10.1). The pen is used to input the values of X1 and Y1. A vector is drawn from X0, Y0 to X1, Y1 (X0 and Y0 are values calculated within the program). As long as the pen is activated, the program continues to draw vectors from successively changing values of X0 and Y0 to whatever X1, Y1 is sent from the pen. If the pen is not activated, no vectors are drawn, no new values of X1, Y1 are picked up from the pen and no values of X0, Y0 are calculated—the user can sit and think.

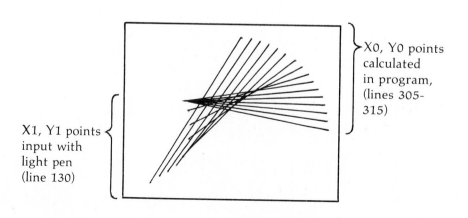

X0, Y0 points calculated in program, (lines 305-315)

X1, Y1 points input with light pen (line 130)

Touching or not touching the forward portion of the Compucolor pen can be programmed to activate it, that is, either the "finger up" or the "finger down" position can mean "draw".

This will be clearer when looking at the listing as a whole.

Explanation of the Listing

Line number   Explanation

20   PLOT 30 means "the next plot code will determine a new background color". INPUT D$ is a "dummy": this statement just stops and lets you use the keyboard to specify the color without generating a syntax error in BASIC. PLOT 12 means "erase the page". What this actually does is fill the screen with blanks of the new background color.

40   Sets up a background and foreground color so that the border will always be white on black. PLOT 29 means "next plot code will be a foreground color". Once the program is running, the user can change the colors of vectors by pressing special color select buttons on the keyboard.

50-60   Border is drawn all around the edges using vector mode.

70   First time flag (see line 220).

90-100   Finds out if pen is activated or not: "let A = the contents of input port #251 logically ANDed with the number 192". Explanation: First you have to know that input port #251 looks like this when the finger is up,

and like this when the finger is down,

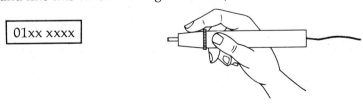

Note: x means either 0 or 1, that is, it's not important for our purposes at this point--these are "don't care" bits.

Secondly, logical ANDing does the following:
0 AND 0 = 0
0 AND 1 = 0
1 AND 0 = 0
1 AND 1 = 1
(no carries)

To examine just the first two bits, we do the AND (also called a "bit-wise AND") between the bits in port #251 and the pattern 11000000 (which is the binary equivalent of decimal 192).

$$11xxxxxx = \text{Port 251 when finger is up}$$
$$\text{AND } 11000000 = 192 \text{ decimal}$$

$$11000000 = 192 \text{ decimal}$$

$$01xxxxxx = \text{Port 251 when finger is down}$$
$$\text{AND } 11000000 = 192 \text{ decimal}$$

$$01000000 \neq 192$$

The test in line 100 therefore means "if finger is up, keep looping back to 90, that is do *not* proceed with the program."

120   means "do nothing 100 times". This empty loop allows time for data to transfer; otherwise "stale" values may be collected from the input ports holding X-Y values from the light pen.

130   Get X1 and Y1 from input ports #252 and #253 (pen).

150,160

170,180   If pen is pointed outside the screen area it will send values outside the proper range (0-159, 0-191) causing wrap-around effects and other confusing errors. These IF statements "push" the values into a slightly smaller range (2-157, 4-187) so vectors will not be drawn over the border.

190   XC and YC are calculated to give a character "cursor" position corresponding to the light pen coordinates X1 and Y1 (see line 250).

200   The Y coordinates from the light pen are designated 0-191 starting at the *upper* left of the screen. Y coordinates for vectors must be designated 0-191 starting at the *lower* left. This calculation translates the Y values from the light pen to proper plotting values for Y.

220,230   F = 0 only for the first vector to be drawn. At that point X0 and Y0 are not calculated yet, and they = 0. This would cause the first vector to always be drawn from the lower left corner (coordinates 0,0) to the light pen point. Line 230 causes the first vector to be drawn as a point at the light pen X,Y.

250	PLOT 3 means "move the cursor to the following values". The next two plot codes must designate X and Y values suitable for characters, i.e., 0-79 and 0-47.
260,270	Draw vector from X0, Y0 to X1, Y1.
305-315	Calculate new values for X0, Y0. In this version, X0 and Y0 define an elipse. Any curve or line can be substituted to create variations. Note: Simply making X0 = X1 and Y0 = Y1 at this point will give a completely user-defined continuous line following the light pen.
400	Go back and check if pen is activated before drawing next vector.

This program contains an infinite loop. It can be easily halted on the Compucolor by pressing the break key, or terminated by pressing the line feed key. Examples of output produced by this program are shown in color plates 9, 10, and 11.

Listing of Light Pen Crayon (with Ellipse)

LIGHT PEN CRAYON

```
10 PRINT"LIGHT PEN CRAYON—DRAWS ON 'FINGER DOWN'"
20 PRINT"KEY IN BACKGROUND COLOR";:PLOT30:INPUT D$:PLOT12
30 REM——-DRAW BORDER——-
40 PLOT 30:PLOT16:PLOT29:PLOT23
50 PLOT2:PLOT0:PLOT0:PLOT242:PLOT159:PLOT0:PLOT159:PLOT191
60 PLOT0:PLOT191:PLOT0:PLOT0:PLOT255
70 F=0
80 REM———IS FINGER UP?——-
90 A=INP(251) AND 192
100 IF A=192 THEN 90
110 REM——-FINGER IS NOW DOWN, GET PEN XY——-
120 FOR Q=1 TO 100:NEXT Q
130 X1=INP(252):Y1=INP(253)
150 IF X1 > 157 THEN X1 = 157
160 IF X1 < 2 THEN X1 = 2
170 IF Y1 > 187 THEN Y1 = 187
180 IF Y1 < 4 THEN Y1 = 4
190 XC = INT(X1/2):YC=INT(Y1/4)
200 Y1=191-Y1
210 REM——-DRAW VECTOR——
220 IF F<>0 THEN 250
230 X0=X1:Y0=Y1
250 PLOT3:PLOTXC:PLOTYC
260 PLOT2:PLOTX0:PLOTY0
270 PLOT242:PLOTX1:PLOTY1:PLOT255
300 F=1
305 R=R+.1
310 X0=70*SIN(R)+80
315 Y0=86*COS(R)+96
400 GOTO 90
```

Computer Music; Speech Synthesis

Computers can be used to control conventional musical instruments, to control electronic music systems, and even to produce new kinds of electrical signals that can be amplified and used for experimental music. The subject is a growing one, and there are now entire journals devoted to computer music. Computers are also of considerable interest as artistic tools, both for composing music and for experimenting with visual art.

A small pipe organ controlled by two microcomputers, with a graphics terminal for composing and editing music.

Low cost plug-in boards that synthesize human speech are now available for microcomputers. These produce good approximations of the basic sounds that people make when speaking. If pitch and stress information is also added, the results are pretty realistic. The reverse problem of recognizing human speech, and using it as input to a computer is a more difficult one. However progress is being made, and both professionals and computer amateurs are contributing new ideas in this area.

Of course recognizing the sounds that make up speech is very different from understanding it. Communicating ideas and feelings—whether through speech or any other medium—is a human art that transcends the capabilities of technology. Which brings us back to a point made much earlier—about ten chapters ago to be exact. While the technology and theory that make personal computing possible are impressive indeed, it's the human connection that counts most. It's the way in which computers can enhance (not replace) human understanding that is significant. The importance of personal computing is that it makes such enhancement the prerogative of everyone.

10.5 PROJECT IDEAS

1. Generalize the Planet-X Lander to work with both X and Y joystick inputs. Try adding sound effects by using a D/A converter to supply a variable frequency voltage to a loudspeaker via an amplifier.

2. If you have access to a special type of input/output device, develop a new computer application based on its use. Then document your work in the form of an article to be submitted to one of the personal computing journals.

3. Develop a proposal for using some special piece(s) of hardware to extend one of the ideas described in the first nine chapters of this book. Your goal should be to remove some of the limitations of an alphanumeric terminal. Your proposal should mix a little bit of fantasy with an awareness of the practical questions that need to be addressed.

4. Modify the Electric Field program of Section 7.3 to run on a color graphics terminal. The color should correspond to electric field potential, and black should be used to help outline the equipotential regions. An example of what the output might look like is shown in color plate 12.

5. Do project #4 in Section 7.6 on a color graphics terminal.

6. Modify the light pen program of Section 10.4 so that the program draws a 3 x 2 Lissajous figure instead of an ellipse. To do this change lines 310 and 315 as follows:

```
310 X0 = 70 * SIN(3*R) + 80
315 Y0 = 86 * COS(2*R) + 96
```

If you don't have a light pen, change line 130 to read:

```
130 X1 = 79: Y1 = 96
```

Also delete lines 80 through 120.

An example of output obtained this way is shown in color plate 13.

APPENDIX A:
EXAMPLE OF USING TIMESHARING

Example of using a large timesharing system:

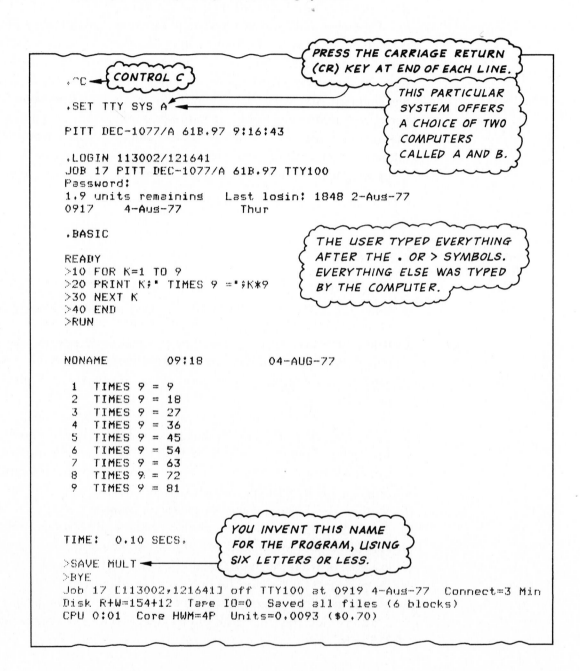

Example of a RUN on the same timesharing system some time later:

```
.SET TTY SYS A

PITT DEC-1077/A 61B.97 10:09:11

.LOGIN 113002/121641
JOB 19 PITT DEC-1077/A 61B.97 TTY100
Password:
1.9 units remaining   Last login: 0916 4-Aug-77
1009    4-Aug-77        Thur

.BASIC
>OLD MULT
>LIST


MULT              10:13            04-AUG-77

10 FOR K=1 TO 9
20 PRINT K;" TIMES 9 =";K*9
30 NEXT K
40 END
>5 PRINT"MULTIPLICATION TABLE FOR 9"
>RUN


MULT              10:14            04-AUG-77

MULTIPLICATION TABLE FOR 9
  1   TIMES 9 = 9
  2   TIMES 9 = 18
  3   TIMES 9 = 27
  4   TIMES 9 = 36
  5   TIMES 9 = 45
  6   TIMES 9 = 54
  7   TIMES 9 = 63
  8   TIMES 9 = 72
  9   TIMES 9 = 81



TIME:  0.12 SECS.
>REPLACE
>BYE
Job 19 [113002,121641] off TTY100 at 1014 4-Aug-77  Connect=6 Min
Disk R+W=153+43  Tape IO=0  Saved all files (12 blocks)
CPU 0:02  Core HWM=4P  Units=0.0124 ($0.93)
```

LOADS THE OLD "MULT" PROGRAM FROM DISK.

A NEW LINE IS PUT IN THE PROGRAM.

REPLACES THE OLD "MULT" PROGRAM ON DISK WITH THE NEW VERSION.

APPENDIX B:
THE ASCII CODES

APPENDIX B 7-Bit ASCII Codes

Binary Form	Meaning of Code	Octal Form	Decimal Form
0000000	NULL (↑@)	000	0
0000001	SOH (↑A)	001	1
0000010	STX (↑B)	002	2
0000011	ETX (↑C)	003	3
0000100	EOT (↑D)	004	4
0000101	ENQ (↑E)	005	5
0000110	ACK (↑F)	006	6
0000111	BELL (↑G)	007	7
0001000	BS (↑H)	010	8
0001001	HT (↑I)	011	9
0001010	LF (↑J)	012	10
0001011	VT (↑K)	013	11
0001100	FF (↑L)	014	12
0001101	CR (↑M)	015	13
0001110	SO (↑N)	016	14
0001111	SI (↑O)	017	15
0010000	DLE (↑P)	020	16
0010001	DC1 (↑Q)	021	17
0010010	DC2 (↑R)	022	18
0010011	DC3 (↑S)	023	19
0010100	DC4 (↑T)	024	20
0010101	NAK (↑U)	025	21
0010110	SYN (↑V)	026	22
0010111	ETB (↑W)	027	23
0011000	CAN (↑X)	030	24
0011001	EM (↑Y)	031	25
0011010	SUB (↑Z)	032	26
0011011	ESC (↑[)	033	27
0011100	FS (↑\)	034	28
0011101	GS (↑])	035	29
0011110	RS (↑∧)	036	30
0011111	US (↑__)	037	31

Binary Form	Meaning of Code	Octal Form	Decimal Form
0100000	SP	040	32
0100001	!	041	33
0100010	"	042	34
0100011	#	043	35
0100100	$	044	36
0100101	%	045	37
0100110	&	046	38
0100111	'	047	39
0101000	(	050	40
0101001	)	051	41
0101010	*	052	42
0101011	+	053	43
0101100	,	054	44
0101101	—	055	45
0101110	.	056	46
0101111	/	057	47
0110000	0	060	48
0110001	1	061	49
0110010	2	062	50
0110011	3	063	51
0110100	4	064	52
0110101	5	065	53
0110110	6	066	54
0110111	7	067	55
0111000	8	070	56
0111001	9	071	57
0111010	:	072	58
0111011	;	073	59
0111100	<	074	60
0111101	=	075	61
0111110	>	076	62
0111111	?	077	63

Control Codes

The codes from octal 000 to octal 037 are used for special control functions. For example, code 002 is used in communications work to mean "start of text" (STX), while on the Compucolor system described in Chapter 10 it means "enter point plot mode".

These codes do not print anything on output devices. However they can be *input* to a computer in two ways.

(1) To input a control code from an ASCII keyboard, type the corresponding *control character* by holding down the key marked control (CTRL), and then simultaneously pressing the character that has a code equal to the control code + 100 octal. For example, to ring the bell (code 007 octal)

Binary Form	Meaning of Code	Octal Form	Decimal Form	Binary Form	Meaning of Code	Octal Form	Decimal Form
1000000	@	100	64	1100000	`	140	96
1000001	A	101	65	1100001	a	141	97
1000010	B	102	66	1100010	b	142	98
1000011	C	103	67	1100011	c	143	99
1000100	D	104	68	1100100	d	144	100
1000101	E	105	69	1100101	e	145	101
1000110	F	106	70	1100110	f	146	102
1000111	G	107	71	1100111	g	147	103
1001000	H	110	72	1101000	h	150	104
1001001	I	111	73	1101001	i	151	105
1001010	J	112	74	1101010	j	152	106
1001011	K	113	75	1101011	k	153	107
1001100	L	114	76	1101100	l	154	108
1001101	M	115	77	1101101	m	155	109
1001110	N	116	78	1101110	n	156	110
1001111	O	117	79	1101111	o	157	111
1010000	P	120	80	1110000	p	160	112
1010001	Q	121	81	1110001	q	161	113
1010010	R	122	82	1110010	r	162	114
1010011	S	123	83	1110011	s	163	115
1010100	T	124	84	1110100	t	164	116
1010101	U	125	85	1110101	u	165	117
1010110	V	126	86	1110110	v	166	118
1010111	W	127	87	1110111	w	167	119
1011000	X	130	88	1111000	x	170	120
1011001	Y	131	89	1111001	y	171	121
1011010	Z	132	90	1111010	z	172	122
1011011	[	133	91	1111011	{	173	123
1011100	\	134	92	1111100	|	174	124
1011101	]	135	93	1111101	}	175	125
1011110	∧	136	94	1111110	~	176	126
1011111	__	137	95	1111111	DEL	177	127

hold down the control key, and then simultaneously press the key for G (code 107 octal). Our table shows control-G as ↑G.

(2) To input a control code from BASIC, use the CHR$(D) function described in Section 4.7, where D is the *decimal* equivalent of the code. For example, to ring the bell use

10 PRINT CHR$(7)

On the Compucolor, you can get the same result with PLOT 7.

APPENDIX C: SUMMARY OF BASIC

Statements

Name	Purpose	Example
(ln means line no.)		
DATA	Holds data for READ.	35 DATA 5,3.14,"SMITH"
DIM	Declares maximum size of array.	35 DIM A(15),X(20,4),N$(25)
END	Last statement in program.	9999 END
FOR...TO...(STEP)	Sets up and controls loop.	35 FOR K=1 TO N STEP 2
GOSUB ln	Branches to subroutine at ln.	35 GOSUB 800
GOTO ln	Branches to ln.	35 GOTO 55
IF...THEN ln	Branches to ln if condition true.	35 IF X-5<=2 THEN 125
IF...THEN stmts	Executes statements if true.	35 IF Z>5 THEN Z=1:PRINT Z
IF...THEN ln ELSE ln	Branches to first ln if true, branches to second ln if false.	35 IF Y=X THEN 85 ELSE 95
IF...THEN stmts ELSE stmts	Does stmts after THEN if true, does stmts after ELSE if false.	35 IF Y>M THEN M=Y ELSE N=Y:D=C
INPUT	Requests data from terminal.	35 INPUT A,B,N$
LET	Assigns value of expression to variable.	35 LET A=3.14*R*R
LINE INPUT	Inputs string containing commas,etc.	35 LINE INPUT A$
NEXT	Marks end of FOR loop.	35 NEXT K
ON X GOSUB...	Branches to Xth subroutine.	35 ON X GOSUB 899,999
ON Y GOTO...	Branches to Yth line number.	35 ON Y GOTO 65,75,85
PRINT	Types strings and/or numbers.	35 PRINT "ANS=";N+1.5,A$
PRINT USING	Types in given format.	35 PRINT USING "##.##";X
READ	Moves values from DATA into variables.	5 READ N,X,A$
RESTORE	Resets DATA pointer to first item.	35 RESTORE
RETURN	Go to statement following last GOSUB.	35 RETURN
STOP	Terminate program.	35 STOP

Special Features

POKE loc, val   PEEK (loc)   OUT port, val   PRINT @ N, exp

Commands

CLEAR, CONT, DELET, EDIT, LIST, LOAD (CLOAD), NEW, OLD, RUN, SAVE (CSAVE)

Numeric Functions

Name	Purpose
ABS(X)	Absolute value of X
ATN(X)	Arctangent of X
COS(X)	Cosine of X
EXP(X)	e to the Xth power
INP(X)	Value at port X
INT(X)	Largest integer <= X
LOG(X)	Natural log of X
RND(1)	0 <= random number < 1
SGN(X)	Sign of X
SIN(X)	Sine of X
SQR(X)	Square root of X
TAN(X)	Tangent of X

String Functions

Name	Purpose
ASC(X$)	Decimal ASCII of 1st character in X$
CHR$(I)	Character with ASCII code I
INSTR(X$,Y$)	Position of Y$ in X$
LEFT$(X$,I)	Leftmost I characters of X$
LEN(X$)	Number of characters in X$
MID$(X$,I,J)	Substring of X$ from I to J
RIGHT$(X$,I)	Rightmost I characters of X$
SPACE$(I)	String with I spaces
STR$(N)	String that looks like N
VAL(X$)	Number that looks like X$

Variables, Operators, Relations

A, Z, A1, Z9, X(I), X(I,J), N(X(I),K), A$, N$(I), Z$(I,J)
$+, -, *, /, \uparrow$
<, <=, =, >=, >, <>

File Features

Vary with systems (see Chapter 8).

SOME TIPS FOR TRS-80 LEVEL II USERS

The programs in this book were written in either BASIC-PLUS or Microsoft Extended BASIC. Radio Shack's Level II BASIC was designed by the same people who did the Microsoft Extended BASIC (which is, in turn, very close to BASIC-PLUS). However there are a few differences which we've illustrated in the program below. We've also shown how to use the special graphical features SET(X,Y) and PRINT @.

You should remember that the TRS-80 has only 64 columns on its screen, so the programs in this book which use 72- or 80-column printers will have to be scaled down. Another problem is the 16-line screen limit. To get around this, try using the following statement to interrupt your output at strategic points:

207 PRINT "PRESS ENTER TO CONTINUE--READY";: INPUT D$

This makes the output stop scrolling until you press ENTER. Try this tip in the program ARRAY SUMS (p. 180) by adding line 207 and a similar line at 247.

```
1 REM ******** ARROW2 (TRAJECTORY GRAPHICS GAME)
2 REM  THIS PROGRAM WAS WRITTEN FOR THE TRS-80 FOR
3 REM  USE WITH THE SET(X,Y) GRAPHICS COMMAND
10 CLS: RANDOM
15 G=32.2
20 PRINT"HOW MANY ARROWS DO YOU WANT";
30 INPUT N
32 D=INT(100 * RND(0) + 50)
33 S1=98/D       'X SCALE FACTOR
34 S2=S1*.5 'Y SCALE FACTOR
35 '============START OF LOOP============
40 FOR L=1 TO N
50 PRINT"YOUR TARGET IS";D;"YARDS AWAY. "
60 PRINT"WHAT ANGLE,VELOCITY WILL YOU USE (E.G.  35,50): ";
70 INPUT A,V
80 IF A>89 OR A<15  PRINT"ANGLE MUST BE 15 TO 89":GOTO 60
90 IF V>100 OR V<50 PRINT"VELOCITY MUST BE 50 TO 100":GOTO 60
95 CLS
100 A = A * 3.14159265/180
110 R = V * V * SIN(2*A)/G
120 H = (V * SIN(A))[2/(2*G)
200 REM-----DISPLAY AXES-----
210 FOR K=1 TO 15: PRINT "!": NEXT K
220 PRINT "%";
230 FOR K=3 TO 50: PRINT "-": NEXT K
240 PRINT @1009, "T--(";RIGHT$(STR$(D),LEN(STR$(D))-1);" YDS)--";
300 REM-----CALCULATE AND PLOT TRAJECTORY-----
310 T1=2*V*SIN(A)/G
320 K1=S1*V*COS(A)
330 K2=S2*V*SIN(A)
340 K3=G*S2/2
350 FOR T=0 TO T1 STEP T1/50
360   X=INT(K1*T+2.5)
370   Y=INT((K2-K3*T)*T+2)
380   IF Y>47 OR Y<0 OR X>127 OR X<0 THEN 395
390   SET(X,47-Y)
395 NEXT T
400 REM------PRINT RESULTS-----
455 PRINT @ 0, "KERPLOP !!!"
460 IF ABS(R-D) <3 PRINT "HIT !!!!!!!!!": GOTO 515
470 PRINT"YOU MISSED BY";R-D;"YDS. "
485 PRINT
490 PRINT"-------YOU HAVE";N-L;"ARROWS LEFT-------"
495 NEXT L
496 REM============END OF MAIN LOOP============
497 PRINT"YOU'RE OUT OF ARROWS--SCORE = 0"
498 PRINT"IF YOU WANT TO TRY AGAIN TYPE RUN. "
500 STOP: REM---CALCULATE SCORES FOR HITS----
515 PRINT"YOU USED";L;"OUT OF YOUR";N;"ARROWS. "
517 PRINT"YOUR FINAL SCORE IS"
520 PRINT 100 * (12 - L)/(L * N)
530 PRINT"POSSIBLE SCORES FOR SOME CHOICES OF ARROWS ARE:"
535 PRINT" 1-ARROW 2-ARROWS 3-ARROWS 4-ARROWS 5-ARROWS 6-ARROWS"
540 FOR K = 1 TO 6
550   FOR N = K TO 6
560     PRINT TAB(9*(N-1)+3);100*(12-K)/(K*N);
570   NEXT N
580 PRINT
590 NEXT K
900 END
```

Line 10 shows the "clear screen" and "randomize" commands for Level II BASIC.

Line 32 shows how to get random numbers from 50 to 149.

IMPORTANT: TRS-80 users should always use RND(0) in programs in this book that use random numbers. Never use RND(1) or RND.

Lines 33, 34, and 35 show how to use the apostrophe (') for remark statements. Incidentally, the [symbol in line 120 is really the up-arrow ↑ (the TRS-80 line printer can't make up-arrows).

Lines 210 and 230 show how a short loop can be written on one line by using the colon (:). Some of the BASIC-PLUS programs in this book (e.g., BUBBLE DEMO, p. 198) use BASIC-PLUS "suffix " statements like
    40 PRINT A(B); FOR B = 1 TO N
    210 D1 = N - B + 1 IF D1 >= N - B
In Level II these should be written as
    40 FOR B = 1 TO N: PRINT A(B);: NEXT B
    210 IF D1 >= N - B THEN D1 = N - B + 1

WARNING: In Level II BASIC, the statement
    FOR E = 1 TO 0: PRINT E: NEXT E
will actually print once (it really shouldn't).

This causes a problem in BUBBLE DEMO. To fix it, two lines are needed:
    215 IF D1 = 0 THEN 230
    220 FOR E=1 TO D1:PRINT TAB(E*6-3);B(E,D);:NEXT E

Lines 240 and 455 show how you can print at any of 1024 positions on the TRS-80 screen with PRINT @.

Lines 380 and 390 show how to use the SET(X,Y) command to plot the arrow trajectory on the TRS-80 screen. This program is much faster than the ARROW program in the book. Part of the reason is that lines 320, 330, and 340 were used to calculate complex quantities outside the plotting loop (350 to 395).

The program shown here is reproduced with permission from the book You Spent $1000 On A Personal WHAT? by T. Dwyer and M. Critchfield.

Index

438

Books in the Microcomputer Books Series, available from your local computer store or bookstore. For more information write:

General Books Division

Addison-Wesley Publishing Company, Inc.
Reading, Massachusetts 01867
(617)944-3700